A RANDOM WALK

DOWN WALL STREET

D0981793

A RANDOM WALK DOWN WALL STREET

The Time-Tested Strategy for
Successful Investing

BURTON G. MALKIEL

W. W. NORTON & COMPANY

Independent Publishers Since 1923

New York · London

For information about permission to reproduce selections from this book, write to Permissions, W. W. Norton & Company, Inc., 500 Fifth Avenue, New York, NY 10110

For information about special discounts for bulk purchases, please contact W. W. Norton Special Sales at specialsales@wwnorton.com or 800-233-4830

Manufacturing by RR Donnelley, Harrisonburg
Book design by Chris Welch
Production manager: Julia Druskin

Library of Congress Cataloging-in-Publication Data

Malkiel, Burton Gordon.
A random walk down Wall Street : the time-tested strategy for successful investing / Burton G. Malkiel. — [Revised and updated edition].
pages cm
Includes index.
ISBN 978-0-393-24611-7 (hardcover)
1. Investments. 2. Stocks. 3. Random walks (Mathematics) I. Title.
HG4521.M284 2015
332.6—dc23
2014041927

ISBN 978-0-393-35224-5 pbk.

W. W. Norton & Company, Inc.
500 Fifth Avenue, New York, N.Y. 10110
www.wwnorton.com

W. W. Norton & Company Ltd.
Castle House, 75/76 Wells Street, London W1T 3QT

1 2 3 4 5 6 7 8 9 0

FOR NANCY AND PIPER

CONTENTS

Part Two

HOW THE PROS PLAY THE BIGGEST GAME IN TOWN

Part Three

THE NEW INVESTMENT TECHNOLOGY

Part Four

A PRACTICAL GUIDE FOR RANDOM WALKERS
AND OTHER INVESTORS

PREFACE

IT HAS NOW been over forty years since the first edition of *A Random Walk Down Wall Street*. The message of the original edition was a very simple one: Investors would be far better off buying and holding an index fund than attempting to buy and sell individual securities or actively managed mutual funds. I boldly stated that buying and holding all the stocks in a broad stock-market average was likely to outperform professionally managed funds whose high expense charges and large trading costs detract substantially from investment returns.

Now, over forty years later, I believe even more strongly in that original thesis, and there's more than a six-figure gain to prove it. I can make the case with great simplicity. An investor with $10,000 at the start of 1969 who invested in a Standard & Poor's 500-Stock Index Fund would have had a portfolio worth $736,196 by June 2014, assuming that all dividends were reinvested. A second investor who instead purchased shares in the average actively managed fund would have seen his investment grow to $501,470. The difference is dramatic. Through June 1, 2014, the index investor was ahead by $234,726, an amount almost 50 percent greater than the final stake of the average investor in a managed fund.

Why, then, an eleventh edition of this book? If the basic message hasn't changed, what has? The answer is that there have been enormous changes in the financial instruments available to the public. A book meant to provide a comprehensive investment guide for individual investors needs to be updated to cover the full range of investment products available. In addition, investors can benefit from a critical analysis of the wealth of new information provided by academic researchers and market professionals—made comprehensible in prose accessible to everyone with an interest in investing. There have been so many bewildering claims about the stock market that it's important to have a book that sets the record straight.

Over the past forty years, we have become accustomed to accepting the rapid pace of technological change in our physical environment. Innovations such as e-mail, the Internet, smartphones, iPads, Kindles, videoconferencing, social networks, and new medical advances ranging from organ transplants and laser surgery to nonsurgical methods of treating kidney stones and unclogging arteries have materially affected the way we live. Financial innovation over the same period has been equally rapid. In 1973, when the first edition of this book appeared, we did not have money-market funds, ATMs, index mutual funds, ETFs, tax-exempt funds, emerging-market funds, target-date funds, floating-rate notes, volatility derivatives, inflation protection securities, equity REITs, asset-backed securities, "smart beta" strategies, Roth IRAs, 529 college savings plans, zero-coupon bonds, financial and commodity futures and options, and new trading techniques such as "portfolio insurance" and "high-frequency trading," to mention just a few of the changes that have occurred in the financial environment. Much of the new material in this book has been included to explain these financial innovations and to show how you as a consumer can benefit from them.

This eleventh edition also provides a clear and easily accessible description of the academic advances in investment theory and practice. Chapter 10 describes the exciting new field of behavioral finance and underscores the important lessons investors should learn from the insights of the behavioralists. Chapter 11 asks whether "smart beta" investment strategies are really smart. In addition, a new section has been added to present practical investment strategies for investors who have retired or are about to retire. So much new material has been added over the years that readers who may have read an earlier edition of this book in college or business school will find this new edition rewarding reading.

This edition takes a hard look at the basic thesis of earlier editions of *Random Walk*—that the market prices stocks so efficiently that a blindfolded chimpanzee throwing darts at the stock listings can select a portfolio that performs as well as those managed by the experts. Through the past forty years, that thesis has held up remarkably well. More than two-thirds of professional portfolio managers have been outperformed by unmanaged broad-based index funds. Nevertheless, there are still both academics and practitioners who doubt the validity of the theory. And the stock-market crash of October 1987, the Internet bubble, and the financial crisis of 2008–09 raised further questions concerning the vaunted efficiency of the market. This edition explains the recent controversy and reexamines the claim that it's possible to "beat the market." I conclude that reports of the death of the efficient-market hypothesis are vastly exaggerated. I will, however, review the evidence on a number of techniques of stock selection that are believed to tilt the odds of success in favor of the individual investor.

The book remains fundamentally a readable investment guide for individual investors. As I have counseled individuals and families about financial strategy, it has become increasingly clear to me that one's capacity for risk-bearing depends importantly upon one's age and ability to earn income from noninvestment sources. It is also the case that the risk involved in many investments decreases with the length of time the investment can be held. For these reasons, optimal investment strategies must be age-related. Chapter 14, entitled "A Life-Cycle Guide to Investing," should prove very helpful to people of all ages. This chapter alone is worth the cost of a high-priced appointment with a personal financial adviser.

My debts of gratitude to those mentioned in earlier editions continue. In addition, I must mention the names of a number of people who were particularly helpful in making special contributions to the eleventh edition. I am especially indebted to Michael Nolan of the Bogle Research Institute, to my Princeton colleagues Harrison Hong and Yacine Aït-Sahalia, and to my research assistants, David Hou, Derek Jun, Michael Lachanski, and Paul Noh. I am also grateful to John Devereaux, Francis Kinniry, Ravi Tolani, and Sarah Hammer of the Vanguard Group for important assistance in providing data.

Karen Neukirchen made an extraordinary contribution to this edition. She was somehow able to decipher my inpenetrable scribbles and turn them into readable text. She also provided research assistance and was responsible for many of the graphic presentations in the book. Sharon Hill added invaluable assistance in the final preparation of the manuscript. My association with W. W. Norton remains a superb collaboration, and I thank Drake McFeely, Otto Sonntag, and Jeff Shreve for their indispensable assistance in bringing this edition to publication. Patricia Taylor continued her association with the project and made extremely valuable editorial contributions to the eleventh edition.

My wife, Nancy Weiss Malkiel, has made by far the most important contributions to the successful completion of the past seven editions. In addition to providing the most loving encouragement and support, she read carefully through various drafts of the manuscript and made innumerable suggestions that clarified and vastly improved the writing. She continues to be able to find errors that have eluded me and a variety of proofreaders and editors. Most important, she has brought incredible joy to my life. No one more deserved the dedication of a book than she and her second-best friend, Piper.

Burton G. Malkiel
Princeton University
August 2014

ACKNOWLEDGMENTS

from Earlier Editions

MY DEBTS OF GRATITUDE to practitioners, financial institutions, and academic colleagues who have helped me with the earlier editions of this book are enormous in both number and degree. Here, I acknowledge the many individuals who offered extremely valuable suggestions and criticisms.

Many research assistants have labored long in compiling information for this book. Especially useful contributions were made by John Americus, Shane Antos, Costin Bontas, Jonathan Curran, Barry Feldman, Ethan Hugo, Amie Ko, Paul Messaris, Matthew Moore, Ker Moua, Christopher Philips, Ellen Renaldi, Cheryl Roberts, Saumitra Sahi, Barry Schwartz, Greg Smolarek, Ray Soldavin, Elizabeth Woods, Yexiao Xu, and Basak Yeltikan. Helen Talar, Phyllis Fafalios, Lugene Whitley, Melissa Orlowski, Diana Prout, and Ellen DiPippo not only faithfully and accurately typed several drafts of the manuscript but also offered extremely valuable research assistance. Elvira Giaimo provided most helpful computer programming. Many of the supporting studies for this book were conducted at Princeton's Bendheim Center for Finance. I am also grateful to Arthur Lipper Corporation for permission to use its mutual-fund rankings.

A vital contribution was made by Patricia Taylor, a professional writer and editor. She read through complete drafts of the book and made innumerable contributions to the style, organization, and content of the manuscript. She deserves much of the credit for whatever lucid writing can be found in these pages.

My association with W. W. Norton & Company has been an extremely pleasant one, and I am particularly grateful to Brendan Curry, Donald Lamm, Robert Kehoe, Ed Parsons, and Deborah Makay, as well as my editor, Starling Lawrence, for his invaluable help.

The contribution of Judith Malkiel was of inestimable importance. She painstakingly edited every page of the manuscript and was helpful in every phase of this undertaking. This acknowledgment of my debt to her is the largest understatement of all.

Finally, I would like to acknowledge with deep gratitude the assistance of the following individuals who made important contributions to earlier editions. They include Peter Asch, Leo Bailey, Howard Baker, Jeffrey Balash, David Banyard, William Baumol, Clair Bien, G. Gordon Biggar Jr., John Bogle, Lynne Brady, John Brennan, Markus Brunnermeier, Claire Cabelus, Lester Chandler, Andrew Clarke, Abby Joseph Cohen, Douglas Daniels, Pia Ellen, Andrew Engel, Steve Feinstein, Barry Feldman, Roger Ford, Stephen Goldfeld, William Grant, Leila Heckman, William Helman, Roger Ibbotson, Deborah Jenkins, Barbara Johnson, George S. Johnston, Kay Kerr, Walter Lenhard, James Litvack, Ian MacKinnon, Barbara Mains, Jonathan Malkiel, Sol Malkiel, Whitney Malkiel, Edward Mathias, Jianping Mei, Melissa McGinnis, Will McIntosh, Kelley Mingone, William Minicozzi, Keith Mullins, Gabrielle Napolitano, James Norris, Gail Paster, Emily Paster, H. Bradlee Perry, George Putnam, Donald Peters, Michelle Peterson, Richard Quandt, James Riepe, Michael Rothschild, Joan Ryan, Robert Salomon Jr., George Sauter, Crystal Shannon, George Smith, Willy Spat, Shang Song, James Stetler, James Stoeffel, H. Barton Thomas, Mark Thompson, Jim Troyer, David Twardock, Linda Wheeler, Frank Wisneski, and Robert Zenowich.

Part One

STOCKS AND

THEIR VALUE

1

FIRM FOUNDATIONS
AND CASTLES IN THE AIR

What is a cynic? A man who knows the price of everything,
and the value of nothing.
—Oscar Wilde, *Lady Windermere's Fan*

IN THIS BOOK I will take you on a random walk down Wall Street, providing a guided tour of the complex world of finance and practical advice on investment opportunities and strategies. Many people say that the individual investor has scarcely a chance today against Wall Street's professionals. They point to professional investment strategies using complex derivative instruments and high-frequency trading. They read news reports of accounting fraud, mammoth takeovers, and the activities of well-financed hedge funds. This complexity suggests that there is no longer any room for the individual investor in today's markets. Nothing could be further from the truth. You can do as well as the experts—perhaps even better. It was the steady investors who kept their heads when the stock market tanked in March 2009, and then saw the value of their holdings eventually recover and continue to produce attractive returns. And many of the pros lost their shirts in 2008 buying derivative securities they failed to understand, as well as during the early 2000s when they overloaded their portfolios with overpriced tech stocks.

This book is a succinct guide for the individual investor. It covers everything from insurance to income taxes. It tells you how to buy life insurance and how to avoid getting ripped off by banks and brokers. It will even tell you what to do about gold and diamonds. But primarily it is a book about common stocks—an investment medium that not only provided generous long-run returns in the past but also appears to represent good possibilities for the years ahead. The life-cycle investment guide described in Part Four gives individuals of all age groups specific portfolio recommendations for meeting their financial goals, including advice on how to invest in retirement.

WHAT IS A RANDOM WALK?

A random walk is one in which future steps or directions cannot be predicted on the basis of past history. When the term is applied to the stock market, it means that short-run changes in stock prices are unpredictable. Investment advisory services, earnings forecasts, and complicated chart patterns are useless. On Wall Street, the term "random walk" is an obscenity. It is an epithet coined by the academic world and hurled insultingly at the professional soothsayers. Taken to its logical extreme, it means that a blindfolded monkey throwing darts at the stock listings could select a portfolio that would do just as well as one selected by the experts.

Now, financial analysts in pin-striped suits do not like being compared to bare-assed apes. They retort that academics are so immersed in equations and Greek symbols (to say nothing of stuffy prose) that they couldn't tell a bull from a bear, even in a china shop. Market professionals arm themselves against the academic onslaught with one of two techniques, called fundamental analysis and technical analysis, which we will examine in Part Two. Academics parry these tactics by obfuscating the random-walk theory with three versions (the "weak," the "semi-strong," and the "strong") and by creating their own theory, called the new investment technology. This last includes a concept called beta, including "smart beta," and I intend to trample on that a bit. By the early 2000s, even some academics had joined the professionals in arguing that the stock market was at least somewhat predictable after all. Still, as you can see, a tremendous battle is going on, and it's fought with deadly intent because the stakes are tenure for the academics and bonuses for the professionals. That's why I think you'll enjoy this random walk down Wall Street. It has all the ingredients of high drama—including fortunes made and lost and classic arguments about their cause.

But before we begin, perhaps I should introduce myself and state my qualifications as guide. I have drawn on three aspects of my background in writing this book; each provides a different perspective on the stock market.

First is my professional experience in the fields of investment analysis and portfolio management. I started my career as a market professional with one of Wall Street's leading investment firms. Later, I chaired the investment committee of a multinational insurance company and for many years served as a director of one of the world's largest investment companies. These perspectives have been indispensable to me. Some things in life can never fully be appreciated or understood by a virgin. The same might be said of the stock market.

Second are my current positions as an economist and chair of several investment committees. Specializing in securities markets and investment behavior, I have acquired detailed knowledge of academic research and new findings on investment opportunities.

Last, and certainly not least, I have been a lifelong investor and successful participant in the market. How successful I will not say, for it is a peculiarity of the academic world that a professor is not supposed to make money. A professor may inherit lots of money, marry lots of money, and spend lots of money, but he or she is never, never supposed to earn lots of money; it's unacademic. Anyway, teachers are supposed to be "dedicated," or so politicians and administrators often say—especially when trying to justify the low academic pay scales. Academics are supposed to be seekers of knowledge, not of financial reward. It is in the former sense, therefore, that I shall tell you of my victories on Wall Street.

This book has a lot of facts and figures. Don't let that worry you. It is specifically intended for the financial layperson and offers practical, tested investment advice. You need no prior knowledge to follow it. All you need is the interest and the desire to have your investments work for you.

INVESTING AS A WAY OF LIFE TODAY

At this point, it's probably a good idea to explain what I mean by "investing" and how I distinguish this activity from "speculating." I view investing as a method of purchasing assets to gain profit in the form of reasonably predictable income (dividends, interest, or rentals) and/or appreciation over the long term. It is the definition of the time period for the investment return and the predictability of the returns that often distinguish an investment from a speculation. A speculator buys stocks hoping for a short-term gain over the next days or weeks. An investor buys stocks likely to produce a dependable future stream of cash returns and capital gains when measured over years or decades.

Let me make it quite clear that this is not a book for speculators: I am not going to promise you overnight riches. I am not promising you stock-market miracles. Indeed, a subtitle for this book might well have been *The Get Rich Slowly but Surely Book*. Remember, just to stay even, your investments have to produce a rate of return equal to inflation.

Inflation in the United States and throughout most of the developed world fell to 2 percent or below in the early 2000s, and some analysts believe that relative price stability will continue indefinitely. They suggest that inflation is the exception rather than the rule and that historical periods of rapid technological progress and peacetime economies were periods of stable or even falling prices. It may well be that little or no inflation will occur during the decades ahead, but I believe investors should not dismiss the possibility that inflation will accelerate again at some time in the future. Although productivity growth accelerated in the 1990s and early 2000s, it has recently slowed, and history tells us that the pace of improvement has always been uneven. Moreover, productivity improvements are harder to come by in some service-oriented activities. It still will take four musicians to play a string quartet and one surgeon to perform an appendectomy throughout the twenty-first century, and if musicians' and surgeons' salaries rise over time, so will the cost of concert tickets and appendectomies. Thus, upward pressure on prices cannot be dismissed.

If inflation were to proceed at a 2 to 3 percent rate—a rate much lower than we had in the 1970s and early 1980s—the effect on our purchasing power would still be devastating. The table on the following page shows what an average inflation rate of close to 4 percent has done over the 1962–2014 period. My morning newspaper has risen 4,900 percent. My afternoon Hershey bar is twenty times more expensive, and it's actually smaller than it was in 1962, when I was in graduate school. If inflation continued at the same rate, today's morning paper would cost more than four dollars by the year 2020. It is clear that if we are to cope with even a mild inflation, we must undertake investment strategies that maintain our real purchasing power; otherwise, we are doomed to an ever-decreasing standard of living.

Investing requires work, make no mistake about it. Romantic novels are replete with tales of great family fortunes lost through neglect or lack of knowledge on how to care for money. Who can forget the sounds of the cherry orchard being cut down in Chekhov's great play? Free enterprise, not the Marxist system, caused the downfall of the Ranevsky family: They had not worked to keep their money. Even if you trust all your funds to an investment adviser or to a mutual fund, you still have to know which adviser or which fund is most suitable to handle your money. Armed with the information contained in this book, you should find it a bit easier to make your investment decisions.

THE BITE OF INFLATION

	Average 1962	Average 2014	Percentage Increase	Compound Annual Rate of Inflation
Consumer Price Index	30.20	236.40	682.8	4.0
Hershey bar	$.05	$1.00	1,900.0	5.9
New York Times	.05	2.50	4,900.0	7.8
First-class postage	.04	0.49	1,125.0	4.9
Gasoline (gallon)	.31	3.40	996.8	4.7
Hamburger (McDonald's double)	.28*	4.00	1,328.6	5.2
Chevrolet	2529.00	24,000.00	849.0	4.4
Refrigerator freezer	470.00	1,249.00	165.7	1.9

*1963 data.
   Source: For 1962 prices, *Forbes*, Nov. 1, 1977, and various government and private sources for 2014 prices.

Most important of all, however, is the fact that investing is fun. It's fun to pit your intellect against that of the vast investment community and to find yourself rewarded with an increase in assets. It's exciting to review your investment returns and to see how they are accumulating at a faster rate than your salary. And it's also stimulating to learn about new ideas for products and services, and innovations in the forms of financial investments. A successful investor is generally a well-rounded individual who puts a natural curiosity and an intellectual interest to work.

INVESTING IN THEORY

All investment returns—whether from common stocks or exceptional diamonds—are dependent, to varying degrees, on future events. That's what makes the fascination of investing: It's a gamble whose success depends on an ability to predict the future. Traditionally, the pros in the investment community have used one of two approaches to asset valuation: the firm-foundation theory or the castle-in-the-air theory. Millions of dollars have been gained and lost on these theories. To add to the drama, they appear to be mutually exclusive. An understanding of these two approaches is essential if you are to make sensible investment decisions. It is also a prerequisite for keeping you safe from serious blunders. Toward the end of the twentieth century, a third theory, born in academia and named the new investment technology, became popular on "the Street." Later in the book, I will describe that theory and its application to investment analysis.

THE FIRM-FOUNDATION THEORY

The firm-foundation theory argues that each investment instrument, be it a common stock or a piece of real estate, has a firm anchor of something called intrinsic value, which can be determined by careful analysis of present conditions and future prospects. When market prices fall below (rise above) this firm foundation of intrinsic value, a buying (selling) opportunity arises, because this fluctuation will eventually be corrected—or so the theory goes. Investing then becomes a dull but straightforward matter of comparing something's actual price with its firm foundation of value.

It is difficult to ascribe to any one individual the credit for originating the firm-foundation theory. S. Eliot Guild is often given this distinction, but the classic development of the technique and particularly of the nuances associated with it was worked out by John B. Williams.

In *The Theory of Investment Value*, Williams presented an actual formula for determining the intrinsic value of stock. Williams based his approach on dividend income. In a fiendishly clever attempt to keep things from being simple, he introduced the concept of "discounting" into the process. Discounting basically involves looking at income backwards. Rather than seeing how much money you will have next year (say $1.05 if you put $1 in a savings certificate at 5 percent interest), you look at money expected in the future and see how much less it is worth currently (thus, next year's $1 is worth today only about 95¢, which could be invested at 5 percent to produce approximately $1 at that time).

Williams actually was serious about this. He went on to argue that the intrinsic value of a stock was equal to the present (or discounted) value of all its future dividends. Investors were advised to "discount" the value of moneys received later. Because so few people understood it, the term caught on and "discounting" now enjoys popular usage among investment people. It received a further boost under the aegis of Professor Irving Fisher of Yale, a distinguished economist and investor.

The logic of the firm-foundation theory is quite respectable and can be illustrated with common stocks. The theory stresses that a stock's value ought to be based on the stream of earnings a firm will be able to distribute in the future in the form of dividends. It stands to reason that the greater the present dividends and their rate of increase, the greater the value of the stock; thus, differences in growth rates are a major factor in stock valuation. Now the slippery little factor of future expectations sneaks in. Security analysts must estimate not only long-term growth rates but also how long an extraordinary growth can be maintained. When the market gets overly enthusiastic about how far in the future growth can continue, it is popularly held on Wall Street that stocks are discounting not only the future but perhaps even the hereafter. The point is that the firm-foundation theory relies on some tricky forecasts of the extent and duration of future growth. The foundation of intrinsic value may thus be less dependable than is claimed.

The firm-foundation theory is not confined to economists alone. Thanks to a very influential book, Benjamin Graham and David Dodd's *Security Analysis*, a whole generation of Wall Street security analysts was converted to the fold. Sound investment management, the practicing analysts learned, simply consisted of buying securities whose prices were temporarily below intrinsic value and selling ones whose prices were temporarily too high. It was that easy. Of course, instructions for determining intrinsic value were furnished, and any analyst worth his or her salt could calculate it with simple arithmetic. Perhaps the most successful disciple of the Graham and Dodd approach was a canny midwesterner named Warren Buffett, who is often called "the sage of Omaha." Buffett compiled a legendary investment record, allegedly following the approach of the firm-foundation theory.

THE CASTLE-IN-THE-AIR THEORY

The castle-in-the-air theory of investing concentrates on psychic values. John Maynard Keynes, a famous economist and successful investor, enunciated the theory most lucidly in 1936. It was his opinion that professional investors prefer to devote their energies not to estimating intrinsic values, but rather to analyzing how the crowd of investors is likely to behave in the future and how during periods of optimism they tend to build their hopes into castles in the air. The successful investor tries to beat the gun by estimating what investment situations are most susceptible to public castle-building and then buying before the crowd.

According to Keynes, the firm-foundation theory involves too much work and is of doubtful value. Keynes practiced what he preached. While London's financial men toiled many weary hours in crowded offices, he played the market from his bed for half an hour each morning. This leisurely method of investing earned him several million pounds for his account and a tenfold increase in the market value of the endowment of his college, King's College, Cambridge.

In the depression years in which Keynes gained his fame, most people concentrated on his ideas for stimulating the economy. It was hard for anyone to build castles in the air or to dream that others would. Nevertheless, in his book *The General Theory of Employment, Interest and Money*, Keynes devoted an entire chapter to the stock market and to the importance of investor expectations.

With regard to stocks, Keynes noted that no one knows for sure what will influence future earnings prospects and dividend payments. As a result, he said, most people are "largely concerned, not with making superior long-term forecasts of the probable yield of an investment over its whole life, but with foreseeing changes in the conventional basis of valuation a short time ahead of the general public." Keynes, in other words, applied psychological principles rather than financial evaluation to the study of the stock market. He wrote, "It is not sensible to pay 25 for an investment of which you believe the prospective yield to justify a value of 30, if you also believe that the market will value it at 20 three months hence."

Keynes described the playing of the stock market in terms readily understandable by his fellow Englishmen: It is analogous to entering a newspaper beauty-judging contest in which one must select the six prettiest faces out of a hundred photographs, with the prize going to the person whose selections most nearly conform to those of the group as a whole.

The smart player recognizes that personal criteria of beauty are irrelevant in determining the contest winner. A better strategy is to select those faces the other players are likely to fancy. This logic tends to snowball. After all, the other participants are likely to play the game with at least as keen a perception. Thus, the optimal strategy is not to pick those faces the player thinks are prettiest, or those the other players are likely to fancy, but rather to predict what the average opinion is likely to be about what the average opinion will be, or to proceed even further along this sequence. So much for British beauty contests.

The newspaper-contest analogy represents the ultimate form of the castle-in-the-air theory of price determination. An investment is worth a certain price to a buyer because she expects to sell it to someone else at a higher price. The investment, in other words, holds itself up by its own bootstraps. The new buyer in turn anticipates that future buyers will assign a still higher value.

In this kind of world, a sucker is born every minute—and he exists to buy your investments at a higher price than you paid for them. Any price will do as long as others may be willing to pay more. There is no reason, only mass psychology. All the smart investor has to do is to beat the gun—get in at the very beginning. This theory might less charitably be called the "greater fool" theory. It's perfectly all right to pay three times what something is worth as long as later on you can find some innocent to pay five times what it's worth.

The castle-in-the-air theory has many advocates, in both the financial and the academic communities. The Nobel laureate Robert Shiller, in his book *Irrational Exuberance*, argues that the mania in Internet and high-tech stocks during the late 1990s can be explained only in terms of mass psychology. At universities, so-called behavioral theories of the stock market, stressing crowd psychology, gained favor during the early 2000s at leading economics departments and business schools across the developed world. The psychologist Daniel Kahneman won the Nobel Prize in Economics in 2002 for his seminal contributions to the field of "behavioral finance." Earlier, Oskar Morgenstern was a leading champion. Morgenstern argued that the search for intrinsic value in stocks is a search for the will-o'-the-wisp. In an exchange economy the value of any asset depends on an actual or prospective transaction. He believed that every investor should post the following Latin maxim above his desk:

Res tantum valet quantum vendi potest.
(A thing is worth only what someone else will pay for it.)

HOW THE RANDOM WALK IS TO BE CONDUCTED

With this introduction out of the way, come join me for a random walk through the investment woods, with an ultimate stroll down Wall Street. My first task will be to acquaint you with the historical patterns of pricing and how they bear on the two theories of pricing investments. It was Santayana who warned that if we did not learn the lessons of the past we would be doomed to repeat the same errors. Therefore, I will describe some spectacular crazes— both long past and recently past. Some readers may pooh-pooh the mad public rush to buy tulip bulbs in the seventeenth-century

Netherlands and the eighteenth-century South Sea Bubble in England. But no one can disregard the new-issue mania of the early 1960s, or the "Nifty Fifty" craze of the 1970s. The incredible boom in Japanese land and stock prices and the equally spectacular crash of those prices in the early 1990s, the "Internet craze" of 1999 and early 2000, and the U.S. real estate bubble that ended in 2007 provide continual warnings that neither individuals nor investment professionals are immune from the errors of the past.

2

THE MADNESS OF CROWDS

October. This is one of the peculiarly dangerous months
to speculate in stocks in. The others are July, January,
September, April, November, May, March, June,
December, August and February.
—Mark Twain, *Pudd'nhead Wilson*

G REED RUN AMOK has been an essential feature of every
spectacular boom in history. In their frenzy, market participants ignore firm foundations of value for the dubious
but thrilling assumption that they can make a killing by building
castles in the air. Such thinking has enveloped entire nations.

The psychology of speculation is a veritable theater of the absurd.
Several of its plays are presented in this chapter. The castles that
were built during the performances were based on Dutch tulip
bulbs, English "bubbles," and good old American blue-chip stocks.
In each case, some of the people made money some of the time, but
only a few emerged unscathed.

History, in this instance, does teach a lesson: Although the
castle-in-the-air theory can well explain such speculative binges,
outguessing the reactions of a fickle crowd is a most dangerous game. "In crowds it is stupidity and not mother-wit that is
accumulated," Gustave Le Bon noted in his 1895 classic on crowd
psychology. It would appear that not many have read the book.
Skyrocketing markets that depend on purely psychic support
have invariably succumbed to the financial law of gravitation.
Unsustainable prices may persist for years, but eventually they

reverse themselves. Such reversals come with the suddenness of an earthquake; and the bigger the binge, the greater the resulting hangover. Few of the reckless builders of castles in the air have been nimble enough to anticipate these reversals and to escape when everything came tumbling down.

THE TULIP-BULB CRAZE

The tulip-bulb craze was one of the most spectacular get-rich-quick binges in history. Its excesses become even more vivid when one realizes that it happened in staid old Holland in the early seventeenth century. The events leading to this speculative frenzy were set in motion in 1593 when a newly appointed botany professor from Vienna brought to Leyden a collection of unusual plants that had originated in Turkey. The Dutch were fascinated with this new addition to the garden—but not with the professor's asking price (he had hoped to sell the bulbs and make a handsome profit). One night a thief broke into the professor's house and stole the bulbs, which were subsequently sold at a lower price but at greater profit.

Over the next decade or so, the tulip became a popular but expensive item in Dutch gardens. Many of these flowers succumbed to a nonfatal virus known as mosaic. It was this mosaic that helped to trigger the wild speculation in tulip bulbs. The virus caused the tulip petals to develop contrasting colored stripes or "flames." The Dutch valued highly these infected bulbs, called bizarres. In a short time, popular taste dictated that the more bizarre a bulb, the greater the cost of owning it.

Slowly, tulipmania set in. At first, bulb merchants simply tried to predict the most popular variegated style for the coming year, much as clothing manufacturers do in gauging the public's taste in fabric, color, and hemlines. Then they would buy an extra-large stockpile to anticipate a rise in price. Tulip-bulb prices began to rise wildly. The more expensive the bulbs became, the more people viewed them as smart investments. Charles Mackay, who chronicled these events in his book *Extraordinary Popular Delusions and the Madness of Crowds*, noted that the ordinary industry of the country was dropped in favor of speculation in tulip bulbs: "Nobles, citizens, farmers, mechanics, seamen, footmen, maidservants, even chimney sweeps and old clotheswomen dabbled in tulips." Everyone imagined that the passion for tulips would last forever.

People who said the prices could not possibly go higher watched with chagrin as their friends and relatives made enormous profits. The temptation to join them was hard to resist. In the last years of the tulip spree, which lasted approximately from 1634 to early 1637, people started to barter their personal belongings, such as land, jewels, and furniture, to obtain the bulbs that would make them even wealthier. Bulb prices reached astronomical levels.

Part of the genius of financial markets is that when there is a real demand for a method to enhance speculative opportunities, the market will surely provide it. The instruments that enabled tulip speculators to get the most action for their money were "call options" similar to those popular today in the stock market.

A call option conferred on the holder the right to buy tulip bulbs (call for their delivery) at a fixed price (usually approximating the current market price) during a specified period. He was charged an amount called the option premium, which might run 15 to 20 percent of the current market price. An option on a tulip bulb currently worth 100 guilders, for example, would cost the buyer only about 20 guilders. If the price moved up to 200 guilders, the option holder would exercise his right; he would buy at 100 and simultaneously sell at the then current price of 200. He then had a profit of 80 guilders (the 100 guilders appreciation less the 20 guilders he paid for the option). Thus, he enjoyed a fourfold increase in his money, whereas an outright purchase would only have doubled his money. Options provide one way to leverage one's investment to increase the potential rewards as well as the risks. Such devices helped to ensure broad participation in the market. The same is true today.

The history of the period was filled with tragicomic episodes.

One such incident concerned a returning sailor who brought news to a wealthy merchant of the arrival of a shipment of new goods. The merchant rewarded him with a breakfast of fine red herring. Seeing what he thought was an onion on the merchant's counter, and no doubt thinking it very much out of place amid silks and velvets, he proceeded to take it as a relish for his herring. Little did he dream that the "onion" would have fed a whole ship's crew for a year. It was a costly Semper Augustus tulip bulb. The sailor paid dearly for his relish—his no longer grateful host had him imprisoned for several months on a felony charge.

Historians regularly reinterpret the past, and some financial historians who have reexamined the evidence about various financial bubbles have argued that considerable rationality in pricing may have existed after all. One of these revisionist historians, Peter Garber, has suggested that tulip-bulb pricing in seventeenth-century Holland was far more rational than is commonly believed.

Garber makes some good points, and I do not mean to imply that there was no rationality at all in the structure of bulb prices during the period. The Semper Augustus, for example, was a particularly rare and beautiful bulb and, as Garber reveals, was valued greatly even in the years before the tulipmania. Moreover, Garber's research indicates that rare individual bulbs commanded high prices even after the general collapse of bulb prices, albeit at levels that were only a fraction of their peak prices. But Garber can find no rational explanation for such phenomena as a twentyfold increase in tulip-bulb prices during January of 1637 followed by an even larger decline in prices in February. Apparently, as happens in all speculative crazes, prices eventually got so high that some people decided they would be prudent and sell their bulbs. Soon others followed suit. Like a snowball rolling downhill, bulb deflation grew at an increasingly rapid pace, and in no time at all panic reigned.

Government ministers stated officially that there was no reason for tulip bulbs to fall in price—but no one listened. Dealers went bankrupt and refused to honor their commitments to buy tulip bulbs. A government plan to settle all contracts at 10 percent of their face value was frustrated when bulbs fell even below this mark. And prices continued to decline. Down and down they went until most bulbs became almost worthless—selling for no more than the price of a common onion.

THE SOUTH SEA BUBBLE

Suppose your broker has called you and recommended that you invest in a new company with no sales or earnings—just great prospects. "What business?" you say. "I'm sorry," your broker explains, "no one must know what the business is, but I can promise you enormous riches." A con game, you say. Right you are, but 300 years ago in England this was one of the hottest new issues of the period. And, just as you guessed, investors got very badly burned. The story illustrates how fraud can make greedy people even more eager to part with their money.

At the time of the South Sea Bubble, the British were ripe for throwing away money. A long period of prosperity had resulted in fat savings and thin investment outlets. In those days, owning stock was considered something of a privilege. As late as 1693, for example, only 499 souls benefited from ownership of East India stock. They reaped rewards in several ways, not least of which was that their dividends were untaxed. Also, their number included women, for stock represented one of the few forms of property that British women could possess in their own right. The South Sea Company, which obligingly filled the need for investment vehicles, had been formed in 1711 to restore faith in the government's ability to meet its obligations. The company took on a government IOU of almost £10 million. As a reward, it was given a monopoly over all trade to the South Seas. The public believed immense riches were to be made in such trade and regarded the stock with distinct favor.

From the very beginning, the South Sea Company reaped profits at the expense of others. Holders of the government securities to be assumed by the company simply exchanged their securities for those of the South Sea Company. Those with prior knowledge of the plan quietly bought up government securities selling as low as £55 and then turned them in at par for £100 worth of South Sea stock when the company was incorporated. Not a single director of the company had the slightest experience in South American trade. This did not stop them from quickly outfitting African slave ships (the sale of slaves being one of the most lucrative features of South American trade). But even this venture did not prove profitable, because the mortality rate on the ships was so high.

The directors were, however, wise in the art of public appearance. An impressive house in London was rented, and the boardroom was furnished with thirty black Spanish upholstered chairs whose beechwood frames and gilt nails made them handsome to look at but uncomfortable to sit in. In the meantime, a shipload of company wool that was desperately needed in Vera Cruz was sent instead to Cartagena, where it rotted on the wharf for lack of buyers. Still, the stock of the company held its own and even rose modestly over the next few years despite the dilutive effect of "bonus" stock dividends and a war with Spain that led to a temporary collapse in trading opportunities. John Carswell, the author of an excellent history, *The South Sea Bubble*, wrote of John Blunt, a director and one of the prime promoters of the securities of the South Sea Company, that "he continued to live his life with a prayer-book in his right hand and a prospectus in his left, never letting his right hand know what his left hand was doing."

Across the Channel, another company was formed by an exiled Englishman named John Law. Law's goal in life was to replace metal as money and create more liquidity through a national paper currency. (Bitcoin promotors are following a long tradition.) To further his purpose, Law acquired a derelict concern called the Mississippi Company and proceeded to build a conglomerate that became one of the largest capital enterprises ever to exist.

The Mississippi Company attracted speculators and their

money from throughout the Continent. The word "millionaire" was invented at this time, and no wonder: The price of Mississippi stock rose from £100 to £2,000 in just two years, even though there was no logical reason for such an increase. At one time the inflated total market value of the stock of the Mississippi Company in France was more than eighty times that of all the gold and silver in the country.

Meanwhile, back on the English side of the Channel, a bit of jingoism now began to appear in some of the great English houses. Why should all the money be going to the French Mississippi Company? What did England have to counter this? The answer was the South Sea Company, whose prospects were beginning to look a bit better, especially with the news that there would be peace with Spain and hence the way to the South American trade would at last be clear. Mexicans supposedly were waiting for the opportunity to empty their gold mines in return for England's abundant supply of cotton and woolen goods. This was free enterprise at its finest.

In 1720, the directors, an avaricious lot, decided to capitalize on their reputation by offering to fund the entire national debt, amounting to £31 million. This was boldness indeed, and the public loved it. When a bill to that effect was introduced in Parliament, the stock promptly rose from £130 to £300.

Various friends and backers who had shown interest in getting the bill passed were rewarded with free stock grants that could be "sold" back to the company when the price went up, with the individual collecting the profit. Among those rewarded were George I's mistress and her "nieces," all of whom bore a startling resemblance to the king.

On April 12, 1720, five days after the bill became law, the South Sea Company sold a new issue of stock at £300. The issue could be bought on the installment plan—£60 down and the rest in eight easy payments. Even the king could not resist; he subscribed for stock totaling £100,000. Fights broke out among other investors surging to buy. To ease the public appetite, the South Sea directors announced another new issue—this one at £400. But the public was ravenous. Within a month the stock was £550. On June 15 yet another issue was floated. This time the payment plan was even easier—10 percent down and not another payment for a year. The stock hit £800. Half the House of Lords and more than half the House of Commons signed on. Eventually, the price rose to £1,000. The speculative craze was in full bloom.

Not even the South Sea Company was capable of handling the demands of all the fools who wanted to be parted from their money. Investors looked for other new ventures where they could get in on the ground floor. Just as speculators today search for the next Google, so in England in the early 1700s they looked for the next South Sea Company. Promoters obliged by organizing and bringing to the market a flood of new issues to meet the insatiable craving for investment.

As the days passed, new financing proposals ranged from ingenious to absurd—from importing a large number of jackasses from Spain (even though there was an abundant supply in England) to making salt water fresh. Increasingly the promotions involved some element of fraud, such as making boards out of sawdust. There were nearly one hundred different projects, each more extravagant and deceptive than the other, but each offering the hope of immense gain. They soon received the name of "bubbles," as appropriate a name as could be devised. Like bubbles, they popped quickly—usually within a week or so.

The public, it seemed, would buy anything. New companies seeking financing during this period were organized for such purposes as the building of ships against pirates; encouraging the breeding of horses in England; trading in human hair; building hospitals for bastard children; extracting silver from lead; extracting sunlight from cucumbers; and even producing a wheel of perpetual motion.

The prize, however, must surely go to the unknown soul who started "A Company for carrying on an undertaking of great advantage, but nobody to know what it is." The prospectus promised unheard-of rewards. At nine o'clock in the morning, when the subscription books opened, crowds of people from all walks of life practically beat down the door in an effort to subscribe. Within five hours, one thousand investors handed over their money for shares in the company. Not being greedy himself, the promoter promptly closed up shop and set off for the Continent. He was never heard from again.

Not all investors in the bubble companies believed in the feasibility of the schemes to which they subscribed. People were "too sensible" for that. They did believe, however, in the "greater fool" theory—that prices would rise, that buyers would be found, and that they would make money. Thus, most investors considered their actions the height of rationality, expecting that they could sell their shares at a premium in the "after market," that is, the trading market in the shares after their initial issue.

Whom the gods would destroy, they first ridicule. Signs that the end was near appeared with the issuance of a pack of South Sea playing cards. Each card contained a caricature of a bubble company, with an appropriate verse inscribed underneath. One of these, the Puckle Machine Company, was supposed to produce machines discharging both round and square cannonballs and bullets. Puckle claimed that his machine would revolutionize the art of war. The eight of spades, shown on the following page, described it as follows:

A rare invention to destroy the crowd,
Of fools at home instead of foes abroad:
Fear not my friends, this terrible machine,
They're only wounded that have shares therein.

Many individual bubbles had been pricked without dampening the speculative enthusiasm, but the deluge came in August with an irreparable puncture to the South Sea Company. Realizing that the price of the shares in the market bore no relationship to the real prospects of the company, the directors and officers sold out in the summer.

Puckle's Machine

A rare invention to Destroy the Crowd,
Of Fools at Home instead of Foes Abroad:
Fear not my Friends, this terrible Machine,
They're only Wounded that have Shares therein.

The news leaked and the stock fell. Soon the price of the shares collapsed and panic reigned. The chart below shows the spectacular rise and fall of the stock of the South Sea Company. Government officials tried in vain to restore confidence, and a complete collapse of the public credit was barely averted. Similarly, the price of Mississippi Company shares fell to a pittance as the public realized that an excess of paper currency creates no real wealth, only inflation. Big losers in the South Sea Bubble included Isaac Newton, who exclaimed, "I can calculate the motions of heavenly bodies, but not the madness of people." So much for castles in the air.

To protect the public from further abuses, Parliament passed the Bubble Act, which forbade the issuing of stock certificates by companies. For more than a century, until the act was repealed in 1825, there were relatively few share certificates in the British market.

BRITISH SOUTH SEA COMPANY PRICE, 1717–1722

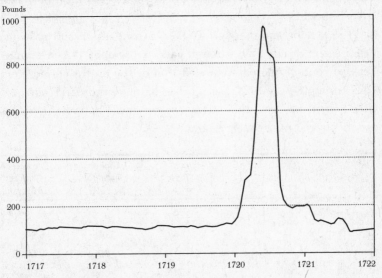

Source: Larry Neal, *The Rise of Financial Capitalism* (Cambridge University Press, 1990).

WALL STREET LAYS AN EGG

The bulbs and bubbles are, admittedly, ancient history. Could the same sort of thing happen in more modern times? Let's turn to more recent events. America, the land of opportunity, had its turn in the 1920s. And given our emphasis on freedom and growth, we produced one of the most spectacular booms and loudest crashes civilization has ever known.

Conditions could not have been more favorable for a speculative craze. The country had been experiencing unrivaled prosperity. One could not but have faith in American business, and as Calvin Coolidge said, "The business of America is business." Businessmen were likened to religious missionaries and almost deified. Such analogies were even made in the opposite direction. Bruce Barton, of the New York advertising agency Batten, Barton, Durstine & Osborn, wrote in *The Man Nobody Knows* that Jesus was "the first businessman" and that his parables were "the most powerful advertisements of all time."

In 1928, stock-market speculation became a national pastime. From early March 1928 through early September 1929, the market's percentage increase equaled that of the entire period from 1923 through early 1928. Stock prices of major industrial corporations sometimes rose 10 or 15 points per day. The price increases are illustrated in the table below.

Security	Opening Price March 3, 1928	High Price September 3, 1929*	Percentage Gain in 18 Months
American Telephone & Telegraph	179½	335⅝	87.0
Bethlehem Steel	56⅞	140⅜	146.8
General Electric	128¾	396¼	207.8
Montgomery Ward	132¾	466½	251.4
National Cash Register	50¾	127½	151.2
Radio Corporation of America	94½	505	434.5

*Adjusted for stock splits and the value of rights received subsequent to March 3, 1928.

Not "everybody" was speculating in the market. Borrowing to buy stocks (buying on margin) did increase from $1 billion in 1921 to almost $9 billion in 1929. Nevertheless, only about one million people owned stocks on margin in 1929. Still, the speculative spirit was at least as widespread as in the previous crazes and was certainly unrivaled in its intensity. More important, stock-market speculation was central to the culture. John Brooks, in *Once in Golconda,** recounted the remarks of a British correspondent newly arrived in New York: "You could talk about Prohibition, or Hemingway, or air conditioning, or music, or horses, but in the end you had to talk about the stock market, and that was when the conversation became serious."

Unfortunately, there were hundreds of smiling operators only too glad to help the public construct castles in the air. Manipulation on the stock exchange set new records for unscrupulousness. No better example can be found than the operation of investment pools. One such undertaking raised the price of RCA stock 61 points in four days.

An investment pool required close cooperation on the one hand and complete disdain for the public on the other. Generally such operations began when a number of traders banded together to manipulate a particular stock. They appointed a pool manager (who justifiably was considered something of an artist) and promised not to double-cross each other through private operations.

The pool manager accumulated a large block of stock through inconspicuous buying over a period of weeks. If possible, he also obtained an option to buy a substantial block of stock at the current market price. Next he tried to enlist the stock's exchange specialist as an ally.

Pool members were in the swim with the specialist on their side. A stock-exchange specialist functions as a broker's broker. If a stock was trading at $50 a share and you gave your broker an order to buy at $45, the broker typically left that order with the specialist.

*Golconda, now in ruins, was a city in India. According to legend, everyone who passed through it became rich.

If and when the stock fell to $45, the specialist then executed the order. All such orders to buy below the market price or sell above it were kept in the specialist's supposedly private "book." Now you see why the specialist could be so valuable to the pool manager. The book gave information about the extent of existing orders to buy and sell at prices below and above the current market. It was always helpful to know as many of the cards of the public players as possible. Now the real fun was ready to begin.

Generally, at this point the pool manager had members of the pool trade among themselves. For example, Haskell sells 200 shares to Sidney at 40, and Sidney sells them back at 40⅛. The process is repeated with 400 shares at prices of 40¼ and 40½. Next comes the sale of a 1,000-share block at 40⅝, followed by another at 40¾. These sales were recorded on ticker tapes across the country, and the illusion of activity was conveyed to the thousands of tape watchers who crowded into the brokerage offices of the country. Such activity, generated by so-called wash sales, created the impression that something big was afoot.

Now tipsheet writers and market commentators under the control of the pool manager would tell of exciting developments in the offing. The pool manager also tried to ensure that the flow of news from the company's management was increasingly favorable. If all went well, and in the speculative atmosphere of the 1928–29 period it could hardly miss, the combination of tape activity and managed news would bring the public in.

Once the public came in, the free-for-all started and it was time discreetly to "pull the plug." As the public did the buying, the pool did the selling. The pool manager began feeding stock into the market, first slowly and then in larger and larger blocks before the public could collect its senses. At the end of the roller-coaster ride, the pool members had netted large profits and the public was left holding the suddenly deflated stock.

But people didn't have to band together to defraud the public. Many individuals, particularly corporate officers and directors, did quite well on their own. Take Albert Wiggin, the head of Chase, the nation's second-largest bank at the time. In July 1929,

Mr. Wiggin became apprehensive about the dizzy heights to which stocks had climbed and no longer felt comfortable speculating on the bull side of the market. (He was rumored to have made millions in a pool boosting the price of his own bank.) Believing that the prospects for his own bank's stock were particularly dim, he sold short more than 42,000 shares of Chase stock. Selling short is a way to make money if stock prices fall. It involves selling stock you do not currently own in the expectation of buying it back later at a lower price. It's hoping to buy low and sell high, but in reverse order.

Wiggin's timing was perfect. Immediately after the short sale, the price of Chase stock began to fall, and when the crash came in the fall the stock dropped precipitously. When the account was closed in November, he had netted a multimillion-dollar profit from the operation. Conflicts of interest apparently did not trouble Mr. Wiggin. In fairness, it should be pointed out that he did retain a net ownership position in Chase stock during this period. Nevertheless, the rules in existence today would not allow an insider to make short-swing profits from trading his own stock.

On September 3, 1929, the market averages reached a peak that was not to be surpassed for a quarter of a century. The "endless chain of prosperity" was soon to break; general business activity had already turned down months before. Prices drifted for the next day, and on the following day, September 5, the market suffered a sharp decline known as the "Babson Break."

This was named in honor of Roger Babson, a frail, goateed, pixyish-looking financial adviser from Wellesley, Massachusetts. At a financial luncheon that day, he had said, "I repeat what I said at this time last year and the year before, that sooner or later a crash is coming." Wall Street professionals greeted the new pronouncements from the "sage of Wellesley," as he was known, with their usual derision.

As Babson implied, he had been predicting the crash for several years and he had yet to be proven right. Nevertheless, at two o'clock in the afternoon, when Babson's words were quoted on the "broad" tape (the Dow Jones financial news tape, which was an essential part of the furniture in every brokerage house), the market went into a nosedive. In the last frantic hour of trading, American Telephone and Telegraph went down 6 points, Westinghouse 7 points, and U.S. Steel 9 points. It was a prophetic episode. After the Babson Break the possibility of a crash, which was entirely unthinkable a month before, suddenly became a common subject for discussion.

Confidence faltered. September had many more bad than good days. At times the market fell sharply. Bankers and government officials assured the country that there was no cause for concern. Professor Irving Fisher of Yale, one of the progenitors of the intrinsic-value theory, offered his soon-to-be-immortal opinion that stocks had reached what looked like a "permanently high plateau."

By Monday, October 21, the stage was set for a classic stock-market break. The declines in stock prices had led to calls for more collateral from margin customers. Unable or unwilling to meet the calls, these customers were forced to sell their holdings. This depressed prices and led to more margin calls and finally to a self-sustaining selling wave.

The volume of sales on October 21 zoomed to more than 6 million shares. The ticker fell way behind, to the dismay of the tens of thousands of individuals watching the tape from brokerage houses around the country. Nearly an hour and forty minutes had elapsed after the close of the market before the last transaction was actually recorded on the stock ticker.

The indomitable Fisher dismissed the decline as a "shaking out of the lunatic fringe that attempts to speculate on margin." He went on to say that prices of stocks during the boom had not caught up with their real value and would go higher. Among other things, the professor believed that the market had not yet reflected the beneficent effects of Prohibition, which had made the American worker "more productive and dependable."

On October 24, later called Black Thursday, the market volume reached almost 13 million shares. Prices sometimes fell $5 and

$10 on each trade. Many issues dropped 40 and 50 points during a couple of hours. On the next day, Herbert Hoover offered his famous diagnosis, "The fundamental business of the country . . . is on a sound and prosperous basis."

Tuesday, October 29, 1929, was among the most catastrophic days in the history of the New York Stock Exchange. Only October 19 and 20, 1987, rivaled in intensity the panic on the exchange. More than 16.4 million shares were traded on that day in 1929. (A 16-million-share day in 1929 would be equivalent to a multi-billion-share day in 2014 because of the greater number of listed shares.) Prices fell almost perpendicularly, and kept on falling, as is illustrated by the following table, which shows the extent of the decline during the autumn of 1929 and over the next three years. With the exception of "safe" AT&T, which lost only three-quarters of its value, most blue-chip stocks had fallen 95 percent or more by the time the lows were reached in 1932.

Security	High Price September 3, 1929*	Low Price November 13, 1929	Low Price for Year 1932
American Telephone & Telegraph	304	197¼	70¼
Bethlehem Steel	140⅜	78¼	7¼
General Electric	396¼	168⅛	8½
Montgomery Ward	137⅞	49¼	3½
National Cash Register	127½	59	6¼
Radio Corporation of America	101	28	2½

*Adjusted for stock splits and the value of rights received subsequent to September 3, 1929.

Perhaps the best summary of the debacle was given by *Variety*, the show-business weekly, which headlined the story "Wall Street Lays an Egg." The speculative boom was dead, and billions of dollars of share values—as well as the dreams of millions—were wiped out. The crash in the stock market was followed by the most devastating depression in history.

Again, there are revisionist historians who say there was a

method to the madness of the stock-market boom of the late 1920s. Harold Bierman Jr., for example, in his book *The Great Myths of 1929*, has suggested that, without perfect foresight, stocks were not obviously overpriced in 1929. After all, very intelligent people, such as Irving Fisher and John Maynard Keynes, believed that stocks were reasonably priced. Bierman goes on to argue that the extreme optimism undergirding the stock market might even have been justified had it not been for inappropriate monetary policies. The crash itself, in his view, was precipitated by the Federal Reserve Board's policy of raising interest rates to punish speculators. There are at least grains of truth in Bierman's arguments, and economists today often blame the severity of the 1930s depression on the Federal Reserve for allowing the money supply to decline sharply. Nevertheless, history teaches us that very sharp increases in stock prices are seldom followed by a gradual return to relative price stability. Even if prosperity had continued into the 1930s, stock prices could never have sustained their advance of the late 1920s.

In addition, the anomalous behavior of closed-end investment company shares (which I will cover in chapter 15) provides clinching evidence of wide-scale stock-market irrationality during the 1920s. The "fundamental" value of these closed-end funds consists of the market value of the securities they hold. In most periods since 1930, these funds have sold at discounts of 10 to 20 percent from their asset values. From January to August 1929, however, the typical closed-end fund sold at a premium of 50 percent. Moreover, the premiums for some of the best-known funds were astronomical. Goldman, Sachs Trading Corporation sold at twice its net asset value. Tri-Continental Corporation sold at 256 percent of its asset value. This meant that you could go to your broker and buy, say, AT&T at whatever its market price was, or you would purchase it through the fund at 2½ times the market value. It was irrational speculative enthusiasm that drove the prices of these funds far above the value at which their individual security holdings could be purchased.

AN AFTERWORD

Why are memories so short? Why do such speculative crazes seem so isolated from the lessons of history? I have no apt answer, but I am convinced that Bernard Baruch was correct in suggesting that a study of these events can help equip investors for survival. The consistent losers in the market, from my personal experience, are those who are unable to resist being swept up in some kind of tulip-bulb craze. It is not hard to make money in the market. What is hard to avoid is the alluring temptation to throw your money away on short, get-rich-quick speculative binges. It is an obvious lesson, but one frequently ignored.

3

SPECULATIVE BUBBLES FROM THE SIXTIES INTO THE NINETIES

Everything's got a moral if only you can find it.
—Lewis Carroll, *Alice's Adventures in Wonderland*

THE MADNESS OF the crowd can be truly spectacular. The examples I have just cited, plus a host of others, have persuaded more and more people to put their money under the care of professional portfolio managers—those who run the large pension and retirement funds, mutual funds, and investment counseling organizations. Although the crowd may be mad, the institution is above all that. Very well, let us then take a look at the sanity of institutions.

THE SANITY OF INSTITUTIONS

By the 1990s, institutions accounted for more than 90 percent of the trading volume on the New York Stock Exchange. One would think that the hardheaded, sharp-penciled reasoning of the pros would guarantee that the extravagant excesses of the past would no longer exist. And yet professional investors participated in several distinct speculative movements from the 1960s through the 1990s. In each case, professional institutions bid actively for stocks not because they felt such stocks were undervalued under the firm-foundation principle, but because they anticipated that some greater fools would take the shares off their hands at even more inflated prices. Because these speculative movements relate to present-day markets, I think you'll find this institutional tour especially useful.

THE SOARING SIXTIES

The New "New Era":
The Growth-Stock/New-Issue Craze

We start our journey when I did—in 1959, when I had just gone to Wall Street. "Growth" was the magic word in those days, taking on an almost mystical significance. Growth companies such as IBM and Texas Instruments sold at price-earnings multiples of more than 80. (A year later they sold at multiples in the 20s and 30s.)

Questioning the propriety of such valuations became almost heretical. Though these prices could not be justified on firm-foundation principles, investors believed that buyers would still eagerly pay even higher prices. Lord Keynes must have smiled quietly from wherever it is that economists go when they die.

I recall vividly one of the senior partners of my firm shaking his head and admitting that he knew of no one with any recollection of the 1929–32 crash who would buy and hold the high-priced growth stocks. But the young Turks held sway. *Newsweek* quoted one broker as saying that speculators have the idea that anything they buy "will double overnight. The horrible thing is, it has happened."

More was to come. Promoters, eager to satisfy the insatiable thirst of investors for the space-age stocks of the Soaring Sixties, created more new issues in the 1959–62 period than at any previous time in history. The new-issue mania rivaled the South Sea Bubble in its intensity and also, regrettably, in the fraudulent practices that were revealed.

It was called the tronics boom, because the stock offerings often included some garbled version of the word "electronics" in their title, even if the companies had nothing to do with the electronics industry. Buyers of these issues didn't really care what the companies made—so long as it sounded electronic, with a suggestion of the esoteric. For example, American Music Guild, whose business consisted entirely of the door-to-door sale of phonograph records and players, changed its name to Space-Tone before "going public." The shares were sold to the public at 2 and, within a few weeks, rose to 14.

Jack Dreyfus, of Dreyfus and Company, commented on the mania as follows:

> Take a nice little company that's been making shoelaces for 40 years and sells at a respectable six times earnings ratio. Change the name from Shoelaces, Inc. to Electronics and Silicon Furth-Burners. In today's market, the words "electronics" and "silicon" are worth 15 times earnings. However, the real play comes from the word "furth-burners," which no one understands. A word that no one understands entitles you to double your entire score. Therefore, we have six times earnings for the shoelace business and 15 times earnings for electronic and silicon, or a total of 21 times earnings. Multiply this by two for furth-burners and we now have a score of 42 times earnings for the new company.

Let the numbers below tell the story. Even Mother's Cookie could count on a sizable gain. Think of the glory it could have achieved if it had called itself Mothertron's Cookitronics. Ten years later, the shares of most of these companies were almost worthless. Today, none exist.

Security	Offering Date	Offering Price	Bid Price on First Day of Trading	High Bid Price 1961	Low Bid Price 1962
Boonton Electronic Corp.	March 6, 1961	5½*	12¼*	24½*	1⅝*
Geophysics Corp.	December 8, 1960	14	27	58	9
Hydro-Space Technology	July 19, 1960	3	7	7	1
Mother's Cookie Corp.	March 8, 1961	15	23	25	7

*Per unit of 1 share and 1 warrant.

Where was the Securities and Exchange Commission (SEC) all this time? Aren't new issuers required to register their offerings with the SEC? Can't they (and their underwriters) be punished for false and misleading statements? Yes, the SEC was there, but by law it had to stand by quietly. As long as a company has prepared (and distributed to investors) an adequate prospectus, the SEC can do nothing to save buyers from themselves. For example, many of the prospectuses of the period contained the following type of warning in bold letters on the cover.

WARNING: THIS COMPANY HAS NO ASSETS OR EARNINGS AND WILL BE UNABLE TO PAY DIVIDENDS IN THE FORESEEABLE FUTURE. THE SHARES ARE HIGHLY RISKY.

But just as the warnings on packs of cigarettes do not prevent many people from smoking, so the warning that this investment may be dangerous to your wealth cannot block a speculator from forking over his money. The SEC can warn fools, but it cannot keep them from parting with their money. And the buyers of new issues were so convinced the stocks would rise in price that the underwriter's problem was not how he could sell the shares but how to allocate them among the frenzied purchasers.

Fraud and market manipulation are different matters. Here the SEC can take and has taken strong action. Indeed, many of the little-known brokerage houses on the fringes of respectability, which were responsible for most of the new issues and for manipulation of their prices, were suspended for a variety of peculations.

The tronics boom came back to earth in 1962. Yesterday's hot issue became today's cold turkey. Many professionals refused to accept the fact that they had speculated recklessly. Very few pointed out that it is always easy to look back and say when prices were too high or too low. Fewer still said that no one seems to know the proper price for a stock at any given time.

Synergy Generates Energy: The Conglomerate Boom

Part of the genius of the financial market is that if a product is demanded, it is produced. The product that all investors desired was expected growth in earnings per share. If growth couldn't be found in a name, it was a good bet that someone would find another way to produce it. By the mid-1960s, creative entrepreneurs suggested that growth could be created by synergism.

Synergism is the quality of having 2 plus 2 equal 5. Thus, two separate companies with an earning power of $2 million each might produce combined earnings of $5 million if the businesses were consolidated. This magical, surefire new creation was called a conglomerate.

Although antitrust laws at that time kept large companies from purchasing firms in the same industry, it was possible to purchase firms in other industries without Justice Department interference. The consolidations were carried out in the name of synergism. Ostensibly, the conglomerate would achieve higher sales and earnings than would have been possible for the independent entities alone.

In fact, the major impetus for the conglomerate wave of the 1960s was that the acquisition process itself could be made to produce growth in earnings per share. Indeed, the managers of conglomerates tended to possess financial expertise rather than the operating skills required to improve the profitability of the acquired companies. By an easy bit of legerdemain, they could put together a group of companies with no basic potential at all and produce steadily rising per-share earnings. The following example shows how this monkey business was performed.

Suppose we have two companies—the Able Circuit Smasher Company, an electronics firm, and Baker Candy Company, which makes chocolate bars. Each has 200,000 shares outstanding. It's 1965 and both companies have earnings of $1 million a year, or $5 per share. Let's assume that neither business is growing and that, with or without merger activity, earnings would just continue along at the same level.

The two firms sell at different prices, however. Because Able Circuit Smasher Company is in the electronics business, the market awards it a price-earnings multiple of 20, which, multiplied by its $5 earnings per share, gives it a market price of $100. Baker Candy Company, in a less glamorous business, has its earnings multiplied at only 10 times and, consequently, its $5 per-share earnings command a market price of only $50.

The management of Able Circuit would like to become a conglomerate. It offers to absorb Baker by swapping stock at the rate of two for three. The holders of Baker shares would get two shares of Able stock—which have a market value of $200—for every three shares of Baker stock—with a total market value of $150. Clearly, Baker's stockholders are likely to accept cheerfully.

We have a budding conglomerate, newly named Synergon, Inc., which now has 333,333 shares outstanding and total earnings of $2 million to put against them, or $6 per share. Thus, by 1966, when the merger has been completed, we find that earnings have risen by 20 percent, from $5 to $6, and this growth seems to justify Able's former price-earnings multiple of 20. Consequently, the shares of Synergon (née Able) rise from $100 to $120, and everyone goes home rich and happy. In addition, the shareholders of Baker who were bought out need not pay any taxes on their profits until they sell their shares of the combined company. The top three lines of the table on page 62 illustrate the transaction.

A year later, Synergon finds Charlie Company, which earns $10 per share, or $1 million with 100,000 shares outstanding. Charlie Company is in the relatively risky military-hardware business, so its shares command a multiple of only 10 and sell at $100. Synergon offers to absorb Charlie Company on a share-for-share exchange basis. Charlie's shareholders are delighted to exchange their $100 shares for the conglomerate's $120 shares. By the end of 1967, the combined company has $3 million in earnings, 433,333 shares outstanding, and $6.92 of earnings per share.

	Company	Earnings Level	Number of Shares Outstanding	Earnings per Share	Price-Earnings Multiple	Price
Before merger 1965	Able	$1,000,000	200,000	$5.00	20	$100
	Baker	1,000,000	200,000	5.00	10	50
After first merger 1966	Synergon (Able and Baker combined)	2,000,000	333,333*	6.00	20	120
	Charlie	1,000,000	100,000	10.00	10	100
After second merger 1967	Synergon (Able, Baker, and Charlie combined)	3,000,000	433,333†	6.92	20	138.4

*The 200,000 original shares of Able plus an extra 133,333, which get printed up to be exchanged for Baker's 200,000 shares according to the terms of the merger.

†The 333,333 shares of Synergon plus the extra 100,000 shares printed up to exchange for Charlie's shares.

Here we have a case where the conglomerate has literally manufactured growth. None of the three companies was growing at all; yet simply by virtue of their merger, our conglomerate will show the following earnings growth:

EARNINGS PER SHARE

	1965	1966	1967
Synergon, Inc.	$5.00	$6.00	$6.92

Synergon is a growth stock, and its record of extraordinary performance appears to have earned it a high and possibly even an increasing multiple of earnings.

The trick that makes the game work is the ability of the electronics company to swap its high-multiple stock for the stock of another company with a lower multiple. The candy company can "sell" its earnings only at a multiple of 10. But when these earnings are averaged with those of the electronics company, the total earnings (including those from selling chocolate bars) could be sold at a multiple of 20. And the more acquisitions Synergon could make, the faster earnings per share would grow and thus the more attractive the stock would look to justify its high multiple.

The whole thing is like a chain letter—no one would get hurt as long as the growth of acquisitions proceeded exponentially. Although the process could not continue for long, the possibilities were mind-boggling for those who got in at the start. It seems difficult to believe that Wall Street professionals could fall for the conglomerate con game, but accept it they did for a period of several years. Or perhaps as subscribers to the castle-in-the-air theory, they only believed that other people would fall for it.

Automatic Sprinkler Corporation (later called A-T-O, Inc., and later still, at the urging of its modest chief executive officer Mr. Figgie, Figgie International) is a real example of how the game of manufacturing growth was actually played. Between 1963 and 1968, the company's sales volume rose by more than 1,400 percent, a phenomenal record due solely to acquisitions. In the middle of 1967, four mergers were completed in a twenty-five-day period. These newly acquired companies, all selling at relatively low price-earnings multiples, helped to produce a sharp growth in earnings per share. The market responded to this "growth" by bidding up the price-earnings multiple to more than 50 times earnings in 1967 and the company's stock price from about $8 per share in 1963 to $73⅝ in 1967.

Mr. Figgie, the president of Automatic Sprinkler, performed the public relations job necessary to help Wall Street build its castle in the air. He automatically sprinkled his conversations with talismanic phrases about the energy of the free-form company and its interface with change and technology. He was careful to point out that he looked at twenty to thirty deals for each one he bought. Wall Street loved every word of it.

Mr. Figgie was not alone in conning Wall Street. Managers of other conglomerates almost invented a new language in the process of dazzling the investment community. They talked about market matrices, core technology fulcrums, modular building blocks, and the nucleus theory of growth. No one from Wall Street really knew what the words meant, but they all got the nice, warm feeling of being in the technological mainstream.

Conglomerate managers also found a new way of describing the businesses they had bought. Their shipbuilding businesses became "marine systems." Zinc mining became the "space minerals division." Steel fabrication plants became the "materials technology division." A lighting fixture or lock company became part of the "protective services division." And if one of the "ungentlemanly" security analysts (somebody from City College of New York rather than Harvard Business School) had the nerve to ask how you can get 15 to 20 percent growth from a foundry or a meat packer, he was told that efficiency experts had isolated millions of dollars of excess costs; that marketing research had found several fresh, uninhabited markets; and that profit margins could be easily tripled within two years. Instead of going down with merger activity, the price-earnings multiples of conglomerate stocks rose for a while. Prices and multiples for a selection of conglomerates in 1967 are shown in the following table.

| | 1967 | | 1969 | |
Security	High Price	Price-Earnings Multiple	Low Price	Price-Earnings Multiple
Automatic Sprinkler (A-T-O, Inc.)	73⅝	51.0	10⅞	13.4
Litton Industries	120½	44.1	55	14.4
Teledyne, Inc.	71½*	55.8	28¼	14.2

*Adjusted for subsequent split.

The music slowed drastically for the conglomerates on January 19, 1968, when the granddaddy of the conglomerates, Litton Industries, announced that earnings for the second quarter of that year would be substantially less than had been forecast. It had recorded 20 percent yearly increases for almost a decade. The market had so thoroughly come to believe in alchemy that the announcement was greeted with disbelief and shock. In the selling wave that followed, conglomerate stocks declined by roughly 40 percent before a feeble recovery set in.

Worse was to come. In July, the Federal Trade Commission announced that it would make an in-depth investigation of the conglomerate merger movement. Again the stocks went tumbling down. The SEC and the accounting profession finally made their move and began to make attempts to clarify the reporting techniques for mergers and acquisitions. The sell orders came flooding in. Shortly afterwards, the SEC and the U.S. Assistant Attorney General in charge of antitrust indicated a strong concern about the accelerating pace of the merger movement.

The aftermath of this speculative phase revealed two disturbing factors. First, conglomerates could not always control their far-flung empires. Indeed, investors became disenchanted with the conglomerate's new math; 2 plus 2 certainly did not equal 5, and some investors wondered whether it even equaled 4. Second, the government and the accounting profession expressed concern about the pace of mergers and about possible abuses. These two worries reduced—and in many cases eliminated—the premium multiples that had been paid in anticipation of earnings growth from the acquisition process alone. This result in itself makes the alchemy game almost impossible, for the acquiring company has to have an earnings multiple larger than the acquired company if the ploy is to work at all.

An interesting footnote to this episode is that during the first two decades of the 2000s deconglomeration came into fashion. Spin-offs of company subsidiaries into separate companies were as a rule rewarded with rising stock prices. The two distinct companies usually had a higher combined market value than the original conglomerate.

Performance Comes to the Market:
The Bubble in Concept Stocks

With conglomerates shattering about them, the managers of investment funds found another magic word, "performance."

Obviously, it would be easier to sell a mutual fund with stocks in its portfolio that went up in value faster than the stocks in its competitors' portfolios.

And perform some funds did—at least over short periods of time. Fred Carr's highly publicized Enterprise Fund racked up a 117 percent total return (including both dividends and capital gains) in 1967 and followed this with a 44 percent return in 1968. The corresponding figures for the Standard & Poor's 500-Stock Index were 25 percent and 11 percent, respectively. This performance brought large amounts of new money into the fund. The public found it fashionable to bet on the jockey rather than the horse.

How did these jockeys do it? They concentrated the portfolio in dynamic stocks, which had a good story to tell, and at the first sign of an even better story, they would quickly switch. For a while the strategy worked well and led to many imitators. The camp followers were quickly given the accolade "go-go funds," and the fund managers often were called "youthful gunslingers." The public's investment dollars flowed into the riskiest of the performance funds.

And so performance investing took hold of Wall Street in the late 1960s. Because near-term performance was especially important (investment services began to publish monthly records of mutual-fund performance), it was best to buy stocks with an exciting concept and a compelling and believable story that the market would recognize now—not far into the future. Hence, the birth of the so-called concept stock.

But even if the story was not totally believable, as long as the investment manager was convinced that the average opinion would think that the average opinion would believe the story, that's all that was needed. The author Martin Mayer quoted one fund manager as saying, "Since we hear stories early, we can figure enough people will be hearing it in the next few days to give the stock a bounce, even if the story doesn't prove out." Many Wall Streeters looked on this as a radical new investment strategy, but John Maynard Keynes had it all spotted in 1936.

Enter Cortes W. Randell. His concept was a youth company

for the youth market. He became founder, president, and major stockholder of National Student Marketing (NSM). First, he sold an image—one of affluence and success. He owned a personal white Learjet named Snoopy, an apartment in New York's Waldorf Towers, a castle with a mock dungeon in Virginia, and a yacht that slept twelve. Adding to his image was an expensive set of golf clubs propped up by his office door. Apparently the only time the clubs were used was at night when the office cleanup crew drove wads of paper along the carpet. Randell spent most of his time visiting institutional fund managers or calling them on the sky phone from his Lear, and he sold the concept of NSM in the tradition of a South Sea Bubble promoter. His real métier was evangelism. The concept that Wall Street bought from Randell was that a single company could specialize in servicing the needs of young people. NSM built its early growth via the merger route, just as the ordinary conglomerates of the 1960s had done. The difference was that each of the constituent companies had something to do with the college-age youth market, from posters and records to sweatshirts and summer job directories. What could be more appealing to a youthful gunslinger than a youth-oriented concept stock—a full-service company to exploit the youth subculture? Glowing press releases and Randell's earnings projections for the company became increasingly optimistic.

The following table clearly shows that institutional investors are at least as adept as the general public at building castles in the air.

Security	High Price 1968–69	Price-Earnings Multiple at High	Number of Institutional Holders Year-End 1969	Low Price 1970	Percentage Decline
National Student Marketing	35¼*	117	31	⅞	98
Performance Systems	23	∞	13	⅛	99

*Adjusted for subsequent stock split.

My favorite example involved Minnie Pearl. Minnie Pearl was a fast-food franchising firm that was as accommodating as all get-out. To please the financial community, Minnie Pearl's chickens became Performance Systems. After all, what better name could be chosen for performance-oriented investors? On Wall Street a rose by any other name does not smell as sweet. The ∞ shown in the table under "price-earnings multiple" indicates that the multiple was infinity. Performance Systems had no earnings at all to divide into the stock's price at the time it reached its high in 1968. As the table indicates, both companies laid an egg—and a bad one at that.

Why did the stocks perform so badly? One general answer was that their price-earnings multiples were inflated beyond reason. If a multiple of 100 drops to a more normal multiple of 20, you have lost 80 percent of your investment right there. In addition, most of the concept companies of the time ran into severe operating difficulties. The reasons were varied: too rapid expansion, too much debt, loss of management control, and so on. These companies were run by executives who were primarily promoters, not sharp-penciled operating managers. Fraudulent practices also were common. For example, NSM's Cortes Randell pleaded guilty to accounting fraud and served eight months in prison.

THE NIFTY FIFTY

In the 1970s, Wall Street's pros vowed to return to "sound principles." Concepts were out and blue-chip companies were in. They would never come crashing down like the speculative favorites of the 1960s. Nothing could be more prudent than to buy their shares and then relax on the golf course.

There were only four dozen or so of these premier growth stocks. Their names were familiar—IBM, Xerox, Avon Products, Kodak, McDonald's, Polaroid, and Disney—and they were called the Nifty Fifty. They were "big capitalization" stocks, which meant that an institution could buy a good-sized position without disturbing the market. And because most pros realized that picking the exact correct time to buy is difficult if not impossible, these stocks seemed to make a great deal of sense. So what if you paid a price that was temporarily too high? These stocks were proven growers, and sooner or later the price would be justified. In addition, these were stocks that—like the family heirlooms—you would never sell. Hence they also were called "one decision" stocks. You made a decision to buy them, once, and your portfolio-management problems were over.

These stocks provided security blankets for institutional investors in another way, too. They were respectable. Your colleagues could never question your prudence in investing in IBM. True, you could lose money if IBM went down, but that was not considered a sign of imprudence (as it would be to lose money in a Performance Systems or a National Student Marketing). Like greyhounds in chase of the mechanical rabbit, big pension funds, insurance companies, and bank trust funds loaded up on the Nifty Fifty one-decision growth stocks. Hard as it is to believe, institutions started to speculate in blue chips. The table below tells the story. Institutional managers blithely ignored the fact that no sizable company could ever grow fast enough to justify an earnings multiple of 80 or 90. They once again proved the maxim that stupidity well packaged can sound like wisdom.

THE DEMISE OF THE NIFTY FIFTY

Security	Price-Earnings Multiple 1972	Price-Earnings Multiple 1980
Sony	92	17
Polaroid	90	16
McDonald's	83	9
Int. Flavors	81	12
Walt Disney	76	11
Hewlett-Packard	65	18

The Nifty Fifty craze ended like all other speculative manias. The same money managers who had worshiped the Nifty Fifty decided that the stocks were overpriced and made a second decision—to sell. In the debacle that followed, the premier growth stocks fell completely from favor.

THE ROARING EIGHTIES

The Return of New Issues

The high-technology, new-issue boom of the first half of 1983 was an almost perfect replica of the 1960s episodes, with the names altered slightly to include the new fields of biotechnology and microelectronics. The 1983 craze made the promoters of the 1960s look like pikers. The total value of new issues during 1983 was greater than the cumulative total of new issues for the entire preceding decade. For investors, initial public offerings (IPOs) were the hottest game in town.

Take, for example, a company that "planned" to mass-produce personal robots, called Androbot, and a chain of three restaurants in New Jersey called Stuff Your Face, Inc. Indeed, the enthusiasm extended to "quality" issues such as Fine Art Acquisitions Ltd. This was not some philistine outfit peddling discount clothing or making computer hardware. This was a truly aesthetic enterprise. Fine Art Acquisitions, the prospectus tells us, was in the business of acquiring and distributing fine prints and Art Deco sculpture replicas. One of the company's major assets consisted of a group of nude photographs of Brooke Shields taken about midway between her time in the stroller and her entrance to Princeton. The pictures were originally owned by—this is absolutely true—a man named Garry Gross. While Fine Arts saw nothing wrong with the pictures of the prepubescent eleven-year-old Brooke, her mother did. The ending, in this case, was a happy one for Brooke: the pictures were returned to Gross and never sold by Fine Arts. The ending was not quite as blissful for Fine Arts, or for most of the other new issues ushered in during the craze. Fine Arts morphed into Dyansen Corporation, complete with gallery in the glitzy Trump Tower, and eventually defaulted in 1993 on a loan made by—are you ready for this?—Chrysler Credit Corporation.

Probably the offering of Muhammad Ali Arcades International burst the bubble. This offering was not particularly remarkable, considering all the other garbage coming out at the time. It was unique, however, in that it showed that a penny could still buy a lot. The company proposed to offer units of one share and two warrants for the modest price of 1¢. Of course, this was 333 times what insiders had recently paid for their own shares, which wasn't unusual either, but when it was discovered that the champ himself had resisted the temptation to buy any stock in his namesake company, investors began to take a good look at where they were. Most did not like what they saw. The result was a dramatic decline in small-company stocks in general and in the market prices of initial public offerings in particular. In the course of a year, many investors lost as much as 90 percent of their money.

The prospectus cover of Muhammad Ali Arcades International featured a picture of the former champ standing over a fallen opponent. In his salad days, Ali used to claim that he could "float like a butterfly and sting like a bee." It turned out that the Ali Arcades offering (as well as the Androbot offering that was scheduled for July 1983) never did get floated. But many others did, particularly stocks of those companies on the bleeding edge of technology. As has been true time and time again, it was the investors who got stung.

Concepts Conquer Again: The Biotechnology Bubble

What electronics was to the 1960s, biotechnology became to the 1980s. The biotech revolution was likened to that of the computer, and optimism regarding the promise of gene-splicing was reflected in the prices of biotech company stocks.

Genentech, the most substantial company in the industry, came to market in 1980. During the first twenty minutes of trading, the stock almost tripled in value. Other new issues of biotech companies were eagerly gobbled up by hungry investors who saw a chance to get into a multibillion-dollar new industry on the ground floor. Interferon, a cancer-fighting drug, drove the first wave of the biotech frenzy. Analysts predicted that its sales would exceed $1 billion by 1982. (In reality, they were barely $200 million in 1989, but there was no holding back the dreams of castles in the air.) Analysts continually predicted an explosion of earnings two years out for the biotech companies and were continually disappointed. But the technological revolution was real, and even weak companies benefited under the umbrella of the technology potential.

Valuation levels of biotechnology stocks reached levels previously unknown to investors. In the 1960s, speculative growth stocks might have sold at 50 times earnings. In the 1980s, some biotech stocks sold at 50 times sales. As a student of valuation techniques, I was fascinated to read how security analysts rationalized these prices. Because biotech companies typically had no current earnings (and realistically no positive earnings expected for several years) and little sales, new valuation methods had to be devised. My favorite was the "product asset valuation" method recommended by one of Wall Street's leading securities houses. Basically, the method involved the estimation of the value of all the products in the "pipeline" of each biotech company. Even if the planned product involved nothing more than the drawings of a genetic engineer, a potential sales volume and a profit margin were estimated. The total value of the "product pipeline" would then give the analyst a fair idea of the price at which the company's stock should sell.

Perhaps U.S. Food and Drug Administration approval would be delayed. (Interferon was delayed for several years.) Would the market bear the projected fancy drug price tags? Would patent protection be possible as virtually every product was being developed simultaneously by several companies, or were patent clashes inevitable? Would much of the potential profit from a successful drug be siphoned off by the marketing partner of the biotech company, usually one of the major drug companies? In the mid-1980s, none of these potential problems seemed real. Indeed, the biotech stocks were regarded by one analyst as less risky than standard drug companies because there were "no old products which need to be offset because of their declining revenues." We had come full circle—having positive sales and earnings was actually considered a drawback because those profits might decline in the future. But during the late 1980s, most biotechnology stocks lost three-quarters of their market value. Even real technology revolutions do not guarantee benefits for investors.

ZZZZ Best Bubble of All

The saga of ZZZZ Best is an incredible Horatio Alger story that captivated investors. In the fast-paced world of entrepreneurs who strike it rich before they can shave, Barry Minkow was a genuine legend of the 1980s. Minkow's career began at age nine. His family could not afford a babysitter, so Barry often went to work at the carpet-cleaning shop managed by his mother. There he began soliciting jobs by phone. By age ten he was actually cleaning carpets. Working evenings and summers, he saved $6,000 within the next four years, and by age fifteen bought some steam-cleaning equipment and started his own carpet-cleaning business in the family's garage. The company was called ZZZZ Best (pronounced "zeee best"). Still in high school and too young to drive, Minkow hired a crew to pick up and clean carpets while he sat in class fretting over each week's payroll. With Minkow working a punishing schedule, the business flourished. He was proud of the fact that he hired his father and mother to work for the business. By age eighteen, Minkow was a millionaire.

Minkow's insatiable appetite for work extended to self-promotion. He drove a red Ferrari and lived in a lavish home with a large pool, which had a big black Z painted on the bottom. He wrote a book entitled *Making It in America*, in which he claimed that teenagers didn't work hard enough. He appeared on *Oprah* as the boy genius of Wall Street and recorded antidrug commercials with the slogan "My act is clean, how's yours?" By this time, ZZZZ Best had 1,300 employees and locations throughout California as well as in Arizona and Nevada.

Was more than 100 times earnings too much to pay for a mundane carpet-cleaning company? Of course not, when the company was run by a spectacularly successful businessman, who could also show his toughness. Minkow's favorite line to his employees was "My way or the highway." And he once boasted that he would fire his own mother if she stepped out of line. When Minkow told Wall Street that his company was better run than IBM and that it was destined to become "the General Motors of carpet cleaning," investors listened raptly. As one security analyst told me, "This one can't miss."

In 1987, Minkow's bubble burst with shocking suddenness. It turned out that ZZZZ Best was cleaning more than carpets—it was also laundering money for the mob. ZZZZ Best was accused of acting as a front for organized-crime figures who would buy equipment for the company with "dirty" money and replace their investment with "clean" cash skimmed from the proceeds of ZZZZ Best's legitimate carpet-cleaning business. The spectacular growth of the company was produced with fictitious contracts, phony credit card charges, and the like. The operation was a giant Ponzi scheme in which money was recycled from one set of investors to pay off another. Minkow was also charged with skimming millions from the company treasury for his own personal use. Minkow and all the investors in ZZZZ Best were in wall-to-wall trouble.

The next chapter of the story (after Chapter Eleven) occurred in 1989 when Minkow, then twenty-three, was convicted of fifty-seven counts of fraud, sentenced to twenty-five years in prison, and required to make restitution of $26 million he was accused of stealing from the company. The U.S. district judge, in rejecting pleas for leniency, told Minkow, "You are dangerous because you have this gift of gab, this ability to communicate." The judge added, "You don't have a conscience."

But the story does not end there. Minkow spent fifty-four months in Lompoc Federal Prison, where he became a born-again Christian, earning bachelor's and master's correspondence school degrees from Liberty University, founded by Jerry Falwell. After his release in December 1994, he became senior pastor at Community Bible Church in California, where he held his congregation in rapt attention with his evangelical style. He wrote several books, including *Cleaning Up and Down, But Not Out*. He was also hired as a special adviser for the FBI on how to spot fraud. In 2006, Minkow's prosecutor, James Asperger, wrote, "Barry has made a remarkable turnaround—both in his personal life and in uncovering more fraud than he ever perpetrated." In 2010, the movie *Minkow* was released. It was billed as "a powerful tale of redemption and inspiration." Unfortunately, the movie story was pure fiction. In 2011, Minkow was sentenced to five years in prison for involvement in a securities fraud; in 2014, he pleaded guilty to embezzling $3 million from the San Diego Community Bible Church, where he had been pastor. Minkow never reformed.

WHAT DOES IT ALL MEAN?

The lessons of market history are clear. Styles and fashions in investors' evaluations of securities can and often do play a critical role in the pricing of securities. The stock market at times conforms well to the castle-in-the-air theory. For this reason, the game of investing can be extremely dangerous.

Another lesson that cries out for attention is that investors should be very wary of purchasing today's hot "new issue." Most initial public offerings underperform the stock market as a whole. And if you buy the new issue after it begins trading, usually at a higher price, you are even more certain to lose. Investors would be well advised to treat new issues with a healthy dose of skepticism.

Certainly investors in the past have built many castles in the air with IPOs. Remember that the major sellers of the stock of IPOs are the managers of the companies themselves. They try to time their sales to coincide with a peak in the prosperity of their companies or with the height of investor enthusiasm for some current fad. In such cases, the urge to get on the bandwagon—even in high-growth industries—produced a profitless prosperity for investors.

The Japanese Yen for Land and Stocks

So far, I have covered only U.S. speculative bubbles. It is important to note that we are not alone. Indeed, one of the largest booms and busts of the late twentieth century involved the Japanese real estate and stock markets. From 1955 to 1990, the value of Japanese real estate increased more than 75 times. By 1990, the total value of all Japanese property was estimated at nearly $20 trillion—equal to more than 20 percent of the entire world's wealth and about double the total value of the world's stock markets. America is twenty-five times bigger than Japan in terms of physical acreage, and yet Japan's property in 1990 was appraised to be worth five times as much as all American property. Theoretically, the Japanese could have bought all the property in America by selling off metropolitan Tokyo. Just selling the Imperial Palace and its grounds at their appraised value would have raised enough cash to buy all of California.

The stock market countered by rising like a helium balloon on a windless day. Stock prices increased 100-fold from 1955 to 1990. At their peak, in December 1989, Japanese stocks had a total market value of about $4 trillion, almost 1.5 times the value of all U.S. equities and close to 45 percent of the world's equity-market capitalization. Firm-foundation investors were aghast at such figures. They read with dismay that Japanese stocks sold at more than 60 times earnings, almost 5 times book value, and more than 200 times dividends. In contrast, U.S. stocks sold at about 15 times earnings, and London equities sold at 12 times earnings. The high prices of Japanese stocks were even more dramatic on a company-by-company comparison. The value of NTT Corporation, Japan's telephone giant, which was privatized during the boom, exceeded the value of AT&T, IBM, Exxon, General Electric, and General Motors put together.

Supporters of the stock market had answers to all the logical objections that could be raised. Were price-earnings ratios in the stratosphere? "No," said the salespeople at Kabuto-cho (Japan's Wall Street). "Japanese earnings are understated relative to U.S. earnings because depreciation charges are overstated and earnings do not include the earnings of partially owned affiliated firms." Price-earnings multiples adjusted for these effects would be much lower. Were yields, at well under ½ of 1 percent, unconscionably low? The answer was that this simply reflected the low interest rates at the time in Japan. Was it dangerous that stock prices were five times the value of assets? Not at all. The book values did not reflect the dramatic appreciation of the land owned by Japanese companies. And the high value of Japanese land was "explained" by both the density of Japanese population and the various regulations and tax laws restricting the use of habitable land.

In fact, none of the "explanations" could hold water. Even when earnings were adjusted, the multiples were still far higher than in other countries and extraordinarily inflated relative to Japan's own history. Moreover, Japanese profitability had been declining, and the strong yen was bound to make it more difficult for Japan to export. Although land was scarce in Japan, its manufacturers, such as its auto makers, were finding abundant land for new plants at attractive prices in foreign lands. And rental income had been rising far more slowly than land values, indicating a falling rate of return on real estate. Finally, the low interest rates that had been underpinning the market had already begun to rise in 1989.

Much to the distress of those speculators who had concluded that the fundamental laws of financial gravity were not applicable to Japan, Isaac Newton arrived there in 1990. Interestingly, it was the government itself that dropped the apple. The Bank of Japan (Japan's Federal Reserve) saw the ugly specter of a general inflation stirring amid the borrowing frenzy and the liquidity boom underwriting the rise in land and stock prices. And so the central bank restricted credit and engineered a rise in interest rates. The hope was that further rises in property prices would be choked off and the stock market might be eased downward.

The stock market was not eased down; instead, it collapsed. The fall was almost as extreme as the U.S. stock-market crash from the end of 1929 to mid-1932. The Japanese (Nikkei) stock-market index reached a high of almost 40,000 on the last trading day of the 1980s. By mid-August 1992, the index had declined to 14,309, a drop of about 63 percent. In contrast, the Dow Jones Industrial Average fell 66 percent from December 1929 to its low in the summer of 1932 (although the decline was over 80 percent from the September 1929 level). The chart below shows quite dramatically that the rise in stock prices during the mid- and late 1980s represented a change in valuation relationships. The fall in stock prices from 1990 on simply reflected a return to the price-to-book-value relationships that were typical in the early 1980s.

The air also rushed out of the real estate balloon during the early 1990s. Various measures of land prices and property values indicate a decline roughly as severe as that of the stock market. The bursting of the bubble destroyed the myth that Japan was different and that its asset prices would always rise. The financial laws of gravity know no geographic boundaries.

THE JAPANESE STOCK-MARKET BUBBLE
JAPANESE STOCK PRICES RELATIVE TO BOOK VALUES, 1980–2000

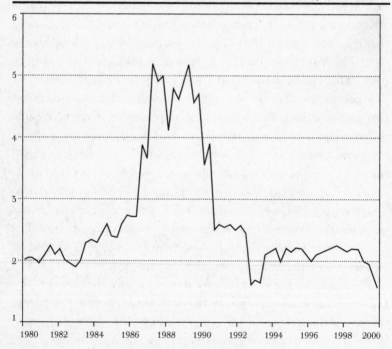

Source: Morgan Stanley Research and author's estimates.

4

THE EXPLOSIVE BUBBLES
OF THE EARLY 2000s

If you can keep your head when all about you
Are losing theirs . . .
Yours is the Earth and everything that's in it . . . .
—Rudyard Kipling, "If—"

FINANCIALLY DEVASTATING AS the bubbles of the last decades of the twentieth century were, they cannot compare with those of the first decade of the twenty-first century. When the Internet bubble popped in the early 2000s, over $8 trillion of market value evaporated. It was as if a year's output of the economies of Germany, France, England, Italy, Spain, the Netherlands, and Russia had completely disappeared. The entire world economy almost crashed when the U.S. real estate bubble popped, and a prolonged world recession followed. Comparing either of these bubbles to the tulip-bulb craze is undoubtedly unfair to the flowers.

THE INTERNET BUBBLE

Most bubbles have been associated with some new technology (as in the tronics and biotech booms) or with some new business opportunity (as when the opening of profitable new trade opportunities spawned the South Sea Bubble). The Internet was associated with both: it represented a new technology, and it offered new business opportunities that promised to revolutionize the way we obtain information and purchase goods and services. The promise of the Internet spawned the largest creation and largest destruction of stock market wealth of all time.

Robert Shiller, in his book *Irrational Exuberance*, describes bubbles in terms of "positive feedback loops." A bubble starts when any group of stocks, in this case those associated with the excitement of the Internet, begin to rise. The updraft encourages more people to buy the stocks, which causes more TV and print coverage, which causes even more people to buy, which creates big profits for early Internet stockholders. The successful investors tell you at cocktail parties how easy it is to get rich, which causes the stocks to rise further, which pulls in larger and larger groups of investors. But the whole mechanism is a kind of Ponzi scheme where more and more credulous investors must be found to buy the stock from the earlier investors. Eventually, one runs out of greater fools.

Even highly respected Wall Street firms joined in the hot-air float. The venerable investment firm Goldman Sachs argued in mid-2000 that the cash burned by the dot-com companies was primarily an "investor sentiment" issue and not a "long-term risk" for the sector or "space," as it was often called. A few months later, hundreds of Internet companies were bankrupt, proving that the Goldman report was inadvertently correct. The cash burn rate was not a long-term risk—it was a short-term risk.

Until that moment, anyone scoffing at the potential for the "New Economy" was a hopeless Luddite. As the chart on page 81 indicates, the NASDAQ Index, an index essentially representing high-tech New Economy companies, more than tripled from late 1998 to March 2000. The price-earnings multiples of the stocks in the index that had earnings soared to over 100.

**NASDAQ COMPOSITE STOCK INDEX,
JULY 1999–JULY 2002**

A Broad-Scale High-Tech Bubble

At the bubble's height, scoffers were hard to find. Surveys of investors in early 2000 revealed that expectations of future stock returns ranged from 15 percent per year to 25 percent or higher. For companies such as Cisco and JDS Uniphase, widely known as producing "the backbone of the Internet," 15 percent returns per year were considered a slam dunk. But Cisco was selling at a triple-digit multiple of earnings and had a market capitalization of almost $600 billion. If Cisco grew its earnings at 15 percent per year, it would still be selling at a well above average multiple ten years later. And if Cisco returned 15 percent per year for the next twenty-five years and the national economy continued to grow at 5 percent over the same period, Cisco would have been bigger than the entire economy. Obviously, there was a complete disconnect between stock-market valuations and any reasonable expectations of future growth. And even blue-chip Cisco lost over 90 percent of its market value when the bubble burst and the forecasted growth never happened. As for JDS Uniphase, the following chart plots its prices against the NASDAQ Index from mid-1997 through mid-2002. By comparison, the bubble in the overall index is hardly noticeable.

COMPARISON OF JDS UNIPHASE STOCK WITH THE NASDAQ COMPOSITE INDEX, JULY 1997–JULY 2002

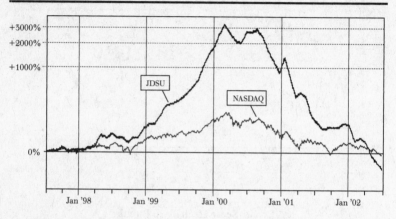

In the name game during the tronics boom, all manner of companies added the suffix "tronics" to increase their attractiveness; the same happened during the Internet mania. Dozens of companies, even those that had little or nothing to do with the Net, changed their names to include web-oriented designations such as dot.com, dotnet, or Internet. Three researchers from Purdue University, M. Cooper, D. Dimitrov, and P. R. Rau, studied sixty-three companies that changed their names in 1998 and 1999 to include some web orientation. Measuring the price change of the companies from five days prior to a name change (when word of the change began to leak out) to five days after the change was announced, they confirmed a remarkable effect. Companies that changed their names enjoyed an increase in price during that ten-day period that was 125 percent greater than that of their peers. This price increase occurred even when the company's core business had nothing whatsoever to do with the Net. In the market decline that followed, shares in these companies became worthless. As the following table shows, investors suffered punishing losses even in the leading Internet companies.

HOW EVEN THE LEADING NEW ECONOMY STOCKS RUINED INVESTORS

Stock	High 2000	Low 2001–2002	Percentage Decline
Amazon.com	75.25	5.51	98.7
Cisco Systems	82.00	11.04	86.5
Corning	113.33	2.80	99.0
JDS Uniphase	297.34	2.24	99.5
Lucent Technologies	74.93	1.36	98.3
Nortel Networks	143.62	.76	99.7
Priceline.com	165.00	1.80	99.4
Yahoo.com	238.00	8.02	96.4

PalmPilot, the maker of Personal Digital Assistants (PDAs), is an example of the insanity that went well beyond irrational exuberance. Palm was owned by a company called 3Com, which decided to spin it off to its shareholders. Since PDAs were touted as a sine qua non of the digital revolution, it was assumed that PalmPilot would be a particularly exciting stock. Little did 3Com know how strongly the market would react.

In early 2000, 3Com sold 5 percent of its shares in Palm in an initial public offering and announced its intention to spin off all the remaining shares to the 3Com shareholders. Palm took off so fast that its market capitalization became twice as large as that of 3Com. It turned out that the market value of the 95 percent of Palm owned by 3Com was almost $25 billion greater than the total market capitalization of 3Com itself. It was as if all of 3Com's other assets had been worth a negative $25 billion. If you wanted to buy PalmPilot, you could have bought 3Com and owned the rest of 3Com's business for minus $61 per share. In its mindless search for riches, the market created anomalies that were even stranger than the fraudulent accounting practices that were soon to be revealed.

Yet Another New-Issue Craze

In the first quarter of 2000, 916 venture capital firms invested $15.7 billion in 1,009 startup Internet companies. Many were playing catch-up: an astonishing 159 initial public offerings (IPOs) had been successfully completed in the preceding quarter. It was as if the stock market was on steroids. As happened during the South Sea Bubble, many companies that received financing were absurd. Almost all turned out to be dot-com catastrophes. Consider the following examples of Internet startups.

- Digiscents offered a peripheral you could plug into your computer that would make websites and computer games smell. The company ran through millions from venture capitalists trying to develop such a product.
- Flooz offered an alternative currency—Flooz—that could be e-mailed to friends and family. It was not quite money, because there were only a few places you could use it, but it sure made a unique gift. In order to jump-start the company, Flooz.com turned to an old business school maxim that "any idiot can sell a one-dollar bill for eighty cents." Flooz.com launched a special offer to American Express platinum card holders allowing them to buy $1,000 of Flooz currency for just $800. Shortly before declaring bankruptcy, Flooz itself was Floozed when Filipino and Russian gangs bought $300,000 of its currency using stolen credit card numbers.
- Consider Pets.com, a real dog if there ever was one. The company had a sock-puppet mascot that starred in its TV commercials and even made an appearance at a Macy's Thanksgiving Day Parade. Unfortunately, the popularity of its mascot did not compensate for the fact that it's hard to make a profit individually shipping low-margin 25-pound bags of kibble.

The names alone of many of the Internet ventures stretch credulity: Bunions.com, Crayfish, Zap.com, Gadzooks, Fogdog, FatBrain, Jungle.com, Scoot.com, mylackey.com, and, moreover, Moreover .com. And then there was ezboard.com, which produced Internet pages called toilet paper, to help you "get the poop" on the online community. These were not business models. They were models for business failure.

Philip J. Kaplan proved to be a brilliant chronicler of the stupidity of the new dot-com financings. Deciding to kill some time during a Memorial Day weekend just after the bubble deflated, he set up a website F**kedcompany.com that offered the latest gossip about sinking dot-com companies as well as a betting pool on when the companies would go under. (The website could be accessed by filling in the expurgated characters censored above.) The site attracted four million viewers. Kaplan then published a book named after the site where he ridiculed a hundred of the most ludicrous of the dot-com business ideas. Here is how Kaplan described the flameout of SwapIt.com.

SO LET ME GET THIS STRAIGHT:

1) I send them a CD.

2) They give me useless "SwapIt Bucks."

3) They go out of business.

4) I get nothing.

Great, sign me up!

SwapIt.com was a fiercely stupid idea. The premise was that people could trade used CDs and video games with one another by physically mailing their crap to SwapIt.com. Users would then be issued "SwapIt Bucks" that they could use to buy other people's crap that had also been sent to the company. . . .

eBay's entire success is based on the fact that they have no inventory. By dealing with all the inventory and fulfillment, SwapIt is like all of the crap with none of the benefit.

TheGlobe.com

My most vivid memory of the IPO boom dates back to an early morning in November 1998, when I was being interviewed on a TV show. While waiting in my suit and tie in the "green room," I thought how out of place it was to be sitting next to two young men dressed in jeans who, while in their early twenties, looked like teenagers. Little did I realize that they were the first superstars of the Internet boom and the featured attractions on the show. Stephan Paternot and Todd Krizelman had formed TheGlobe.com in Todd's dorm room at Cornell. The company was an online message board system that hoped to generate large revenues from selling banner advertising. In earlier times, one needed actual revenues and profits to come to market with an IPO. TheGlobe.com had neither. Nevertheless, its bankers, Credit Suisse First Boston, brought it to market at a price of $9 per share. The price immediately soared to $97, at that time the largest first-day gain in history, giving the company a market value of nearly $1 billion and making the two founders multimillionaires. That day we learned that investors would throw money at businesses that only five years before would not have passed normal due diligence hurdles.

The initial public offering of TheGlobe.com was the catalyst that launched the pathological phase of the Internet bubble. The relationship between profits and share price had been severed, and a wave of money-losing ventures rushed to the market with IPOs. As for Paternot, a CNN segment in 1999 caught him at a trendy New York nightclub dancing on a table, in shiny plastic black pants, with his trophy model girlfriend. On camera Paternot was heard to say, "Got the girl, got the money. Now I'm ready to live a disgusting, frivolous life." Paternot and Krizelman became known as the "global poster boys of Internet excess." TheGlobe.com closed its website in 2001. And though Paternot may no longer be living a "disgusting" life, in 2010, he was serving as executive producer of the independent film *Down and Dirty Pictures*.

While the party was still going strong in early 2000, John Doerr, a leading venture capitalist with the preeminent firm of Kleiner Perkins, called the rise in Internet-related stocks "the greatest legal creation of wealth in the history of the planet." In 2002, he neglected to write that it was also the greatest legal destruction of wealth on the planet.

Doonesbury

Source: Doonesbury © 1998 G. B. Trudeau. Reprinted with permission of UNIVERSAL UCLICK. All rights reserved.

Security Analysts $peak Up

Wall Street's high-profile securities analysts provided much of the hot air floating the Internet bubble. Mary Meeker of Morgan Stanley, Henry Blodgett of Merrill Lynch, and Jack Grubman of Salomon Smith Barney became household names and were accorded superstar status. Meeker was dubbed by *Barron's* the "Queen of the 'Net." Blodgett was known as "King Henry," while Grubman acquired the sobriquet "Telecom Guru." Like sports heroes, each of them was earning a multimillion-dollar salary. Their incomes, however, were based not on the quality of their analysis but rather on their ability to steer lucrative investment banking business to their firms by implicitly promising that their ongoing favorable research coverage would provide continuing support for the initial public offerings in the after market.

Traditionally, a "Chinese Wall" was supposed to separate the research function of Wall Street firms, which is supposed to work for the benefit of investors, from the very profitable investment banking function, which works for the benefit of corporate clients. But during the bubble, that wall became more like Swiss cheese.

Analysts were the very public cheerleaders for the boom. Blodgett flatly stated that traditional valuation metrics were not relevant in "the big-bang stage of an industry." Meeker suggested, in a flattering *New Yorker* profile in 1999, that "this is a time to be rationally reckless." Their public comments on individual stocks made prices soar. And why not? Stock selections were described in terms of powerful baseball hits: A stock that would be expected to quadruple was a "Four Bagger." More exciting stocks might be "Ten Baggers."

Securities analysts always find reasons to be bullish. They seldom utter the four-letter "sell" word, because they do not want to endanger current or future investment banking relationships or to offend corporate chief financial officers. Traditionally, ten stocks were rated "buys" for each one rated "sell." But during the bubble, the ratio was almost a hundred to one. And as stocks soared, Americans became convinced that investing was easy. They watched

CNBC's interviews with their favorite investment gurus, devouring the fluff the analysts were peddling. When the bubble burst, the celebrity analysts faced death threats and lawsuits; and their firms faced investigations and fines by the SEC and the New York State Attorney General Eliot Spitzer. Blodgett was renamed the "clown prince" of the Internet bubble by the *New York Post*. Grubman was ridiculed before a congressional committee for his continuous touting of WorldCom stock and investigated for changing his stock ratings to help obtain investment banking business. Both Blodgett and Grubman left their firms. *Fortune* magazine summed it all up with a picture of Mary Meeker on the cover and the caption "Can We Ever Trust Wall Street Again?"

New Valuation Metrics

In order to justify ever higher prices for Internet-related companies, security analysts began to use a variety of "new metrics" that could be used to value the stocks. After all, the New Economy stocks were a breed apart—they should certainly not be held to the fuddy-duddy old-fashioned standards such as price-earnings multiples that had been used to value traditional old-economy companies.

Somehow, in the brave new Internet world, sales, revenues, and profits were irrelevant. In order to value Internet companies, analysts looked instead at "eyeballs"—the number of people viewing a web page or "visiting" a website. Particularly important were numbers of "engaged shoppers"—those who spent at least three minutes on a website. Mary Meeker gushed enthusiastically about Drugstore.com because 48 percent of the eyeballs viewing the site were "engaged shoppers." No one cared whether the engaged shopper ever forked over any greenbacks. Sales were so old-fashioned. Drugstore.com hit $67.50 during the height of the bubble of 2000. A year later, when eyeballs started looking at profits, it was a "penny" stock.

"Mind share" was another popular nonfinancial metric that convinced me that investors had lost their collective minds. For example, the online home seller Homestore.com was highly recommended in October 2000 by Morgan Stanley because 72 percent of all the time spent by Internet users on real estate websites was spent on properties listed by Homestore.com. But "mind share" did not lead Internet users to make up their minds to buy the properties listed and did not prevent Homestore.com from falling 99 percent from its high during 2001.

Special metrics were established for telecom companies. Security analysts clambered into tunnels to count the miles of fiber-optic cable in the ground rather than examining the tiny fraction that was actually lit up with traffic. Each telecom company borrowed money with abandon, and enough fiber was laid to circle the earth 1,500 times. As a sign of the times, the telecom and Internet service provider PSI Net (now bankrupt) put its name on the Baltimore Ravens' football field. As the prices of telecom stocks continued to skyrocket well past any normal valuation standards, security analysts did what they often do—they just lowered their standards.

The ease with which telecoms could raise money from Wall Street led to massive oversupply—too much long-distance fiber-optic cable, too many computers, and too many telecom companies. In 2002, mighty WorldCom declared bankruptcy. And the big equipment companies such as Lucent and Nortel, which had engaged in risky vendor financing deals, suffered staggering losses. Most of the trillion dollars thrown into telecom investments during the bubble vaporized. One of the jokes making the rounds of the Internet in 2001 went as follows:

> *Tip of the Week*
>   *If you bought $1,000 worth of Nortel stock one year ago, it would now be worth $49.*
>   *If you bought $1,000 worth of Budweiser (the beer, not the stock) one year ago, drank all the beer, and traded in the cans for the nickel deposit, you would have $79.*
>   *My advice to you . . . start drinking heavily.*

By the fall of 2002, the $1,000 put into Nortel stock was worth only $3.

The Writes of the Media

The bubble was aided and abetted by the media, which turned us into a nation of traders. Like the stock market, journalism is subject to the laws of supply and demand. Since investors wanted more information about Internet investing opportunities, the supply of magazines increased to fill the need. And since readers were not interested in downbeat skeptical analyses, they flocked to those publications that promised an easy road to riches. Investment magazines featured stories such as "Internet stocks likely to double in the months ahead." As Jane Bryant Quinn remarked, it was "investment pornography"—"soft core rather than hard core, but pornography all the same."

A number of business and technology magazines devoted to the Internet sprang up to satisfy the insatiable public desire for more information. *Wired* described itself as the vanguard of the digital revolution. The *Industry Standard*'s IPO tracker was the most widely followed index in Silicon Valley. *Business 2.0* prided itself as the "oracle of the New Economy." The proliferation of publications was a classic sign of a speculative bubble. The historian Edward Chancellor pointed out that during the 1840s, fourteen weeklies and two dailies were introduced to cover the new railroad industry. During the financial crisis of 1847, many of the rail publications perished. When the *Industry Standard* failed in 2001, the *New York Times* editorialized, "it may well go down as the day the buzz died."

The Internet itself became the media. No longer did the individual investor have to consult the *Wall Street Journal* or call a broker to get a stock's price quote. All the information needed was available online in real time. The web provided stock summaries, analyst ratings, past stock charts, forecasts of next quarter's earnings and long-term growth, and instant access to any news items about most any stock. The Internet had democratized the investment process, and it played an important enabling role in perpetuating the bubble.

Online brokers were also a critical factor in fueling the Internet boom. Trading was cheap, at least in terms of the small dollar amount of commissions charged. (Actually, the costs of trading were larger than most online brokers advertised, since much of the cost is buried in the spread between a dealer's "bid" price, the price at which a customer could sell, and the "asked" price, the price at which a customer could buy.) The discount brokerage firms advertised heavily and made it seem that it was easy to beat the market. In one commercial, the customer boasted that she did not simply want to beat the market but to "throttle its scrawny little body to the ground and make it beg for mercy." In another popular TV commercial, Stuart, the cybergeek from the mailroom, was encouraging his old-fashioned boss to make his first online stock purchase with the exhortation "Let's light this candle." When the boss protested that he knew nothing about the stock, Stuart said, "Let's research it." After one click on the keyboard, the boss, thinking himself much wiser, bought his first hundred shares.

Cable networks such as CNBC and Bloomberg became cultural phenomena. Across the world, health clubs, airports, bars, and restaurants were permanently tuned in to CNBC. The stock market was treated like a sports event with a pre-game show (what to expect before the market opened), a play-by-play during trading hours, and a post-game show to review the day's action and to prepare investors for the next. CNBC implied that listening would put you "ahead of the curve." Most guests were bullish. CNBC's former commentator Maria (the money honey) Bartiromo particularly favored scheduling interviews with analysts who could say with confidence that some $50 dot-com stock would soon go to $500. There was no need to remind a CNBC anchor that, just as the family dog that bites the baby is likely to have a short tenure, sourpuss skeptics did not encourage high ratings.

The market was a hotter story than sex. Even Howard Stern would interrupt more usual discussions about porn queens and body parts to muse about the stock market and then to tout some particular Internet stocks.

Turnover reached an all-time high. The average holding period for a typical stock was no longer years or months but days and even hours. Redemption ratios of mutual funds (the percentage of the funds' assets redeemed) soared, and the volatility of individual stock prices exploded. The ten most volatile stocks in each trading day used to rise or fall by 5 percent. By early 2000, the biggest price changes were 50 percent or more. And there were 10 million Internet "day traders," many of whom had quit their jobs to go down the easy path to riches. For them, the long term meant later in the morning. It was lunacy. People who would spend hours researching the pros and cons of buying a $50 kitchen appliance would risk tens of thousands on a chat-room tip. Terrance Odean, a finance professor who studies investor behavior, found with his colleagues that most Internet traders actually lost money even during the bubble, systematically buying and selling the wrong stocks, and that they performed worse the more they traded. The average survival time for day traders was about six months.

Fraud Slithers In and Strangles the Market

Speculative manias, such as the Internet bubble, bring out the worst aspects of our system. Let there be no mistake: It was the extraordinary New Economy mania that encouraged a string of business scandals that shook the capitalist system to its roots.

Many businesses were managed not for the creation of long-run value but for the immediate gratification of speculators. When Wall Street's conflicted sell-side analysts looked for high short-term forecasted earnings to justify outlandishly high stock prices, many corporate managers willingly obliged. And if aggressive earnings targets proved hard to meet, "creative accounting" could be used so that not only the published street estimates but even the "whisper numbers" could be surpassed. One spectacular example was the rise and subsequent bankruptcy of Enron—at one time the seventh-largest corporation in America. The collapse of Enron, where over $65 billion of market value was wiped out, can be understood only in the context of the enormous bubble in the New Economy part of the stock market. Enron was seen as the perfect New Economy stock that could dominate the market not just for energy but also for broadband communications, widespread electronic trading, and commerce.

Enron was a clear favorite of Wall Street analysts. Even after it began to unravel during the fall of 2001, sixteen out of seventeen security analysts covering Enron had "buy" or "strong buy" ratings on the stock. Old utility and energy companies were likened by *Fortune* magazine to "a bunch of old fogies and their wives shuffling around to the sounds of Guy Lombardo." Enron was likened to a young Elvis Presley "crashing through the skylight" in his skintight gold-lamé suit. The writer left out the part where Elvis ate himself to death. Enron set the standard for thinking outside the box—the quintessential killer app, paradigm-shifting company. Unfortunately, it also set new standards for obfuscation and deception.

One of the scams perpetrated by Enron management was the establishment of a myriad of complex partnerships that obfuscated the true financial position of the firm and led to an overstatement of Enron's earnings. Here is how one of the simpler ones worked. Enron formed a joint venture with Blockbuster to rent out movies online. The deal failed several months later. But after the venture was formed, Enron secretly set up a partnership with a Canadian bank that essentially lent Enron $115 million in exchange for future profits from the Blockbuster venture. Of course, the Blockbuster deal never made a nickel, but Enron counted the $115 million loan as a "profit." Wall Street analysts applauded and called Ken Lay, Enron's chairman, the "mastermind of the year."

Other partnerships, with names like Cheruco (named for Chewbacca, the *Star Wars* Wookie), Raptor, and Jedi, had similar effects, since the Force was clearly with Enron. And the Force was generous. Before the law caught up with him, Andrew Fastow, Enron's chief financial officer, made $30 million in fees for running "independent" partnerships. The partnerships were kept off Enron's financial statements, which had the effect of inflating earnings and obscuring losses and indebtedness. The accounting firm of Arthur Andersen certified the books as "fairly stating" Enron's financial condition. And Wall Street was delighted to collect lucrative fees from the creative partnerships that were established.

Deception appeared to be a way of life at Enron. The *Wall Street Journal* reported that Ken Lay and Jeff Skilling, Enron's top executives, were personally involved in establishing a fake trading room to impress Wall Street security analysts, in an episode employees referred to as "The Sting." The best equipment was purchased, employees were given parts to play arranging fictitious deals, and even the phone lines were painted black to make the operation look particularly slick. The whole thing was an elaborate charade. In 2006, Lay and Skilling were convicted of conspiracy and fraud. A broken man, Ken Lay died later that year.

One employee, who lost his job and his retirement savings when Enron collapsed into bankruptcy, took to the web, where he sold T-shirts with the message "I got lay'd by enron."

But Enron was only one of a number of accounting frauds that were perpetrated on unsuspecting investors. Various telecom companies overstated revenues through swaps of fiber-optic capacity at inflated prices. Tyco created "cookie jar" reserves and accelerated pre-merger outlays to "springload" earnings from acquisitions. WorldCom admitted that it had overstated profits and cash flow by $7 billion, by classifying ordinary expenses, which should have been charged against earnings, as capital investments, which were not deducted from the bottom line. In far too many cases, corporate chief executive officers (CEOs) acted more like chief embezzlement officers, and some chief financial officers (CFOs) could more appropriately be called corporate fraud officers. While analysts were praising stocks like Enron and WorldCom to the skies, some corporate officers were transforming the meaning of EBITDA from earnings before interest, taxes, depreciation, and amortization to "earnings before I tricked the dumb auditor."

Should We Have Known the Dangers?

Fraud aside, we should have known better. We should have known that investments in transforming technologies have often proved unrewarding for investors. In the 1850s, the railroad was widely expected to greatly increase the efficiency of communications and commerce. It certainly did so, but it did not justify the prices of railroad stocks, which rose to enormous speculative heights before collapsing in August 1857. A century later, airlines and television manufacturers transformed our country, but most of the early investors lost their shirts. The key to investing is not how much an industry will affect society or even how much it will grow, but rather its ability to make and sustain profits. And history tells us that eventually all excessively exuberant markets succumb to the laws of gravity. The consistent losers in the market, from my personal experience, are those who are unable to resist being swept up in some kind of tulip-bulb craze. It is not hard, really, to make money in the market. As we shall see later, an investor who simply buys and holds a broad-based portfolio of stocks can make reasonably generous long-run returns. What is hard to avoid is the alluring temptation to throw your money away on short, get-rich-quick speculative binges.

There were many villains in this morality tale: the fee-obsessed underwriters who should have known better than to peddle all of the crap they brought to market; the research analysts who were the cheerleaders for the banking departments and who were eager to recommend Net stocks that could be pushed by commission-hungry brokers; corporate executives using "creative accounting" to inflate their profits. But it was the infectious greed of individual investors and their susceptibility to get-rich-quick schemes that allowed the bubble to expand.

And yet the melody lingers on. I have a friend who built a modest investment stake into a small fortune with a diversified portfolio of bonds, real estate funds, and stock funds that owned a broad selection of blue-chip companies. But he was restless. At cocktail parties he kept running into people boasting about this

Internet stock that tripled or that telecom chipmaker that doubled. He wanted some of the action. Along came a stock called Boo.com, an Internet retailer that planned to sell with no discounts "urban chic clothing—that was so cool it wasn't even cool yet." In other words, Boo.com was going to sell at full price clothes that people were not yet wearing. But my friend had seen the cover of *Time* with the headline "Kiss Your Mall Goodbye: Online Shopping Is Faster, Cheaper, and Better." The prestigious firm of JP Morgan had invested millions in the company, and *Fortune* called it one of the "cool companies of 1999."

My friend was hooked. "This Boo.com story will have all the tape watchers drooling with excitement and conjuring up visions of castles in the air. Any delay in buying would be self-defeating." And so my friend had to rush in before greater fools would tread.

The company blew through $135 million in two years before going bankrupt. The co-founder, answering charges that her firm spent too extravagantly, explained, "I only flew Concorde three times, and they were all special offers." Of course, my friend had bought in just at the height of the bubble, and he lost his entire investment when the firm declared bankruptcy. The ability to avoid such horrendous mistakes is probably the most important factor in preserving one's capital and allowing it to grow. The lesson is so obvious and yet so easy to ignore.

THE U.S. HOUSING BUBBLE AND CRASH OF THE EARLY 2000s

Although the Internet bubble may have been the biggest stock-market bubble in the United States, the bubble in single-family home prices that inflated during the early years of the new millennium was undoubtedly the biggest U.S. real estate bubble of all time. Moreover, the boom and later collapse in house prices had far greater significance for the average American than any gyrations in the stock market. The single-family home represents the largest asset in the portfolios of most ordinary investors, so falling home prices have an immediate impact on family wealth and sense of well-being. The deflation of the housing bubble almost brought down the U.S. (as well as the international) financial system and ushered in a sharp and painful worldwide recession. In order to understand how this bubble was financed and why it created such far-reaching collateral damage, we need to understand the fundamental changes in the banking and financial systems.

A story I like to tell concerns a middle-aged woman who has a serious heart attack. As she is lying in the emergency room, she has a near-death experience in which she comes face to face with God. "Is this it?" she asks. "Am I about to die?" God assures her that she will survive and that she has thirty more years to live. Sure enough, she does survive, gets stents put in to open up her clogged arteries, and feels better than ever. She then says to herself, "If I have thirty more years to live, I might as well make the most of it." And since she's already in the hospital, she decides to undergo what might charitably be called "comprehensive cosmetic surgery." Now she looks and feels great. With a jaunty step she bounds out of the hospital, only to be hit by a speeding ambulance and instantly killed. She goes to the Pearly Gates and again meets God. "What happened?" she asks. "I thought I had thirty more years to live." "I'm terribly sorry, Madam," God responds. "I didn't recognize you."

The New System of Banking

If a financier had awakened from a thirty-year nap during the early 2000s, the financial system would have appeared unrecognizable as well. Under the old system, which might be called the "originate and hold" system, banks would make mortgage loans (as well as loans to businesses and consumers) and hold those loans as assets until they were repaid. In such an environment, bankers were very careful about the loans they made. After all, if a mortgage loan went into default, someone would come back to the loan officer who made the loan and question the original credit judgment. In this environment, both substantial down payments and documentation were required to verify the creditworthiness of the borrower.

This system fundamentally changed in the early 2000s to what might be called the "originate and distribute" model of banking. Mortgage loans were still made by banks (as well as by big specialized mortgage companies). But the loans were held by the originating institution for only a few days, until they could be sold to an investment banker. The investment banker would then assemble packages of these mortgages and issue mortgage-backed securities—derivative bonds "securitized" by the underlying mortgages. These collateralized securities relied on the payments of interest and principal from the underlying mortgages to service the interest payment on the new mortgage-backed bonds that were issued.

To make matters even more complicated, there was not just one bond issued against a package of mortgages. The mortgage-backed securities were sliced into different "tranches," each tranche with different claim priority against payments from the underlying mortgages and each with a different bond rating. It was called "financial engineering." Even if the underlying mortgage loans were of low quality, the bond-rating agencies were happy to bestow an AAA rating on the bond tranches with the first claims on the payments of interest and principal from the underlying mortgages. The system should more accurately be called "financial alchemy," and the alchemy was employed not only with mortgages but with all sorts of underlying instruments, such as credit card loans and automobile loans. These derivative securities were in turn sold all over the world.

It gets even murkier. Second-order derivatives were sold on the derivative mortgage-backed bonds. Credit-default swaps were issued as insurance policies on the mortgage-backed bonds. Briefly, the swap market allowed two parties—called counterparties—to bet for or against the performance of the mortgage bonds, or the bonds of any other issuer. For example, suppose I hold bonds issued by General Electric and I begin to worry about GE's creditworthiness. I could buy and hold an insurance policy from a company like AIG (the biggest issuer of credit default swaps) that would pay me if GE defaulted. The problems with this market lay in the fact that the issuers of the insurance such as AIG had inadequate reserves to pay the claims if trouble occurred. And anyone from any country could buy the insurance, even without owning the underlying bonds. Eventually, the credit-default swaps trading in the market grew to as much as ten times the value of the underlying bonds, pushed by demand from institutions around the world. This change, where the derivative markets grew to a large multiple of the underlying markets, was a crucial feature of the new finance system. It made the world's financial system very much riskier and much more interconnected.

Looser Lending Standards

To round out this dangerous picture, the financiers created structured investment vehicles, or SIVs, that kept derivative securities off their books, in places where the banking regulators couldn't see them. The mortgage-backed security SIV would borrow the money needed to buy the derivatives, and all that showed up on the investment bank's balance sheet was a small investment in the equity of the SIV. In the past, banking regulators might have flagged the vast leverage and the risk it carried, but that was overlooked in the new finance system.

This new system led to looser and looser lending standards by bankers and mortgage companies. If the only risk a lender took was the risk that a mortgage loan would go bad in the few days before it could be sold to the investment banker, the lender did not need to be as careful about the creditworthiness of the borrower. And so the standards for making mortgage loans deteriorated sharply. When I took out my first home mortgage, the lender insisted on *at least* a 30 percent down payment. But in the new system loans were made with no equity down in the hopes that housing prices would rise forever. Moreover, so-called NINJA loans were common—those were loans to people with no income, no job, and no assets. Increasingly, lenders did not even bother to ask for documentation about ability to pay. Those were called NO-DOC loans. Money for housing was freely available, and housing prices rose rapidly.

The government itself played an active role in inflating the housing bubble. Under pressure by Congress to make mortgage loans easily available, the Federal Housing Administration was directed to guarantee the mortgages of low-income borrowers. Indeed, almost two-thirds of the bad mortgages on the financial system as of the start of 2010 were bought by government agencies or required by government regulations. The government not only failed as a regulator of financial institutions but also contributed to the bubble by its own policies. No accurate history of the housing bubble can fail to recognize that it was not simply "predatory lenders" but the government itself that caused many mortgage loans to be made to people who did not have the wherewithal to service them.

The Housing Bubble

The combination of government policies and changed lending practices led to an enormous increase in the demand for houses. Fueled by easy credit, house prices began to rise rapidly. The initial rise in prices encouraged even more buyers. Buying houses or apartments appeared to be risk free as house prices appeared consistently to go up. And some buyers made their purchases with the objective not of finding a place to live but rather of quickly selling (flipping) the house to some future buyer at a higher price. The pattern was eerily similar to that of the bubbles described earlier.

The graph on page 102 illustrates the dimensions of the bubble. The data come from the Case-Shiller inflation-adjusted home-price indexes. The adjustment works by considering that if house prices increased by 5 percent when prices in general increased by

5 percent, no inflation-adjusted housing price increase occurred. If house prices went up by 10 percent, however, then the inflation-adjusted price would be recorded as a 5 percent increase.

The graph shows that for the hundred-year period from the late 1800s to the late 1900s, inflation-adjusted house prices were stable. House prices went up, but only as much as the general price level. Prices did dip during the Great Depression of the 1930s, but they ended the century at the same level at which they started. In the early 2000s, the house price index doubled. This index is a composite index of prices in twenty cities. In some cities, prices increased far more than the national average.

INFLATION-ADJUSTED HOME PRICES

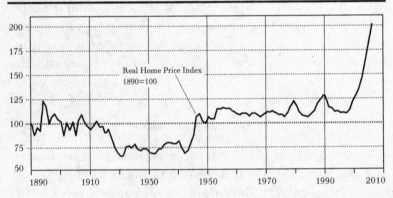

Source: Case-Shiller.

What we know about all bubbles is that eventually they pop. The next graph depicts the damage. The decline was broad-based and devastating. Many home buyers found that the amount of their mortgage far exceeded the value of their home. Increasingly, they defaulted and returned the house keys to the lender. In an instance of macabre financial humor, bankers referred to this practice as "jingle mail." On average, home prices declined by one-third, not only wiping out the real estate equity of millions of Americans but bankrupting many of the largest financial institutions.

THE BURSTING OF THE BUBBLE

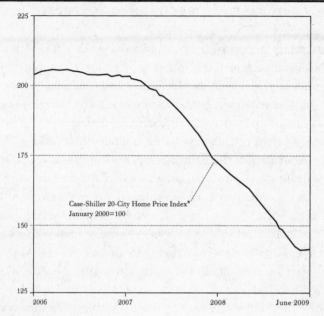

Case-Shiller 20-City Home Price Index*
January 2000=100

Data: Standard and Poor's.
*Seasonally adjusted

The effects on the economy were devastating. As home equity collapsed, consumers pulled in their horns and went on a spending strike. And consumers who previously might have taken out a second mortgage on a home equity loan on their house were no longer able to finance their consumption in that manner.

The drop in house prices destroyed the value of the mortgage-backed securities as well as the leveraged financial institutions that had eaten their own cooking and that held vast amounts of these toxic assets with borrowed money. Spectacular bankruptcies ensued, and some of our largest financial institutions had to be rescued by the government. Lending institutions turned full circle, and credit was shut off both to small businesses and to consumers. The recession that followed in the United States was painful and prolonged, exceeded in its intensity only by the Great Depression of the 1930s.

BUBBLES AND ECONOMIC ACTIVITY

Our survey of historical bubbles makes clear that the bursting of bubbles has invariably been followed by severe disruptions in real economic activity. The fallout from asset-price bubbles has not been confined to speculators. Bubbles are particularly dangerous when they are associated with a credit boom and widespread increases in leverage both for consumers and for financial institutions.

The experience of the United States during the early 2000s provides a dramatic illustration. Increased demand for housing raised home prices, which in turn encouraged further mortgage lending, which led to further price increases in a continuing positive feedback loop. The cycle of increased leverage involved loosening credit standards and even further increase in leverage. At the end of the process, individuals and institutions alike became dangerously vulnerable.

When the bubble bursts, the feedback loop goes into reverse. Prices decline and individuals find not only that their wealth has declined but that in many cases their mortgage indebtedness exceeds the value of their houses. Loans then go sour, and consumers reduce their spending. Overly leveraged financial institutions begin a deleveraging process. The attendant tightening of credit weakens economic activity further, and the outcome of the negative feedback loop is a severe recession. Credit boom bubbles are the ones that pose the greatest danger to real economic activity.

Does This Mean That Markets Are Inefficient?

This chapter's review of the Internet and housing bubbles seems inconsistent with the view that our stock and real estate markets are rational and efficient. The lesson, however, is not that markets occasionally can be irrational and that we should therefore abandon the firm-foundation theory of the pricing of financial assets. Rather, the clear conclusion is that, in every case, the market did correct itself. The market eventually corrects any irrationality—albeit in its own slow, inexorable fashion. Anomalies can crop up, markets can get irrationally optimistic, and often they attract unwary investors. But, eventually, true value is recognized by the market, and this is the main lesson investors must heed.

I am also persuaded by the wisdom of Benjamin Graham, author of *Security Analysis*, who wrote that in the final analysis the stock market is not a voting mechanism but a weighing mechanism. Valuation metrics have not changed. Eventually, every stock can only be worth the present value of the cash flow it is able to earn for the benefit of investors. In the final analysis, true value will win out. The important investment question is how you can estimate true value. More about this in chapter 5, where we will take a closer look at how professionals attempt to determine what a stock is truly worth.

Markets can be highly efficient even if they make errors. Some are doozies, as when Internet stocks in the early 2000s appeared to discount not only the future but the hereafter. How could it be otherwise? Stock valuations depend upon estimations of the earning power of companies many years into the future. Such forecasts are invariably incorrect. Moreover, investment risk is never clearly perceived, so the appropriate rate at which the future should be discounted is never certain. Thus, market prices must always be wrong to some extent. But at any particular time, it is not obvious to anyone whether they are too high or too low. The evidence I will present next shows that professional investors are not able to adjust their portfolios so that they hold only "undervalued" stocks and avoid "overvalued" ones. The fact that the best and the brightest on Wall Street cannot consistently distinguish correct valuations from incorrect ones shows how hard it is to beat the market. There is no evidence that anyone can generate excess returns by making consistently correct bets against the collective wisdom of the market. Markets are not always or even usually correct. But NO ONE PERSON OR INSTITUTION CONSISTENTLY KNOWS MORE THAN THE MARKET.

Nor does the unprecedented bubble and bust in house prices during the first decade of the 2000s drive a stake through the heart of the efficient-market hypothesis. If individuals are given an opportunity to buy houses with no money down, it can be the height of rationality to be willing to pay an inflated price. If the house continues to escalate in value, the buyer will profit. If the bubble bursts and the house price declines, the buyer walks away and leaves the lender (and perhaps ultimately the government) with the loss. Yes, the incentives were perverse. And in retrospect, regulation was lax and some government policies were ill considered. But in no sense was this sorry episode and the deep recession that followed caused by a blind faith in the efficient-market hypothesis.

Part Two

HOW THE PROS
PLAY THE BIGGEST
GAME IN TOWN

5

TECHNICAL AND
FUNDAMENTAL ANALYSIS

A picture is worth ten thousand words.
—Old Chinese proverb

The greatest of all gifts is the power to estimate
things at their true worth.
—La Rochefoucauld, *Réflexions; ou sentences et maximes morales*

ON A TYPICAL trading day, shares with a total market value of hundreds of billions are traded on the New York Stock Exchange, the NASDAQ market, and various electronic crossing networks across the country. Including markets for futures, options, and swaps, trillions of dollars of transactions take place each day. Professional investment analysts and counselors are involved in what has been called the biggest game in town.

If the stakes are high, so are the rewards. When Wall Street is having a good year, new trainees from the Harvard Business School routinely draw salaries of $200,000 per year. At the top of the salary scale are the high-profile money managers themselves— the men and women who run the large mutual and pension funds and who manage the trillions of dollars of hedge-fund and private equity assets. "Adam Smith," after writing *The Money Game*, boasted that he would make a quarter of a million dollars from his best-selling book. His Wall Street friends retorted, "You're only going to make as much as a second-rate institutional salesman." Although not the oldest, the profession of high finance is certainly one of the most generously compensated.

Part Two of this book concentrates on the methods used by

professional portfolio managers. It shows how academics have analyzed their investment results and have concluded that they are not worth the money you pay for them. It then introduces the efficient-market hypothesis (EMH) and its practical implication: Stock investors can do no better than simply buying and holding an index fund that owns a portfolio consisting of all the stocks in the market.

TECHNICAL VERSUS FUNDAMENTAL ANALYSIS

The attempt to predict accurately the future course of stock prices and thus the appropriate time to buy or sell a stock must rank as one of investors' most persistent endeavors. This search for the golden egg has spawned a variety of methods, ranging from the scientific to the occult. There are people today who forecast future stock prices by measuring sunspots, looking at the phases of the moon, or measuring the vibrations along the San Andreas Fault. Most, however, opt for one of two methods: technical or fundamental analysis.

The alternative techniques used by the investment pros are related to the two theories of the stock market I covered in Part One. Technical analysis is the method of predicting the appropriate time to buy or sell a stock used by those believing in the castle-in-the-air view of stock pricing. Fundamental analysis is the technique of applying the tenets of the firm-foundation theory to the selection of individual stocks.

Technical analysis is essentially the making and interpreting of stock charts. Thus, its practitioners, a small but abnormally dedicated cult, are called chartists or technicians. They study the past—both the movements of common-stock prices and the volume of trading—for a clue to the direction of future change. Many chartists believe that the market is only 10 percent logical and 90 percent psychological. They generally subscribe to the castle-in-the-air school and view the investment game as one of anticipating how the other players will behave. Charts, of course, tell only what the other players have been doing in the past. The chartist's hope, however, is that a careful study of what the other players are doing will shed light on what the crowd is likely to do in the future.

Fundamental analysts take the opposite tack, believing that the market is 90 percent logical and only 10 percent psychological. Caring little about the particular pattern of past price movements, fundamentalists seek to determine a stock's proper value. Value in this case is related to a company's assets, its expected growth rate of earnings and dividends, interest rates, and risk. By studying these factors, the fundamentalist arrives at an estimate of a security's intrinsic value or firm foundation of value. If this is above the market price, then the investor is advised to buy. Fundamentalists believe that eventually the market will reflect the security's real worth. Perhaps 90 percent of the Wall Street security analysts consider themselves fundamentalists. Many would argue that chartists are lacking in dignity and professionalism.

WHAT CAN CHARTS TELL YOU?

The first principle of technical analysis is that all information about earnings, dividends, and the future performance of a company is automatically reflected in the company's past market prices. A chart showing these prices and the volume of trading already comprises all the fundamental information, good or bad, that the security analyst can hope to know. The second principle is that prices tend to move in trends: A stock that is rising tends to keep on rising, whereas a stock at rest tends to remain at rest.

A true chartist doesn't even care to know what business or industry a company is in, as long as he or she can study its stock chart. A chart shaped in the form of an "inverted bowl" or "pennant" means the same for Microsoft as it does for Coca-Cola. Fundamental information on earnings and dividends is considered at best to be useless—and at worst a positive distraction. It is either of inconsequential importance for the pricing of the stock or, if it is important, it has already been reflected in the market days, weeks, or even months in advance. Many chartists will not even read the newspaper or check the financial web services.

One of the original chartists, John Magee, operated from a small office in Springfield, Massachusetts, where even the windows were boarded up to prevent any outside influences from distracting his analysis. Magee was once quoted as saying, "When I come into this office I leave the rest of the world outside to concentrate entirely on my charts. This room is exactly the same in a blizzard as on a moonlit June evening. In here I can't possibly do myself and my clients the disservice of saying 'buy' simply because the sun is out or 'sell' because it is raining."

The figures that follow show how easy it is to construct a chart. Simply draw a vertical line whose bottom is the stock's low for the day and whose top is the high. This line is crossed to indicate the closing price for the day. The process can be repeated for each trading day and can be used for individual stocks or for a stock index.

Often the chartist will indicate the volume of shares of stock traded during the day by another vertical line at the bottom of the chart. Gradually, the highs and lows on the chart of the stock in question jiggle up and down sufficiently to produce patterns. To

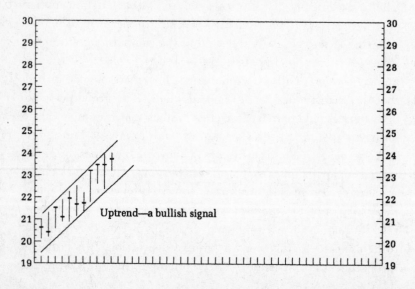

the chartist, these patterns have the same significance as X-ray plates to a surgeon.

One of the first things the chartist looks for is a trend. The preceding figure shows one in the making. It is the record of price changes for a stock over a number of days—and the prices are obviously on the way up. The chartist draws two lines connecting the tops and bottoms, creating a "channel" to delineate the uptrend. Because the presumption is that momentum in the market will tend to perpetuate itself, the stock can be expected to continue to rise. As Magee wrote in the bible of charting, *Technical Analysis of Stock Trends*, "Prices move in trends, and trends tend to continue until something happens to change the supply-demand balance."

Suppose, however, that at about 24, the stock finally runs into trouble and is unable to gain any further ground. This is called a resistance level. The stock may wiggle around a bit and then turn downward. One pattern, which chartists claim reveals a clear signal that the market has topped out, is a head-and-shoulders formation (shown in the figure below).

The stock first rises and then falls slightly, forming a rounded shoulder. It rises again, going slightly higher, before once more receding, forming a head. Finally the right shoulder is formed, and

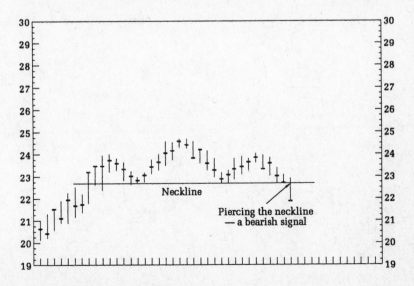

chartists wait with bated breath for the sell signal, which sounds loud and clear when the stock "pierces the neckline." With the glee of Count Dracula surveying one of his victims, the chartists are off and selling, anticipating that a prolonged downtrend will follow as it allegedly has in the past. Of course, sometimes the market surprises the chartist. For example, the stock may make an end run up to 30 right after giving a bear signal, as shown in the following chart. This is called a bear trap or, to the chartist, the exception that tests the rule.

It follows from the technique that the chartist is a trader, not a long-term investor. The chartist buys when the auguries look favorable and sells on bad omens. He flirts with stocks just as some flirt with the opposite sex, and his scores are successful in-and-out trades, not rewarding long-term commitments. Indeed, the psychiatrist Don D. Jackson, author with Albert Haas Jr. of *Bulls, Bears and Dr. Freud*, suggested that such an individual may be playing a game with overt sexual overtones.

When the chartist chooses a stock, there is typically a period of observation and flirtation before he commits himself, because for the chartist—as in romance and sexual conquest—timing is essential. There is mounting excitement as the stock penetrates the

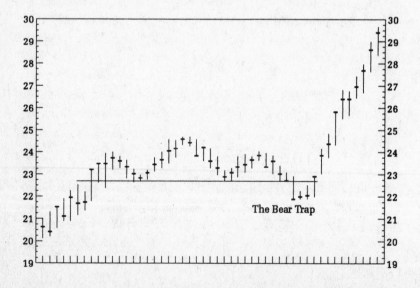

The Bear Trap

base formation and rises higher. Finally, if the affair has gone well, there is the moment of fulfillment—profit-taking, and the release and afterglow that follow. The chartist's vocabulary features such terms as "double bottoms," "breakthrough," "violating the lows," "firmed up," "big play," "ascending peaks," and "buying climax." And all this takes place under the pennant of that great symbol of sexuality: the bull.

THE RATIONALE FOR THE CHARTING METHOD

Why is charting supposed to work? Many chartists freely admit that they don't know why charting should work—history just has a habit of repeating itself.

To me, the following three explanations of technical analysis appear to be the most plausible. First, it has been argued that the crowd instinct of mass psychology makes trends perpetuate themselves. When investors see the price of a speculative favorite going higher and higher, they want to jump on the bandwagon and join the rise. Indeed, the price rise itself helps fuel the enthusiasm in a self-fulfilling prophecy. Each rise in price just whets the appetite and makes investors expect a further rise.

Second, there may be unequal access to fundamental information about a company. When some favorable piece of news occurs, such as the discovery of a rich mineral deposit, it is alleged that the insiders are the first to know, and they act, buying the stock and causing its price to rise. The insiders then tell their friends, who act next. Then the professionals find out the news, and the big institutions put blocks of the shares in their portfolios. Finally, the poor slobs like you and me get the information and buy, pushing the price still higher. This process is supposed to result in a rather gradual increase in the price of the stock when the news is good and a decrease when the news is bad.

Third, investors often underreact initially to new information. There is some evidence that when earnings are announced that beat (trail) Wall Street estimates (positive or negative "earnings surprises"), the stock price reacts positively (negatively), but the initial adjustment is incomplete. Thus, the stock market will often adjust to earnings information only gradually, resulting in a sustained period of price momentum.

Chartists also believe that people have a nasty habit of remembering what they paid for a stock, or the price they wish they had paid. For example, suppose a stock sold for about $50 a share for a long period of time, during which a number of investors bought in. Suppose then that the price drops to $40.

The chartists claim that the public will be anxious to sell out the shares when they rise back to the price at which they were bought, and thus break even on the trade. Consequently, the price of $50 at which the stock sold initially becomes a "resistance area." Each time the resistance area is reached and the stock turns down, the resistance level becomes harder to cross, because more investors get the idea that the market or the individual stock in question cannot go any higher.

A similar argument lies behind the notion of "support levels." Chartists say that many investors who failed to buy when the market fluctuated around a relatively low price level will feel they have missed the boat when prices rise. Presumably such investors will jump at the chance to buy when prices drop back to the original low level. In chart theory, a support area that holds on successive declines becomes stronger and stronger. So if a stock declines to a support area and then begins to rise, the traders will jump in, believing that the stock is just "coming off the pad." Another bullish signal is flashed when a stock finally breaks through a resistance area. In the lexicon of the chartists, the former resistance area becomes a support area, and the stock should have no trouble gaining further ground.

WHY MIGHT CHARTING FAIL TO WORK?

There are many logical arguments against charting. First, note that the chartist buys only after price trends have been established, and sells only after they have been broken. Because sharp reversals in the market may occur quite suddenly, the chartist often misses the boat. By the time an uptrend is signaled, it may already have taken place. Second, such techniques must ultimately be self-defeating. As more and more people use it, the value of any technique depreciates. No buy or sell signal can be worthwhile if everyone tries to act on it simultaneously.

Moreover, traders tend to anticipate technical signals. If they see a price about to break through a resistance area, they tend to buy before, not after, it breaks through. This suggests that others will try to anticipate the signal still earlier. Of course, the earlier they anticipate, the less certain they are that the signal will occur and that the trade will be profitable.

Perhaps the most telling argument against technical methods comes from the logical implications of profit-maximizing behavior. Suppose that Universal Polymers is selling at around 20 when Sam, the chief research chemist, discovers a new production technique that promises to double the company's earnings. Sam is convinced that the price of Universal will hit 40 when the news of his discovery comes out. Because any purchases below 40 will provide a swift profit, he may well buy up all the stock he can until the price hits 40, a process that could take no longer than a few minutes.

Even if Sam doesn't have enough money to drive up the price himself, surely his friends and professional traders do have the funds to move the price so rapidly that no chartist could get into the act before the whole play is gone. The market may well be a most efficient mechanism. If some people know that the price will go to 40 tomorrow, it will go to 40 today.

FROM CHARTIST TO TECHNICIAN

Although chartists are not held in high repute on Wall Street, their colorful methods have attracted a wide following. The companies that distribute stock charts, the computer programmers who provide charting software, and financial news networks such as CNBC and Bloomberg have enjoyed a boom in their sales, and chartists themselves still find excellent employment opportunities with brokerage firms.

In the days before the computer, the laborious task of charting a course through the market was done by hand. Chartists were often viewed as peculiar people with green eyeshades who were tucked away in a small closet at the back of the office. Now chartists have computer services hooked into a variety of data networks and replete with a large display terminal that, at the tap of a finger, can produce every conceivable chart. The chartist (now called a technician) can, with the glee of a child playing with a new electric train, produce a complete chart of a stock's past performance, including measures of volume, the 200-day moving average (an average of prices over the previous 200 days recalculated each day), the strength of the stock relative to the market and its industry, and literally hundreds of other averages, ratios, oscillators, and indicators. Moreover, individuals can access a variety of charts for different time periods through Internet sites such as Yahoo!

THE TECHNIQUE OF FUNDAMENTAL ANALYSIS

Fred Schwed Jr., in his charming and witty exposé of the financial community in the 1930s, *Where Are the Customers' Yachts?*, tells of a Texas broker who sold some stock to a customer at $760 a share at the moment when it could have been purchased at $730. When the outraged customer found out what had happened, he complained bitterly to the broker. The Texan cut him short. "Suh," he boomed, "you-all don't appreciate the policy of this firm. This heah firm selects investments foh its clients not on the basis of Price, but of Value."

In a sense, this story illustrates the difference between the technician and the fundamentalist. The technician is interested only in the record of the stock's price, whereas the fundamentalist's primary concern is with what a stock is really worth. The fundamentalist strives to be relatively immune to the optimism and pessimism of the crowd and makes a sharp distinction between a stock's current price and its true value.

In estimating the firm-foundation value of a stock, the fundamentalist's most important job is to estimate the firm's future stream of earnings and dividends. The worth of a share is taken to be the present or discounted value of all the cash flows the investor is expected to receive. The analyst must estimate the firm's sales level, operating costs, tax rates, depreciation, and the sources and costs of its capital requirements.

Basically, the security analyst must be a prophet without the benefit of divine inspiration. As a poor substitute, the analyst turns to a study of the past record of the company, a review of the company's income statements, balance sheets, and investment plans, and a firsthand visit to and appraisal of the company's management team. The analyst must then separate the important facts from the unimportant ones. As Benjamin Graham put it in *The Intelligent Investor*, "Sometimes he reminds us a bit of the erudite major general in 'The Pirates of Penzance,' with his 'many cheerful facts about the square of the hypotenuse.'"

Because the general prospects of a company are strongly influenced by the economic position of its industry, the starting point for the security analyst is a study of industry prospects. Indeed, security analysts usually specialize in particular industry groups. The fundamentalist hopes that a thorough study of industry conditions will produce valuable insights into factors that are not yet reflected in market prices.

The fundamentalist uses four basic determinants to help estimate the proper value for any stock.

Determinant 1: The expected growth rate. Most people don't recognize the implications of compound growth for financial decisions. Albert Einstein once described compound interest as the "greatest mathematical discovery of all time." It is often said that the Native American who sold Manhattan Island in 1626 for $24 was rooked by the white man. In fact, he may have been an extremely sharp salesman. Had he put his $24 away at 6 percent interest, compounded semiannually, it would now be worth more than $100 billion, and with it his descendants could buy back much of the now improved land. Such is the magic of compound growth!

Compounding is the process that makes 10 plus 10 equal 21 rather than 20. Suppose you invest $100 this year and next year in an investment that produces a 10 percent annual return. How much have you made by the end of year two? If you answered 21 percent, then you deserve a gold star and a trip to the head of the class.

The algebra is simple. Your $100 grows to $110 at the end of year one. Next year, you also earn 10 percent on the $110 you start with, so you have $121 at the end of year two. Thus, the total return over the two-year period is 21 percent. The reason it works is that the interest you earn from your original investment also earns interest. Carrying it out in year three, you have $133.10. Compounding is powerful indeed.

A useful rule, called "the rule of 72," provides a shortcut way to determine how long it takes for money to double. Take the interest rate you earn and divide it into the number 72, and you get the number of years it will take to double your money. For example, if the interest rate is 15 percent, it takes a bit less than five years for your money to double (72 divided by 15 = 4.8 years). The implications of various growth rates for the size of future dividends are shown in the table below.

Growth Rate of Dividends	Present Dividend	Dividend in Five Years	Dividend in Ten Years	Dividend in Twenty-Five Years
5%	$1.00	$1.28	$1.63	$3.39
15%	1.00	2.01	4.05	32.92
25%	1.00	3.05	9.31	264.70

The catch (and doesn't there always have to be at least one, if not twenty-two?) is that dividend growth does not go on forever, for the simple reason that corporations have life cycles similar to most living things. Consider the leading corporations in the United States over a hundred years ago. Such names as Eastern Buggy Whip Company, La Crosse and Minnesota Steam Packet

Company, Savannah and St. Paul Steamboat Line, and Hazard Powder Company would have ranked high in a Fortune top 500 list of that era. All are now deceased.

And even if the natural life cycle doesn't get a company, there's always the fact that it gets harder and harder to grow at the same percentage rate. A company earning $1 million need increase its earnings by only $100,000 to achieve a 10 percent growth rate, whereas a company starting from a base of $10 million in earnings needs $1 million in additional earnings to produce the same record.

The nonsense of relying on very high long-term growth rates is nicely illustrated by working with population projections for the United States. If the populations of the nation and of California continue to grow at their recent rates, 120 percent of the United States population will live in California by the year 2045!

Hazardous as projections may be, share prices must reflect differences in growth prospects if any sense is to be made of market valuations. Also, the probable length of the growth phase is very important. If one company expects to enjoy a rapid 20 percent growth rate for ten years, and another growth company expects to sustain the same rate for only five years, the former company is, other things equal, more valuable to the investor than the latter. The point is that growth rates are general rather than gospel truths. And this brings us to the first fundamental rule for evaluating securities:

Rule 1: A rational investor should be willing to pay a higher price for a share the larger the growth rate of dividends and earnings.

To this is added an important corollary:

Corollary to Rule 1: A rational investor should be willing to pay a higher price for a share the longer an extraordinary growth rate is expected to last.

Does this rule seem to conform to actual practices? Let's first reformulate the question in terms of price-earnings (P/E) multiples rather than market prices. This provides a good yardstick for comparing stocks—which have different prices and earnings—against one another. A stock selling at $100 per share with earnings of $10 per share would have the same P/E multiple (10) as a stock selling at $40 with earnings of $4 per share. It is the P/E multiple, not the price, that really tells you how a stock is valued in the market.

Our reformulated question now reads: Are actual price-earnings multiples higher for stocks for which a high growth rate is anticipated? A study by John Cragg and myself strongly indicates that the answer is yes.

It was easy to collect data on prices and earnings required to calculate P/E multiples. To obtain expected long-term growth rates, we surveyed eighteen leading investment firms. From each firm we obtained estimates of the five-year growth rates anticipated for a large sample of stocks.

I will not bore you with the details of the actual statistical study that was performed. The results of a similar 2014 study involving a few representative securities are shown in the following chart. It is clear that, just as Rule 1 asserts, high P/E ratios are associated with high expected growth rates.

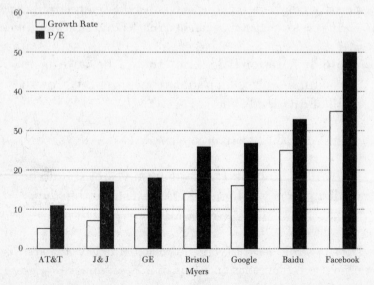

In addition to demonstrating how the market values different growth rates, the chart can also be used as a practical investment guide. Suppose you were considering the purchase of a stock with an anticipated 8½ percent growth rate and you knew that, on average, stocks with 8½ percent growth sold, like General Electric, at 18 times earnings. If the stock you were considering sold at a price-earnings multiple of 20, you might reject the idea of buying the stock in favor of one more reasonably priced in terms of current market norms. If, on the other hand, your stock sold at a multiple below the average in the market for that growth rate, the security is said to represent good value for your money.

Determinant 2: The expected dividend payout. The amount of dividends you receive at each payout—as contrasted to their growth rate—is readily understandable as being an important factor in determining a stock's price. The higher the dividend payout, other things equal, the greater the value of the stock. The catch here is the phrase "other things equal." Stocks that pay out a high percentage of earnings in dividends may be poor investments if their growth prospects are unfavorable. Conversely, many companies in their most dynamic growth phase often pay no dividends. Many companies tend to buy back their shares rather than increasing their dividends. For two companies whose expected growth rates are the same, you are better off with the one that returns more cash to the shareholders.

Rule 2: A rational investor should pay a higher price for a share, other things equal, the larger the proportion of a company's earnings paid out in cash dividends or used to buy back stock.

Determinant 3: The degree of risk. Risk plays an important role in the stock market, no matter what your overeager broker may tell you. There is always a risk—and that's what makes the market so fascinating. Risk also affects the valuation of a stock. Some people think risk is the only aspect of a stock to be examined.

The more respectable a stock is—that is, the less risk it has—the higher its quality. Stocks of the so-called blue-chip companies, for example, are said to deserve a quality premium. (Why high-quality stocks are given an appellation derived from the poker tables is a fact known only to Wall Street.) Most investors prefer less risky stocks, and these stocks can therefore command higher price-earnings multiples than their risky, low-quality counterparts.

Although there is general agreement that the compensation for higher risk must be greater future rewards (and thus lower current prices), measuring risk is well-nigh impossible. This has not daunted the economist, however. A great deal of attention has been devoted to risk measurement by both academic economists and practitioners.

According to one well-known theory, the bigger the swings—relative to the market as a whole—in an individual company's stock prices (or in its total yearly returns, including dividends), the greater the risk. For example, a nonswinger such as Johnson & Johnson gets the Good Housekeeping seal of approval for "widows and orphans." That's because its earnings are relatively stable during recessions, and its dividend is secure. Therefore, when the market goes down 20 percent, J&J usually trails with perhaps only a 10 percent decline. Thus, the stock qualifies as one with less than average risk. Salesforce.com, on the other hand, has a very volatile past record, and it characteristically falls by 30 percent or more when the market declines by 20 percent. The investor gambles in owning stock in such a company, particularly if he may be forced to sell out during a time of unfavorable market conditions.

When business is good and the market mounts a sustained upward drive, however, Salesforce.com can be expected to outdistance J&J. But if you are like most investors, you value stable returns over speculative hopes, freedom from worry about your portfolio over sleepless nights, and limited loss exposure over the possibility of a downhill roller-coaster ride. This leads to a third basic rule of security valuation:

Rule 3: A rational (and risk-averse) investor should pay a higher price for a share, other things equal, the less risky the company's stock.

I should warn the reader that a "relative volatility" measure may not fully capture the relevant risk of a company. Chapter 9 will present a thorough discussion of this important risk element in stock valuation.

Determinant 4: The level of market interest rates. The stock market does not exist as a world unto itself. Investors should consider how much profit they can obtain elsewhere. Interest rates, if they are high enough, can offer a stable, profitable alternative to the stock market. Consider periods such as the early 1980s when yields on prime-quality corporate bonds soared to close to 15 percent. The expected returns from stock prices had trouble matching these bond rates; money flowed into bonds while stock prices fell sharply. Finally, stock prices reached such a low level that a sufficient number of investors were attracted to stem the decline. Again in 1987, interest rates rose substantially, preceding the great stock-market crash of October 19. To put it another way, to attract investors from high-yielding bonds, stock must offer bargain-basement prices.*

---

*The point can be made another way by noting that because higher interest rates enable us to earn more now, any deferred income should be "discounted" more heavily. Thus, the present value of any flow of future dividend returns will be lower when current interest rates are relatively high. The relationship between interest rates and stock prices is somewhat more complicated, however, than this discussion may suggest. Suppose investors expect that the rate of inflation will increase from 5 percent to 10 percent. Such an expectation is likely to drive interest rates up by about 5 percentage points to compensate investors for holding fixed-dollar-obligation bonds whose purchasing power will be adversely affected by greater inflation. Other things being the same, this should make stock prices fall. But with higher expected inflation, investors may reasonably project that corporate earnings and dividends will also increase at a faster rate, causing stock prices to rise. A fuller discussion of inflation, interest rates, and stock prices is contained in chapter 13.

On the other hand, when interest rates are very low, fixed-interest securities provide very little competition for the stock market and stock prices tend to be relatively high. This provides justification for the last basic rule of fundamental analysis:

Rule 4: A rational investor should pay a higher price for a share, other things equal, the lower the interest rates.

THREE IMPORTANT CAVEATS

The four valuation rules imply that a security's firm-foundation value (and its price-earnings multiple) will be higher the larger the company's growth rate and the longer its duration; the larger the dividend payout for the firm; the less risky the company's stock; and the lower the general level of interest rates.

In principle, such rules are very useful in suggesting a rational basis for stock prices and in giving investors some standard of value. But before we even think of using these rules, we must bear in mind three important caveats.

Caveat 1: Expectations about the future cannot be proven in the present. Predicting future earnings and dividends is a most hazardous occupation. It is extremely difficult to be objective; wild optimism and extreme pessimism constantly battle for top place. In 2008, the economy was suffering from severe recession and a worldwide credit crisis. The best that investors could do that year was to project modest growth rates for most corporations. During the Internet bubble in the late 1990s and early 2000, investors convinced themselves that a new era of high growth and unlimited prosperity was a foregone conclusion.

The point to remember is that no matter what formula you use for predicting the future, it always rests in part on the indeterminate premise. Although many Wall Streeters claim to see into the future, they are just as fallible as the rest of us. As Samuel Goldwyn used to say, "Forecasts are difficult to make—particularly those about the future."

Caveat 2: Precise figures cannot be calculated from undetermined data. It stands to reason that you can't obtain precise figures by using indefinite factors. Yet to achieve desired ends, investors and security analysts do this all the time.

Take a company that you've heard lots of good things about. You study the company's prospects, and you conclude that it can maintain a high growth rate for a long period. How long? Well, why not ten years?

You then calculate what the stock should be "worth" on the basis of the current dividend payout, the expected future growth rate, and the general level of interest rates, perhaps making an allowance for the riskiness of the shares. It turns out to your chagrin that the price the stock is worth is just slightly less than its present market price.

You now have two alternatives. You could regard the stock as overpriced and refuse to buy it, or you could say, "Perhaps this stock could maintain a high growth rate for eleven years rather than ten. After all, the ten was only a guess in the first place, so why not eleven years?" And so you go back to your computer, and lo and behold you now come up with a worth for the shares that is larger than the current market price. Armed with this "precise" knowledge, you make your "sound" purchase.

The reason the game worked is that the longer one projects extraordinary growth, the greater is the stream of future dividends. Thus, the present value of a share is at the discretion of the calculator. If eleven years was not enough to do the trick, twelve or thirteen might well have sufficed. There is always some combination of growth rate and growth period that will produce any specific price. In this sense, it is intrinsically impossible to calculate the intrinsic value of a share. There is, I believe, a fundamental indeterminateness about the value of common shares even in principle. God Almighty does not know the proper price-earnings multiple for a common stock.

Caveat 3: What's growth for the goose is not always growth for the gander. The difficulty comes with the value the market puts on specific fundamentals. It is always true that the market values growth, and that higher growth rates and larger multiples go hand in hand. But the crucial question is: How much more should you pay for higher growth?

There is no consistent answer. In some periods, as in the early 1960s and 1970s, when growth was thought to be especially desirable, the market was willing to pay an enormous price for stocks exhibiting high growth rates. At other times, such as the late 1980s and early 1990s, high-growth stocks commanded only a modest premium over the multiples of common stocks in general. By early 2000, the growth stocks making up the NASDAQ 100 Index sold at triple-digit price-earnings multiples. Growth can be as fashionable as tulip bulbs, as investors in growth stocks learned painfully.

From a practical standpoint, the rapid changes in market valuations that have occurred suggest that it would be very dangerous to use any one year's valuation relationships as an indication of market norms. However, by comparing how growth stocks are currently valued with historical precedent, investors should at least be able to isolate those periods when a touch of the tulip bug has smitten investors.

WHY MIGHT FUNDAMENTAL ANALYSIS FAIL TO WORK?

Despite its plausibility and scientific appearance, there are three potential flaws in this type of analysis. First, the information and analysis may be incorrect. Second, the security analyst's estimate of "value" may be faulty. Third, the market may not correct its "mistake," and the stock price may not converge to its value estimate.

The security analyst studying each company and consulting with industry specialists will receive a great deal of fundamental information. Some critics have suggested that, taken as a whole, this information will be worthless. What investors make on the valid news (assuming it is not yet recognized by the market) they lose on the bad information. Moreover, the analyst wastes considerable effort collecting the information, and investors pay transactions fees acting on it. Security analysts may also be unable to translate correct facts into accurate estimates of future earnings. A faulty analysis of valid information could throw estimates of the rate of growth of earnings and dividends far wide of the mark.

The second problem is that even if the information is correct and its implications for future growth are properly assessed, the analyst might make a faulty value estimate. It is virtually impossible to translate specific estimates of growth into a single estimate of intrinsic value. Indeed, attempts to obtain a measure of fundamental value may be an unrewarding search for a will-o'-the-wisp. All the information available to the security analyst may already be reflected accurately by the market. Any difference between a security's price and its "value" may result from an incorrect estimate of value.

The final problem is that, even with correct information and value estimates, the stock you buy might still go down. For example, suppose that Biodegradable Bottling Company is selling at 30 times earnings, and the analyst estimates that it can sustain a long-term growth rate of 25 percent. If, on average, stocks with 25 percent anticipated growth rates are selling at 40 times earnings, the fundamentalist might conclude that Biodegradable was a "cheap" stock and recommend purchase.

But suppose, a few months later, stocks with 25 percent growth rates are selling in the market at only 20 times earnings. Even if the analyst was correct in his growth-rate estimate, his customers might not gain, because the market revalued its estimates of what growth stocks were worth. The market might correct its "mistake" by revaluing all stocks downward, rather than raising the price for Biodegradable Bottling.

Such changes in valuation are not extraordinary—these are the routine fluctuations in market sentiment that were experienced in the past. Not only can the average multiple change rapidly for stocks in general, but so can the premium assigned to growth. Clearly, then, one should not take the success of fundamental analysis for granted.

USING FUNDAMENTAL AND
TECHNICAL ANALYSIS TOGETHER

Many analysts use a combination of techniques to judge whether individual stocks are attractive for purchase. One of the most sensible procedures can easily be summarized by the following three rules. The persistent, patient reader will recognize that the rules are based on principles of stock pricing I have developed above.

Rule 1: Buy only companies that are expected to have above-average earnings growth for five or more years. An extraordinary long-run earnings growth rate is the single most important element contributing to the success of most stock investments. Google and practically all the other really outstanding common stocks of the past were growth stocks. Difficult as the job may be, picking stocks whose earnings grow is the name of the game. Consistent growth not only increases the earnings and dividends of the company but may also increase the multiple that the market is willing to pay for those earnings. Thus, the purchaser of a stock whose earnings begin to grow rapidly has a chance at a potential double benefit—both the earnings and the multiple may increase.

Rule 2: Never pay more for a stock than its firm foundation of value. While I have argued, and I hope persuasively, that you can never judge the exact intrinsic value of a stock, many analysts feel that you can roughly gauge when a stock seems to be reasonably priced. Generally, the earnings multiple for the market as a whole is a helpful benchmark. Growth stocks selling at multiples in line with or not very much above this multiple often represent good value.

There are important advantages to buying growth stocks at very reasonable earnings multiples. If your growth estimate turns out to be correct, you may get the double bonus I mentioned in connection with Rule 1: The price will tend to go up simply because the earnings went up, but also the multiple is likely to expand in recognition of the growth rate that is established. Hence, the double bonus. Suppose, for example, you buy a stock earning $1 per share and selling at $7.50. If the earnings grow to $2 per share and if the price-earnings multiple increases from 7½ to 15 (in recognition that the company now can be considered a growth stock), you don't just double your money—you quadruple it. That's because your $7.50 stock will be worth $30 (15, the multiple, times $2, the earnings).

Now consider the other side of the coin. There are special risks involved in buying "growth stocks" when the market has already recognized the growth and has bid up the price-earnings multiple to a hefty premium over that accorded more run-of-the-mill stocks. The problem is that the very high multiples may already fully reflect the growth that is anticipated, and if the growth does not materialize and earnings in fact go down (or even grow more slowly than expected), you will take a very unpleasant bath. The double benefits that are possible if the earnings of low-multiple stocks grow can become double damages if the earnings of high-multiple stocks decline.

What is proposed, then, is a strategy of buying unrecognized growth stocks whose earnings multiples are not at any substantial premium over the market. Of course, it is very hard to predict growth. But even if the growth does not materialize and earnings decline, the damage is likely to be only single if the multiple is low to begin with, whereas the benefits may double if things do turn out as you expected. This is an extra way to put the odds in your favor.

Peter Lynch, the very successful but now retired manager of the Magellan Fund, used this technique to great advantage during the fund's early years. Lynch calculated each potential stock's P/E-to-growth ratio (or PEG ratio) and would buy for his portfolio only those stocks with high growth relative to their P/Es. This was not simply a low P/E strategy, because a stock with a 50 percent growth rate and a P/E of 25 (PEG ratio of ½) was deemed far better than a stock with 20 percent growth and a P/E of 20 (PEG ratio of 1). If one is correct in one's growth projections, and for a while Lynch was, this strategy can produce excellent returns.

We can summarize the discussion thus far by restating the first two rules: *Look for growth situations with low price-earnings multiples. If the growth takes place, there's often a double bonus—both the earnings and the multiple rise, producing large gains. Beware of very high multiple stocks in which future growth is already discounted. If growth doesn't materialize, losses are doubly heavy—both the earnings and the multiples drop.*

Rule 3: Look for stocks whose stories of anticipated growth are of the kind on which investors can build castles in the air. I have stressed the importance of psychological elements in stock-price determination. Individual and institutional investors are not computers that calculate warranted price-earnings multiples and print out buy and sell decisions. They are emotional human beings—driven by greed, gambling instincts, hope, and fear in their stock-market decisions. This is why successful investing demands both intellectual and psychological acuteness.

Stocks that produce "good feelings" in the minds of investors can sell at premium multiples for long periods, even if the growth rate is only average. Those not so blessed may sell at low multiples for long periods, even if their growth rate is above average. To be sure, if a growth rate appears to be established, the stock is almost certain to attract some type of following. The market is not irrational. But stocks are like people—what stimulates one may leave another cold, and the multiple improvement may be smaller and slower to be realized if the story never catches on.

So Rule 3 says to ask yourself whether the story about your stock is one that is likely to catch the fancy of the crowd. Is it a story from which contagious dreams can be generated? Is it a story on which investors can build castles in the air—but castles in the air that really rest on a firm foundation?

You don't have to be a technician to follow Rule 3. You might simply use your intuition or speculative sense to judge whether the "story" on your stock is likely to catch the fancy of the crowd—particularly the notice of institutional investors. Technical analysts, however, would look for some tangible evidence before they could be convinced that the investment idea was, in fact, catching on. This tangible evidence is, of course, the beginning of an uptrend or a technical signal that could "reliably" predict that an uptrend would develop.

Although the rules I have outlined seem sensible, the important question is whether they really work. After all, lots of other people are playing the game, and it is by no means obvious that anyone can win consistently.

In the next two chapters, I shall look at the actual record. Chapter 6 will consider the question: Does technical analysis work? Chapter 7 looks at the performance record of fundamentalists. Together they should help us evaluate how much confidence we should have in the advice of professional investment people.

6

TECHNICAL ANALYSIS AND
THE RANDOM-WALK THEORY

Things are seldom what they seem.
Skim milk masquerades as cream.
—Gilbert and Sullivan, *H.M.S. Pinafore*

NOT EARNINGS, NOR dividends, nor risk, nor gloom of high interest rates stay the technicians from their assigned task: studying the price movements of stocks. Such single-minded devotion to numbers has yielded the most colorful theories and folk language of Wall Street: "Hold the winners, sell the losers," "Switch into the strong stocks," "Sell this issue, it's acting poorly," "Don't fight the tape." All are popular prescriptions of technical analysts. They build their strategies upon dreams of castles in the air and expect their tools to tell them which castle is being built and how to get in on the ground floor. The question is: Do they work?

HOLES IN THEIR SHOES AND
AMBIGUITY IN THEIR FORECASTS

University professors are sometimes asked by their students, "If you're so smart, why aren't you rich?" The question usually rankles professors, who think of themselves as passing up worldly riches to engage in such an obviously socially useful occupation as teaching.

The same question is more appropriately addressed to technicians. Since the whole point of technical analysis is to make money, one would expect that those who preach it should practice it successfully.

On close examination, technicians are often seen with holes in their shoes and frayed shirt collars. I personally have never known a successful technician, but I have seen the wrecks of several unsuccessful ones. Curiously, however, the broke technician is never apologetic. If you commit the social error of asking him why he is broke, he will tell you quite ingenuously that he made the all-too-human error of not believing his own charts. To my great embarrassment, I once choked conspicuously at the dinner table when a chartist made such a comment. I have since made it a rule never to eat with a chartist. It's bad for digestion.

Although technicians might not get rich following their own advice, their store of words is precious indeed. Consider this advice offered by one technical service:

> The market's rise after a period of reaccumulation is a bullish sign. Nevertheless, fulcrum characteristics are not yet clearly present and a resistance area exists 40 points higher in the Dow, so it is clearly premature to say the next leg of the bull market is up. If, in the coming weeks, a test of the lows holds and the market breaks out of its flag, a further rise would be indicated. Should the lows be violated, a continuation of the intermediate term downtrend is called for. In view of the current situation, it is a distinct possibility that traders will sit in the wings awaiting a clearer delineation of the trend and the market will move in a narrow trading range.

If you ask me what this means, I cannot tell you, but I think the technician probably had the following in mind: "If the market does not go up or go down, it will remain unchanged." Even the weather forecaster can do better than that.

Obviously, I'm biased. This is not only a personal bias but a professional one as well. Technical analysis is anathema to much of the academic world. We love to pick on it. We have two main reasons: (1) after paying transactions costs and taxes, the method does not do better than a buy-and-hold strategy; and (2) it's easy to pick on. And while it may seem a bit unfair, just remember that it's your money we're trying to save.

Although the computer perhaps enhanced the standing of the technician for a time, and while charting services are widely available on the Internet, technology has ultimately proved to be the technician's undoing. Just as fast as he (or she) creates charts to show where the market is going, the academic gets busy constructing charts showing where the technician has been. Because it's so easy to test all the technical trading rules on the computer, it has become a favorite pastime for academics to see whether they really work.

IS THERE MOMENTUM IN THE STOCK MARKET?

The technician believes that knowledge of a stock's past behavior can help predict its probable future behavior. In other words, the sequence of price changes before any given day is important in predicting the price change for that day. This might be called "the wallpaper principle." The technical analyst tries to predict future stock prices just as we might predict that the pattern of wallpaper behind the mirror is the same as the pattern above the mirror. The basic premise is that there are repeatable patterns in space and time.

Chartists believe momentum exists in the market. Supposedly, stocks that have been rising will continue to do so, and those that begin falling will go on sinking. Investors should therefore buy stocks that start rising and continue to hold their strong stocks. Should the stock begin to fall, investors are advised to sell.

These technical rules have been tested exhaustively by using stock-price data on the major exchanges going back as far as the beginning of the twentieth century. The results reveal that past movements in stock prices cannot be used reliably to foretell future movements. The stock market has little, if any, memory. While the market does exhibit some momentum from time to time, it does not occur dependably, and there is not enough persistence in stock prices to make trend-following strategies consistently profitable. Although there is some short-term momentum in the stock market, as will be described more fully in chapter 11, any investor who pays transactions costs and taxes cannot benefit from it.

Economists have also examined the technician's thesis that there are often sequences of price changes in the same direction over several days (or several weeks or months). Stocks are likened to fullbacks who, once having gained some momentum, can be expected to carry on for a long gain. It turns out that this is simply not the case. Sometimes one gets positive price changes (rising prices) for several days in a row; but sometimes when you are flipping a fair coin you also get a long string of "heads" in a row, and you get sequences of positive (or negative) price changes no more frequently than you can expect random sequences of heads or tails in a row. What are often called "persistent patterns" in the stock market occur no more frequently than the runs of luck in the fortunes of any gambler. This is what economists mean when they say that stock prices behave very much like a random walk.

JUST WHAT EXACTLY IS A RANDOM WALK?

To many people this appears to be errant nonsense. Even the most casual reader of the financial pages can easily spot patterns in the market. For example, look at the stock chart on page 138.

The chart seems to display obvious patterns. After an initial rise the stock turned down, and then headed persistently downhill. Later, the decline was arrested and the stock had another sustained upward move. One cannot look at a stock chart like this without noticing the self-evidence of these statements. How can the economist be so myopic that he cannot see what is so plainly visible to the naked eye?

The persistence of this belief in repetitive stock-market patterns is due to statistical illusion. To illustrate, let me describe an experiment in which I asked my students to participate. The students were asked to construct a stock chart showing the movements of a hypothetical stock initially selling at $50. For each successive trading day, the closing stock price would be determined by the flip of a coin. If the toss was a head, the students assumed that the stock closed ½ point higher than the preceding close. If the flip was a tail, the price was assumed to be down by ½. The chart below is the hypothetical stock chart derived from one of these experiments.

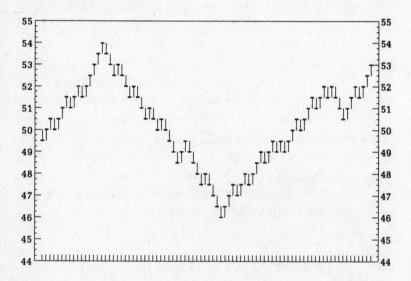

The chart derived from random coin tossings looks remarkably like a normal stock price chart and even appears to display cycles. Of course, the pronounced "cycles" that we seem to observe in coin tossings do not occur at regular intervals as true cycles do, but neither do the ups and downs in the stock market.

It is this lack of regularity that is crucial. The "cycles" in the stock charts are no more true cycles than the runs of luck or misfortune of the ordinary gambler. And the fact that stocks seem to be in an uptrend, which looks just like the upward move in some earlier period, provides no useful information on the dependability or duration of the current uptrend. Yes, history does tend to repeat itself in the stock market, but in an infinitely surprising variety of ways that confound any attempts to profit from a knowledge of past price patterns.

In other simulated stock charts derived from student coin-tossings, there were head-and-shoulders formations, triple tops and bottoms, and other more esoteric chart patterns. One chart showed a beautiful upward breakout from an inverted head and shoulders (a very bullish formation). I showed it to a chartist friend of mine who practically jumped out of his skin. "What is this company?" he exclaimed. "We've got to buy immediately. This pattern's a classic. There's no question the stock will be up 15 points next week." He did not respond kindly when I told him the chart had been produced by flipping a coin. Chartists have no sense of humor. I got my comeuppance when *BusinessWeek* hired a technician adept at hatchet work to review the first edition of this book.

My students used a completely random process to produce their stock charts. With each toss, as long as the coins used were fair, there was a 50 percent chance of heads, implying an upward move in the price of the stock, and a 50 percent chance of tails and a downward move. Even if they flipped ten heads in a row, the chance of getting a head on the next toss was still 50 percent. Mathematicians call a sequence of numbers produced by a random process (such as those on our simulated stock chart) a random walk. The next move on the chart is completely unpredictable on the basis of what has happened before.

The stock market does not conform perfectly to the mathematician's ideal of the complete independence of present price movements from those in the past. There is some momentum in stock prices. When good news arises, investors often only partially adjust their estimates of the appropriate price of the stock. Slow adjustment can make stock prices rise steadily for a period, imparting a degree of momentum. The failure of stock prices to measure up perfectly to the definition of a random walk led the financial economists Andrew Lo and A. Craig MacKinlay to publish a book entitled *A Non-Random Walk Down Wall Street.* In addition to some evidence of short-term momentum, there has been a long-run uptrend in most averages of stock prices in line with the long-run growth of earnings and dividends.

But don't count on short-term momentum to give you some sure-fire strategy to allow you to beat the market. For one thing, stock prices don't always underreact to news—sometimes they overreact and price reversals can occur with terrifying suddenness. We shall see in chapter 11 that investment funds managed in accordance with a momentum strategy started off with subpar results. And even during periods when momentum is present (and the market fails to behave like a random walk), the systematic relationships that exist are often so small that they are not useful to investors. The transactions charges and taxes involved in trying to take advantage of these dependencies are far greater than any profits that might be obtained. Thus, an accurate statement of the "weak" form of the random-walk hypothesis goes as follows:

> The history of stock price movements contains no useful information that will enable an investor consistently to out-perform a buy-and-hold strategy in managing a portfolio.

If the weak form of the random-walk hypothesis is valid, then, as my colleague Richard Quandt says, "Technical analysis is akin to astrology and every bit as scientific."

I am not saying that technical strategies never make money. They very often do make profits. The point is rather that a simple buy-and-hold strategy (that is, buying a stock or group of stocks and holding on for a long period of time) typically makes as much or more money.

When scientists want to test the efficacy of some new drug, they usually run an experiment in which two groups of patients are administered pills—one containing the drug in question, the other a worthless placebo (a sugar pill). The results of the admin-istration to the two groups are compared, and the drug is deemed effective only if the group receiving the drug did better than the group getting the placebo. Obviously, if both groups got better in the same period of time, the drug should not be given the credit, even if the patients did recover.

In the stock-market experiments, the placebo with which the technical strategies are compared is the buy-and-hold strategy. Technical schemes often do make profits for their users, but so does a buy-and-hold strategy. Indeed, as we shall see later, a simple buy-and-hold strategy using a portfolio consisting of all the stocks in a broad stock-market index has provided investors with an average annual rate of return of about 10 percent over the past eighty years. Only if technical schemes produce better returns than the market can they be judged effective. To date, none has consistently passed the test.

SOME MORE ELABORATE TECHNICAL SYSTEMS

Devotees of technical analysis may argue with some justification that I have been unfair. The simple tests I have just described do not do justice to the "richness" of technical analysis. Unfortunately for the technician, even more elaborate trading rules have been subjected to scientific testing. Let's examine a few popular ones in detail.

The Filter System

Under the popular "filter" system, a stock that has reached a low and has moved up, say 5 percent (or any other percent you wish to name), is said to be in an uptrend. A stock that has moved down 5 percent from a peak is said to be in a downtrend. You're supposed to buy any stock that has moved up 5 percent from its low and hold it until the price moves down 5 percent from a subsequent high, at which time you sell and, perhaps, even sell short. The short position is maintained until the price rises at least 5 percent from a subsequent low.

This scheme is very popular with brokers. Indeed, the filter method lies behind the popular "stop-loss" order favored by brokers, where the client is advised to sell his stock if it falls 5 percent below his purchase price to "limit his potential losses." The argument is that presumably a stock that falls by 5 percent will be going into a downtrend.

Exhaustive testing of various filter rules has been undertaken. The percentage drop or rise that filters out buy and sell candidates has been allowed to vary from 1 percent to 50 percent. The tests covered different time periods and involved individual stocks as well as stock indexes. The results are remarkably consistent. When the higher transactions charges incurred under the filter rules are taken into consideration, these techniques cannot consistently beat a policy of simply buying the individual stock (or the stock index) and holding it over the period during which the test is performed. The individual investor would do well to avoid using any filter rule and, I might add, any broker who recommends it.

The Dow Theory

The Dow theory is a great tug-of-war between resistance and support. When the market tops out and moves down, that previous peak defines a resistance area, because people who missed selling at the top will be anxious to do so if given another opportunity. If the market then rises again and nears the previous peak, it is said to be "testing" the resistance area. Now comes the moment of truth. If the market breaks through the resistance area, it is likely to keep going up for a while and the previous resistance area becomes a support area. If, on the other hand, the market "fails to penetrate the resistance area" and instead falls through the preceding low where there was previous support, a bear-market signal is given and the investor is advised to sell.

The basic Dow principle implies a strategy of buying when the market goes higher than the last peak and selling when it sinks through the preceding valley. There are various wrinkles to the theory, but the basic idea is part of the gospel of charting.

Unhappily, the signals generated by the Dow mechanism

have no significance for predicting future price movements. The market's performance after sell signals is no different from its performance after buy signals. Relative to simply buying and holding the representative list of stocks in the market averages, the Dow follower actually comes out a little behind, because the strategy entails a number of extra brokerage costs as the investor buys and sells when the strategy decrees.

The Relative-Strength System

In the relative-strength system, an investor buys and holds those stocks that are acting well, that is, outperforming the general market indexes. Conversely, the stocks that are acting poorly relative to the market should be avoided or, perhaps, even sold short. While there do seem to be some time periods when a relative-strength strategy would have outperformed a buy-and-hold strategy, there is no evidence that it can do so consistently. As indicated earlier, there is some evidence of momentum in the stock market. Nevertheless, a computer test of relative-strength rules over a twenty-five-year period suggests that such rules are not, after accounting for transactions charges and taxes, useful for investors.

Price-Volume Systems

Price-volume systems suggest that when a stock (or the general market) rises on large or increasing volume, there is an unsatisfied excess of buying interest and the stock will continue its rise. Conversely, when a stock drops on large volume, selling pressure is indicated and a sell signal is given.

Again, the investor following such a system is likely to be disappointed in the results. The buy and sell signals generated by the strategy contain no information useful for predicting future price movements. As with all technical strategies, however, the investor is obliged to do a great deal of in-and-out trading, and thus his transactions costs and taxes are far in excess of those necessitated in a buy-and-hold strategy. After accounting for these costs, the investor does worse than he would by simply buying and holding a diversified group of stocks.

Reading Chart Patterns

Perhaps some of the more complicated chart patterns, such as those described in the preceding chapter, are able to reveal the future course of stock prices. For example, is the downward penetration of a head-and-shoulders formation a reliable bearish omen? As one of the gospels of charting, *Technical Analysis*, puts it, "One does not bring instantly to a stop a heavy car moving at seventy miles per hour and, all within the same split second, turn it around and get it moving back down the road in the opposite direction." Before the stock turns around, its price movements are supposed to form one of a number of extensive reversal patterns as the smart-money traders slowly "distribute" their shares to the "public." Of course, we know some stocks do reverse directions in quite a hurry (this is called an "unfortunate V formation"), but perhaps some chart configurations can, like the Roman soothsayers, accurately foretell the future. Alas, the computer has even tested more arcane charting techniques, and the technician's tool has again betrayed him.

In one elaborate study, the computer was programmed to draw charts for 548 stocks traded on the New York Stock Exchange over a five-year period. It was instructed to scan all the charts and identify any one of thirty-two of the most popularly followed chart patterns. The computer was told to be on the lookout for heads and shoulders, triple tops and bottoms, channels, wedges, diamonds, and so forth. Because the machine is a very thorough (though rather dull) worker, we can be sure that it did not miss any significant chart patterns.

When the machine found that one of the bearish chart patterns such as a head and shoulders was followed by a downward move through the neckline toward décolletage (a most bearish omen), it recorded a sell signal. If, on the other hand, a triple bottom was followed by an upside breakout (a most favorable augury), a buy signal was recorded. The computer then followed the performance of the stocks for which buy and sell signals were given and compared them with the performance record of the general market.

Again, there seemed to be no relationship between the technical signal and subsequent performance. If you had bought only those stocks with buy signals, and sold on a sell signal, your performance after transactions costs would have been no better than that achieved with a buy-and-hold strategy.

Randomness Is Hard to Accept

Human nature likes order; people find it hard to accept the notion of randomness. No matter what the laws of chance might tell us, we search for patterns among random events wherever they might occur—not only in the stock market but even in interpreting sporting phenomena.

In describing an outstanding performance by a basketball player, reporters and spectators commonly use expressions such as "LeBron James has the hot hand" or "Kobe Bryant is a streak shooter." Those who play, coach, or follow basketball are almost universally convinced that if a player has successfully made his last shot, or last few shots, he is more likely to make his next shot. A study by a group of psychologists, however, suggests that the "hot hand" phenomenon is a myth.

The psychologists did a detailed study of every shot taken by the Philadelphia 76ers over a full season and a half. They found no positive correlation between the outcomes of successive shots. Indeed, they found that a hit by a player followed by a miss was actually a bit likelier than the case of making two baskets in a row. Moreover, the researchers looked at sequences of more than two shots. Again, they found that the number of long streaks (that is, hitting of several baskets in a row) was no greater than could have been expected in a random set of data (such as flipping coins in which every event was independent of its predecessor). Although the event of making one's last two or three shots influenced the player's perception of whether he would make his next shot, the hard evidence was that there was no effect. The researchers then confirmed their study by examining the free-throw records of the Boston Celtics and by conducting controlled shooting experiments with the men and women of the Cornell University varsity basketball teams.

These findings do not imply that basketball is a game of chance rather than skill. Obviously there are some players who are more adept at making baskets and free throws than others. The point is, however, that the probability of making a shot is independent of the outcome of previous shots. The psychologists conjecture that the persistent belief in the hot hand could be due to memory bias. If long sequences of hits or misses are more memorable than alternating sequences, observers are likely to overestimate the correlation between successive shots. When events sometimes do come in clusters and streaks, people refuse to believe that they are random, even though such clusters and streaks do occur frequently in random data such as are derived from the tossing of a coin.

A GAGGLE OF OTHER TECHNICAL THEORIES TO HELP YOU LOSE MONEY

Once the academic world polished off most of the standard technical trading rules, it turned its august attention toward some of the more fanciful schemes. The world of financial analysis would be much quieter and duller without the chartists, as the following techniques amply demonstrate.

The Hemline Indicator

Not content with price movements, some technical analysts have broadened their investigations to include other movements as well. One of the most charming of these schemes has been called by the author Ira Cobleigh the "bull markets and bare knees" theory. Check the hemlines of women's dresses in any given year, and you'll have an idea of the direction of stock prices. The following chart suggests a loose tendency for bull markets to be associated with bare knees and depressed markets to be associated with bear markets for girl watchers.

For example, in the late nineteenth century and early part of the twentieth, the stock market was rather dull, and so were hemlines. But then came rising hemlines and the great bull market of the 1920s, to be followed by long skirts and the crash of the 1930s. (Actually, the chart cheats a bit: hemlines fell in 1927, before the most dynamic phase of the bull market.)

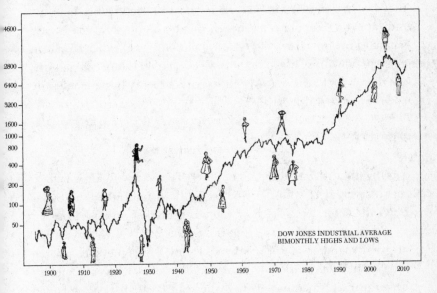

DOW JONES INDUSTRIAL AVERAGE
BIMONTHLY HIGHS AND LOWS

Things did not work out as well in the post–World War II period. The market declined sharply during the summer of 1946, well in advance of the introduction of the "New Look" featuring longer skirts in 1947. Similarly, the sharp stock-market decline that began at the end of 1968 preceded the introduction of the midiskirt, which was high fashion in 1969 and especially in 1970.

How did the theory work out during the crash of 1987? You might think the hemline indicator failed. After all, in the spring of 1987, when designers began shipping their fall lines, very short skirts were decreed as the fashion for the time. But along about the beginning of October, when the first chill winds began blowing across the country, a strange thing happened: Most women decided that miniskirts were not for them. As women went back to long skirts, designers quickly followed suit. The rest is stock-market history. And how about the severe bear markets of the first decade of the 2000s? Unfortunately, you guessed it, pants became the fashion. Women business leaders and politicians always appeared in pants suits. Now we know the real culprit for the punishing bear markets of the period.

Even though there does seem to be some evidence in favor of the theory, don't be too optimistic about expecting the hemline indicator to give you a leg up on market timing. No longer are women imprisoned by the tyranny of hemlines. As *Vogue* put it, you can now dress like a man or woman, and all hemline lengths are now okay. I'm afraid this stock-market theory has undoubtedly outlived its usefulness.

The Super Bowl Indicator

Why did the market go up in 2009? That's easy to answer for a technical analyst who uses the Super Bowl indicator. The Super Bowl indicator forecasts how the stock market will perform on the basis of which team wins the Super Bowl. A victory by an original member of the National Football League such as the Steelers in 2009 predicts a bull market in stocks, whereas a victory by an original member of the American Football League is bad news for stock market investors. In 2002 the Patriots (AFL team) defeated the Rams (NFL), and the market responded correctly by falling sharply. Although the indicator sometimes fails, it has been correct far more often than it has been wrong. Naturally, it makes no sense. The results of the Super Bowl indicator simply illustrate nothing more than the fact that it's sometimes possible to correlate two completely unrelated events. Indeed, Mark Hulbert reports that the stock-market researcher David Leinweber found that the indicator most closely correlated with the S&P 500 Index is the volume of butter production in Bangladesh.

The Odd-Lot Theory

The odd-lot theory holds that except for the investor who is always right, no one can contribute more to a successful investment strategy than an investor who is invariably wrong. The "odd-lotter," according to popular superstition, is that kind of person. Thus, success is assured by buying when the odd-lotter sells and selling when the odd-lotter buys.

Odd-lotters are the people who trade stocks in less than 100-share lots (called round lots). Many amateurs in the stock market cannot afford the $5,000 investment to buy a round lot (100 shares) of stock selling at $50 a share. They are more likely to buy, say, ten shares for a more modest investment of $500.

By examining the ratio of odd-lot purchases (the number of shares these amateurs bought during a particular day) to odd-lot sales (the number of shares they sold) and by looking at what particular stocks odd-lotters buy and sell, one can supposedly make money. These uninformed amateurs, presumably acting solely out of emotion and not with professional insight, are lambs in the street being led to slaughter. They are, according to legend, invariably wrong.

It turns out that the odd-lotter isn't such a stupendous dodo after all. A little stupid? Maybe. There is some indication that the performance of odd-lotters might be slightly worse than the stock averages. However, the available evidence indicates that knowledge of odd-lotters' actions is not useful for the formulation of investment strategies.

Dogs of the Dow

This interesting strategy capitalized on a general contrarian conviction that out-of-favor stocks eventually tend to reverse direction. The strategy entailed buying each year the ten stocks in the Dow Jones 30-Stock Industrial Average that had the highest dividend yields. The idea was that these ten stocks were the most out of favor, so they typically had low price-earnings multiples and low price-to-book-value ratios as well. The theory is attributed to a money manager named Michael O'Higgins, who publicized the technique in his book *Beating the Dow*. James O'Shaughnessy tested the theory as far back as the 1920s; he found that the Dogs of the Dow had beaten the overall index by over 2 percentage points per year with no additional risk.

Members of the canine contingent of Wall Street analysts raised their ears and marketed billions of dollars of mutual funds on the basis of the principle. And then, just as might be expected, success bit the dogs. The Dogs of the Dow consistently underperformed the overall market. As the Dogs star O'Higgins opined, "the strategy became too popular" and ultimately self-destructed. The Dogs of the Dow no longer hunt.

January Effect

A number of researchers have found that January has been a very unusual month for stock-market returns. Stock-market returns have tended to be especially high during the first two weeks of January. The effect appears to be particularly strong for smaller firms. Even after one adjusts for risk, small firms appear to offer investors abnormally generous returns—with the excess returns produced largely during the first few days of the year. Such an effect has also been documented for several foreign stock markets. This led to the publication of one book with the provocative title *The Incredible January Effect*. Investors and especially stockbrokers, with visions of large commissions dancing around in their heads, designed strategies to capitalize on this "anomaly" believed to be so dependable.

Unfortunately, however, the transactions costs of trading in the stocks of small companies are substantially higher than those for larger companies (because of higher bid-ask spreads and lower liquidity), and there appears to be no way any ordinary investor could exploit this anomaly. Moreover, the effect is not dependable in each year. In other words, the January "loose change" costs too much to pick up, and in some years it turns out to be a mirage.

A Few More Systems

To continue this review of technical schemes would soon generate rapidly diminishing returns. Probably few people seriously believe that the sunspot theory of stock-market movements can make money for them. But do you believe that by following the ratio of advancing to declining stocks on the New York Stock Exchange you can find a reliable leading indicator of general stock-market peaks? A careful computer study says no. Do you think that a rise in short interest (the number of shares of a stock sold short) is a bullish signal (because eventually the stock will be repurchased by the short seller to cover his or her position)? Exhaustive testing indicates no relationship either for the stock market as a whole or for individual issues. Do you think that a moving-average system as espoused by some of the financial television networks (for example, buy a stock if its price or its fifty-day average price goes higher than its average price over the past 200 days and sell it if it goes below the average) can lead you to extraordinary stock-market profits? Not if you have to pay transactions charges—to buy and sell! Do you think you should "Sell in May and Go Away" until October? In fact, the market rises between May and October more often than not.

Technical Market Gurus

Technicians may not make accurate predictions, but the early ones were certainly colorful. During the 1980s, for example, the most influential market guru was Robert Prechter. Prechter became interested in the parallels between social psychology and the stock market while a Yale undergraduate. After college, Prechter spent four years playing drums in a rock band, after which he joined Merrill Lynch as a junior technical analyst. There Prechter stumbled on the work of an obscure accountant, R. N. Elliott, who had devised an arcane theory that he modestly entitled the Elliott wave theory. Elliott's premise was that there were predictable waves of investor psychology and that they steered the market with natural ebbs and flows. By watching them, Elliott believed, one could call major shifts in the market. Prechter was so excited about this discovery that he quit Merrill Lynch in 1979 to write an investor newsletter from the unlikely location of Gainesville, Georgia.

Prechter's initial predictions were uncannily accurate. Early in the 1980s, he predicted a major bull market with the Dow expected to rise to the 3,600 level. Prechter was the golden knight of the day by keeping his followers fully invested through his predicted "interim stop" at 2,700.

Tarnish set in after October 1987. To Prechter's credit, he did say that there was "a 50/50 risk of a 10% decline" in the market on October 5, 1987. But he advised institutional investors to hang on for the ultimate target of 3,686 in the Dow. After the crash, with the Dow near 2,000, Prechter turned bearish for the long term and recommended holding Treasury bills. He predicted that "the great bull market is probably over" and that by the early 1990s the Dow Jones Industrial Average would plunge below 400. Prechter missed out on the entire bull market of the 1990s. This was a mortal wound for a golden guru. Prechter remained a consistent bear, however, and did gain some renewed following during the market's meltdown of the early 2000s. This only proves that if one keeps predicting a market decline (or rise) one is bound to be correct at some time.

Prechter was succeeded by Elaine Garzarelli, then an executive vice president of the investment firm of Lehman Brothers. Garzarelli was not a one-indicator woman. She plunged into the ocean of financial data and used thirteen different indicators to predict the course of the market. Garzarelli always liked to study vital details. As a child, she would get animal organs from the local butcher and dissect them.

Garzarelli was the Roger Babson of the 1987 crash. Turning bearish in August, she was recommending by September 1 that her clients get out of the stock market. By October 11, she was confident that a crash was imminent. Two days later, in a forecast almost frighteningly prescient, she told *USA Today* that a drop of more than 500 points in the Dow was coming. Within a week, her predictions were realized.

But the crash was Garzarelli's last hurrah. Just as the media were coronating her as the "Guru of Black Monday" and adulatory articles appeared in magazines ranging from *Cosmopolitan* to *Fortune*, she drowned in her prescience—or her notoriety. After the crash, she said she wouldn't touch the market and predicted that the Dow would fall another 200 to 400 points. Thus, Garzarelli missed the bounce-back in the market. Moreover, those who put money in her hands were sadly disappointed. In explaining her lack of consistency, she gave the time-honored explanation of technicians: "I failed to believe my own charts."

Perhaps the most colorful investment gurus of the mid-1990s were the homespun, grandmotherly (median age seventy) Beardstown Ladies. Called by publicists "the greatest investment minds of our generation," these celebrity grannies cooked up profits and hype, selling more than a million books and appearing frequently on national television shows and in weekly magazines. They mixed explanations of their investment success ("heartland" virtues of hard work and churchgoing) with yummy cooking recipes (such as stock-market muffins—guaranteed to rise). In their best-selling 1995 book, *The Beardstown Ladies Common-Sense Investment Guide*, they claimed that their investment returns were 23.9 percent per year over the preceding decade, far eclipsing the 14.9 annual percent return of the S&P 500 Index. What a great story: Little old midwestern ladies using common sense could beat the pants off the overpaid investment pros of Wall Street and could even put index funds to shame.

Unfortunately, the ladies were discovered to be cooking the books as well. Apparently, members of the Beardstown group were counting their investment club dues as part of their stock-market profits. The accounting firm Price Waterhouse was called in, and it calculated the ladies' true investment return over the decade to be 9.1 percent per year—almost 6 points below the overall market. So much for getting rich by worshiping investment idols.

The moral to the story is obvious. With large numbers of techni-

cians predicting the market, there will always be some who have
called the last turn or even the last few turns, but none will be
consistently accurate. To paraphrase the biblical warning, "He
who looks back at the predictions of market gurus dies of remorse."

WHY ARE TECHNICIANS STILL HIRED?

It seems very clear that under scientific scrutiny chart reading
must share a pedestal with alchemy. There has been a remarkable uniformity in the conclusions of studies done on all forms
of technical analysis. Not one has consistently outperformed the
placebo of a buy-and-hold strategy. Technical methods cannot be
used to make useful investment strategies. This is the fundamental conclusion of the random-walk theory.

A former colleague of mine believed that the capitalist system
would weed out all useless growths such as the flourishing technicians. "The days of these modern-day soothsayers on Wall Street
are numbered," he would say. "Brokers will soon learn they can
easily do without the technicians' services." The chartist's durabil-
ity suggests that the capitalist system may garden like most of
the rest of us. We like to see our best plants grow, but, as summer
wears on, the weeds frequently get the best of us.

The point is, the technicians often play an important role in
the greening of the brokers. Chartists recommend trades—almost
every technical system involves some degree of in-and-out trading.
Trading generates commissions, and commissions are the lifeblood
of many brokerage houses. The technicians do not help produce
yachts for the customers, but they do help generate the trading
that provides yachts for the brokers.

APPRAISING THE COUNTERATTACK

As you might imagine, the random-walk theory's dismissal of
charting is not altogether popular among technicians. Academic

proponents of the theory are greeted in some Wall Street quarters with as much enthusiasm as Bernie Madoff addressing the Better Business Bureau from his jail cell. Technical analysts consider the theory "just plain academic drivel." Let us pause, then, and appraise the counterattack by beleaguered technicians.

Perhaps the most common complaint about the weakness of the random-walk theory is based on a distrust of mathematics and a misconception of what the theory means. "The market isn't random," the complaint goes, "and no mathematician is going to convince me it is." Even so astute a commentator on the Wall Street scene as "Adam Smith" displays this misconception when he writes, "I suspect that even if the random walkers announced a perfect mathematical proof of randomness I would go on believing that in the long run future earnings influence present value, and that in the short run the dominant factor is the temper of the crowd."

Of course, earnings and dividends influence market prices, and so does the temper of the crowd. We saw ample evidence of this in earlier chapters of the book. But, even if markets were dominated during certain periods by irrational crowd behavior, the stock market might well still be approximated by a random walk. The original illustrative analogy of a random walk concerned a drunken man staggering around an empty field. He is not rational, but he's not predictable either.

Moreover, new fundamental information about a company (a big mineral strike, the death of the president, etc.) is also unpredictable. It will occur randomly over time. Indeed, successive appearances of news items must be random. If an item of news were not random, that is, if it were dependent on an earlier item of news, then it wouldn't be news at all. The weak form of the random-walk theory says only that stock prices cannot be predicted on the basis of past stock prices.

The technical analyst will also cite chapter and verse that the academic world has certainly not tested every technical scheme that has been devised. No economist or mathematician, however skillful, can prove conclusively that technical methods can never work. All that can be said is that the small amount of information contained in stock-market pricing patterns has not been shown to be sufficient to overcome the transactions costs and taxes involved in acting on that information.

Each year a number of eager people visit the gambling parlors of Las Vegas and Atlantic City and examine the last several hundred numbers of the roulette wheel in search of some repeating pattern. Usually they find one. And so they stay until they lose everything because they do not retest the pattern.* The same thing is true for technicians.

If you examine past stock prices in any given period, you can almost always find some kind of system that would have worked in a given period. If enough different criteria for selecting stocks are tried, one will eventually be found that selects the best ones of that period. The real problem is, of course, whether the scheme works in a different time period. What most advocates of technical analysis usually fail to do is to test their schemes with market data derived from periods other than those during which the scheme was developed.

Even if the technician follows my advice, tests his scheme in many different time periods, and finds it a reliable predictor of stock prices, I still believe that technical analysis must ultimately be worthless. For the sake of argument, suppose the technician had found a reliable year-end rally, that is, every year stock prices rose between Christmas and New Year's Day. The problem is that once such a regularity is known to market participants, people will act in a way that prevents it from happening in the future.†

Any successful technical scheme must ultimately be self-defeating. The moment I realize that prices will be higher after New Year's

---

*Edward O. Thorp actually did find a method to win at blackjack. Thorp wrote it all up in *Beat the Dealer*. Since then, casinos switched to the use of several decks of cards to make it more difficult for card counters and, as a last resort, they banished the counters from the gaming tables.

†If such a regularity was known to only one individual, he would simply practice the technique until he had collected a large share of the marbles. He surely would have no incentive to share a truly useful scheme by making it available to others.

Day than they are before Christmas, I will start buying before Christmas ever comes around. If people know a stock will go up tomorrow, you can be sure it will go up today. Any regularity in the stock market that can be discovered and acted upon profitably is bound to destroy itself. This is the fundamental reason why I am convinced that no one will be successful in using technical methods to get above-average returns in the stock market.

IMPLICATIONS FOR INVESTORS

The past history of stock prices cannot be used to predict the future in any meaningful way. Technical strategies are usually amusing, often comforting, but of no real value. This is the weak form of the efficient market hypothesis. Technical theories enrich only the people preparing and marketing the technical service or the brokerage firms who hire technicians in the hope that their analyses may help encourage investors to do more in-and-out trading and thus generate commission business for the brokerage firm.

Using technical analysis for market timing is especially danger-ous. Because there is a long-term uptrend in the stock market, it can be very risky to be in cash. An investor who frequently carries a large cash position to avoid periods of market decline is very likely to be out of the market during some periods where it rallies smartly. Professor H. Negat Seybun of the University of Michigan found that 95 percent of the significant market gains over a thirty-year period came on 90 of the roughly 7,500 trading days. If you happened to miss those 90 days, just over 1 percent of the total, the generous long-run stock-market returns of the period would have been wiped out. Studying a longer period, Laszlo Birinyi, in his book *Master Trader*, has calculated that a buy-and-hold investor would have seen one dollar invested in the Dow Jones Industrial Average in 1900 grow to $290 by the start of 2013. Had that inves-tor missed the best five days each year, however, that dollar invest-ment would have been worth less than a penny in 2013. The point is that market timers risk missing the infrequent large sprints that are the big contributors to performance.

The implications of this analysis are simple. If past prices contain little or no useful information for the prediction of future prices, there is no point in following any technical trading rule for the timing of purchases or sales. A simple policy of buying and holding will be at least as good as any technical procedure. Moreover, buying and selling, to the extent that it is profitable at all, tends to generate capital gains, which are subject to tax. By following any technical strategy, you are likely to realize short-term capital gains and pay larger taxes (as well as paying them sooner) than you would under a buy-and-hold strategy. Thus, simply buying and holding a diversified portfolio suited to your objectives will enable you to save on investment expense, brokerage charges, and taxes.

7

HOW GOOD IS
FUNDAMENTAL ANALYSIS?
THE EFFICIENT-MARKET
HYPOTHESIS

How could I have been so mistaken as
to have trusted the experts?
—John F. Kennedy after the Bay of Pigs fiasco

I N THE BEGINNING he was a statistician. He wore a white starched
shirt and threadbare blue suit. He quietly put on his green
eyeshade, sat down at his desk, and recorded meticulously the
historical financial information about the companies he followed.
The result: writer's cramp. But then a metamorphosis began to set
in. He rose from his desk, bought blue button-down shirts and gray
flannel suits, threw away his eyeshade, and began to make field
trips to visit the companies that previously he had known only as
a collection of financial statistics. His title now became security
analyst.

As time went on, his salary and perks attracted the attention
of his female cohorts, and they too donned suits. And just about
everybody who was anybody was now flying first-class and talking
money, money, money. The new generation was hip; suits were
out, and Gucci shoes and Armani slacks were in. They were so
incredibly brilliant and knowledgeable that portfolio managers
relied on their recommendations and Wall Street firms used them
increasingly to cultivate investment banking clients. They were
now equity research stars. Some, however, whispered unkindly
that they were investment banking whores.

THE VIEWS FROM WALL STREET
AND ACADEMIA

No matter what title, derogatory or otherwise, these individuals hold, the great majority are fundamentalists. Thus, studies casting doubt on the efficacy of technical analysis would not be considered surprising by most professionals. At heart, the Wall Street pros are fundamentalists. The really important question is whether fundamental analysis is any good.

Two opposing views have been taken about the efficacy of fundamental analysis. Wall Streeters feel that fundamental analysis is becoming more powerful all the time. The individual investor has scarcely a chance against the professional portfolio manager and a team of fundamental analysts.

Many in the academic community sneer at such pomposity. Some academicians have gone so far as to suggest that a blindfolded monkey throwing darts at the stock listings can select stocks with as much success as professional portfolio managers. They have argued that fund managers and their analysts can do no better at picking stocks than a rank amateur. This chapter will recount the major battle in an ongoing war between academics and market professionals, explain what is meant by "the efficient market hypothesis," and tell you why it is important to your wallet.

ARE SECURITY ANALYSTS
FUNDAMENTALLY CLAIRVOYANT?

Forecasting future earnings is the security analysts' raison d'être. As *Institutional Investor* put it, "Earnings are the name of the game and always will be."

To predict future directions, analysts generally start by looking at past wanderings. "A proven score of past performance in earnings growth is," one analyst told me, "a most reliable indicator of future earnings growth." If management is really skillful, there is no reason to think that it will lose its Midas touch in the future. If the same adroit management team remains at the helm, the course of future earnings growth should continue as it has in the past, or so the argument goes. While it sounds suspiciously like an argument used by technical analysts, fundamentalists pride themselves on the fact that it is based on specific, proven company performance.

Such thinking flunks in the academic world. Calculations of past earnings growth are no help in predicting future growth. If you had known the growth rates of all companies during, say, the 1980–90 period, this would not have helped you at all in predicting what growth they would achieve in the 1990–2000 period. And knowing the fast growers of the 1990s did not help analysts find the fast growers of the first decade of the twenty-first century. This startling result was first reported by British researchers for companies in the United Kingdom in an article charmingly titled "Higgledy Piggledy Growth." Learned academicians at Princeton and Harvard applied the British study to U.S. companies—and, surprise, the same was true here!

"IBM," the cry immediately went up, "remember IBM." I do remember IBM: a steady high grower for decades. For a while it was a glaring exception. But after the mid-1980s, even the mighty IBM failed to continue its dependable growth pattern. I also remember Polaroid, Kodak, Nortel Networks, Xerox, and dozens of other firms that chalked up consistent high growth rates until the roof fell in. I hope you remember not the current exceptions, but rather the rule: Many in Wall Street refuse to accept the fact that no reliable pattern can be discerned from past records to aid the analyst in predicting future growth. Even during the boom years of the 1990s, only one in eight large companies managed to achieve consistent yearly growth. And not even one continued to enjoy growth into the first years of the new millennium. Analysts can't predict consistent long-run growth, because it does not exist.

A good analyst will argue, however, that there's much more to predicting than just examining the past record. Some will even admit that the past record is not a perfect measurement. Rather than examine every factor that goes into the actual forecasting process, John Cragg and I decided to concentrate on the end result: the prediction itself.

Donning our cloak of academic detachment, we wrote to nineteen of the most respected Wall Street firms engaged in fundamental analysis. We asked these firms for their estimates of the future one-year and five-year earnings for a large sample of S&P 500 companies. These estimates, made at several different times, were then compared with actual results to see how well the analysts forecast short-run and long-run earnings changes. The results were surprising.

Bluntly stated, the careful estimates of security analysts (based on industry studies, plant visits, etc.) do little better than those that would be obtained by simple extrapolation of past trends, which we have already seen are no help at all. Indeed, when compared with actual earnings growth rates, the five-year estimates of security analysts were actually worse than the predictions from several naive forecasting models.

Our method of determining the efficacy of the security analyst's diagnoses of his companies is exactly the same as was used before in evaluating the technicians' medicine. We compared the results obtained by following the experts with the results from some naive mechanism involving no expertise at all. Sometimes these naive predictors work very well. For example, if you want to forecast the weather tomorrow, you will do a pretty good job by predicting that it will be exactly the same as today. Although this system misses every turning point in the weather, most days it is quite reliable. How many weather forecasters do you suppose do any better?

When confronted with the poor record of their five-year growth estimates, the security analysts honestly, if sheepishly, admitted that five years ahead is really too far in advance to make reliable projections. They felt that they really ought to be judged on their ability to project earnings changes one year ahead. Believe it or not, it turned out that their one-year forecasts were even worse than their five-year projections.

The analysts fought back gamely. They complained that it was unfair to judge their performance on a wide cross section of industries, because earnings for high-tech firms and various "cyclical" companies are notoriously hard to forecast. "Try us on utilities," one analyst confidently asserted. So we tried it and they didn't like it. Even the forecasts for the "stable" utilities were far off the mark. This led to the second major finding of our study: Not one industry is easy to predict.

Moreover, no analysts proved consistently superior to the others. Of course, in each year some analysts did much better than average, but no consistency in their pattern of performance was found. Analysts who did better than average one year were no more likely than the others to make superior forecasts in the next year.

These findings have been confirmed by several other researchers. For example, Michael Sandretto of Harvard and Sudhir Milkrishnamurthi of MIT completed a massive study of the one-year forecasts of the 1,000 most widely followed companies. Their staggering conclusion was that the error rates each year were remarkably consistent and that the average annual error of the analysts was 31.3 percent over a five-year period. Financial forecasting appears to be a science that makes astrology look respectable.

Amid all these accusations is a deadly serious message: Security analysts have enormous difficulty in performing their basic function of forecasting company earnings prospects. Investors who put blind faith in such forecasts in making their investment selections are in for some rude disappointments.

WHY THE CRYSTAL BALL IS CLOUDED

It is always somewhat disturbing to learn that highly trained and well-paid professionals may not be terribly skillful at their calling. Unfortunately, this is hardly unusual. Similar types of findings exist for most groups of professionals. There is a classic example in medicine. At a time when tonsillectomies were very fashionable, the American Child Health Association surveyed a group of 1,000 children, eleven years of age, from the public schools of New York

City, and found that 611 of these had had their tonsils removed. The remaining 389 were then examined by a group of physicians, who selected 174 of these for tonsillectomies and declared that the rest had no tonsil problem. The remaining 215 were reexamined by another group of doctors, who recommended 99 of these for tonsillectomies. When the 116 "healthy" children were examined a third time, a similar percentage were told their tonsils had to be removed. After three examinations, only 65 children remained who had not been recommended for tonsillectomies. These remaining children were not examined further, because the supply of examining physicians ran out.

Numerous studies have shown similar results. Radiologists have failed to recognize the presence of lung disease in about 30 percent of the X-ray plates they read, despite the clear presence of the disease on the X-ray film. Another experiment proved that professional staffs in psychiatric hospitals could not tell the sane from the insane. The point is that we should not take for granted the reliability and accuracy of any judge, no matter how expert. When one considers the low reliability of so many kinds of judgments, it does not seem too surprising that security analysts, with their particularly difficult forecasting job, should be no exception.

There are, I believe, five factors that help explain why security analysts have such difficulty in predicting the future. These are (1) the influence of random events, (2) the production of dubious reported earnings through "creative" accounting procedures, (3) errors made by the analysts themselves, (4) the loss of the best analysts to the sales desk or to portfolio management, and (5) the conflicts of interest facing securities analysts at firms with large investment banking operations. Each factor deserves some discussion.

1. The Influence of Random Events

Many of the most important changes that affect the basic prospects for corporate earnings are essentially random, that is, unpredictable. Take the utility industry, to which I referred earlier. Presumably it is one of the most stable and dependable groups of companies. But, in fact, many important unpredictable events made earnings even for this industry enormously difficult to forecast. Unexpected unfavorable rulings of state public utility commissions often made it impossible for utilities to translate rapid growth in demand into higher profits. In the 1970s and early 2000s, forecasts were very wide of the mark as analysts failed to predict the increased fuel costs resulting from the sharp increase in the international price of oil.

Forecasting problems have been even more difficult in other industries. As we saw in chapter 4, growth forecasts made in early 2000 for a wide variety of high-tech and telecom companies were egregiously wrong. U.S. government budgetary, contract, legal, and regulatory decisions can have enormous implications for the fortunes of individual companies. So can the incapacitation of key members of management, the discovery of a major new product, a major oil spill, terrorist attacks, the entry of new competitors, price wars, and natural disasters such as floods and hurricanes, among others. The biotech industry is notoriously difficult to forecast. Potential blockbuster new drugs often fail Phase III trials because of failure to improve mortality or because of unexpected toxic side effects. In 2013, Celsion Corporation announced that its trial of a promising liver cancer drug had failed to meet its primary endpoint. The stock quickly lost 90 percent of its value. The stories of unpredictable events affecting earnings are endless.

2. The Production of Dubious Reported Earnings through "Creative" Accounting Procedures

A firm's income statement may be likened to a bikini—what it reveals is interesting but what it conceals is vital. Enron, one of the most ingeniously corrupt companies I have come across, led the beauty parade in this regard. Alas, Enron was far from unique. During the great bull market of the late 1990s, companies increasingly used aggressive fictions to report the soaring sales and earnings needed to propel their stock prices upward.

In the hit musical *The Producers*, Leo Bloom decides he can make more money from a flop than from a hit. He says, "It's all a matter of creative accounting." Bloom's client Max Bialystock sees the potential immediately. Max fleeces buckets of money from rich widows to finance a Broadway musical, *Springtime for Hitler.* He hopes for a total flop, so that no one will ask questions about where the money went.

Actually, Bloom doesn't begin to match the tricks that have been used by companies to pump up earnings and to fool investors and security analysts alike. In chapter 3, I described how Barry Minkow's late 1980s carpet-cleaning empire, ZZZZ Best, was built on a mosaic of phony credit card billings and fictitious contracts. But accounting abuses appear to have become even more frequent during the 1990s and early twenty-first century. Failing dot-coms, high-tech leaders, and even old-economy blue chips all tried to hype earnings and mislead the investment community.

Here's but a small number of examples of how companies have often stretched accounting rules like taffy to mislead analysts and the public as to the true state of their operations.

- In September 2001, Enron and Qwest needed to show that their revenues and profits were still growing rapidly. They figured out a great way to make their statements look as if business was proceeding well. They swapped fiber-optic network capacity at an exaggerated value of $500 million, and each company recorded the transaction as a sale. This inflated profits and masked a deteriorating position for both companies. Qwest already had a surfeit of capacity and, with an enormous glut of fiber in the market, the valuation put on the trade had no justification.
- Motorola, Lucent, and Nortel all boosted sales and earnings by lending large amounts to their customers. Many of these accounts became uncollectable and had to be written off later.
- Xerox boosted its profits in the short term by allowing its overseas units in Europe and Latin America, as well as in Canada, to book as one-time revenue all the cash to be paid over several years for long-term copier leases.

- "Chainsaw Al" Dunlap, the CEO of Sunbeam, needed a boost during the winter quarter to satisfy Wall Street's need for steadily growing earnings. He hit upon the ingenious idea of convincing retailers to buy backyard grills in the middle of winter. Chainsaw sweetened the deal by saying that the retailer would not have to actually pay for the grills until later and that all purchases could be stored in Sunbeam warehouses. Eventually, Dunlap ran out of tricks and fled, leaving Sunbeam a cut-up wreck that finally went bankrupt.

- Diamond Foods (maker of snack foods such as Pop•Secret microwave popcorn) underreported costs by pushing payments to suppliers into future years. This allowed the company to beat analyst estimates and sent the stock price to $90 per share. It also allowed top executives to pull in big bonuses. When the SEC discovered the fraud, it prosecuted the CEO and CFO and forced Diamond to restate earnings in 2012. The stock then fell to $12 per share

- Groupon, the online coupon service that offers deals on restaurants, retail goods, and services, had an initial public offering (IPO) in November 2011 and promptly rose about 35 percent over its offering price. But just a few months later the company announced a "material weakness" in its critical accounting controls that led it to overstate revenues and earnings. By mid-2014, the stock had lost 80 percent of its post-IPO value.

- Then there is the pension gambit. Many companies estimated that their pension plans were overfunded, and therefore they eliminated the companies' contribution to the plans, thus boosting profits. Often these gains were hidden in the footnotes. When the market suffered a sharp decline during the early 2000s, the companies discovered that their plans were actually underfunded and what investors assumed were sustainable profits turned out to be transitory.

A major problem that the analyst has in interpreting current and projecting future earnings is the tendency of companies to report so-called pro forma earnings as opposed to actual earnings computed in accordance with generally accepted accounting principles. In pro forma earnings, companies decide to ignore certain costs that are considered unusual; in fact, no rules or guidelines exist. Pro forma earnings are often called "earnings before all the bad stuff," and give firms license to exclude any expenses they deem to be "special," "extraordinary," and "non-recurring." Depending on what expenses are considered to be improperly ignored, companies can report a substantial overstatement of earnings. Small wonder that security analysts have extraordinary difficulty estimating what future earnings are likely to be.

3. Errors Made by the Analysts Themselves

To be perfectly blunt, many security analysts are not particularly perceptive or critical, and they often make egregious errors. I found this out early in the game as a young Wall Street trainee. In attempting to learn the techniques of the pros, I tried to duplicate some analytic work done by Louie, a metals specialist. Louie had figured that for each 10¢ increase in the price of copper, a particular copper producer's earnings would increase by $1 per share. Because he expected a $1 increase in the price of copper, he reasoned that this particular stock was "an unusually attractive purchase candidate."

In redoing the calculation, I found that Louie had misplaced a decimal point. A 10¢ increase in the price of copper would increase earnings by 10¢, not by $1. When I pointed this out to Louie (assuming he would put out a correction immediately), he simply shrugged his shoulders and declared, "Well, the recommendation sounds more convincing if we leave the report as is." Attention to detail was not Louie's forte.

Louie's lack of attention to detail revealed his lack of understanding of the industry he was covering. But he was not unique. In an article written for *Barron's*, Dr. Lloyd Kriezer, a plastic surgeon, examined some reports written by biotech analysts. Kriezer paid particular attention to analysts' coverage of those biotech companies that were creating artificial skin for use in the treatment of chronic wounds and burns—a field in which he had considerable expertise. He found the security analysts' diagnoses of stocks far wide of the mark. First, he added the assumptions made of the market share predicted for competing companies. The predicted shares of the five biotech companies competing in the market for artificial skin added up to well over 100 percent. Moreover, the analysts' prediction of the absolute size of the potential market bore little relationship to data on the number of actual burn victims, even though accurate data were easily available. Moreover, in examining the various analyst reports on the companies, Dr. Kriezer concluded, "They clearly did not understand the industry." One is reminded of words attributed to the legendary baseball manager Casey Stengel: "Can't anybody here play this game?"

Many analysts emulate Louie. Generally too lazy to make their own earnings projections, they prefer to copy the forecasts of other analysts or to swallow the "guidance" released by corporate managements without even chewing. Then it's very easy to know whom to blame if something goes wrong. And it's much easier to be wrong when your professional colleagues all agree with you. As Keynes put it, "Worldly wisdom teaches that it is better for reputation to fail conventionally than to succeed unconventionally."

Security analysts continue to make devastating forecasting errors. Apollo Group, owner of the University of Phoenix, was a Wall Street darling in early 2012. Analysts gushed at the huge earnings potential for this leader in the for-profit college industry and projected large investor returns. Reports of high student loan defaults, low graduation rates, and predatory recruiting practices were ignored. But such problems were confirmed by a widely distributed congressional report. The bad publicity and resulting new government regulations led to a sharp drop in enrollments and an even sharper 80 percent drop in Apollo's stock price.

I do not mean to imply that most Wall Street analysts parrot back what managements tell them. But I do imply that the average analyst is just that—a well-paid and usually highly intelligent person who has an extraordinarily difficult job and does it in a rather mediocre fashion. Analysts are often misguided, sometimes sloppy, perhaps self-important, and at times susceptible to the same pressures as other people. In short, they are really very human beings.

4. The Loss of the Best Analysts to the Sales Desk, to Portfolio Management, or to Hedge Funds

My fourth argument against the profession is a paradoxical one: Many of the best security analysts are not paid to analyze securities. They are often very high-powered institutional salespeople, or they are promoted to the prestigious and lucrative position of portfolio manager.

Investment firms known for their research prowess often send a security analyst to chaperone the regular salesperson on a call to a financial institution. Institutional investors like to hear about a new investment idea right from the horse's mouth, so the regular salesperson usually sits back and lets the analyst do the talking. The most articulate analysts find that their time is spent with institutional clients, not with financial reports.

During the 2000s, many analysts were seduced away from research to take highly compensated positions in portfolio management for hedge funds. The late Barton Biggs left Morgan Stanley to form his own hedge fund. He wrote about his experiences in *Hedgehogging*. It's far more exciting, prestigious, and remunerative to "run money" in the line position of hedge-fund portfolio manager than only to advise in the staff position of security analyst. Small wonder that many of the best-respected security analysts do not remain long in their jobs.

5. The Conflicts of Interest between Research and Investment Banking Departments

The analyst's goal is to ring as many cash registers as possible, and the fullest cash registers for the major brokers are to be found in the investment banking division. It wasn't always that way. In the 1970s, before the demise of fixed commissions and the introduction of "discount" brokerage firms, the retail brokerage operation paid the tab and analysts could feel they were really working for their customers—the retail and institutional investors. But that profit center faded in importance with competitive commissions, and the only gold mines left were trading profits and the underwriting of new issues for new or existing firms (where fees can run to hundreds of millions of dollars) and advising firms on borrowing facilities, restructuring, acquisitions, etc. And so it came to pass that "ringing the cash registers" meant helping the brokerage firm obtain and nurture banking clients. And that's how the conflicts arose. Analysts' salaries and bonuses were determined in part by their role in assisting the underwriting department. When such business relationships existed, analysts became nothing more than tools of the investment banking division.

One indication of the tight relationship between security analysts and their investment banking operations has been the traditional paucity of sell recommendations. There has always been some bias in the ratio of buy to sell recommendations, since analysts do not want to offend the companies they cover. But as investment banking revenues became a major source of profits for the major brokerage firms, research analysts were increasingly paid to be bullish rather than accurate. In one celebrated incident, an analyst who had the chutzpah to recommend that Trump's Taj Mahal bonds be sold because they were unlikely to pay their interest was summarily fired by his firm after threats of legal retaliation from "The Donald" himself. (Later, the bonds did default.) Small wonder that most analysts have purged their prose of negative comments that might give offense to current or prospective investment banking clients. During the Internet bubble, the ratio of buy to sell recommendations climbed to 100 to 1, particularly for firms with large investment banking businesses.

To be sure, when an analyst says "buy" he may mean "hold," and when he says "hold" he probably means this as a euphemism for "dump this piece of crap as soon as possible." But investors should not need a course in deconstruction semantics to understand the recommendations, and most individual investors sadly took the analysts at their word during the Internet bubble.

There is convincing evidence that analyst recommendations are tainted by the very profitable investment banking relationships of the brokerage firms. Several studies have assessed the accuracy of analysts' stock selections. Brad Barber of the University of California studied the performance of the "strong buy" recommendations of Wall Street analysts and found it nothing short of "disastrous." Indeed, the analysts' strong buy recommendations underperformed the market as a whole by 3 percent per month, while their sell recommendations outperformed the markets by 3.8 percent per month. Even worse, researchers at Dartmouth and Cornell found that stock recommendations of Wall Street firms without investment banking relationships did much better than the recommendations of brokerage firms that were involved in profitable investment banking relationships with the companies they covered. A study from Investors.com found that investors lost over 50 percent when they followed the advice of an analyst employed by a Wall Street firm that managed or co-managed the initial public offering of the recommended stock. Research analysts were basically paid to tout the stocks of the firm's underwriting clients. And analysts lick the hands that feed them.

In 2002, the attorney general of the state of New York found a smoking gun. While Henry Blodgett and other analysts at Merrill Lynch were officially recommending a number of Internet and New Economy stocks, the same analysts were referring to the stocks disparagingly in e-mail messages as "junk," "dogs," or less attractive epithets. Merrill did not admit guilt, but it settled with New York and other states for $100 million. It also promised certain reforms such as not directly tying analysts' pay to investment banking revenues, clarifying its stock recommendations, and better disclosing potential conflicts of interest. Other firms such as Goldman Sachs quickly embraced the Merrill proposals.

The situation today is somewhat improved. Outright "sell" recommendations have become more common, although the bias to "buy" advice remains. But the Sarbanes-Oxley legislation, which followed the scandals associated with the Internet bubble, made the job of the analyst more difficult by limiting the extent to which corporate financial officers could talk to Wall Street analysts. The SEC has promulgated a policy of "fair disclosure," whereby any relevant company information must be made public immediately and thus disclosed to the whole market. While such a policy can help make the stock market even more efficient, many disgruntled security analysts dubbed the situation as one of "no disclosure." Security analysts could no longer have early access to privileged information. Thus, there is no reason to believe that the recommendations of security analysts will improve in the future.

Conflicts of interest and analysts' lack of independent questioning did not disappear after Sarbanes-Oxley. In 2010, immediately following announcement of the explosion and oil spill from British Petroleum's Deepwater Horizon drilling platform, BP's stock fell 10 points, from $60 to $50 per share. Yet the nearly unanimous verdict of the Wall Street analyst community was that the stock price had overreacted and that BP was a "screaming buy." As one analyst put it, the decline was "disproportionate to the likely costs to the company (estimated to be $450 million), even assuming damages can be claimed." Of the thirty-four analysts who covered the stock, twenty-seven rated it a "buy." The other seven had "hold" ratings. There was not a single "sell" recommendation. And even the hyperactive TV host Jim Cramer told his viewers that his charitable trust was purchasing BP shares. The stock eventually dropped into the 20s, a loss of almost $100 billion in market value. (By February 2013, BP had made payments and provisions of $42.2 billion and the costs were continuing to rise. The British newspaper *The Telegraph*, during the same month, estimated that the final total cost was likely to be $90 billion.)

The pervasiveness of the error indicates that conflicts of interest have not been eliminated. BP is a major issuer of securities that generate large underwriting fees for Wall Street. Analysts are still influenced by the fear that very negative comments about a company could result in a loss of underwriting business in the future.

Finally, the ability of professional fund managers to make correct decisions in moving money from cash or bonds to equities on the basis of their forecasts of economic conditions has been egregiously poor. Peaks in mutual-fund cash positions have generally coincided with market troughs. Conversely, cash positions were invariably low when the market was at its highs.

DO SECURITY ANALYSTS PICK WINNERS?
THE PERFORMANCE OF THE MUTUAL FUNDS

I can almost hear the chorus in the background as I write these words. It goes something like this: The real test of the analyst lies in the performance of the stocks he recommends. Maybe "Sloppy Louie," the copper analyst, did mess up his earnings forecast with a misplaced decimal point, but if the stocks he recommended made money for his clients, his lack of attention to detail can surely be forgiven. "Analyze investment performance," the chorus is saying, "not earnings forecasts."

Fortunately, the records of one group of professionals—the mutual funds—are publicly available. Better still for my argument, the men and women at the funds are some of the best analysts and portfolio managers in the business. As one investment manager recently put it, "It will take many years before the general level of competence rises enough to overshadow the startling advantage of today's aggressive investment manager."

Statements like these were just too tempting to the lofty-minded in the academic world. Given the wealth of available data, the time available to conduct such research, and the overwhelming desire to prove academic superiority in such matters, it was only natural that academia would zero in on mutual-fund performance.

Again, the evidence from several studies is remarkably uniform. Investors have done no better with the average mutual fund than they could have done by purchasing and holding an unmanaged broad stock index. In other words, over long periods of time, mutual-fund portfolios have not outperformed randomly selected groups of stocks. Although funds may have very good records for certain short time periods, superior performance is not consistent, and there is no way to predict how funds will perform in any given future period.

The table below shows the returns from the average equity mutual fund over a twenty-year period to December 31, 2013. As a comparison, the Standard & Poor's 500 Index is used to represent the broad market. Similar results have been found for different time periods and for pension-fund managers as well as mutual-fund managers. Simply buying and holding the stocks in a broad market index is a strategy that is very hard for the professional portfolio manager to beat.

MUTUAL FUNDS VS. THE MARKET INDEX

	20 years to December 31, 2013
S&P 500 Index	9.22%
Average Equity Fund	8.36%
Index Advantage (percentage points)	0.86%

Sources: Lipper and Vanguard.

In addition to the scientific evidence that has been accumulated, several less formal tests have verified this finding. For example, in the early 1990s, the *Wall Street Journal* started a dartboard contest in which each month the selections of four experts were pitted against the selections of four darts. The *Journal* kindly let me throw the darts for the first contest. By the early 2000s, the experts appeared to be somewhat ahead of the darts. If, however, the performance of the experts was measured from the day their selections and their attendant publicity was announced in the *Journal* (rather than from the preceding day), the darts were actually slightly ahead. Does this mean that the wrist is mightier than the brain? Perhaps not, but I think *Forbes* magazine raised a very valid question when one journalist concluded, "It would seem that a combination of luck and sloth beats brains."

How can this be? Every year one can read the performance rankings of mutual funds. These always show many funds beating the averages—some by significant amounts. The problem is that there is no consistency to performance. Just as past earnings growth cannot predict future earnings, neither can past fund performance predict future results. Fund managements are also subject to random events: They may grow fat, become lazy, or break up. An investment approach that works very well for one period can easily turn sour the next. One is tempted to conclude that a very important factor in determining performance ranking is our old friend Lady Luck.

This conclusion is not a recent one. It has held throughout the past forty years, a period of great change in the market and in the percentage of the general public holding stocks. Again and again yesterday's star fund has proven to be today's disaster. During the late 1960s, the go-go funds with their youthful gunslingers turned in spectacular results, and their fund managers were written up like sports celebrities. But when the next bear market hit from 1969 through 1976, it was fly now, pay later. The top funds of 1968 had a perfectly disastrous subsequent performance.

The Mates Fund, for example, was number one in 1968. At the end of 1974, the fund had lost 93 percent of its 1968 value, and Fred Mates finally threw in the towel. He left the investment community to start a singles' bar in New York City appropriately named Mates. Indeed, most of the top-performing funds of the late 1960s were out of business by the mid-1970s.

The illustration from the late 1960s appeared in the first edition of this book. Similar results continue to hold. The following table presents the 1980 to 1990 performance for the twenty top funds of the 1970–80 period. Again, there is no consistency. Many of the top funds of the 1970s ranked close to the bottom during the 1980s. There was, however, one striking exception. The Magellan Fund, managed by Peter Lynch, was a superior performer in both the 1970s and 1980s. But Lynch retired in 1990 at the ripe old age of forty-six, and we will never know if he would have continued to beat the Street.

**HOW THE TOP 20 EQUITY FUNDS OF THE 1970s
PERFORMED DURING THE 1980S**

	Average Annual Return	
	1970s	*1980s*
Top 20 funds of the 1970s	+19.0%	+11.1%
Average of all equity funds	+10.4%	+11.7%

In case you think the picture changed during the decade of the 1990s, the next table shows the top twenty mutual-fund performers of the decade of the 1980s and the deterioration of their performance in the 1990s. The results are distressingly similar. Financial magazines and newspapers will keep singing the praises of particular mutual-fund managers who have recently produced above-average returns. As long as there are averages, some managers will outperform. But good performance in one period does not predict good performance in the next.

**HOW THE TOP 20 EQUITY FUNDS OF THE 1980s
PERFORMED DURING THE 1990s**

	Average Annual Return	
	1980s	*1990s*
Top 20 funds of the 1980s	+18.0%	+13.7%
S&P 500-Stock Index	+14.1%	+14.9%

Similarly, the best-performing general equity funds during the 1990s performed worse than the market during the 2000–09 period—a decade I have called "the naughties." We find that the twenty hottest funds earned rates of return during the 1990s that were well above the return for the market. These were the "genius" fund managers interviewed adoringly on CNBC and featured in articles in investment magazines. In fact, these funds had simply loaded up their portfolios with New Economy stocks. They had ridden the Internet bubble up, but when the bubble burst, they collapsed as well. On average, during the first decade of the 2000s, these funds performed far worse than the market as a whole.

Investors learned that making 100 percent one year and losing 50 percent the next left them exactly where they started out.

HOW THE TOP 20 EQUITY FUNDS OF THE 1990s PERFORMED DURING THE NAUGHTIES

	Average Annual Return	
	1990–99	2000–09
Top 20 funds of the 1990s	+18.0%	−2.2%
S&P 500-Stock Index	+14.9%	−0.9%

Moreover, the top mutual funds during the naughties tended to have well below average returns during the 2010s. To be sure, some funds have recorded above-average returns for two decades in a row. But they are few and far between, and their numbers are no greater than might be expected according to the laws of chance.

Perhaps the laws of chance should be illustrated. Let's engage in a coin-flipping contest. Those who can consistently flip heads will be declared winners. The contest begins and 1,000 contestants flip coins. Just as would be expected by chance, 500 of them flip heads and these winners are allowed to advance to the second stage of the contest and flip again. As might be expected, 250 flip heads. Operating under the laws of chance, there will be 125 winners in the third round, 63 in the fourth, 32 in the fifth, 16 in the sixth, and 8 in the seventh.

By this time, crowds start to gather to witness the surprising ability of these expert coin-flippers. The winners are overwhelmed with adulation. They are celebrated as geniuses in the art of coin-flipping, their biographies are written, and people urgently seek their advice. After all, there were 1,000 contestants and only 8 could consistently flip heads. The game continues and some contestants eventually flip heads nine and ten times in a row.* The point of this analogy is not to indicate that investment-fund

---

*If we had let the losers continue to play (as mutual-fund managers do, even after a bad year), we would have found several more contestants who flipped eight or nine heads out of ten and were therefore regarded as expert coin-flippers.

managers can or should make their decisions by flipping coins, but that the laws of chance do operate and that they can explain some amazing success stories.

It is the nature of an average that some investors will beat it. With large numbers of players in the money game, chance will—and does—explain some extraordinary performances. The very great publicity given occasional success in stock selection reminds me of the story of the doctor who claimed he had developed a cure for cancer in chickens. He proudly announced that in 33 percent of the cases tested remarkable improvement was noted. In another one-third of the cases, he admitted, there seemed to be no change in condition. He then rather sheepishly added, "And I'm afraid the third chicken ran away."

The *Wall Street Journal* did an interesting story in 2009 showing how fleeting extraordinary investment performance is likely to be. The paper noted that fourteen mutual funds had beaten the S&P for nine consecutive years through 2007. But only one continued that feat in 2008, as is shown in the table below. It is simply impossible to count on any fund or any investment manager to consistently beat the market—even when the past record suggests some unusual investment skill.

IT'S DOWN TO ONE

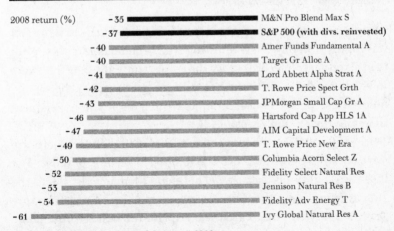

2008 return (%)	
-35	M&N Pro Blend Max S
-37	S&P 500 (with divs. reinvested)
-40	Amer Funds Fundamental A
-40	Target Gr Alloc A
-41	Lord Abbett Alpha Strat A
-42	T. Rowe Price Spect Grth
-43	JPMorgan Small Cap Gr A
-46	Hartsford Cap App HLS 1A
-47	AIM Capital Development A
-49	T. Rowe Price New Era
-50	Columbia Acorn Select Z
-52	Fidelity Select Natural Res
-53	Jennison Natural Res B
-54	Fidelity Adv Energy T
-61	Ivy Global Natural Res A

Source: *The Wall Street Journal*, January 5, 2009.

The evidence in favor of index investing grows stronger over time. Standard & Poor's publishes reports each year comparing all actively managed funds with various Standard & Poor's 500 stock indexes. The 2014 report is shown below. When one looks at a five-year period, over two-thirds of active managers are outperformed by their benchmark indexes. And each year's report is much the same. Every time I do a revision of this book, the results are similar. The index performance is not mediocre—it exceeds the results achieved by the typical active manager. And the result holds for big stocks and small, domestic as well as international. Moreover, the same result obtains if one looks at ten- or twenty-year results. And it works for the bond market as well as the stock market. Index investing is smart investing.

STANDARD & POOR'S INDICES VERSUS ACTIVE FUNDS

Percentage of Active Funds Outperformed by Benchmarks

	One Year	Three Years	Five Years
All Large-Cap Funds vs. S&P 500	55.8	80.0	72.7
All Small-Cap Funds vs. S&P Small Cap 500	52.8	80.4	71.7
Global Funds vs. S&P Global 1200	54.1	71.8	66.2
Emerging-Market Funds vs. S&P IFCI Composite	57.5	60.9	80.0

Source: S&P SPIVA Report—March 2014.

I am not suggesting that it is impossible to beat the market. But it is highly unlikely. An interesting way to demonstrate this result is to examine the records of *all* the equity mutual funds that were in existence in 1970 (when I first began work on this book) and follow their performance through 2013. This is the experiment shown in the exhibit on page 181.

In 1970, 358 equity mutual funds existed. (Today there are thousands.) We can measure the long-term records of only 84 of those original funds because 274 of them no longer exist. Thus, the data in the exhibit suffer from "survivorship bias." You can be sure that the surviving funds are the ones with the best records. There is a nasty secret in the mutual-fund industry that if you have a poorly performing fund, it does not reflect well on the managers of the mutual-fund complex. So the poorly performing funds tend to get merged into funds with better records, thereby killing off their embarrassing records. The surviving funds, measured in the exhibit, are the better-performing ones. But even with this survivorship bias in the data, observe how few of the original funds actually had superior records. You can count on the fingers of one hand the number of funds from the original 358 that actually beat the market index by 2 percentage points or more.

THE ODDS OF SUCCESS: RETURNS OF SURVIVING FUNDS

Mutual Funds 1970 to 2013—Compared with S&P 500 returns

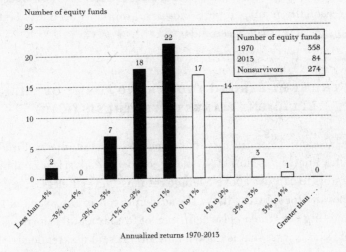

Source: Lipper.

The point is that it is highly unlikely you can beat the market. It is so rare that it's like looking for a needle in a haystack. A strategy far more likely to be optimal is to buy the haystack itself: that is, buy an index fund—a fund that simply buys and holds all the stocks in a broad stock-market index. Fortunately, more and more investors are doing just that. During 2014, about one-third of the money invested by individuals and institutions was invested in index funds. And that percentage continues to grow each year.

Although the preceding discussion has focused on mutual funds, it should not be assumed that the funds are simply the worst of the whole lot of investment managers. In fact, the mutual funds have had a somewhat better performance record than many other professional investors. The records of life insurance companies, property and casualty insurance companies, pension funds, foundations, state and local trust funds, personal trusts administered by banks, and individual discretionary accounts handled by investment advisers have all been studied. No sizable differences in the investment performance of common-stock portfolios exist among these professional investors or between these groups and the market as a whole. Exceptions are very rare. No scientific evidence has yet been assembled to indicate that the investment performance of professionally managed portfolios as a group has been any better than that of a broad-based index.

THE SEMI-STRONG AND STRONG FORMS OF THE EFFICIENT-MARKET HYPOTHESIS (EMH)

The academic community has rendered its judgment. Fundamental analysis is no better than technical analysis in enabling investors to capture above-average returns. Nevertheless, given its propensity for splitting hairs, the academic community soon fell to quarreling over the precise definition of fundamental information. Some said it was what is known now; others said it extended to the hereafter. It was at this point that what began as the strong form of the efficient-market hypothesis split into two. The "semi-strong" form says that no public information will help the analyst select undervalued securities. The argument here is that the structure of market prices already takes into account any public information that may be contained in balance sheets, income statements, dividends, and so forth; professional analyses of these data will be useless. The "strong" form says that absolutely nothing that is known or even knowable about a company will benefit the fundamental analyst. According to the strong form of the theory, not even "inside" information can help the investors.

The strong form of the EMH is obviously an overstatement. It does not admit the possibility of gaining from inside information. Nathan Rothschild made millions in the market when his carrier pigeons brought him the first news of Wellington's victory at Waterloo before other traders were aware of the victory. But today, the information superhighway carries news far more swiftly than carrier pigeons. And Regulation FD (Fair Disclosure) requires companies to make prompt public announcements of any material news items that may affect the price of their stock. Moreover, insiders who do profit from trading on the basis of nonpublic information are breaking the law. The Nobel laureate Paul Samuelson summed up the situation as follows:

> If intelligent people are constantly shopping around for good value, selling those stocks they think will turn out to be overvalued and buying those they expect are now undervalued, the result of this action by intelligent investors will be to have existing stock prices already have discounted in them an allowance for their future prospects. Hence, to the passive investor, who does not himself search for under- and overvalued situations, there will be presented a pattern of stock prices that makes one stock about as good or bad a buy as another. To that passive investor, chance alone would be as good a method of selection as anything else.

This is a statement of the EMH—the efficient-market hypothesis. The "narrow" (weak) form of the EMH says that technical analysis—looking at past stock prices—cannot help investors. Prices move from period to period very much like a random walk. The "broad" (semi-strong and strong) forms state that fundamental analysis is not helpful either. All that is known concerning the expected growth of the company's earnings and dividends, all of the possible favorable and unfavorable developments affecting the company that might be studied by the fundamental analyst, is already reflected in the price of the company's stock. Thus, purchasing a fund holding all the stocks in a broad-based index will produce a portfolio that can be expected to do as well as any managed by professional security analysts.

The efficient-market hypothesis does not, as some critics have proclaimed, state that stock prices move aimlessly and erratically and are insensitive to changes in fundamental information. On the contrary, the reason prices move randomly is just the opposite. The market is so efficient—prices move so quickly when information arises—that no one can buy or sell fast enough to benefit. And real news develops randomly, that is, unpredictably. It cannot be predicted by studying either past technical or fundamental information.

Even the legendary Benjamin Graham, heralded as the father of fundamental security analysis, reluctantly came to the conclusion that fundamental security analysis could no longer be counted on to produce superior investment returns. Shortly before he died in 1976, he was quoted in an interview in the *Financial Analysts Journal* as saying, "I am no longer an advocate of elaborate techniques of security analysis in order to find superior value opportunities. This was a rewarding activity, say, 40 years ago, when Graham and Dodd was first published; but the situation has changed. . . . [Today] I doubt whether such extensive efforts will generate sufficiently superior selections to justify their cost. . . . I'm on the side of the 'efficient market' school of thought." And Peter Lynch, just after he retired from managing the Magellan Fund, as well as the legendary Warren Buffett, admitted that most investors would be better off in an index fund rather than investing in an actively managed equity mutual fund.

A Note on High-Frequency Trading (HFT)

A popular book published in 2014, *Flash Boys*, shined a spotlight on high-frequency trading and unleashed a firestorm of criticism against the technique. High-frequency trading (HFT) has been alleged to give a select group of traders an unfair advantage over the public and even over institutional investors such as mutual funds and pension funds.

HFT involves the placement of high-speed computers in close

proximity to stock-market servers to give some participants the ability to buy and sell stocks faster than the blink of an eye. In a sense, it is merely the next development in response to investors' ever-increasing appetite for speed. From shouting orders from office buildings to traders standing under a buttonwood tree on Wall Street in 1792, technology has dramatically improved the efficiency of trading, reducing transaction costs and increasing liquidity for all investors. It has also helped ensure that market-moving news is reflected in stock prices as rapidly as possible.

It's easy to stir up fear over such trading activity, but most stock-market volume is conducted over these high-speed networks. And whether you're buying 100 shares of a stock or 100,000 shares, you directly or indirectly participate. We're all high-frequency traders now.

Another major advantage of HFT is that it ensures that the exchange-traded broad-based index funds, which I recommend for individual investors, are appropriately priced. Any discrepancy between the price of the ETF and the underlying stocks can be quickly arbitraged away. Thus, HFT, rather than harming individual investors, actually benefits them by assuring that ETFs are fairly priced.

That doesn't mean that HFT is completely benign. Right now, as critics note, optimally positioned traders can see trade orders from other investors before they are executed. They can execute a purchase just ahead of those orders and run the price up just a bit, pocketing the difference. This kind of scalping, called "front-running," is a form of insider trading. If someone else is able to know that I want to buy 10,000 shares of a stock before I actually buy the shares, that's insider information, and it should be illegal to trade on such information. The SEC needs to address these practices and find regulatory solutions. But critics of HFT are wrong to assert that the practice has harmed individual investors. Investors both small and large have always been well served by technological advances that improve liquidity, make trades at better prices, and speed up the trading process. HFT makes markets more efficient and reinforces the advantage of index-fund investing.

Part Three

THE NEW INVESTMENT
TECHNOLOGY

8

A NEW WALKING SHOE: MODERN PORTFOLIO THEORY

> ... Practical men, who believe themselves to be quite
> exempt from any intellectual influence, are usually the
> slaves of some defunct economist. Madmen in authority,
> who hear voices in the air, are distilling their frenzy from
> some academic scribbler of a few years back.
> —J. M. Keynes, *The General Theory of Employment,*
> *Interest and Money*

THROUGHOUT THIS BOOK, I have attempted to explain the theories used by professionals—simplified as the firm-foundation and the castle-in-the-air theories—to predict the valuation of stocks. As we have seen, many academics have earned their reputations by attacking these theories and maintaining that they cannot be relied on to yield extraordinary profits.

As graduate schools continued to grind out bright young financial economists, the attacking academics became so numerous that it seemed obvious that a new strategy was needed; ergo, the academic community busily went about erecting its own theories of stock-market valuation. That's what this part of the book is all about: the rarefied world of the "new investment technology" created within the towers of the academy. One insight—modern portfolio theory (MPT)—is so basic that it is now widely followed on the Street. The others remain controversial enough to continue to generate thesis material for students and hefty lecture fees for their advisers.

This chapter is about modern portfolio theory, whose insights will enable you to reduce risk while possibly earning a higher return. In chapter 9, I turn to the academics who have suggested that investors can increase their returns by assuming a certain kind of risk. Then, in chapters 10 and 11, I cover the arguments of some academics and practitioners who conclude that psychology, not rationality, rules the market, and that there is no such thing as a random walk. They argue that markets are not efficient, that market prices are predictable, and that a number of investment strategies can be followed to "beat the market." These include a number of "smart beta" strategies that have become popular on Wall Street. Then I conclude by showing that, despite all the critics, traditional index funds remain the undisputed champions in taking the most profitable stroll through the market.

THE ROLE OF RISK

The efficient-market hypothesis explains why the random walk is possible. It holds that the stock market is so good at adjusting to new information that no one can predict its future course in a superior manner. Because of the actions of the pros, the prices of individual stocks quickly reflect all the news that is available. Thus, the odds of selecting superior stocks or anticipating the general direction of the market are even. Your guess is as good as that of the ape, your stockbroker, or even mine.

Hmmm. "I smell a rat," as Samuel Butler wrote long ago. Money is being made in the market; some stocks do outperform others. Common sense attests that some people can and do beat the market. It's not all chance. Many academics agree; but the method of beating the market, they say, is not to exercise superior clairvoyance but rather to assume greater risk. Risk, and risk alone, determines the degree to which returns will be above or below average.

DEFINING RISK: THE DISPERSION OF RETURNS

Risk is a most slippery and elusive concept. It's hard for investors—let alone economists—to agree on a precise definition. The *American Heritage Dictionary* defines risk as "the possibility of suffering harm or loss." If I am able to buy one-year Treasury bills to yield 2 percent and hold them until they mature, I am virtually certain of earning a 2 percent monetary return, before income taxes. The possibility of loss is so small as to be considered nonexistent. If I hold common stock in my local electric utility for one year, anticipating a 5 percent dividend return, the possibility of loss is greater. The dividend of the company may be cut and, more important, the market price at the end of the year may be much lower, causing me to suffer a net loss. Investment risk, then, is the chance that expected security returns will not materialize and, in particular, that the securities you hold will fall in price.

Once academics accepted the idea that risk for investors is related to the chance of disappointment in achieving expected security returns, a natural measure suggested itself—the probable dispersion of future returns. Thus, financial risk has generally been defined as the variance or standard deviation of returns. Being long-winded, we use the accompanying exhibit to illustrate what we mean. A security whose returns are not likely to depart much, if at all, from its average (or expected) return is said to carry little or no risk. A security whose returns from year to year are likely to be quite volatile (and for which sharp losses occur in some years) is said to be risky.

Illustration: Expected Return and Variance Measures of Reward and Risk

This simple example will illustrate the concept of expected return and variance and how these are measured. Suppose you buy a stock from which you expect the following overall returns (including both dividends and price changes) under different economic conditions:

Business Conditions	Possibility of Occurrence	Expected Return
"Normal" economic conditions	1 chance in 3	10%
Rapid real growth without inflation	1 chance in 3	30%
Recession with inflation (stagflation)	1 chance in 3	–10%

If, on average, a third of past years have been "normal," another third characterized by rapid growth without inflation, and the remaining third characterized by "stagflation," it might be reasonable to take these relative frequencies of past events and treat them as our best guesses (probabilities) of the likelihood of future business conditions. We could then say that an investor's expected return is 10 percent. One-third of the time the investor gets 30 percent, another one-third 10 percent, and the rest of the time she suffers a 10 percent loss. This means that, on average, her yearly return will turn out to be 10 percent.

$$Expected\ return = \tfrac{1}{3}(0.30) + \tfrac{1}{3}(0.10) + \tfrac{1}{3}(-0.10) = 0.10.$$

The yearly returns will be quite variable, however, ranging from a 30 percent gain to a 10 percent loss. The "variance" is a measure of the dispersion of returns. It is defined as the average squared deviation of each possible return from its average (or expected) value, which we just saw was 10 percent.

$$Variance = \tfrac{1}{3}(0.30-0.10)^2 + \tfrac{1}{3}(0.10-0.10)^2 + \tfrac{1}{3}(-0.10-0.10)^2$$
$$= \tfrac{1}{3}(0.20)^2 + \tfrac{1}{3}(0.00)^2 + \tfrac{1}{3}(-0.20)^2 = 0.0267.$$

The square root of the variance is known as the standard deviation. In this example, the standard deviation equals 0.1634.

Dispersion measures of risk such as variance and standard deviation have failed to satisfy everyone. "Surely riskiness is not related to variance itself," the critics say. "If the dispersion results from happy surprises—that is, from outcomes turning out better than expected—no investors in their right minds would call that risk."

It is, of course, quite true that only the possibility of downward disappointments constitutes risk. Nevertheless, as a practical matter, as long as the distribution of returns is symmetric—that is, as long as the chances of extraordinary gain are roughly the same as the probabilities for disappointing returns and losses—a dispersion or variance measure will suffice as a risk measure. The greater the dispersion or variance, the greater the possibilities for disappointment.

Although the pattern of historical returns from individual securities has not usually been symmetric, the returns from well-diversified portfolios of stocks are at least roughly symmetric. The following chart shows the distribution of monthly security returns for a portfolio invested in the S&P 500-Stock Index over seventy

DISTRIBUTION OF MONTHLY RETURNS FOR A PORTFOLIO INVESTED IN THE S&P 500-STOCK INDEX, JANUARY 1940–MAY 2014

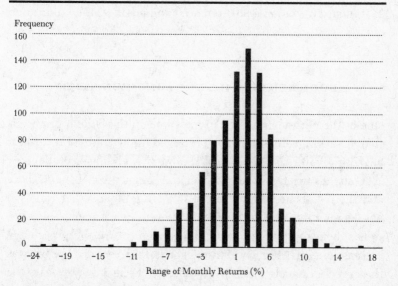

Source: Global Financial Data.

years. It was constructed by dividing the range of returns into equal intervals (of approximately 1¼ percent) and then noting the frequency (the number of months) with which the returns fell within each interval. On average, the portfolio returned close to 1 percent per month or about 11 percent per year. In periods when the market declined sharply, however, the portfolio also plunged, losing more than 20 percent in a single month.

For reasonably symmetric distributions such as this one, a helpful rule of thumb is that two-thirds of the monthly returns tend to fall within one standard deviation of the average return and 95 percent of the returns fall within two standard deviations. Recall that the average return for this distribution was close to 1 percent per month. The standard deviation (our measure of portfolio risk) turns out to be about 4½ percent per month. Thus, in two-thirds of the months the returns from this portfolio were between +5½ percent and −3½ percent, and 95 percent of the returns were between 10 percent and −8 percent. Obviously, the higher the standard deviation (the more spread out the returns), the more probable it is (the greater the risk) that at least in some periods you will take a real bath in the market. That's why a measure of variability such as standard deviation is so often used and justified as an indication of risk.

DOCUMENTING RISK: A LONG-RUN STUDY

One of the best-documented propositions in the field of finance is that, on average, investors have received higher rates of return for bearing greater risk. The most thorough study has been done by Ibbotson Associates. Its data cover the period 1926 through 2013, and the results are shown in the following table. What Ibbotson Associates did was to take several different investment vehicles— stocks, bonds, and Treasury bills—and measure the percentage increase or decrease each year for each item. A rectangle or bar was then erected on the baseline to indicate the number of years the returns fell between 0 and 5 percent; another rectangle indicated the number of years the returns fell between 5 and 10 percent; and so on, for both positive and negative returns. The result is a series of bars showing the dispersion of returns and from which the standard deviation can be calculated.

BASIC SERIES: SUMMARY STATISTICS OF ANNUAL TOTAL RETURNS FROM 1926 TO 2013

Series	Geometric Mean (%)	Arithmetic Mean (%)	Standard Deviation (%)	Distribution (%)
Large-company stocks	10.1	12.1	20.2	
Small-company stocks*	12.3	16.9	32.3	
Long-term corporate bonds	6.0	6.3	8.4	
Long-term government bonds	5.5	5.9	9.8	
Intermediate-term government bonds	5.3	5.4	5.7	
U.S. Treasury bills	3.5	3.5	3.1	
Inflation	3.0	3.0	4.1	

-90%   0%   90%

Data from 1926 to 2013.
*The 1933 Small-Company Stocks Total Return was 142.9 percent.

A quick glance shows that over long periods of time, common stocks have, on average, provided relatively generous total rates of return. These returns, including dividends and capital gains, have exceeded by a substantial margin the returns from long-term bonds, Treasury bills, and the inflation rate as measured by the annual rate of increase in consumer prices. Thus, stocks have tended to provide positive "real" rates of return, that is, returns after washing out the effects of inflation. The data show, however, that common-stock returns are highly variable, as indicated by the standard deviation and the range of annual returns, shown in adjacent columns of the table. Returns from equities have ranged from a gain of more than 50 percent (in 1933) to a loss of almost the same percentage (in 1931). Clearly, the extra returns that have been available to investors from stocks have come at the expense of assuming considerably higher risk. Note that small-company stocks have provided an even higher rate of return since 1926, but the dispersion (standard deviation) of those returns has been even larger than for equities in general. Again, we see that higher returns have been associated with higher risks.

There have been several periods of five years or longer when common stocks have produced negative rates of return. The period 1930–32 was extremely poor for stock-market investors. The early 1970s also produced negative returns. The one-third decline in the broad stock-market averages during October 1987 is the most dramatic change in stock prices during a brief period since the 1930s. And stock investors know only too well how poorly stocks performed during the first decade of the 2000s. Still, over the long haul, investors have been rewarded with higher returns for taking on more risk. However, there are ways in which investors can reduce risk. This brings us to the subject of modern portfolio theory, which has revolutionized the investment thinking of professionals.

REDUCING RISK:
MODERN PORTFOLIO THEORY (MPT)

Portfolio theory begins with the premise that all investors are like my wife—they are risk-averse. They want high returns and guaranteed outcomes. The theory tells investors how to combine stocks in their portfolios to give them the least risk possible, consistent with the return they seek. It also gives a rigorous mathematical justification for the time-honored investment maxim that diversification is a sensible strategy for individuals who like to reduce their risks.

The theory was invented in the 1950s by Harry Markowitz, and for his contribution he was awarded the Nobel Prize in Economics in 1990. His book *Portfolio Selection* was an outgrowth of his PhD dissertation at the University of Chicago. His experience has ranged from teaching at UCLA to designing a computer language at RAND Corporation. He even ran a hedge fund, serving as president of Arbitrage Management Company. What Markowitz discovered was that portfolios of risky (volatile) stocks might be put together in such a way that the portfolio as a whole could be less risky than the individual stocks in it.

The mathematics of modern portfolio theory (also known as MPT) is recondite and forbidding; it fills the journals and, incidentally, keeps a lot of academics busy. That in itself is no small accomplishment. Fortunately, there is no need to lead you through the labyrinth of quadratic programming for you to understand the core of the theory. A single illustration will make the whole game clear.

Let's suppose we have an island economy with only two businesses. The first is a large resort with beaches, tennis courts, and a golf course. The second is a manufacturer of umbrellas. Weather affects the fortunes of both. During sunny seasons, the resort does a booming business and umbrella sales plummet. During rainy seasons, the resort owner does very poorly, while the umbrella manufacturer enjoys high sales and profits. The table below shows some hypothetical returns for the two businesses during the different seasons:

	Umbrella Manufacturer	Resort Owner
Rainy Season	50%	−25%
Sunny Season	−25%	50%

Suppose that, on average, one-half of the seasons are sunny and one-half are rainy (i.e., the probability of a sunny or rainy season is ½). An investor who bought stock in the umbrella manufacturer would find that half the time he earned a 50 percent return and half the time he lost 25 percent of his investment. On average, he would earn a return of 12½ percent. This is what we have called the investor's expected return. Similarly, investment in the resort would produce the same results. Investing in either one of these businesses would be fairly risky, however, because the results are quite variable and there could be several sunny or rainy seasons in a row.

Suppose, however, that instead of buying only one security, an investor with two dollars diversified and put half his money in the umbrella manufacturer's and half in the resort owner's business. In sunny seasons, a one-dollar investment in the resort would produce a 50-cent return, whereas a one-dollar investment in the umbrella manufacturer would lose 25 cents. The investor's total return would be 25 cents (50 cents minus 25 cents), which is 12½ percent of his total investment of two dollars.

Note that during rainy seasons, exactly the same thing happens—only the names are changed. Investment in the umbrella manufacturer produces a 50 percent return, while the investment in the resort loses 25 percent. Again, the diversified investor makes a 12½ percent return on his total investment.

This simple illustration points out the basic advantage of diversification. Whatever happens to the weather, and thus to the island economy, by diversifying investments over both of the firms, an investor is sure of making a 12½ percent return each year. The trick that made the game work was that although both companies were risky (returns were variable from year to year), the companies were affected differently by weather conditions. (In statistical terms, the two companies had a negative covariance.)* As long as

---

*Statisticians use the term "covariance" to measure what I have called the degree of parallelism between the returns of the two securities. If we let R stand for the actual return from the resort and R^- be the expected or average

there is some lack of parallelism in the fortunes of the individual companies in the economy, diversification can reduce risk. In the present case, where there is a perfect negative relationship between the companies' fortunes (one always does well when the other does poorly), diversification can totally eliminate risk.

Of course, there's always a rub, and in this case it's that the fortunes of most companies move pretty much in tandem. When there is a recession and people are unemployed, they may buy neither summer vacations nor umbrellas. Therefore, one shouldn't expect in practice to get the neat kind of total risk elimination just shown. Nevertheless, because company fortunes don't always move completely in parallel, investment in a diversified portfolio of stocks is likely to be less risky than investment in one or two single securities.

It is easy to carry the lessons of this illustration to actual portfolio construction. Suppose you were considering combining Ford Motor Company and its major supplier of new tires in a stock portfolio. Would diversification be likely to give you much risk reduction? Probably not. If Ford's sales slump, Ford will be buying fewer new tires from the tire manufacturer. In general, diversification will not help much if there is a high covariance (high correlation) between the returns of the two companies.

---

return, whereas U stands for the actual return from the umbrella manufacturer and U^- *is* the average return, we define the covariance between U and R (or COV_{UR}) as follows:

$$\text{COV}_{UR} = \text{Prob. rain } (U, \text{ if rain} - U^-) (R, \text{ if rain} - R^-) +$$
$$\text{Prob. sun } (U, \text{ if sun} - U^-) (R, \text{ if sun} - R^-).$$

From the preceding table of returns and assumed probabilities, we can fill in the relevant numbers:

$$\text{COV}_{UR} = \tfrac{1}{2}(0.50 - 0.125)(-0.25 - 0.125) + \tfrac{1}{2}(-0.25 - 0.125)(0.50 - 0.125) = -0.141.$$

Whenever the returns from two securities move in tandem (when one goes up, the other always goes up), the covariance number will be a large positive number. If the returns are completely out of phase, as in the present example, the two securities are said to have negative covariance.

On the other hand, if Ford was combined with a government contractor in a depressed area, diversification might reduce risk substantially. If consumer spending is down (or if oil prices sky-rocket), Ford's sales and earnings are likely to be down and the nation's level of unemployment up. If the government makes a habit during times of high unemployment of giving out contracts to the depressed area (to alleviate some of the unemployment miseries there), it could well be that the returns of Ford and those of the contractor do not move in phase. The two stocks might have very little covariance or, better still, negative covariance.

The example may seem a bit strained, and most investors will realize that when the market gets clobbered, just about all stocks go down. Still, at least at certain times, some stocks and some classes of assets do move against the market; that is, they have negative covariance or (and this is the same thing) they are negatively cor-related with each other.

THE CORRELATION COEFFICIENT AND THE ABILITY OF DIVERSIFICATION TO REDUCE RISK

Correlation Coefficient	Effect of Diversification on Risk
+1.0	No risk reduction is possible.
+0.5	Moderate risk reduction is possible.
0	Considerable risk reduction is possible.
−0.5	Most risk can be eliminated.
−1.0	All risk can be eliminated.

Now comes the real kicker; negative correlation is not neces-sary to achieve the risk reduction benefits from diversification. Markowitz's great contribution to investors' wallets was his dem-onstration that anything less than perfect positive correlation can potentially reduce risk. His research led to the results presented in the preceding table. As shown, it demonstrates the crucial role of the correlation coefficient in determining whether adding a security or an asset class can reduce risk.

DIVERSIFICATION IN PRACTICE

To paraphrase Shakespeare, can there be too much of a good thing? In other words, is there a point at which diversification is no longer a magic wand safeguarding returns? Numerous studies have demonstrated that the answer is yes. As shown in the following chart, the golden number for American xenophobes—those fearful of looking beyond our national borders—is at least fifty equal-sized and well-diversified U.S. stocks (clearly, fifty oil stocks or fifty electric utilities would not produce an equivalent amount of risk reduction). With such a portfolio, the total risk is reduced by over 60 percent. And that's where the good news stops, as further increases in the number of holdings do not produce much additional risk reduction.

THE BENEFITS OF DIVERSIFICATION

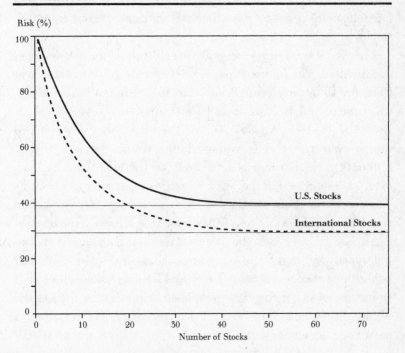

Those with a broader view—investors who recognize that the world has changed considerably since Markowitz first enunciated his theory—can reap even greater protection because the movement of foreign economies is not always synchronous with that of the U.S. economy, especially those in emerging markets. For example, increases in the price of oil and raw materials have a negative effect on Europe, Japan, and even the United States, which is at least partially self-sufficient. On the other hand, oil price increases have a very positive effect on Indonesia and oil-producing countries in the Middle East. Similarly, increases in mineral and other raw-material prices have positive effects on nations rich in natural resources such as Australia and Brazil.

It turns out that about fifty is also the golden number for global-minded investors. Such investors, however, get more protection for their money, as shown in the preceding chart. Here, the stocks are drawn not simply from the U.S. stock market but from the international markets as well. As expected, the international diversified portfolio tends to be less risky than the one drawn purely from U.S. stocks.

The benefits of international diversification have been well documented. The figure on page 203 shows the gains realized over the more than forty-year period from 1970 through 2013. During this time period, foreign stocks (as measured by the Morgan Stanley EAFE [Europe, Australasia, and Far East] Index of developed foreign countries) had an average annual return that was slightly higher than the U.S. stocks in the S&P 500 Index. U.S. stocks, however, were safer in that their year-to-year returns were less volatile. The correlation between the returns from the two indexes during this time period was around 0.5—positive but only moderately high. The figure shows the different combinations of return and risk (volatility) that could have been achieved if an investor had held different combinations of U.S. and EAFE (developed foreign country) stocks. At the right-hand side of the figure, we see the higher return and higher risk level (greater volatility) that would have been achieved with a portfolio of only EAFE stocks. At the left-hand side of the figure, the return and risk level of a totally domestic portfolio of U.S. stocks are shown. The solid dark line indicates the different combinations of return and volatility that would result from different portfolio allocations between domestic and foreign stocks.

Note that as the portfolio shifts from a 100 percent domestic allocation to one with gradual additions of foreign stocks, the return tends to increase because EAFE stocks produced a slightly higher return than domestic stocks over this period. The significant point, however, is that adding some of these riskier securities actually reduces the portfolio's risk level—at least for a while. Eventually, however, as larger and larger proportions of the riskier EAFE stocks are put into the portfolio, the overall risk rises with the overall return.

**DIVERSIFICATION OF U.S. AND DEVELOPED
FOREIGN COUNTRY STOCKS, JANUARY 1970–DECEMBER 2013**

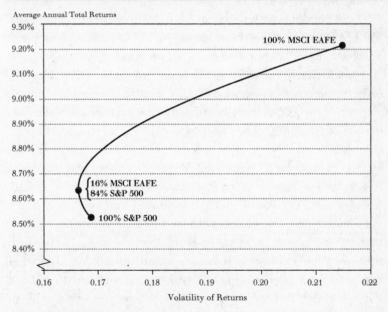

Source: DATASTREAM.

The paradoxical result of this analysis is that overall portfolio risk is reduced by the addition of a small amount of riskier foreign securities. Good returns from Japanese automakers balanced out poor returns from domestic ones when the Japanese share of the U.S. market increased. On the other hand, good returns from U.S. manufacturers offset poor returns from foreign manufacturers when the dollar became more competitive and Japan and Europe remained in a recession as the U.S. economy boomed. It is precisely these offsetting movements that reduced the overall volatility of the portfolio.

It turns out that the portfolio with the least risk had 17 percent foreign securities and 83 percent U.S. securities. Moreover, adding 17 percent EAFE stocks to a domestic portfolio also tended to increase the portfolio return. International diversification provided the closest thing to a free lunch available in our world securities markets. When higher returns can be achieved with lower risk by adding international stocks, no investor should fail to take notice.

Some portfolio managers have argued that diversification has not continued to give the same degree of benefit as was previously the case. Globalization led to an increase in the correlation coefficients between the U.S. and foreign markets as well as between stocks and commodities. The following three charts indicate how correlation coefficients have risen over the first decade of the 2000s. The charts show the correlation coefficients calculated over every twenty-four-month period between U.S. stocks (as measured by the S&P 500-Stock Index) and the EAFE index of developed foreign stocks, between U.S. stocks and the broad (MSCI) index of emerging-market stocks, and between U.S. stocks and the Goldman Sachs (GSCI) index of a basket of commodities such as oil, metals, and the like. Particularly upsetting for investors is that correlations have been high when markets have been falling. During the global credit crisis of 2007–09, all markets fell in unison. There was apparently no place to hide. Small wonder that some investors came to believe that diversification no longer seemed to be as effective a strategy to decrease risk.

TWO-YEAR ROLLING CORRELATION BETWEEN
S&P 500 AND MSCI EAFE INDEX

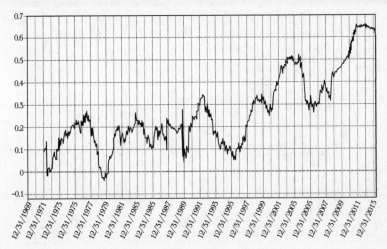

TWO-YEAR ROLLING CORRELATION BETWEEN
S&P 500 AND MSCI EMERGING-MARKETS INDEX

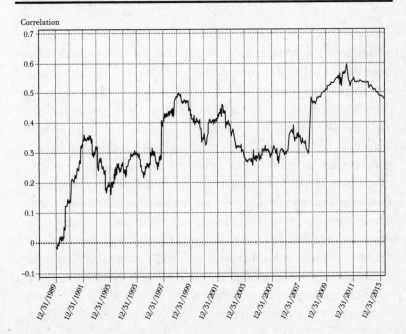

TWO-YEAR ROLLING CORRELATION BETWEEN
S&P 500 AND GSCI COMMODITY INDEX

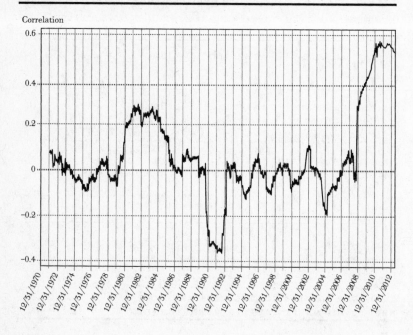

But note that even though correlations between markets have risen, they are still far from perfectly correlated, and broad diversification will still tend to reduce the volatility of a portfolio. And even over periods when different equity markets tended to zig and zag together, diversification still provided substantial benefits. Consider the first decade of the twenty-first century, which was widely referred to as a "lost decade" for U.S. equity investors. Markets in developed countries—the United States, Europe, and Japan—ended the decade at or below their levels at the start of the decade. Investors who limited their portfolios to stocks in developed economies failed to earn satisfactory returns. But over that same decade, investors who included equities from emerging markets (which were easily available through low-cost, broadly diversified emerging-market equity index funds) enjoyed quite satisfactory equity investment performance.

The following graph shows that an investment in the S&P 500 did not make any money during the first decade of the 2000s. But investment in a broad emerging-market index produced quite satisfactory returns. Broad international diversification would have been of enormous benefit to U.S. investors, even during "the lost decade."

**DIVERSIFICATION INTO EMERGING MARKETS
HELPED DURING "THE LOST DECADE":
CUMULATIVE RETURNS FROM ALTERNATIVE MARKETS**

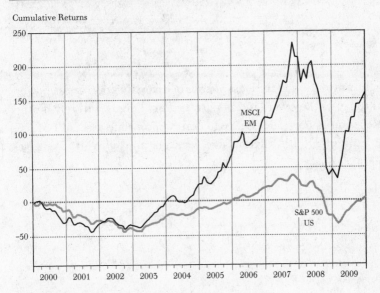

Source: Vanguard, Datastream, Morningstar.

Moreover, safe bonds proved their worth as a risk reducer. The graph on page 208 shows how correlation coefficients between U.S. Treasury bonds and large capitalization U.S. equities fell during the 2008–09 financial crisis. Even during the horrible stock market of 2008, a broadly diversified portfolio of bonds invested in the Barclay's Capital broad bond index returned 5.2 percent. There was a place to hide during the financial crisis. Bonds (and bond-like securities to be covered in Part Four) have proved their worth as an effective diversifier.

TIME VARYING STOCK-BOND CORRELATION

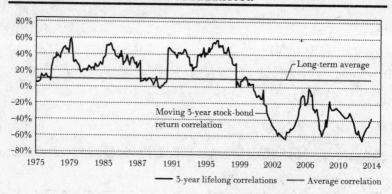

Source: Vanguard.

In summary, the timeless lessons of diversification are as powerful today as they were in the past. In Part Four, I will rely on this
discussion of portfolio theory to craft appropriate asset allocations
for individuals in different age brackets and with different risk
tolerances.

9

REAPING REWARD
BY INCREASING RISK

*Theories that are right only 50 percent of the time
are less economical than coin-flipping.*
—George J. Stigler, *The Theory of Price*

As every reader should know by now, risk has its rewards. Thus, both within academia and on the Street, there has long been a scramble to exploit risk to earn greater returns. That's what this chapter covers: the creation of analytical tools to measure risk and, with such knowledge, reap greater rewards.

We begin with a refinement to modern portfolio theory. As I mentioned in the last chapter, diversification cannot eliminate all risk—as it did in my mythical island economy—because all stocks tend to move up and down together. Thus, diversification in practice reduces some but not all risk. Three academics—the former Stanford professor William Sharpe and the late finance specialists John Lintner and Fischer Black—focused their intellectual energies on determining what part of a security's risk can be eliminated by diversification and what part cannot. The result is known as the capital-asset pricing model. Sharpe received a Nobel Prize for his contribution to this work at the same time Markowitz was honored in 1990.

The basic logic behind the capital-asset pricing model is that there is no premium for bearing risks that can be diversified away. Thus, to get a higher average long-run rate of return, you need to increase the risk level of the portfolio that cannot be diversified away. According to this theory, savvy investors can outperform the overall market by adjusting their portfolios with a risk measure known as beta.

BETA AND SYSTEMATIC RISK

Beta? How did a Greek letter enter this discussion? Surely it didn't originate with a stockbroker. Can you imagine any stockbroker saying, "We can reasonably describe the total risk of any security (or portfolio) as the total variability (variance or standard deviation) of the returns from the security"? But we who teach say such things often. We go on to say that part of total risk or variability may be called the security's *systematic risk* and that this arises from the basic variability of stock prices in general and the tendency for all stocks to go along with the general market, at least to some extent. The remaining variability in a stock's returns is called *unsystematic risk* and results from factors peculiar to that particular company—for example, a strike, the discovery of a new product, and so on.

Systematic risk, also called market risk, captures the reaction of individual stocks (or portfolios) to general market swings. Some stocks and portfolios tend to be very sensitive to market movements. Others are more stable. This relative volatility or sensitivity to market moves can be estimated on the basis of the past record, and is popularly known by—you guessed it—the Greek letter beta.

You are now about to learn all you ever wanted to know about beta but were afraid to ask. Basically, beta is the numerical description of systematic risk. Despite the mathematical manipulations involved, the basic idea behind the beta measurement is one of putting some precise numbers on the subjective feelings money managers have had for years. The beta calculation is essentially a comparison between the movements of an individual stock (or portfolio) and the movements of the market as a whole.

The calculation begins by assigning a beta of 1 to a broad

market index. If a stock has a beta of 2, then on average it swings twice as far as the market. If the market goes up 10 percent, the stock tends to rise 20 percent. If a stock has a beta of 0.5, it tends to go up or down 5 percent when the market rises or declines 10 percent. Professionals call high-beta stocks aggressive investments and label low-beta stocks as defensive.

Now, the important thing to realize is that systematic risk cannot be eliminated by diversification. It is precisely because all stocks move more or less in tandem (a large share of their variability is systematic) that even diversified stock portfolios are risky. Indeed, if you diversified perfectly by buying a share in the Total Stock Market index (which by definition has a beta of 1), you would still have quite variable (risky) returns because the market as a whole fluctuates widely.

Unsystematic risk is the variability in stock prices (and, there-fore, in returns from stocks) that results from factors peculiar to an individual company. Receipt of a large new contract, the find-ing of mineral resources, labor difficulties, accounting fraud, the discovery that the corporation's treasurer has had his hand in the company till—all can make a stock's price move independently of the market. The risk associated with such variability is precisely the kind that diversification can reduce. The whole point of port-folio theory is that, to the extent that stocks don't always move in tandem, variations in the returns from any one security tend to be washed away by complementary variation in the returns from others.

The chart on page 212, similar to the one on page 201, illustrates the important relationship between diversification and total risk. Suppose we randomly select securities for our portfolio that on average are just as volatile as the market (the average betas for the securities in our portfolio will be equal to 1). The chart shows that as we add more securities, the total risk of our portfolio declines, especially at the start.

When thirty securities are selected for our portfolio, a good deal of the unsystematic risk is eliminated, and additional diversifica-tion yields little further risk reduction. By the time sixty well-diversified securities are in the portfolio, the unsystematic risk is substantially eliminated and our portfolio (with a beta of 1) will tend to move up and down essentially in tandem with the market. Of course, we could perform the same experiment with stocks whose average beta is 1½. Again, we would find that diversification quickly reduced unsystematic risk, but the remaining systematic risk would be larger. A portfolio of sixty or more stocks with an average beta of 1½ would tend to be 50 percent more volatile than the market.

HOW DIVERSIFICATION REDUCES RISK:
RISK OF PORTFOLIO (STANDARD DEVIATION OF RETURN)

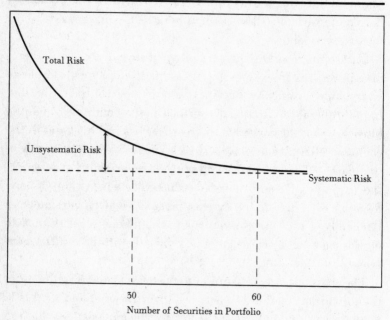

Now comes the key step in the argument. Financial theorists and practitioners agree that investors should be compensated for taking on more risk with a higher expected return. Stock prices must, therefore, adjust to offer higher returns where more risk is perceived, to ensure that all securities are held by someone. Obviously, risk-averse investors wouldn't buy securities with extra risk without the expectation of extra reward. But not all of the risk of individual securities is relevant in determining the premium for bearing risk. The unsystematic part of the total risk is easily eliminated by adequate diversification. So there is no reason to think that investors will receive extra compensation for bearing unsystematic risk. The only part of total risk that investors will get paid for bearing is systematic risk, the risk that diversification cannot help. Thus, the capital-asset pricing model says that returns (and, therefore, risk premiums) for any stock (or portfolio) will be related to beta, the systematic risk that cannot be diversified away.

THE CAPITAL-ASSET PRICING MODEL (CAPM)

The proposition that risk and reward are related is not new. Finance specialists have agreed for years that investors do need to be compensated for taking on more risk. What is different about the new investment technology is the definition and measurement of risk. Before the advent of the capital-asset pricing model, it was believed that the return on each security was related to the total risk inherent in that security. It was believed that the return from a security varied with the variability or standard deviation of the returns it produced. The new theory says that the total risk of each individual security is irrelevant. It is only the systematic component that counts as far as extra rewards go.

Although the mathematical proof of this proposition is forbidding, the logic behind it is fairly simple. Consider two groups of securities—Group I and Group II—with sixty securities in each. Suppose that the systematic risk (beta) for each security is 1; that is, each of the securities in the two groups tends to move up and down in tandem with the general market. Now suppose that, because of factors peculiar to the individual securities in Group I, the total risk for each of them is substantially higher than the total risk for each security in Group II. Imagine, for example, that in addition to general market factors the securities in Group I are also particularly susceptible to climatic variations, to changes in exchange rates, and to natural disasters. The specific risk for each of the securities in Group I will, therefore, be very high. The specific risk for each of the securities in Group II, however, is assumed to be very low, and, hence, the total risk for each of them will be very low. Schematically, this situation appears as follows:

Group I (60 Securities)	Group II (60 Securities)
Systematic risk (beta) = 1 for each security	Systematic risk (beta) = 1 for each security
Specific risk is high for each security	Specific risk is low for each security
Total risk is high for each security	Total risk is low for each security

Now, according to the old theory, commonly accepted before the advent of the capital-asset pricing model, returns should be higher for a portfolio made up of Group I securities, because each security in Group I has a higher total risk than each security in Group II, and risk, as we know, has its reward. With a wave of their intellectual wands, the academics changed that sort of thinking. Under the capital-asset pricing model, returns from the two portfolios should be equal. Why?

First, remember the preceding chart on page 212. (The forgetful can take another look.) There we saw that as the number of securities in the portfolio approached sixty, the total risk of the portfolio was reduced to its systematic level. The conscientious reader will now note that in the schematic illustration, the number of securities in each portfolio is sixty. All unsystematic risk has essentially been washed away: An unexpected weather calamity is balanced by a favorable exchange rate, and so forth. What remains is only the systematic risk of each stock in the portfolio, which is given by its beta. But in these two groups, each of the stocks has a beta of 1. Hence, a portfolio of Group I securities and a portfolio of Group II securities will perform exactly the same with respect to risk (standard deviation), even though the stocks in Group I display higher total risk than the stocks in Group II.

The old and the new views now meet head on. Under the old system of valuation, Group I securities were regarded as offering a higher return because of their greater risk. The capital-asset pricing model says there is no greater risk in holding Group I securities if they are in a diversified portfolio. Indeed, if the securities of Group I did offer higher returns, then all rational investors would prefer them over Group II securities and would attempt to rearrange their holdings to capture the higher returns from Group I. But by this very process, they would bid up the prices of Group I securities and push down the prices of Group II securities until, with the attainment of equilibrium (when investors no longer want to switch from security to security), the portfolios for each group had identical returns, related to the systematic component of their risk (beta) rather than to their total risk (including the unsystematic or specific portions). Because stocks can be combined in portfolios to eliminate specific risk, only the undiversifiable or systematic risk will command a risk premium. Investors will not get paid for bearing risks that can be diversified away. This is the basic logic behind the capital-asset pricing model.

In a big fat nutshell, the proof of the capital-asset pricing model (henceforth to be known as CAPM because we economists love to use letter abbreviations) can be stated as follows: If investors did get an extra return (a risk premium) for bearing unsystematic risk, it would turn out that diversified portfolios made up of stocks with large amounts of unsystematic risk would give larger returns than equally risky portfolios of stocks with less unsystematic risk. Investors would snap at the chance to have these higher returns, bidding up the prices of stocks with large unsystematic risk and selling stocks with equivalent betas but lower unsystematic risk. This process would continue until the prospective returns of stocks with the same betas were equalized and no risk premium could be obtained for bearing unsystematic risk. Any other result would be inconsistent with the existence of an efficient market.

The key relationship of the theory is shown in the following diagram. As the systematic risk (beta) of an individual stock (or portfolio) increases, so does the return an investor can expect. If an investor's portfolio has a beta of zero, as might be the case if all her funds were invested in a government-guaranteed bank savings certificate (beta would be zero because the returns from the certificate would not vary at all with swings in the stock market), the investor would receive some modest rate of return, which is generally called the risk-free rate of interest. As the individual takes on more risk, however, the return should increase. If the investor holds a portfolio with a beta of 1 (as, for example, holding a share in a broad stock-market index fund), her return will equal the general return from common stocks. This return has over long periods of time exceeded the risk-free rate of interest, but the investment is a risky one. In certain periods, the return is much less than the risk-free rate and involves taking substantial losses. This is precisely what is meant by risk.

The diagram shows that a number of different expected returns are possible simply by adjusting the beta of the portfolio. For example, suppose the investor put half of her money in a savings certificate and half in a share of an index fund representing the broad stock market. In this case, she would receive a return midway between the risk-free return and the return from the market, and her portfolio would have an average beta of 0.5.* The CAPM then asserts that to get a higher average long-run rate of return, you should just increase the beta of your portfolio. An investor can get a portfolio with a beta larger than 1 either by buying high-beta stocks or by purchasing a portfolio with average volatility on margin (see the diagram on page 217 and the table on page 218).

---

*In general, the beta of a portfolio is simply the weighted average of the betas of its component parts.

RISK AND RETURN ACCORDING TO THE
CAPITAL-ASSET PRICING MODEL*

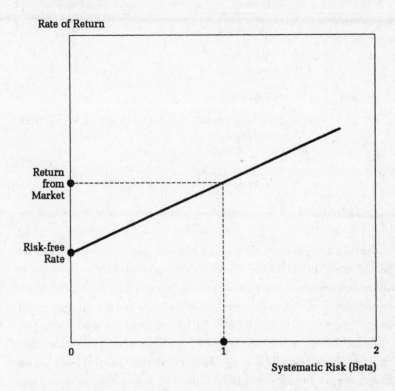

*Those who remember their high school algebra will recall that any straight line can be written as an equation. The equation for the straight line in the diagram is:

Rate of Return = Risk-free Rate + Beta (Return from Market – Risk-free Rate).

Alternatively, the equation can be written as an expression for the risk premium, that is, the rate of return on a portfolio of stocks or any individual stock over and above the risk-free rate of interest:

Rate of Return – Risk-free Rate = Beta (Return from Market – Risk-free Rate).

The equation says that the risk premium you get on any stock or portfolio increases directly with the beta value you assume. Some readers may wonder what relationship beta has to the covariance concept that was so critical in our discussion of portfolio theory. The beta for any security is essentially the same thing as the covariance between that security and the market index as measured on the basis of past experience.

ILLUSTRATION OF PORTFOLIO BUILDING*

Desired Beta	Composition of Portfolio	Expected Return from Portfolio
0	$1 in risk-free asset	10%
½	$.50 in risk-free asset $.50 in market portfolio	½ (0.10) + ½ (0.15) = 0.125, or 12½ %†
1	$1 in market portfolio	15%
1½	$1.50 in market portfolio borrowing $.50 at an assumed rate of 10 percent	1½ (0.15) − ½ (0.10) = 0.175, or 17½ %

* Assuming expected market return is 15 percent and risk-free rate is 10 percent.

† We can also derive the figure for expected return using directly the formula that accompanies the preceding chart:

Rate of Return = 0.10 + ½ (0.15 − 0.10) = 0.125 or 12½ %.

Just as stocks had their fads, so beta came into high fashion in the early 1970s. *Institutional Investor*, the prestigious magazine that spent most of its pages chronicling the accomplishments of professional money managers, put its imprimatur on the movement by featuring on its cover the letter beta on top of a temple and including as its lead story "The Beta Cult! The New Way to Measure Risk." The magazine noted that money men whose mathematics hardly went beyond long division were now "tossing betas around with the abandon of PhDs in statistical theory." Even the SEC gave beta its approval as a risk measure in its *Institutional Investors Study Report*.

On Wall Street, the early beta fans boasted that they could earn higher long-run rates of return simply by buying a few high-beta stocks. Those who thought they were able to time the market thought they had an even better idea. They would buy high-beta stocks when they thought the market was going up, switching to low-beta ones when they feared the market might decline. To accommodate the enthusiasm for this new investment idea, beta measurement services proliferated among brokers, and it was a symbol of progressiveness for an investment house to provide its own beta estimates. Today, you can obtain beta estimates from brokers such as Merrill Lynch and investment advisory services such as Value Line and Morningstar. The beta boosters on the Street oversold their product with an abandon that would have shocked even the most enthusiastic academic scribblers intent on spreading the beta gospel.

LET'S LOOK AT THE RECORD

In Shakespeare's *Henry IV, Part I*, Glendower boasts to Hotspur, "I can call spirits from the vasty deep." "Why, so can I, or so can any man," says Hotspur, unimpressed. "But will they come when you do call for them?" Anyone can theorize about how security markets work. CAPM is just another theory. The really important question is: Does it work?

Certainly many institutional investors have embraced the beta concept. Beta is, after all, an academic creation. What could be more staid? Simply created as a number that describes a stock's risk, it appears almost sterile in nature. The closet chartists love it. Even if you don't believe in beta, you have to speak its language because, back on the nation's campuses, my colleagues and I have been producing a long line of PhDs and MBAs who spout its terminology. They now use beta as a method of evaluating a portfolio manager's performance. If the realized return is larger than that predicted by the portfolio beta, the manager is said to have produced a positive alpha. Lots of money in the market sought out managers who could deliver the largest alpha.

But is beta a useful measure of risk? Is it true that high-beta portfolios will provide larger long-term returns than lower-beta ones, as the capital-asset pricing model suggests? Does beta alone summarize a security's total systematic risk, or do we need to consider other factors as well? In short, does beta really deserve an alpha? These are subjects of intense current debate among practitioners and academics.

In a study published in 1992, Eugene Fama and Kenneth French divided all traded stocks into deciles according to their beta measures over the 1963–90 period. Decile 1 contained the 10 percent of all stocks that had the lowest betas; decile 10 contained the 10 percent that had the highest betas. The remarkable result, shown in the chart below, is that there was essentially no relationship between the return of these decile portfolios and their beta measures. I found a similar result for the relationship between return and beta for mutual funds. There was no relationship between returns for stocks or portfolios and their beta risk measures.

AVERAGE MONTHLY RETURN VS. BETA: 1963–90 (FAMA AND FRENCH STUDY)

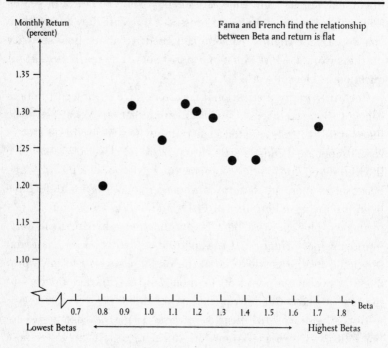

Because their comprehensive study covered a period of almost thirty years, Fama and French concluded that the relationship between beta and return is essentially flat. Beta, the key analytical tool of the capital-asset pricing model, is not a useful single measure to capture the relationship between risk and return. And so, by the mid-1990s, not only practitioners but even many academics as well were ready to assign beta to the scrap heap. The financial press, which earlier had chronicled the ascendancy of beta, now ran feature stories with titles such as "The Death of Beta," "Bye, Bye Beta," and "Beta Beaten." Typical of the times was a letter quoted in *Institutional Investor* from a writer known only as "Deep Quant."* The letter began, "There is a very big story breaking in money management. The Capital-Asset Pricing Model is dead." The magazine went on to quote one "turncoat quant" as follows: "Advanced mathematics will become to investors what the Titanic was to sailing." And so the whole set of tools making up the new investment technology—including even modern portfolio theory—came under a cloud of suspicion.

AN APPRAISAL OF THE EVIDENCE

My own guess is that the "turncoat quant" is wrong. The unearthing of serious cracks in the CAPM will not lead to an abandonment of mathematical tools in financial analysis and a return to traditional security analysis. The financial community is not ready to write an obituary for beta at this time. There are many reasons, I believe, to avoid a rush to judgment.

First, it is important to remember that stable returns are preferable, that is, less risky than very volatile returns. Clearly, if one could earn only the same return drilling for oil as from a riskless government security, only those who loved gambling for gambling's sake alone would drill for oil. If investors really did not worry at all about volatility, the multitrillion-dollar derivative-securities markets would not be thriving as they are. Thus, the beta measure of relative volatility does capture at least some aspects of what we normally think of as risk. And portfolio betas from the past do a reasonably good job of predicting relative volatility in the future.

*"Quant" is the Wall Street nickname for the quantitatively inclined financial analyst who devotes attention largely to the new investment technology.

"Does it bother you at all that when you say MPT quickly it comes out 'empty'?"

Second, as Professor Richard Roll of UCLA has argued, we must keep in mind that it is very difficult (indeed probably impossible) to measure beta with any degree of precision. The S&P 500 Index is not "the market." The Total Stock Market contains many thousands of additional stocks in the United States and thousands more in foreign countries. Moreover, the total market includes bonds, real estate, commodities, and assets of all sorts, including one of the most important assets any of us has—the human capital built up by education, work, and life experiences. Depending on exactly how you measure the "market," you can obtain very different beta values. One's conclusions about the capital-asset pricing model and beta as a measure of risk depend very much on how you measure beta. Two economists from the University of Minnesota, Ravi Jagannathan and Zhenyu Wang, find that when the market index (against which we measure beta) is redefined to include human capital and when betas are allowed to vary with cyclical fluctuations in the economy, the support for the CAPM and beta as a predictor of returns is quite strong.

Finally, investors should be aware that even if the long-run relationship between beta and return is flat, beta can still be a useful investment management tool. Were it in fact the case that low-beta stocks will dependably earn rates of return at least as large as those of high-beta stocks (a very big "if" indeed), then beta would be even more valuable as an investment tool than if the capital-asset pricing model held. Investors should scoop up low-beta stocks and earn returns as attractive as for the market as a whole but with much less risk. And investors who do wish to seek higher returns by assuming greater risk should buy and hold low-beta stocks on margin, thereby increasing their risk and returns. We shall see in chapter 11 that some "smart beta" strategies are designed to execute that exact strategy. What is clear, however, is that beta, as usually measured, is not a substitute for brains and cannot be relied on as a simple predictor of long-run future returns.

THE QUANT QUEST FOR BETTER MEASURES OF RISK: ARBITRAGE PRICING THEORY

If beta is damaged as an effective quantitative measure of risk, is there anything to take its place? One of the pioneers in the field of risk measurement is Stephen Ross. Ross has developed a theory of pricing in the capital markets called arbitrage pricing theory (APT). To understand the logic of APT, one must remember the correct insight underlying the CAPM: The only risk that investors should be compensated for bearing is the risk that cannot be diversified away. Only systematic risk will command a risk premium. But the systematic elements of risk in particular stocks and portfolios may be too complicated to be captured by beta—the tendency of the stocks to move more or less than the market. This is especially so because any particular stock index is an imperfect representative of the general market. Hence, beta may fail to capture a number of important systematic elements of risk.

Let's take a look at several of these other systematic risk elements. Changes in national income undoubtedly affect returns from individual stocks in a systematic way. This was shown in our illustration of a simple island economy in chapter 8. Also, changes in national income mirror changes in the personal income of individuals, and the systematic relationship between security returns and salary income can be expected to have a significant effect on individual behavior. For example, the laborer in a Ford plant will find that holding Ford common stock is particularly risky, because job layoffs and poor returns from Ford stock are likely to occur at the same time. Changes in national income may also reflect changes in other forms of property income and may, therefore, be relevant for institutional portfolio managers as well.

Changes in interest rates also systematically affect the returns from individual stocks and are important nondiversifiable risk elements. To the extent that stocks tend to suffer as interest rates go up, equities are a risky investment, and those stocks that are particularly vulnerable to increases in the general level of interest rates are especially risky. Thus, some stocks and fixed-income investments tend to move in parallel, and these stocks will not be helpful in reducing the risk of a bond portfolio. Because fixed-income securities are a major part of the portfolios of many institutional investors, this systematic risk factor is particularly important for some of the largest investors in the market.

Changes in the rate of inflation will similarly tend to have a systematic influence on the returns from common stocks. This is so for at least two reasons. First, an increase in the rate of inflation tends to increase interest rates and thus tends to lower the prices of some equities, as just discussed. Second, the increase in inflation may squeeze profit margins for certain groups of companies—public utilities, for example, which often find that rate increases lag behind increases in costs. On the other hand, inflation may benefit the prices of common stocks in the natural resource industries. Thus, again there are important systematic relationships between stock returns and economic variables that may not be captured adequately by a simple beta measure of risk.

Statistical tests of the influence on security returns of several systematic risk variables have shown somewhat promising results. Better explanations than those given by the CAPM can be obtained for the variation in returns among different securities by using, in addition to the traditional beta measure of risk, a number of systematic risk variables, such as sensitivity to changes in national income, in interest rates, and in the rate of inflation. Of course, the APT measures of risk are beset by some of the same problems faced by the CAPM beta measure.

THE FAMA-FRENCH THREE-FACTOR MODEL

Eugene Fama and Kenneth French have proposed a factor model, like arbitrage pricing theory, to account for risk. Two factors are used in addition to beta to describe risk. The factors derive from their empirical work showing that returns are related to the size of the company (as measured by the market capital-ization) and to the relationship of its market price to its book value. Fama-French argue that smaller firms are relatively risky. One explanation might be that they will have more difficulty sustaining themselves during recessionary periods and thus may have more systematic risk relative to fluctuations in GDP. Fama-French also argue that stocks with low market prices relative to their book values may be in some degree of "financial distress." These views are hotly debated, and not everyone agrees that the Fama-French factors measure risk. But certainly regarding early 2009, when the stocks of major banks sold at very low prices relative to their book values, it is hard to argue that investors did not consider them in danger of going bankrupt. And even those who would argue that low-market-to-book-value stocks provide higher returns because of investor irrationality find the Fama-French risk factors useful.

THE FAMA-FRENCH RISK FACTORS

- Beta: from the Capital-Asset Pricing Model
- Size: measured by total equity market capitalization
- Value: measured by the ratio of market to book value

Some analysts would add further variables to the Fama-French three-factor risk model. A momentum factor could be added to capture the tendency for rising or falling stocks to continue moving in the same direction. In addition, a liquidity factor could be added to reflect the fact that investors need to be paid a return premium to induce them to hold illiquid securities. A further factor that has been suggested is the "quality" of the company as measured by such indicators as the stability of its earnings and sales growth and its low amount of debt. Factor models are extensively used now to measure investment performance and to design "smart beta" portfolios, as will be discussed in chapter 11.

A SUMMING UP

Chapters 8 and 9 have been an academic exercise in the modern theory of capital markets. The stock market appears to be an efficient mechanism that adjusts quite quickly to new information. Neither technical analysis, which analyzes the past price movements of stocks, nor fundamental analysis, which analyzes more basic information about the prospects for individual companies and the economy, seems to yield consistent benefits. It appears that the only way to obtain higher long-run investment returns is to accept greater risks.

Unfortunately, a perfect risk measure does not exist. Beta, the risk measure from the capital-asset pricing model, looks nice on the surface. It is a simple, easy-to-understand measure of market sensitivity. Alas, beta also has its warts. The actual relationship between beta and rate of return has not corresponded to the relationship predicted in theory during long periods of the twentieth century. Moreover, betas for individual stocks are not stable over time, and they are very sensitive to the market proxy against which they are measured.

I have argued here that no single measure is likely to capture adequately the variety of systematic risk influences on individual stocks and portfolios. Returns are probably sensitive to general market swings, to changes in interest and inflation rates, to changes in national income, and, undoubtedly, to other economic factors such as exchange rates. Moreover, there is evidence that returns are higher for stocks with lower price-book ratios and smaller size. The mystical perfect risk measure is still beyond our grasp.

To the great relief of assistant professors who must publish or perish, there is still much debate within the academic community on risk measurement, and much more empirical testing needs to be done. Undoubtedly, there will yet be many improvements in the techniques of risk analysis, and the quantitative analysis of risk measurement is far from dead. My own guess is that future risk measures will be even more sophisticated—not less so. Nevertheless, we must be careful not to accept beta or any other measure as an easy way to assess risk and to predict future returns with any certainty. You should know about the best of the modern techniques of the new investment technology—they can be useful aids. But there is never going to be a handsome genie who will appear and solve all our investment problems. And even if he did, we would probably foul it up—as did the little old lady in the following favorite story of Robert Kirby of Capital Guardian Trust:

> She was sitting in her rocking chair on the porch of the retirement home when a little genie appeared and said, "I've decided to grant you three wishes."
>
> The little old lady answered, "Buzz off, you little twerp, I've seen all the wise guys I need to in my life."
>
> The genie answered, "Look, I'm not kidding. This is for real. Just try me."
>
> She shrugged and said, "Okay, turn my rocking chair into solid gold."

When, in a puff of smoke, he did it, her interest picked up noticeably. She said, "Turn me into a beautiful young maiden."

Again, in a puff of smoke, he did it. Finally, she said, "Okay, for my third wish turn my cat into a handsome young prince."

In an instant, there stood the young prince, who then turned to her and asked, "Now aren't you sorry you had me fixed?"

10

BEHAVIORAL
FINANCE

*Behavioral finance is not a branch of standard finance: it is
its replacement with a better model of humanity.*
—Meir Statman

THUS FAR I have described stock-market theories and techniques based on the premise that investors are completely rational. They make decisions with the objective of maximizing their wealth and are constrained only by their tolerance for bearing risk. Not so, declares a new school of financial economists who came to prominence in the early part of the twenty-first century. Behavioralists believe that many (perhaps even most) stock-market investors are far from fully rational. After all, think of the behavior of your friends and acquaintances, your fellow workers and your supervisors, your parents and (dare I say) spouse (children, of course, are another matter). Do any of these people act rationally? If your answer is "no" or even "sometimes no," you will enjoy this journey down the less than rational byways of behavioral finance.

Efficient-market theory, modern portfolio theory, and various asset-pricing relationships between risk and return all are built on the premise that stock-market investors are rational. As a whole, they make reasonable estimates of the present value of stocks, and their buying and selling ensures that the prices of stocks fairly represent their future prospects.

By now, it should be obvious that the phrase "as a whole" represents the economists' escape hatch. That means they can admit that some individual market participants may be less than rational. But they quickly wriggle out by declaring that the trades of irrational investors will be random and therefore cancel each other out without affecting prices. And even if investors are irrational in a similar way, efficient-market theory believers assert that smart rational traders will correct any mispricings that might arise from the presence of irrational traders.

Psychologists will have none of this economic claptrap. Two in particular—Daniel Kahneman and Amos Tversky—blasted economists' views about how investors behave and in the process are credited with fathering a whole new economic discipline, called behavioral finance.

The two argued quite simply that people are not as rational as economic models assume. Although this argument is obvious to the general public and non-economists, it took over twenty years for it to become widely accepted in academia. Tversky died in 1996, just as it was gaining increased credibility. Six years later, Kahneman won the Nobel Memorial Prize in Economic Sciences for the work. The award was particularly notable in that it was not given to an economist. Upon hearing the news, Kahneman commented, "The prize . . . is quite explicitly for joint work, but unfortunately there is no posthumous prize."

Though the insights expounded by Kahneman and Tversky affected all social sciences dealing with the process of decision making, they had a particularly strong impact on economics departments and business schools across the country. Imagine—a whole new field in which to publish papers, give lectures for hefty fees, and write graduate theses.

While that may be all well and good for the professors and the students, what about all the other people who want to invest in stocks. How can behavioral finance help them? More to the point, what's in it for you? Actually, quite a bit.

Behavioralists believe that market prices are highly imprecise. Moreover, people deviate in systematic ways from rationality, and the irrational trades of investors tend to be correlated. Behavioral finance then takes that statement further by asserting that it is possible to quantify or classify such irrational behavior. Basically, there are four factors that create irrational market behavior: over-confidence, biased judgments, herd mentality, and loss aversion.

Well, yes, believers in efficient markets say. But—and we believers always have a but—the distortions caused by such factors are countered by the work of arbitrageurs. This last is the fancy word used to describe people who profit from any deviation of market prices from their rational value.

In a strict sense, the word "arbitrage" means profiting from prices of the same good that differ in two markets. Suppose in New York you can buy or sell British pounds for $1.50, while in London you can trade dollars for pounds at a $2.00 exchange rate. The arbitrageur would then take $1.50 in New York and buy a pound and simultaneously sell it in London for $2.00, making a 50¢ profit. Similarly, if a common stock sold at different prices in New York and London, it would be justifiable to buy it in the cheap market and sell it in the expensive one. The term "arbitrage" is generally extended to situations where two very similar stocks sell at different valuations or where one stock is expected to be exchanged for another stock at a higher price if a planned merger between the two companies is approved. In the loosest sense of the term, "arbitrage" is used to describe the buying of stocks that appear "undervalued" and the selling of those that have gotten "too high." In so doing, hardworking arbitrageurs can smooth out irrational fluctuations in stock prices and create an efficiently priced market.

On the other hand, behavioralists believe there are substantial barriers to efficient arbitrage. We cannot count on arbitrage to bring prices in line with rational valuation. Market prices can be expected to deviate substantially from those that could be expected in an efficient market.

The remainder of this chapter explores the key arguments of behavioral finance in explaining why markets are not efficient and why there is no such thing as a random walk down Wall Street. I'll also explain how an understanding of this work can help protect individual investors from some systematic errors that investors are prone to.

THE IRRATIONAL BEHAVIOR OF INDIVIDUAL INVESTORS

As Part One made abundantly clear, there are always times when investors are irrational. Behavioral finance, however, says that this behavior is continual rather than episodic.

Overconfidence

Researchers in cognitive psychology have documented that people deviate in systematic ways from rationality in making judgments amid uncertainty. One of the most pervasive of these biases is the tendency to be overconfident about beliefs and abilities and overoptimistic about assessments of the future.

One class of experiments illustrating this syndrome consists of asking a large group of participants about their competence as automobile drivers in relation to the average driver in the group or to everyone who drives a car. Driving an automobile is clearly a risky activity where skill plays an important role. Answers to this question easily reveal whether people have a realistic conception of their own skill in relationship to others. In the case of college students, 80 to 90 percent of respondents invariably say that they are more skillful, safer drivers than others in the class. As in Lake Wobegon, (almost) all the students consider themselves above average.

In another experiment involving students, respondents were asked about likely future outcomes for themselves and their roommates. They typically had very rosy views about their own futures, which they imagined to include successful careers, happy marriages, and good health. When asked to speculate about their roommates' futures, however, their responses were far more realistic. The roommates were believed to be far more likely to become alcoholics, suffer illnesses, get divorced, and experience a variety of other unfavorable outcomes.

These kinds of experiments have been repeated many times and in several different contexts. For example, in the business management best-seller *In Search of Excellence*, Peters and Waterman report that a random sample of male adults were asked to rank themselves in terms of their ability to get along with others. One hundred percent of the respondents ranked themselves in the top half of the population. Twenty-five percent believed that they were in the top 1 percent of the population. Even in judging athletic ability, an area where self-deception would seem more difficult, at least 60 percent of the male respondents ranked themselves in the top quartile. Even the klutziest deluded themselves about their athletic ability. Only 6 percent of male respondents believed that their athleticism was below average.

Daniel Kahneman has argued that this tendency to overconfidence is particularly strong among investors. More than most other groups, investors tend to exaggerate their own skill and deny the role of chance. They overestimate their own knowledge, underestimate the risks involved, and exaggerate their ability to control events.

Kahneman's tests show how well investors' probability judgments are calibrated by asking experimental subjects for confidence intervals. He asks a question such as the following:

> *What is your best estimate of the value of the Dow Jones one month from today?* Next pick a high value, such that you are 99% sure (but not absolutely sure) that the Dow Jones a month from today will be lower than that value. Now pick a low value, such that you are 99% sure (but no more) that the Dow Jones a month from today will be higher than that value.

If the instructions are carried out properly, the probability that the Dow will be higher (lower) than your high (low) estimate should be only 1 percent. In other words, the investor should be 98 percent confident that the Dow will be within the given range. Similar experiments have been carried out on estimates for interest rates, the rate of inflation, individual stock prices, and the like.

In fact, few investors are able to set accurate confidence intervals. Correct intervals would lead to actual outcomes being outside the predicted range only 2 percent of the time. Actual surprises do occur close to 20 percent of the time. This is what psychologists mean by overconfidence. If an investor tells you he is 99 percent sure, he would be better off assuming that he was only 80 percent sure. Such precision implies that people tend to put larger stakes on their predictions than are justified. And men typically display far more overconfidence than women, especially about their prowess in money matters.

What should we conclude from these studies? It is clear that people set far too precise confidence intervals for their predictions. They exaggerate their skills and tend to have a far too optimistic view of the future. These biases manifest themselves in various ways in the stock market.

First and foremost, many individual investors are mistakenly convinced that they can beat the market. As a result, they speculate more than they should and trade too much. Two behavioral economists, Terrance Odean and Brad Barber, examined the individual accounts at a large discount broker over a substantial period of time. They found that the more individual investors traded, the worse they did. And male investors traded much more than women, with correspondingly poorer results.

This illusion of financial skill may well stem from another psychological finding, called hindsight bias. Such errors are sustained by having a selective memory of success. You remember your successful investments. And in hindsight, it is easy to convince yourself that you "knew Google was going to quintuple right after its initial public offering." People are prone to attribute any good outcome to their own abilities. They tend to rationalize bad outcomes as resulting from unusual external events. History does not move us as much as a couple of anecdotes of success. Hindsight promotes overconfidence and fosters the illusion that the world is far more predictable than it really is. The people who sell worthless financial advice may even believe that it is good advice. Steve Forbes, the longtime publisher of *Forbes* magazine, liked to quote the advice he received at his grandfather's knee: "It's far more profitable to sell advice than to take it."

Many behavioralists believe that overconfidence in the ability to predict the future growth of companies leads to a general tendency for so-called growth stocks to be overvalued. If the exciting new computer technology, medical device, or retail outlet catches the public fancy, investors will usually extrapolate success and project high growth rates for the companies involved and hold such beliefs with far more confidence than is justified. The high-growth forecasts lead to higher valuations for growth stocks. But the rosy forecasts are often not realized. The earnings may fall, and so may the price-earnings multiples of the shares, which will lead to poor investment results. Overoptimism in forecasting the growth for exciting companies could then be one explanation for the tendency of "growth" stocks to underperform "value" stocks.

Biased Judgments

I meet investors every day who are convinced that they can "control" their investment results. This is especially true of chartists who are confident that they can define the future by looking at past prices.

Larry Swedroe, in his *Rational Investing in Irrational Times*, provides a wonderful illustration of how hot streaks occur with much greater frequency than people believe.

Each year a statistics professor begins her class by asking each student to write down the sequential outcome of a series of one hundred imaginary coin tosses. One student, however, is chosen to flip a real coin and chart the outcome. The professor then leaves the room and returns in fifteen minutes with the outcomes waiting for her on her desk. She tells the class that she will identify the one real coin toss out of the thirty submitted with just one guess. With great persistence

she amazes the class by getting it correct. How does she perform this seemingly magical act? She knows that the report
with the longest consecutive streak of H (heads) or T (tails)
is highly likely to be the result of the real flip. The reason is
that, when presented with a question like which of the following sequences is more likely to occur, HHHHHTTTTT
or HTHTHTHTHT, despite the fact that statistics show that
both sequences are equally likely to occur, the majority of
people select the latter "more random" outcome. They thus
tend to write imaginary sequences that look much more like
HHTTHTHTTT than HHHTTTHHHH.

Aside from the long-term positive direction of the stock market,
streaks of excessively high stock returns do not persist—they are
typically followed by lower future returns. There is reversion to
the mean. Similarly, the laws of financial gravity also operate in
reverse. At least for the stock market as a whole, what goes down
eventually comes back up. Yet each era's conventional wisdom
typically assumes that unusually good markets will get better and
unusually bad markets will get worse.

Psychologists have long identified a tendency for individuals to
be fooled by the illusion that they have some control over situations
where, in fact, none exists. In one study, subjects were seated in
front of a computer screen divided by a horizontal line, with a ball
fluctuating randomly between two halves. The people were given
a device to press to move the ball upward, but they were warned
that random shocks would also influence the ball so that they did
not have complete control. Subjects were then asked to play a game
with the object of keeping the ball in the upper half of the screen as
long as possible. In one set of experiments, the device was not even
attached, so the players had absolutely no control over the movements of the ball. Nevertheless, when subjects were questioned
after a period of playing the game, they were convinced that they
had a good deal of control over the movement of the ball. (The only
subjects not under such an illusion turned out to be those who had
been clinically diagnosed with severe depression.)

In another experiment, an office lottery was conducted with two identical sets of baseball cards. One set was placed in a bin from which one card was to be selected by chance. The other set was distributed to the participants. Half the participants were given a choice of which card to take, while the other half were simply given a card. Participants were told that the winner would be the person holding the card that matched the one that would be selected by chance from the bin. The individuals were then told that while all the cards had been distributed, a new player wanted to buy a card. Participants were faced with a choice—sell their cards at some negotiated price or hold on to them and hope to win. Obviously, each card had the same probability of winning. Nevertheless, the prices at which players were willing to sell their cards were systematically higher for those who chose their cards than for the group who had simply been given a card. Insights such as this led to the decision to let state lottery buyers pick their own numbers even though luck alone determines lottery winners.

It is this illusion of control that can lead investors to see trends that do not exist or to believe that they can spot a stock-price pattern that will predict future prices. In fact, despite considerable efforts to tease some form of predictability out of stock-price data, the development of stock prices from period to period is very close to a random walk, where price changes in the future are essentially unrelated to changes in the past.

Biases in judgments are compounded (get ready for some additional jargon) by the tendency of people mistakenly to use "similarity" or "representativeness" as a proxy for sound probabilistic thinking. A famous Kahneman and Tversky experiment best illustrates this "heuristic." Subjects are shown the following description of Linda:

> Linda is 31 years old, single, outspoken and very bright. She majored in philosophy. As a student, she was deeply concerned with issues of discrimination and social justice, and also participated in anti-nuclear demonstrations.

Subjects were then asked to rate the relative likelihood that eight different statements about Linda were true. Two of the statements on the list were "Linda is a bank teller" and "Linda is a bank teller and is active in the feminist movement." Over 85 percent of subjects judged it more likely that Linda was both a bank teller and a feminist than that she was a bank teller. But this answer is a violation of a fundamental axiom of probability theory (the conjunction rule): the probability that somebody belongs to both category A and category B is less than or equal to the probability that she belongs to category A alone. Obviously, few respondents had learned much probability theory.

The description of Linda made her seem like a feminist, so being a bank teller and a feminist seems a more natural description, and thus more representative of Linda, than simply being a bank teller. This experiment has been replicated many times with naive and sophisticated subjects (including those who had backgrounds in probability but who had not studied all its nuances).

Kahneman and Tversky came up with the term "representative heuristic" to describe this finding. Its application leads to a number of other biases in judgment—for example, the underuse of base-rate probabilities. One cardinal rule of probability (Bayes' law) tells us that our assessment of the likelihood that someone belongs to a particular group should combine "representativeness" with base rates (the percentage of the population falling into various groups). In everyday English, this means that if we see somebody who looks like a criminal (seems to represent our idea of a criminal type), our assessment of the probability that he is a criminal also requires knowledge about base rates—that is, the percentage of people who are criminals. But in experiment after experiment, subjects have been shown to underuse the knowledge of base rates when making predictions. Arcane as this all may seem, the representativeness heuristic is likely to account for a number of investing mistakes such as chasing hot funds or excessive extrapolation from recent evidence.

Herding

In general, research shows that groups tend to make better decisions than individuals. If more information is shared, and if differing points of view are considered, informed discussion of the group improves the decision-making process.

The wisdom of crowd behavior is perhaps best illustrated in the economy as a whole by the free-market price system. A variety of individual decisions by consumers and producers leads the economy to produce the goods and services that people want to buy. Responding to the forces of demand and supply, the price system guides the economy through Adam Smith's invisible hand to produce the correct quantity of products. As communist economies have discovered to their dismay, an all-powerful central planner cannot possibly achieve any semblance of market efficiency in deciding what goods to produce and how resources should be allocated.

Similarly, millions of individual and institutional investors by their collective buying and selling decisions produce a tableau of stock-market prices that appear to make one stock just as good a buy as another. And while market forecasts of future returns are often erroneous, as a group they appear to be more correct than the forecasts made by any individual investor. Most active portfolio managers must hold their heads in shame when their returns are compared with the results of investing in a low-cost, broad-based equity index fund.

As all readers of this book recognize, the market as a whole does not invariably make correct pricing decisions. At times, there is a madness to crowd behavior, as we have seen from seventeenth-century tulip bulbs to twenty-first-century Internet stocks. It is this occasional pathological crowd behavior that has attracted the attention of behavioral finance.

One widely recognized phenomenon in the study of crowd behavior is the existence of "group think." Groups of individuals will sometimes reinforce one another into believing that some incorrect point of view is, in fact, the correct one. Surely, the wildly overoptimistic group forecasts regarding the earnings potential of the Internet and the incorrect pricing of New Economy stocks during early 2000 are examples of the pathology of herd behavior.

The social psychologist Solomon Asch was one of the first to study how group behavior may lead to incorrect decision making. During the 1950s, Asch conducted a famous laboratory experiment in which a group of participants was asked to answer a simple question that any child could answer correctly. The subjects were shown two cards with vertical lines such as the cards shown below. The card on the left showed one vertical line. The subjects were asked which line on the card on the right was the same length as the line on the first card. Seven subjects participated in a series of such questions.

But Asch added a diabolical twist to the experiment. In some of the experiments, he recruited six of the seven participants to deliberately give the wrong answer and to do so before the seventh participant had a chance to express an opinion. The results were astonishing. The seventh participant would often give the incorrect answer. Asch conjectured that social pressure caused participants to pick the wrong line even when they knew that their answer was incorrect.

SAMPLE CARDS USED IN ASCH EXPERIMENT

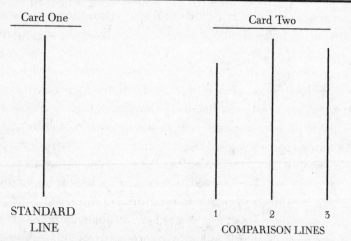

Card One   Card Two

STANDARD LINE   1   2   3

COMPARISON LINES

Source: Solomon E. Asch, *Social Psychology* (Oxford, 1987). By permission of Oxford University Press, http://www.oup.com.

A 2005 study by Gregory Berns, a neuroscientist, used MRI scanners to examine the workings of the brain to determine whether people gave in to the group knowing that their answers were incorrect or whether their perceptions had actually changed. If caving in to the group was the result of social pressure, the study reasoned, one should see changes in the area of the forebrain involved in monitoring conflicts. But if the conformity stemmed from actual changes in perception, one would expect changes in the posterior brain areas dedicated to vision and spatial perception. In fact, the study found that when people went along with the group in giving wrong answers, activity increased in the area of the brain devoted to spatial awareness. In other words, it appeared that what other people said actually changed what subjects believed they saw. It seems that other people's errors actually affect how someone perceives the external world.

In another study, social psychologists put a single person on a street corner and asked him to look up at an empty sky for sixty seconds. The psychologists then observed that a tiny fraction of the pedestrians on the street stopped to see what the person was looking at, but most simply walked past. Then the psychologists put five people on the corner looking at the sky; this time four times as many people stopped by to gaze at an empty sky. When the psychologists put fifteen people on the corner looking at the sky, almost half of the passersby stopped. Increasing the number of people looking skyward increased the number of gazing pedestrians even more.

Clearly, the Internet bubble of the 1999–early 2000 period provides a classic example of incorrect investment judgments leading people to go mad in herds. Individual investors, excited by the prospect of huge gains from stocks catering to the New Economy, got infected with an unreasoning herd mentality. Word-of-mouth communications from friends at the golf club, associates at work, and fellow card players provided a powerful message that great wealth was being created by the growth of the Internet. Investors then began to purchase common stocks for no other reason than that prices were rising and other people were making money, even if the price increases could not be justifiable by fundamental reasons such as the growth of earnings and dividends. As the economic historian Charles Kindleberger has stated, "There is nothing so disturbing to one's well-being and judgment as to see a friend get rich." And as Robert Shiller, author of the best-selling *Irrational Exuberance*, has noted, the process feeds on itself in a "positive feedback loop." The initial price rise encourages more people to buy, which in turn produces greater profits and induces a larger and larger group of participants. The phenomenon is another example of the Ponzi scheme that I described in chapter 4, in connection with the Internet bubble. Eventually one runs out of greater fools.

Such herding is not limited to unsophisticated individual investors. Mutual-fund managers have a tendency to follow the same strategies and herd into the same stocks. Indeed, a study by Harrison Hong, Jeffrey Kubik, and Jeremy Stein, three leaders in the field of behavioral finance, determined that mutual-fund managers were more likely to hold similar stocks if other managers in the same city were holding similar portfolios. Such results are consistent with an epidemic model, in which investors quickly and irreversibly spread information about stocks by word of mouth. Such herding has had devastating effects for the individual investor. Although long-run returns from the stock market have been generous, the returns for the average investor have been significantly poorer. This is because investors tended to buy equity mutual funds just when exuberance had led to market peaks. During the twelve months ending in March of 2000, more new cash flow went into equity mutual funds than during any preceding period. But while the market was reaching troughs in the falls of 2002 and 2008, individuals made significant withdrawals from their equity investments. A study by Dalbar Associates suggests that the average investor may earn a rate of return 5 percentage points lower than the average market return because of this timing penalty.

In addition, investors tend to put their money into the kinds of mutual funds that have recently had good performance. For example, the large inflows into equity mutual funds in the first quarter of 2000 went entirely into high-tech "growth" funds. So-called "value" funds experienced large fund outflows. Over the subsequent two years, the growth funds declined sharply in value, while the value funds actually produced positive returns. This selection penalty exacerbates the timing penalty described above. One of the most important lessons of behavioral finance is that individual investors must avoid being carried away by herd behavior.

Loss Aversion

Kahneman and Tversky's most important contribution is called prospect theory, which describes individual behavior in the face of risky situations where there are prospects of gains and losses. In general, financial economists such as Harry Markowitz constructed models where individuals made decisions based on the likely effect of those choices on the person's final wealth. Prospect theory challenges that assumption. People's choices are motivated instead by the values they assign to gains and losses. Losses are considered far more undesirable than equivalent gains are desirable. Moreover, the language used to present the possible gains and losses will influence the final decision that is made. In psychological terms, this is known as "how the choice is framed."

For example, you are told that a fair coin will be flipped and that if it comes up heads you will be given $100. If the coin comes up tails, however, you must pay $100. Would you accept such a gamble? Most people would say no, even though the gamble is a fair one in the sense that in repeated trials you would end up even. Half the time you would gain $100 and half the time you would lose $100. In mathematical terms, the gamble has an "expected value" of zero, calculated as follows:

$$Probability\ of\ heads \times payoff\ if\ heads + probability\ of\ tails \times payoff\ if\ tails = Expected\ value.$$
$$Expected\ value = \tfrac{1}{2}(\$100) + \tfrac{1}{2}(-\$100) = 0.$$

Kahneman and Tversky then tried this experiment with many different subjects, varying the amount of the positive payoff to test what it would take to induce people to accept the gamble. They found that the positive payoff had to be about $250. Note that the expected value of the gain from such a gamble is $75, so this is a very favorable bet.

$$Expected\ value = \frac{1}{2}(\$250) + \frac{1}{2}(-\$100) = \$75.$$

Kahneman and Tversky concluded that losses were 2½ times as undesirable as equivalent gains were desirable. In other words, a dollar loss is 2½ times as painful as a dollar gain is pleasurable. People exhibit extreme loss aversion, even though a change of $100 of wealth would hardly be noticed for most people with substantial assets. We'll see later how loss aversion leads many investors to make costly mistakes.

Interestingly, however, when individuals faced a situation where sure losses were involved, the psychologists found that they were overwhelmingly likely to take the gamble. Consider the following two alternatives:

1. A sure loss of $750.

2. A 75 percent chance to lose $1,000 and a 25 percent chance to lose nothing.

Note that the expected values of the two alternatives are the same—that is, a loss of $750. But almost 90 percent of the subjects tested chose alternative (2), the gamble. In the face of sure losses, people seem to exhibit risk-seeking behavior.

Kahneman and Tversky also discovered a related and important "framing" effect. The way choices are framed to the decision maker can lead to quite different outcomes. They posed the following problem.

Imagine that the U.S. is preparing for the outbreak of an unusual Asian disease, which is expected to kill 600 people. Two alternative programs to combat the disease have been proposed. Assume that the exact scientific estimates of the consequences of the programs are as follows:

If Program A is adopted, 200 people will be saved.

If Program B is adopted, there is a one-third probability that 600 people will be saved and a two-thirds probability that no people will be saved.

Note first that the expected value of the number of people saved is the same 200 in both programs. But according to prospect theory, people are risk-averse when considering possible gains from the two programs, and, as expected, about two-thirds of the respondents to this question picked Program A as the more desirable.

But suppose we framed the problem differently.

If Program A* is adopted, 400 people will die.

If Program B* is adopted, there is a one-third probability that nobody will die and a two-thirds probability that 600 people will die.

Note that the options A and A* as well as B and B* are identical. But the presentation in the second problem is in terms of the risks of people's dying. When the problem was framed in this way, over 75 percent of the subjects chose Program B*. This illustrated the effect of "framing" as well as risk-seeking preferences in the domain of losses. When doctors are faced with decisions regarding treatment options for people with cancer, different choices tend to be made if the problem is stated in terms of survival probabilities rather than mortality probabilities.

Pride and Regret

Behavioralists also stress the importance of the emotions of pride and regret in influencing investor behavior. Investors find it very difficult to admit, even to themselves, that they have made a bad stock-market decision. Feelings of regret may be amplified if such an admission had to be made to friends or a spouse. On the other hand, investors are usually quite proud to tell the world about their successful investments that produced large gains.

Many investors may feel that if they hold on to a losing position, it will eventually recover and feelings of regret will be avoided. These emotions of pride and regret may be behind the tendency of investors to hold on to their losing positions and to sell their winners. The Barber and Odean study of the trading records of 10,000 clients of a large discount brokerage firm found a pronounced "disposition effect." There was a clear disposition among investors to sell their winning stocks and to hold on to their losing investments. Selling a stock that has risen enables investors to realize profits and build their self-esteem. If they sold their losing stocks, they would realize the painful effects of regret and loss.

This reluctance to take losses is clearly non-optimal according to rational investment theory and stupid in commonsense terms. Selling stocks with gains (outside tax-advantaged retirement accounts) involves paying capital gains taxes. Selling stock on which losses have been realized involves reducing taxes on other realized gains or a tax deduction, up to certain limits. Even if the investor believed that his losing stock would recover in the future, it would pay to sell the stock and purchase a stock in the same industry with similar prospects and risk characteristics. A similar reluctance to take losses appears to be evident in the residential housing market. When house prices are rising, the volume of sales rises and houses tend to sell quickly at asking prices or higher. During periods of falling prices, however, sales volumes decline and individuals let their homes sit on the market for long periods of time with asking prices well above market prices. Extreme loss aversion helps explain sellers' reluctance to sell their properties at a loss.

BEHAVIORAL FINANCE AND SAVINGS

Behavioral-finance theory also helps explain why many people refuse to join a 401(k) savings plan at work, even when their company matches their contributions. If one asks an employee who has become used to a particular level of take-home pay to increase his allocation to a retirement plan by one dollar, he will view the resulting deduction (even though it is less than a dollar because contributions to retirement plans are deductible from taxable income up to certain generous amounts) as a loss of current spending availability. Individuals weigh these losses much more heavily than gains. When this loss aversion is coupled with the difficulty of exhibiting self-control, the ease of procrastinating, and the ease of making no changes (status quo bias), it becomes, as psychologists teach us, perfectly understandable why people tend to save too little.

Two suggestions have been made to overcome people's reluctance to save. The first is to overcome inertia and status quo bias by changing the framing of the choice. We know that if we ask employees actively to sign up for a 401(k) savings plan, many will decline to join. But if the problem is framed differently, so that one must actively "opt out" of the savings plan, participation rates will be much greater. Corporations that frame their 401(k) savings plans with an automatic enrollment feature (where a conscious decision must be made to fill out an "opt out" declaration) have far higher participation rates than do plans where employees must actively "opt in" to the plan.

Another brilliant enticement has been developed by the economists Richard Thaler and Shlomo Benartzi. Some employees will decline to save even with plans that have automatic enrollment because they can barely make ends meet with their current salary. The essence of the Thaler-Benartzi "Save More Tomorrow" plan is to have employees commit in advance to allocate a portion of any salary increases toward retirement savings. If employees join the plan, their contribution to their retirement savings plan is increased, beginning with the first paycheck after a raise. This feature mitigates the perceived loss aversion of a cut in take-home pay. The contribution rate continues to increase on each scheduled raise until it reaches the maximum tax-deductible amount allowed by law. In this way, inertia and status quo bias work toward keeping people in the plan. The employee is allowed to opt out of the plan at any time.

Thaler and Benartzi first implemented their plan in 1998 at a midsize manufacturing company. The company was suffering from low participation in its retirement savings plan at the time. The Save More Tomorrow plan proved to be very popular. More than three-quarters of the employees of the firm agreed to join. In addition, over 80 percent of those employees stayed with it through subsequent pay raises. Even those who withdrew did not reduce their contribution rates to the original levels; they merely stopped the future increases from taking place. Thus, even these workers were saving significantly more than they had been before joining the plan.

THE LIMITS TO ARBITRAGE

Thus far we have considered the cognitive biases that influence investors and, therefore, security prices. The actions of individual investors are often irrational, or at least not fully consistent with the economist's ideal of optimal decision making. In perhaps the most pathological case, individuals appear to go mad in herds and bid some categories of stocks to unreasonable heights. Since the errors of irrational investors do not cancel out but often reinforce each other, how can stocks be efficiently priced? Believers in efficient markets rotely state that "arbitrage" will make the market efficient even if many individual investors are irrational. Arbitrageurs, such as professional Wall Street traders and hedge-fund managers, are expected to take offsetting positions—such as selling overpriced stocks short and buying underpriced ones—so that any mispricing caused by irrational investors is quickly corrected. Rational traders are expected to offset the impact of behavioral traders. Thus, the second major pillar on which some behavioralists rest their case against efficient markets is that such arbitrage is severely constrained. Behavioralists believe that important limits to arbitrage exist that prevent out-of-whack prices from being corrected.

Suppose irrational investors cause an oil company security to become overpriced relative to both its fundamental value and its peer oil companies. Arbitrageurs can simply sell the overpriced security short and buy a similar substitute oil company security. Thus, the arbitrageur is hedged in the sense that favorable or unfavorable events affecting the oil industry will influence both companies. A rise in the price of oil that makes the shorted security rise will make the arbitrageur's long position rise as well.

But this kind of arbitrage is extremely risky. Suppose the "overpriced" security reports some unusually good news, such as a significant oil strike that was not anticipated. Or suppose the "fairly valued" security suffers some unforeseen setback, such as the explosion of a deep-water oil well, which causes its price to fall. The arbitrageur could conceivably lose on both sides of the trade. The security that had been sold short could rise, and the security held long could fall. The kind of arbitrage required to correct perceived mispricings is extremely risky.

The trader who tries to "correct" perceived mispricings also runs the risk that investors will become even more overenthusiastic about the prospects for the "overpriced" security. Suppose an arbitrageur was convinced during 1999 that Internet stocks were outrageously overpriced. The trader might sell short the Internet favorites, hoping to buy them back later at lower prices. But as enthusiasm for the New Economy continued to grow, the prices of these stocks rose even further—many of them doubling and then doubling again. Only in retrospect do we know that the bubble burst during 2000. In the meantime, many traders lost their shirts. The market can remain irrational longer than the arbitrageur can remain solvent. This is especially true when the arbitrageur is credit constrained. Long Term Capital Management, a hedge fund in which Nobel laureates devised the strategies, found itself in an untenable position when the prices of its hedges moved against it and it had insufficient capital to keep them afloat.

The natural players in the game of selling overpriced securities short and buying underpriced ones are global hedge funds, with trillions of dollars to invest. One might suppose that these funds would have recognized the unsustainability of the prices of Internet stocks and exploited the mispricing by selling short. A study by Markus Brunnermeier and Stefan Nagel examined hedge-fund behavior during the 1998–2000 period to see whether these funds restrained the rise in speculative favorites.

The findings were surprising. Sophisticated speculators such as hedge funds were not a correcting force during the bubble period. They actually helped inflate the bubble by riding it rather than attacking it. Hedge funds were net buyers of Internet stocks throughout the 1998–early 2000 period. Their strategy reflected their belief that contagious enthusiasm and herding of unsophisticated investors would cause the mispricing to grow. They were playing the game described earlier in Keynes's famous newspaper beauty contest. While a stock selling at $30 might be "worth" only $15, it would be a good buy if some greater fools would be willing to pay $60 for the stock at some future time.

It appears that hedge funds also played a destabilizing role in the oil market during 2005 and 2006. From 2004 to 2006 the price of a barrel of crude oil more than doubled. Although economic forces such as the growth of the world economy provided some fundamental reasons for the upward price pressure, it seems that speculative activity, especially by hedge funds, helped fuel the advance. And the few hedge funds that went short in the oil futures market experienced substantial losses. It is clear that arbitrage trades to correct a perceived price bubble are inherently risky.

And there are also times when short selling is not possible or at least severely constrained. Typically in selling short, the security that is shorted is borrowed in order to deliver it to the buyer. If, for example, I sell short 100 shares of IBM, I must borrow the securities to be able to deliver them to the buyer. (I must also pay the buyer any dividends that are declared on the stock during the period I hold the short position.) In some cases it may be impossible to find stock to borrow, and thus it is technically impossible even to execute a short sale. In some of the most glaring examples of inefficient pricing, technical constraints on short selling prevented arbitrageurs from correcting the mispricing.

Arbitrages may also be hard to establish if a close substitute for the overpriced security is hard to find. For an arbitrage to be effective, there must be a similar fairly priced security that can be bought to offset the short position and that can be expected to rise if some favorable event occurs that influences the whole market or the sector to which the security belongs.

One of the best examples used by behavioralists to show that market prices can be inefficient is the case of two identical shares that do not trade at identical prices. Royal Dutch Petroleum and Shell Transport are considered Siamese twin companies. These companies agreed in 1907 to form an alliance and to split their after-tax profits 60 percent for Royal Dutch, 40 percent for Shell. In an efficient market, the market value of Royal Dutch should always be 1½ times as great as the market value of Shell. In fact, Royal Dutch has often traded at a premium to Shell of up to 20 percent over fair value. In efficient markets, the same cash flows ought to sell at equivalent valuations.

The problem with this example is that the two securities trade in different national markets with different rules and possibly different future restrictions. But even if Royal Dutch and Shell were considered equivalent in all respects, the arbitrage between the two securities would be inherently risky. If Royal Dutch sells at a 10 percent premium to Shell, the appropriate arbitrage is to sell the overpriced Royal Dutch shares short and buy the cheap Shell shares. The arbitrage is risky, however. An overpriced security can always become more overpriced, causing losses for the short seller. Bargains today can become better bargains tomorrow. It is clear that one cannot rely completely on arbitrage to smooth out any deviations of market prices from fundamental value. Constraints on short selling undoubtedly played a role in the propagation of the housing bubble during the end of the first decade of the 2000s. When it is virtually impossible to short housing in specific areas of the country, only the votes of the optimists get counted. When the optimists are able to leverage themselves easily with mortgage loans, it is easy to see why a housing bubble is unlikely to be constrained by arbitrage.

WHAT ARE THE LESSONS FOR INVESTORS FROM BEHAVIORAL FINANCE?

Night owls like myself often watch the late-night TV shows. One of the funnier bits from David Letterman's show was the segment "Stupid Pet Tricks," where pet owners have their animals perform all manner of dumb antics. Unfortunately, investors often act very much like the owners and pets on the TV show—and it isn't funny. They are overconfident, get trampled by the herd, harbor illusions of control, and refuse to recognize their investment mistakes. The pets actually look smart in comparison.

We have just seen how various aspects of human behavior influence investing. In investing, we are often our worst enemy. As Pogo put it, "We have met the enemy and it is us." An understanding of how vulnerable we are to our own psychology can help us avoid the stupid investor delusions that can screw up our financial security. There is an old adage about the game of poker: If you sit down at the table and can't figure out who the sucker is, get up and leave because it's you. These insights about investor psychology can keep you from being the patsy.

Charles Ellis, a longtime observer of stock markets and author of the brilliant investing book *Winning the Loser's Game*, observes that, in the game of amateur tennis, most points are won not by adroit plays on your part but rather by mistakes on the part of your opponent. So it is in investing. Ellis argues that most investors beat themselves by engaging in mistaken stock-market strategies rather than accepting the passive buy-and-hold indexing approach recommended in this book. The way most investors behave, the stock market becomes a loser's game.

How easy it was in early 2000, when the tech stock you bought moved persistently higher, to convince yourself that you were an investment genius. How easy it was then to convince yourself that chasing the last period's best-performing mutual fund was a sure strategy for success. And for the few who gave up their jobs during the bubble to engage in day-trading, how exhilarating it was to buy a stock at 10:00 a.m. and find that it had risen 10 percent by noon. All of these strategies ended in disaster. Frequent traders invariably earn lower returns than steady buy-and-hold investors.

The first step in dealing with the pernicious effects of our behavioral foibles is to recognize them. Bow to the wisdom of the market. Just as the tennis amateur who simply tries to return the ball with no fancy moves is the one who usually wins, so does the investor who simply buys and holds a diversified portfolio comprising all of the stocks that trade in the market. Don't be your own worst enemy: Avoid stupid investor tricks. Here are the most important insights from behavioral finance.

1. Avoid Herd Behavior

Behavioral financial economists understand the feedback mechanisms that lead investors to follow the crowd. When Internet stocks were consistently rising, it was hard not to get swept up in the euphoria—especially when all your friends were boasting of their spectacular stock-market profits. A large literature documents the pervasiveness of the influence of friends on one's investment decisions. Robert Shiller and John Pound surveyed 131 individual investors and asked what had drawn their attention to the stock they had most recently purchased. A typical response was that a personal contact, such as a friend or relative, had recommended the purchase. Hong, Kubik, and Stein provided more systematic evidence as to the importance of friends in influencing investors' decisions. They found that social households—those who interact with their neighbors, or attend church—are substantially more likely to invest in the market than nonsocial households, controlling for wealth, race, education, and risk tolerance.

Any investment that has become a topic of widespread conversation is likely to be especially hazardous to your wealth. It was true of gold in the early 1980s and Japanese real estate and stocks in the late 1980s. It was true of Internet-related stocks in the late 1990s and early 2000 and condominiums in California, Nevada, and Florida in the first decade of the 2000s.

Invariably, the hottest stocks or funds in one period are the worst performers in the next. And just as herding induces investors to take greater and greater risks during periods of euphoria, so the same behavior often leads many investors simultaneously to throw in the towel when pessimism is rampant. The media tend to encourage such self-destructive behavior by hyping the severity of market declines and blowing the events out of proportion to gain viewers and listeners. Even without excessive media attention, large market movements encourage buy and sell decisions that are based on emotion rather than on logic.

Because of bad timing, the typical mutual-fund investor earns a rate of return from the stock market far below the returns that would be earned by simply buying and holding a market index fund. This is because investors tend to put their money into mutual funds at or near market tops (when everyone is enthusiastic) and to pull their money out at market bottoms (when pessimism reigns). The exhibit on page 255 makes the point. In the chart, we see that net new cash flow into mutual funds peaked when the market reached a high in early 2000. At the market trough in the fall of 2002, investors pulled their money out. In late 2008 and early 2009, just at the bottom of the market during the financial crisis, more money went out of the market than ever before. You can see the effects of this timing penalty in the chart.

There is also a selection penalty. At the peak of the market in early 2000, money flowed into "growth"-oriented mutual funds, typically those associated with high technology and the Internet, and flowed out of "value" funds, those funds holding old-economy stocks that sold at low prices relative to their book values and earnings. Over the next three years, the "value" funds provided generous positive returns to their investors, and "growth" funds declined sharply. During the third quarter of 2002, after an 80 percent decline from the peak of the NASDAQ Index, there were large redemptions out of growth funds. Chasing today's hot investment usually leads to tomorrow's investment freeze.

DO NOT TRY TO TIME THE MARKET:
FLOWS TO EQUITY FUNDS RELATED TO GLOBAL STOCK-PRICE
PERFORMANCE

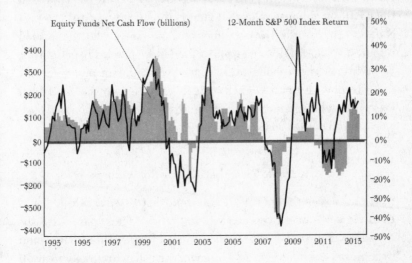

2. Avoid Overtrading

Behavioral finance specialists have found that investors tend to be overconfident in their judgments and invariably do too much trading for their own financial well-being. Many investors move from stock to stock or from mutual fund to mutual fund as if they were selecting and discarding cards in a game of gin rummy. Investors accomplish nothing from this behavior except to incur transactions costs and to pay more in taxes. Short-term gains are taxed at regular income tax rates. The buy-and-hold investor defers any tax payments on the gains and may avoid taxes completely if stocks are held until distributed as part of one's estate. Remember the advice of the legendary investor Warren Buffett: Lethargy bordering on sloth remains the best investment style. The correct holding period for the stock market is forever.

The cost of overtrading is quite substantial. Using data on the trading behavior of approximately 66,000 households during the period 1991–96, Barber and Odean found that the average household in the sample earned an annual return of 16.4 percent, while the market returned 17.9 percent. In contrast, the annual return to the portfolio of households that traded the most was only 11.4 percent. In other words, the portfolios of those households that traded the most substantially underperformed more passive benchmarks. In addition, men tended to be more overconfident and trade far more frequently than women. Odean's advice to investors: If you are contemplating making a stock trade (and you are married), ask your wife whether you should do it.

3. If You Do Trade: Sell Losers, Not Winners

We have seen that people are far more distressed at taking losses than they are overjoyed at realizing gains. Thus, paradoxically, investors might take greater risks to avoid losses than they would to achieve equivalent gains. Moreover, investors are likely to avoid selling stocks or mutual funds that went down, in order to avoid the realization of a loss and the necessity of admitting that they made a mistake. On the other hand, investors are generally willing to discard their winners because that enables them to enjoy the success of being correct.

Sometimes, it is sensible to hold on to a stock that has declined during a market meltdown, especially if you have reason to believe the company is still successful. Moreover, you would suffer double the regret if you sold it and the stock subsequently went up. But it makes no sense to hold on to losing stocks such as Enron and WorldCom because of the mistaken belief that if you don't sell, you have not taken a loss. A "paper loss" is just as real as a realized loss. The decision not to sell is exactly the same as the decision to buy the stock at the current price. Moreover, if you own the stock in a taxable account, selling allows you to take a tax loss, and the government will help cushion the blow by lowering the amount of your taxes. Selling your winners will add to your tax burden.

4. Other Stupid Investor Tricks

Be Wary of New Issues. Do you think you can make lots of money by getting in on the ground floor of the initial public offering (IPO) of a company just coming to market? Particularly during the great Internet bubble that collapsed in 2000, it seemed that IPOs were the sure path to riches. Some successful IPOs began trading at two, three, and (in one case) even seven times the price at which they were first offered to the public. No wonder some investors came to believe that getting in on an IPO was the easiest way to coin money in the stock market.

My advice is that you should not buy IPOs at their initial offering price and that you should never buy an IPO just after it begins trading at prices that are generally higher than the IPO price. Historically, IPOs have been a bad deal. In measuring all IPOs five years after their initial issuance, researchers have found that IPOs underperform the total stock market by about 4 percentage points per year. The poor performance starts about six months after the issue is sold. Six months is generally set as the "lock-up" period, where insiders are prohibited from selling stock to the public. Once that constraint is lifted, the price of the stock often tanks.

The investment results are even poorer for individual investors. You will never be allowed to buy the really good IPOs at the initial offering price. The hot IPOs are snapped up by the big institutional investors or the very best wealthy clients of the underwriting firm. If your broker calls to say that IPO shares will be available for you, you can bet that the new issue is a dog. Only if the brokerage firm is unable to sell the shares to the big institutions and the best individual clients will you be offered a chance to buy at the initial offering price. Hence, it will systematically turn out that you will be buying only the poorest of the new issues. There is no strategy I am aware of likely to lose you more money, except perhaps the horse races or the gaming tables of Las Vegas.

Stay Cool to Hot Tips. We've all heard the stories. Your uncle Gene knows about a diamond mine in Zaire that's a guaranteed winner. Please remember that a mine is usually a hole in the ground with a liar standing in front of it. Your cousin's sister-in-law Gertrude was told confidentially about an undiscovered little biotech company. "It's a screaming bargain. It's selling at only a dollar a share, and they're ready to announce a cure for cancer. Think, for $2,000 you can buy 2,000 shares." Tips come at you from all fronts—friends, relatives, the telephone, even the Internet. Don't go there. Steer clear of any hot tips. They are overwhelmingly likely to be the poorest investments of your life. And remember: Never buy anything from someone who is out of breath.

Distrust Foolproof Schemes. You will be told by amateurs and professionals alike that schemes exist to pick the best fund managers and to keep you out of the market when prices are falling. The sad fact is that it can't be done. Sure, there are portfolio strategies that in hindsight produced above-average returns, but they all self-destruct over time. There are even market-timing strategies that have been successful for years and even decades. In the long run, though, I agree with Bernard Baruch, a legendary investor of the early twentieth century, who said, "Market timing can only be accomplished by liars." And Jack Bogle, a legend of the late twentieth century, has remarked, "I do not know of anybody who has done it [market timing] successfully and consistently."

Investors should also never forget the age-old maxim "If something is too good to be true, it is too good to be true." Heeding this maxim could have saved investors from falling prey to the largest Ponzi scheme ever: the Bernard L. Madoff fraud uncovered in 2008, in which $50 billion was said to have been lost. The real con in the Madoff affair is that people fell for the myth that Madoff could consistently earn between 10 and 12 percent a year for investors in his fund.

The "genius" of the fraud was that Madoff offered what seemed to be a modest and safe return. Had he offered a 50 percent return, people might well have been skeptical of such pie-in-the-sky promises. But consistent returns of 10 to 12 percent per year seemed well within the realm of possibility. In fact, however, earning such returns year after year in the stock market (or in any other market) is not remotely possible, and such claims should have been a dead giveaway. The U.S. stock market may have averaged over 9 percent a year over long periods of time, but only with tremendous volatility, including years when investors have lost as much as 40 percent of their capital. The only way Madoff could report such a performance was by cooking the books. And don't count on the regulators to protect you from such fraudulent schemes. The SEC was warned that Madoff's results were impossible, but the agency failed to act. Your only protection is to realize that anything that seems too good to be true undoubtedly is untrue.

DOES BEHAVIORAL FINANCE TEACH
WAYS TO BEAT THE MARKET?

Some behavioralists believe that the systematic errors of investors can provide opportunities for unemotional, rational investors to beat the market. They believe that irrational trading creates predictable stock-market patterns that can be exploited by wise investors. These ideas are far more controversial than the lessons provided above, and we will examine some of them in the next chapter.

11

IS "SMART BETA" REALLY SMART?

The clairvoyant society of London will not meet Tuesday
because of unforeseen circumstances.
—An advertisement in the *Financial Times*

THERE IS A new hotshot investment strategy in portfolio management called "smart beta." With the implicit promise that it can improve portfolio performance, it has attracted hundreds of billions of dollars in assets and is growing by leaps and bounds. It is important that investors be aware of the strengths and weaknesses of "smart beta" strategies and the role they might play in their investment plans.

This chapter explains what "smart beta" is, what kinds of funds pursue this strategy, and why so many people are excited about it. It shows why "smart beta" flunks a safety test, and why it is not as smart as it claims to be. The chapter concludes that "smart beta" is not a smart way to go for the individual investor, and it argues that the tried-and-true approach—investing in low-cost, broad-based, capitalization-weighted index funds—is still the best way to build an investment portfolio.

WHAT IS "SMART BETA"?

There is no universally accepted definition of "smart beta" investment strategies. What most people who use the term have in mind is that it may be possible to gain excess (greater than market) returns by using a variety of relatively passive investment strategies that involve no more risk than would be assumed by investing in a low-cost Total Stock Market index fund.

I have argued in earlier chapters that the core of every investment portfolio should consist of low-cost, tax-efficient, broad-based index funds. Indeed, from the first edition of this book in 1973—even before index funds existed—I urged that they be created because such funds would serve investors far better than expensive, tax-inefficient, actively managed funds. By holding a portfolio containing all the stocks in the market, in proportion to their relative size or capitalization (the number of shares outstanding times the price of their shares), the investor would be guaranteed to receive the market return. Such a fund would minimize trading costs and be tax efficient. If one company doubled in value (and therefore its weight in the index increased), the investor's portfolio would automatically reflect the change, and no trading would be required. Moreover, the substantial evidence cited in earlier chapters makes clear that index funds generally provide higher net returns for investors than actively managed funds that try to beat the market.

If an investor buys a low-cost Total (U.S.) Stock Market index fund, as I have recommended, she will receive the market rate of return as well as assume the risks of the characteristic ups and downs of the U.S. stock market. Remember that the volatility of the market is measured by beta and that the beta of the market is defined to have a value of 1, as presented in the discussion of the capital-asset pricing model in chapter 9. Now what the "smart beta" investment managers would have us believe is that pure indexing, where each company has a weight in the portfolio given by the size of the company's total capitalization, is not an optimal strategy. They claim that one doesn't have to be a stock picker, as most active portfolio managers are, to be able to beat the market. Rather, you can manage a relatively passive (low turnover) portfolio to accomplish good results more dependably without assuming any extra risk. And you can do so at a fee well below that charged by active managers. The trick is to tilt (or flavor) the portfolio in some direction such as "value" versus "growth," smaller versus larger companies, relatively strong stocks versus weak, and low-volatility stocks versus high-volatility ones.

Other tilts or flavors that have been suggested include "quality" (encompassing attributes such as stable sales and earnings growth, and low leverage), profitability, high dividends, and liquidity. Just as good cooking blends a number of food flavors, some "smart beta" portfolios mix two or more flavors together. There are portfolios that blend "value" and "small size" as well as those that mix several of the flavors mentioned above. Moreover, all this can be accomplished without increasing the expected volatility (beta level) of the "smart beta" portfolio.*

FOUR TASTY FLAVORS: THEIR PROS AND CONS

1. Value Wins

The Positives. In 1934, David L. Dodd and Benjamin Graham published a manifesto for investors that has attracted strong adherents, including the legendary Warren Buffett. They argued that "value" wins over time. To find "value," investors should look for stocks with low price-earnings ratios and low prices relative to book value. "Value" is based on current realities rather than on projections of future growth. The resulting theory is consistent with the views of behavioralists that investors tend to be overconfident in their ability to project high earnings growth and thus overpay for "growth" stocks.

I have considerable intellectual sympathy with this approach. One of my cardinal rules of stock selection is to look for companies with

---

*"Smart beta" strategies are related to the multifactor models discussed in chapter 9. If one assumes that the beta of the capital-asset pricing model is an incomplete measure of risk, the tilts or flavors listed above can be considered additional risk factors. By tilting the portfolio toward smaller companies, for example, the investor is making a bet that the risk premium that is available from smaller companies can enhance returns. Here, of course, "smart beta" is interpreted as a technique to enhance returns by assuming additional risk.

good growth prospects that have yet to be discovered by the stock market and sell at relatively low earning multiples. This approach is often described as GARP, "growth at a reasonable price." I have warned investors repeatedly about the dangers of fashionable high-multiple stocks. Particularly because earnings growth is so hard to forecast, it's far better to be in low-multiple stocks. If growth does materialize, both the earnings and the earnings multiple will likely increase, giving the investor a double benefit. Buying a high-multiple stock whose earnings growth fails to materialize subjects investors to a double whammy. Both the earnings and the multiple can fall.

There is some evidence that a portfolio of stocks with relatively low earnings multiples (as well as low multiples of book value, cash flow, and/or sales) produces above-average rates of return even after adjustment for risk, as measured by the capital-asset pricing model. For example, the figure that follows shows the return from ten equal-sized groups of stocks, ranked by their P/E ratios. Group 1 had the lowest P/Es, Group 2 the second lowest, and so on. The figure shows that as the P/E of a group of stocks increased, the return decreased.

AVERAGE ANNUAL RETURNS VS. P/E RATIO

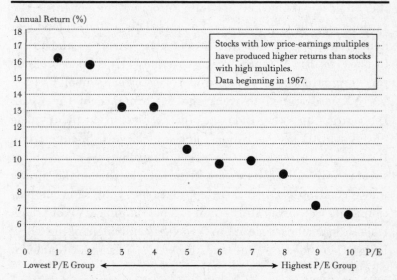

Source: Stern School of Business, New York University.

Another predictable pattern of return is the relationship between the ratio of a stock's price to its book value (the value of the company's assets as recorded on its books) and its later return. Stocks that sell at low ratios of price to book value tend to produce higher future returns. This pattern appears to hold for both U.S. and many foreign stock markets, as has been shown by Fama and French, whose work was described in chapter 9.

The Negatives. Never forget that low P/E multiples and low price-to-book-value (P/BV) ratios can reflect risk factors that are priced into the market. Companies in some degree of financial distress are likely to sell at low prices relative to earnings and book values. For example, the big money center banks such as Citigroup and Bank of America sold at prices well below their reported book values during 2009, when it appeared that these institutions could quite possibly be taken over by the government and the stockholders' equity be wiped out.

Portfolio Examples. It is possible to purchase portfolios that divide the broad stock-market portfolio into two components—the "value" and the "growth" components. The "value" component holds those stocks with the lowest price-earnings and price-to-book ratios. A representative "value" ETF sponsored by the Vanguard Group trades under the ticker symbol VVIAX. VVIAX is designed to track the performance of the CRSP U.S. LargeCap Value Index, a broadly diversified index made up predominantly of "value" stocks of large U.S. companies. It attempts to replicate the target index by investing all, or substantially all, of its assets in the stocks that make up the index, holding each stock in approximately the same proportion as its weighting in the index. The Vanguard VIGAX ETF tracks the performance of the "growth" component of the CRSP Large-Cap Index. "Value" and "growth" ETFs are available for smallcap broad indexes as well.

2. Smaller Is Better

The Positives. Another pattern that academic investigators have found in stock returns is the tendency over long periods of time for small-company stocks to generate larger returns than those of large-company stocks. Since 1926, according to Ibbotson Associates, small company stocks in the United States have produced rates of return about 2 percentage points higher than the returns from large-company stocks. The diagram that follows shows the work of Fama and French, who divided stocks into deciles according to their size. They found that decile 1, the 10 percent of stocks with the smallest total capitalization, produced the highest rates of return, whereas decile 10, the largest capitalization stocks, produced the lowest rate of return. Moreover, small firms tended to outperform larger firms with the same beta levels.

AVERAGE MONTHLY RETURNS VS. SIZE: 1963–1990

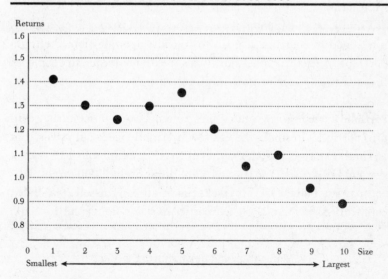

Portfolios of smaller firms have tended to produce higher rates of return than portfolios of larger firms.

Source: Fama and French, "The Cross-Section of Expected Stock Returns," *Journal of Finance* (June 1992).

The Negatives. Nevertheless, we need to remember that small firms may be riskier than larger firms and deserve to give investors a higher rate of return. Thus, even if the "small-firm effect" were to persist in the future, such a finding would not violate market efficiency. A finding that small-company stocks outperform the stocks of larger companies on a risk-adjusted basis depends upon how one measures risk. Beta, the risk measure typically used in the studies that have found "excess" returns from small firms, may be an incomplete measure of risk. We cannot distinguish whether the abnormal returns are truly the result of inefficiencies, or whether they result from inadequacies in our measure of risk. The higher returns for smaller companies may simply be the requisite reward owed to investors for assuming greater risk. Moreover, the small-firm effect found in some studies may simply flow from what is called survivorship bias. Today's list of companies includes only small firms that have survived—not the small firms that later went bankrupt.

Finally, the dependability of the small-firm effect and its likelihood to continue is open to considerable question. Buying a portfolio of small firms is hardly a surefire technique to enable an investor to earn abnormally high returns.

Portfolio Examples. Investable instruments are available that contain portfolios of stocks skewed toward small-sized companies, that is, small-cap stocks. For example, the ETF trading under the ticker symbol IWB tracks the Russell 1000 Index of the 1,000 largest U.S. companies. The ETF IWN tracks the small-cap Russell 2000 Index containing the next 2,000 companies in size (total capitalization).

3. Momentum and Reversion to the Mean

The Positives. The earliest empirical work on the behavior of stock prices, going back to the early 1900s, found that a sequence of random numbers had the same appearance as a time series of stock prices. But even though the earliest studies supported a general finding of randomness, more recent work indicated that the random-walk model does not strictly hold. Some patterns appear to exist in the development of stock prices. Over short holding periods, there is some evidence of momentum in the stock market. Increases in stock prices are slightly more likely to be followed by further increases than by price declines. For longer holding periods, reversion to the mean appears to be present. When large price increases have been experienced over a period of months or years, such increases are often followed by sharp reversals.

Two possible explanations for the existence of momentum have been offered: the first is based on behavioral considerations; the second, on sluggish responses to new information. Robert Shiller, one of the leaders in the field of behavioral finance, emphasized in 2000 a psychological feedback mechanism imparting a degree of momentum into stock prices, especially during periods of extreme enthusiasm. Individuals see stock prices rising and are drawn into the market in a kind of "bandwagon effect." The second explanation is based on the argument that investors do not adjust their expectations immediately when news arises—especially news of company earnings that exceeded (or fell short of) anticipation. Some investigators have found that abnormally high returns follow positive earnings surprises as market prices appear to respond only gradually to earnings information.

While there is some evidence supporting the existence of short-term momentum in the stock market, other studies have documented negative serial correlation—that is, return reversals—over longer holding periods. A considerable amount of the variation in long holding period returns can be predicted in terms of a negative correlation with past returns.

Some studies have attributed this forecastability to the tendency of stock-market prices to "overreact." They argue that investors are subject to waves of optimism and pessimism that cause prices to deviate systematically from their fundamental values and later to exhibit reversion to the mean. They suggest that such overreaction to past events is consistent with behavioral factors, where investors are systematically overconfident of their ability to forecast either future stock prices or future corporate earnings. These findings give some support to investment techniques that rest on a "contrarian" strategy, that is, buying those stocks, or groups of stocks, that have been out of favor for long periods of time.

The Negatives. However, the findings of short-term momentum and longer-term reversion to the mean are not uniform across studies and are quite a bit weaker in some periods than in others. Moreover, it may not be possible to profit from the tendency for individual stocks to exhibit return reversals. A study of mine simulated a strategy of buying stocks over a thirteen-year period that had particularly poor returns over the preceding three to five years. The study found that stocks with very low returns over the preceding three to five years had higher returns in the next period and that stocks with very high returns over the preceding three to five years had lower returns in the next period. Thus, there was very strong *statistical* evidence of return reversals. However, the returns in the next period were similar for both groups. A contrarian approach, therefore, did not yield higher-than-average returns. There was a statistically strong pattern of return reversal, but not one that implied an inefficiency in the market that would enable investors to make excess returns.

Portfolio Examples. There are investment funds and ETFs that tilt the portfolio toward stocks that are exhibiting relative strength compared with the whole market. The fund AMOMX, sponsored by the investment firm AQR, invests in large-cap and mid-cap companies traded on a principal U.S. exchange or the over-the-counter market that are determined to have positive momentum. Positive momentum is often considered to be strong relative to performance over the preceding twelve months (not including the most recent month, to allow for any short-term return reversals).

4. Low Volatility Can Produce High Returns

The Positives. In order to understand the rationale for various low-volatility "smart beta" strategies, we need to refer back to the capital-asset pricing model (CAPM), covered in chapter 9. According to CAPM, risk and return are related to beta, a measure of the relative volatility (or nondiversifiable risk) of any stock or portfolio. According to the theory, the higher the beta (risk) of any stock or portfolio, the higher should be the return. As was shown in chapter 9, however, the empirical support for the theory is weak. High-beta portfolios do not produce higher returns than low-beta ones. The relationship between beta and return is relatively flat both in the United States and internationally.

Investors can use this fact to fashion a variety of "betting against beta" portfolio strategies. For example, suppose very low beta portfolios have a beta of ½ (they are half as volatile as the broad market portfolio) but produce the same return as the market, which by definition has a beta of 1. Suppose the market return was 10 percent. By buying a low-beta portfolio on margin (putting up fifty cents for each dollar of market value), an investor could double the beta and double the return of the low-beta portfolio as is illustrated below.

LEVERAGING A LOW-BETA PORTFOLIO

	Buy the Market Portfolio	Buy the Low-Beta Portfolio	Buy the Low-Beta* Portfolio on Margin
Average Return	+10%	+10%	+20%
Beta	1	½	1

* To keep the illustration simple we assume zero interest is paid on the margin loan.

It is easy to see how the margin borrowing increases both the return and the volatility of the portfolios. For every $100 of value purchased, the investor puts up only $50 and borrows the other $50. The $100 portfolio increases 10 percent, to $110. But the investor's ownership stake increases 20 percent as shown below.

EFFECT OF LEVERAGE ON GAIN AND BETA

	Before	After 10% Gain	Percentage Gain
Portfolio Value	$100	$110	10%
Borrowing	50	50	–
Investor's Equity	50	60	20%

Of course, the enhanced gain is realized at the expense of double the volatility. If the portfolio value decreased by 10 percent, to $90, the investor's stake would be reduced to $40, a 20 percent decline. Therefore, the low-volatility portfolio (with a beta of ½) will have double the underlying volatility of the stocks held.

The Negatives. There are other flavors of the low-volatility strategy. For example, an investor might buy (go long) the 10 percent of the stocks with the lowest volatility and sell short the 10 percent of the stocks with the highest volatility. Whichever strategy the investor employs, she ends up with quite a different and less diversified portfolio than if she bought and held the market portfolio, the strategy favored in this book. Low-volatility portfolios tend to be concentrated in utility stocks as well as in large pharmaceutical companies. Relatively undiversified portfolios are a characteristic of all the "smart beta" strategies.

Portfolio Examples. Low-volatility ETFs hold portfolios of stocks with the lowest measured volatility relative to their benchmarks. For example, the SPLV ETF sponsored by PowerShares holds the 100 least-volatile stocks in the S&P 500. It does not adjust for resulting sector biases and thus holds nearly one-third of its portfolio in utility stocks. An investor could buy SPLV on margin to replicate a strategy of leveraging the portfolio up to a beta of 1.

Blended Flavors and Strategies

Dimensional Fund Advisors Funds. Dimensional Fund Advisors (DFA) offers mutual funds sold through investment advisers. The funds are formed by selecting stocks quantitatively based on the Fama-French criteria of value and size discussed in chapter 9. The DFA funds contain stocks having the lowest ratios of price-to-book value, as well as those with the lowest market capitalization (size). The DFA large-cap value fund (DFLVX) is a value-tilted portfolio of large-cap stocks. DFSVX is a value-tilted portfolio of small-cap stocks designed to capture both the "size" and the "value" effects. The Fama-French work suggests that the effects exist not only in the United States but internationally as well. Thus, DFA offers international funds and domestic ones. DFA states that they may also blend other flavors into their portfolios, such as "quality," when conditions warrant.

RAFI "Fundamental Indexes."™ The firm Research Affiliates has designed both domestic and international portfolios based on "trademarked indexes" it believes are vastly superior to standard indexes, which are capitalization weighted. The RAFI ETF PRF weights stocks in the Russell 1000 Index not by total capitalization but by their "economic footprint." The RAFI Fundamental Index™ weights each stock by fundamental measures of worth such as sales, earnings, and book values, rather than by total capitalization.

In fact, the RAFI procedures tilt the portfolio toward the same value and size factors that are present in other "smart beta" portfolios. Consider two companies with equal earnings, but company A sells at 25 times earnings while company B sells at 12½ times earnings. With capitalization weighting, company A gets twice the weight of company B. Under Fundamental Indexing they both get the same weight. Thus, value stocks (with low P/Es) and small-capitalization stocks are overweighted relative to their weights in standard cap-weighted indexes.

Equal-Weighted Indexes. As the name implies, these portfolios give equal weight to all the stocks contained in the index. The ETF EWRI sponsored by Guggenheim Investments gives equal weight to each of the stocks in the Russell 1000 large-cap index. As with the RAFI portfolio, this procedure introduces both a size and a value tilt to the ETF.

"SMART BETA" FUNDS FLUNK THE RISK TEST

Appraisal of "Smart Beta"

All "smart beta" strategies represent active management rather than indexing. Capitalization-weighted portfolios are the market. If you believe a subset of securities will give you superior returns, you are counting on some "dumb" investors to hold portfolios producing poorer returns. Some "smart beta" advocates have been quite explicit in suggesting who these dumb investors might be. They claim that the investors in traditional capitalization index funds are the dumb beta investors, since by holding the broad index they will be holding a number of overvalued growth stocks. *But that argument must be false.* The holder of a broad-based index fund will by definition achieve the average return for the market. If "smart beta" funds generate above average returns, it can't be at the expense of traditional index-fund investors—it must be at the expense of all active managers who do not hold the market portfolio.

- To the extent that "smart beta" funds do generate excess returns, it is most likely because they are assuming greater risks. By tilting in one direction or another—small size, for example—investors will be less diversified and exposed to greater risk than those associated with the broad-market portfolio. Managers such as DFA readily admit that whatever higher returns such funds may generate are simply compensation for the extra risks assumed. Over its history, the entire above-market returns for the RAFI Fundamental Index™ portfolio were achieved during 2009, when the proportion of bank stocks in the portfolio was more than twice as large as the weight in the benchmark index and almost 15 percent of the portfolio was invested in two stocks, Citigroup and Bank of America. The "bet" worked but was certainly risky, since it was unclear whether banks would avoid nationalization and a "zeroing out" of the banks' shareholders. "Smart beta" portfolios may not have high betas, but they do carry considerable risk.
- When "smart beta" portfolios are assessed with multifactor risk models (such as the Fama-French three-factor model or extensions of it), the typical finding is that no excess risk-adjusted performance is demonstrated. "Smart beta" portfolios do not produce alphas.
- "Smart beta" funds require periodic rebalancing. For example,

in order for an equally weighted fund to maintain its equal weighting, stocks that have gone up more than average must be pared back. In a rising market, the trading involves transactions costs and short-term capital gains taxes. "Smart beta" funds and ETFs also carry considerably higher management expenses than traditional capitalization-weighted index funds.

- All "smart beta" portfolios have undergone long periods of underperformance. There is considerable evidence of "reversion to the mean," and periods of excess performance are often followed by periods of disappointing results.

- Mutual funds (and ETFs) designed to capture momentum and low-beta effects have not demonstrated superior performance. Often real money results differ from those simulated returns demonstrated in academic studies.

- Whether "smart beta" strategies will perform well in the future depends crucially on the market valuations existing at the time the strategy is implemented. "Value" strategies performed extraordinarily well coming out of the Internet bubble when high-tech "growth" stocks were priced extremely richly relative to "value" stocks. Similarly, small-company stocks did particularly well when they were inexpensively priced relative to large-cap stocks. Particularly as these strategies become increasingly popular, the stocks favored by those techniques will become more richly priced, and results could prove disappointing. No strategy will be effective irrespective of valuation relationships.

- Finally, many of the "smart beta" ETFs are more costly to buy and sell than their traditional cap-weighted brethren. Plain vanilla, such as S&P 500, index ETFs trade at prices essentially the same as their net asset values because any differences tend to be quickly arbitraged away. Many "smart beta" ETFs follow nonstandard indexes that are far more difficult to hedge against. Hence, their prices are more likely to deviate from fair value and often trade at significant premiums or discounts from the value of their underlying holdings. Moreover, the successful "smart beta" funds offered by DFA can only be purchased from investment advisers, adding an additional layer of fees.

HOW WELL HAVE FACTOR TILTS WORKED
IN PRACTICE?

Mutual funds and exchange-traded funds are available that allow investors to implement each of the "smart beta" strategies considered above. Here we will examine the actual records of some of the funds and ETFs that mimic each of the four major strategies (portfolio flavors or tilts) that have been advocated, as well as some that employ blended flavors. Information about each of the funds or ETFs listed can be found in the Random Walker's Address Book included as an appendix.

Value and Size Tilts

Mutual Fund and ETF Portfolios. The strongest academic evidence supporting "smart beta" portfolios is the tendency of "value" stocks to outperform "growth" stocks and the tendency of "small-cap" portfolios to outperform "large-cap" ones. Here is where the academic literature is unambiguously supportive.

But we must remember that the results of published studies— even those done over decades—may still be time dependent, and we must ask whether the return patterns of academic studies can actually be generated with real money. The chart that follows presents average actual returns generated by mutual funds classified by either their "growth" or their "value" objectives. "Value" funds are so classified if they buy stocks with low P/E multiples and low P/BV ratios. We see that over a period going back to the 1930s, it does not appear that investors could actually have realized higher rates of return from mutual funds specializing in "value" stocks. Indeed, the chart suggests that the period studied by Fama and French from the early 1960s (demonstrating a strong "value" effect) may have been a unique period in which "value" stocks rather consistently produced higher rates of return.

The top chart on the next page was compiled from the records of actively managed funds. For more-recent periods, we can repeat the analysis with "smart beta" indexed ETFs, which now exist. The bottom chart shows the exact same pattern repeated with indexed

"GROWTH" FUNDS VS. "VALUE" FUNDS, 1937–2013

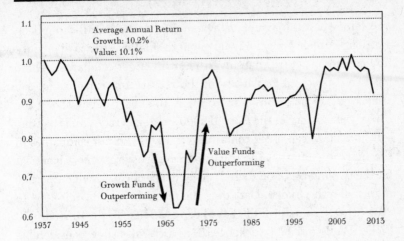

The chart shows the return of "Value" mutual funds divided by the return of "Growth" mutual funds. A number above (below) 1 indicates that "Value" is outperforming (underperforming) "Growth."
Source: Bogle Research Institute.

ETF portfolios that were available during the ten years from 2004 to 2013. Investors looking for a decade of outperformance with "value" ETFs would have been disappointed. Neither the mutual funds nor the ETFs with a "value" mandate would have produced above-average returns.

REVERSION TO THE MEAN: "GROWTH" INDEX VS. "VALUE" INDEX ETFs 2004–2013

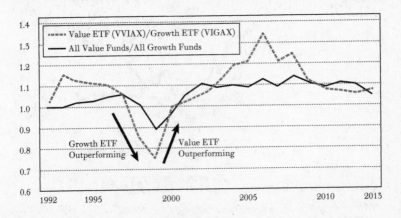

The chart shows the return of "Value" mutual funds (Value ETF) divided by the return of "Growth" mutual funds (Growth ETF). A number above (below) 1 indicates that "Value" is outperforming (underperforming) "Growth."
Source: Bogle Research Institute.

A somewhat similar story can be told about the "small-cap" effect. The long-run tendency for investment in smaller firms is to produce higher rates of return than investments in larger companies. There has been substantial volatility in the relative returns of small-cap and large-cap portfolios. For example, the chart below shows the thirty-year history of the Russell 2000 small-cap index and the Russell 1000 large-cap index containing the 1,000 largest companies in the market. Note that the thirty-year returns are almost identical for the two indexes, and there is no evidence of consistent outperformance of either index. Data over the ten-year period from 2004 to 2014, when investable ETFs have been available for the Russell 1000 (ticker IWB) and 2000 (ticker IMB) indexes, also show considerable reversion to the mean, although smaller companies have produced average annual returns almost 1 percentage point greater than the returns for larger companies during this period.

RUSSELL 2000 (SMALL-CAP) INDEX VS. RUSSELL 1000 (LARGE-CAP) INDEX (30-YEAR)

IWM (RUSSELL 2000) ETF VS. IWB (RUSSELL 1000) ETF (10-YEAR)

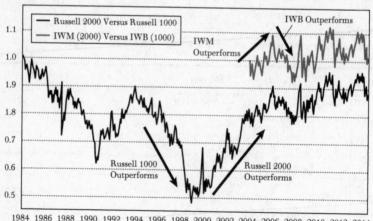

Russell 2000 Average Annual Return (since 04/02/1984): 8.31%
Russell 1000 Average Annual Return (since 04/02/1984): 8.78%

IWM 2000 Average Annual Return (since 04/01/2004): 8.07%
IWB 1000 Average Annual Return (since 04/01/2004): 7.97%

The chart shows the returns of the Russell 2000 index (ETF) divided by the returns of the Russell 1000 index (ETF). A number above (below) 1 indicates that the Russell 2000 is outperforming (underperforming) the Russell 1000.
Source: Morningstar.

BLENDED HYBRID STRATEGIES

We have called blended strategies those that depart indirectly from capitalization weighting in an attempt to benefit from the factor tilts of "value" and "size" that have figured prominently in the academic literature. The two principal strategies are those of equal weighting and the Research Affiliates Fundamental Index™. Both give the portfolio a (small) "size" and "value" tilt.

The Dimensional Fund Advisors (DFA) Portfolios. DFA funds have experienced somewhat better performance than many of the other "smart beta" offerings available to investors. They are generally low cost with expense ratios only moderately higher than the fees of broad-based capitalization-weighted ETFs. However, they are sold only through investment advisers. The investment advisers from whom DFA funds are available are "fee only"—that is, they do not collect extra commissions for placing investors in particular funds. Thus, these advisers tend to be unconflicted, unlike other advisers. Nevertheless, they charge advisory fees that could range up to 1 percent or more, and therefore the extra returns that have been available from many DFA funds need to be reduced by these advisory fees. Do-it-yourself investors who do not need the hand-holding services of an adviser can avoid this substantial extra layer of costs by buying standard index funds.

On page 278 we show the performance of two DFA funds over a ten-year period ending in April 2014. Note that both the DFA small-cap value fund (ticker DFSVX) and the large-cap value fund (ticker DFLVX) have outperformed their benchmarks by over 1 percentage point. Again, however, we need to emphasize that DFA is quite explicit that any extra returns represent an appropriate compensation for the added risk of the portfolios. Note also that the DFA funds, like all the "smart beta" funds, experience periods of underperformance.

DFA LARGE-CAP VALUE (DFLVX) AND DFA SMALL-CAP VALUE (DFSVX) VS. BENCHMARKS (10-YEAR)

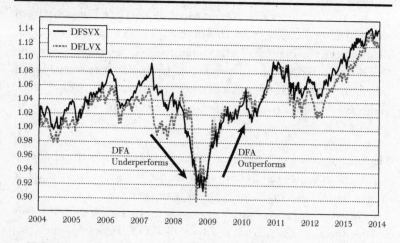

DFLVX Benchmark: IWD   DFSVX Benchmark: IWN

DFA Large-Cap Value Annual Return (since 04/01/2004): 8.92%
Russell 1000 Value Annual Return (since 04/01/2004): 7.65%

DFA Small-Cap Value Annual Return (since 04/01/2004): 9.12%
Russell 2000 Value Annual Return (since 04/01/2004): 7.49%

The chart shows the return of the "smart beta" strategy divided by the return of the benchmark index. A number above (below) 1 indicates that the "smart beta" fund is outperforming (underperforming) the benchmark index.
Source: Morningstar.

Research Affiliates Fundamental Index™ (RAFI)

By the criterion of commercial success, the RAFI "smart beta" funds are among the most impressive of all the new fund offerings. The founder of Research Affiliates, Robert Arnott, is able to hold audiences spellbound as he argues that cap weighting implies that holders of such portfolios will always be holding too big a share of overpriced growth stocks. He avoids this problem by adjusting the weight of each stock to its economic footprint such as earnings, assets, and the like. Of course, this weighting gives the RAFI portfolios a tilt toward value and small size. As of the start of 2014, Research Affiliates managed $1.66 billion of assets.

The RAFI ETF (ticker PRF) has indeed outperformed its benchmark, the Russell 1000 Index, by about 1 percentage point over its seven-year history to early 2014. Research Affiliates claims the excess return results from its avoidance of the overpriced stocks in the benchmark that have higher market capitalizations than are justified by "fundamental" valuation metrics. An analysis of the RAFI's results suggests, however, that the excess performance results from the assumption of higher risk.

The chart below shows the quarterly excess return of the RAFI portfolio (PRF) over its benchmark portfolio, the Russell 1000 Index (ETF IWB). The chart indicates that there are usually small quarterly differences over time that are more likely to represent underperformance by RAFI rather than excess performance. There is, however, one notable exception during 2009 when PRF delivered extraordinary excess returns that were entirely responsible for the seven-year RAFI excess return.

FUNDAMENTAL INDEX (PRF) AND EQUAL WEIGHT (EWRI) VS. RUSSELL 1000 (IWB)

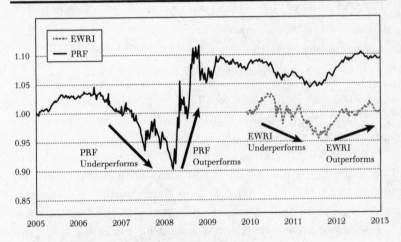

Fundamental Index Average Annual Return (since 12/19/2005): 8.77%
Russell 1000 Average Annual Return (since 12/19/2005): 7.71%

Equal Weight Average Annual Return (since 12/03/2010): 16.44%
Russell 1000 Average Annual Return (since 12/03/2010): 16.23%

The chart shows the return of the "smart beta" strategy divided by the return of the benchmark index. A number above (below) 1 indicates that the "smart beta" fund is outperforming (underperforming) the benchmark index.
Source: Morningstar.

The RAFI portfolio substantially overweighted large-bank stocks in 2009, coming out of the financial crisis, since these stocks sold at unusually large discounts from their book (asset) "values." As mentioned above, the RAFI Fundamental Index™ portfolio had about 15 percent of its portfolio in two stocks (Citigroup and Bank of America) at that time. It turned out that such an overweighting helped produce excellent returns. But it was far from clear at the time that the troubled banks would avoid nationalization. In any event, the strategy involved considerable risk. It is hard to avoid the conclusion that whatever success RAFI has had in generating excess returns resulted from the assumption of greater risk rather than from the mispricing of growth stocks.

A statistical analysis of the RAFI results also supports the risk explanation. If one performs a statistical analysis of the PRF's returns, explaining them via the Fama-French three-factor risk model (where "value" and "size" are considered risk factors), the RAFI excess performance (its "alpha") is estimated to be zero. The performance chart also indicates long periods of underperformance during the history of the ETF.

Equally Weighted Portfolio Strategies

As was shown for the RAFI ETF, equally weighted portfolios have delivered somewhat similar returns. We can illustrate the performance of these portfolios with the Guggenheim Equal Weight 1000 ETF (ticker symbol EWRI) compared with its benchmark, the Russell 1000 capitalization-weighted ETF (ticker IWB). A short, three-year history is shown in the chart on page 279. Again, we see alternating periods of overperformance and underperformance, with equal weighting producing a slightly larger average annual return. Of course, the two portfolios do not have the same characteristics. Equally weighted portfolios give far greater weight to the smallest companies and hence have diversification and risk characteristics quite different from those of capitalization-weighted portfolios. They are also tax inefficient, as indicated earlier.

OTHER FACTOR TILTS

Other "smart beta" portfolios have attempted to exploit the tendency for low-volatility strategies to provide attractive returns and for stock returns to exhibit momentum over time. A variety of ETFs are now trading that give investors the opportunity to put real money to work in these strategies, so we can analyze their performance as well. Here the results are not as good.

Low-Beta (Low-Volatility) Strategies

Several ETFs are marketed that attempt to provide investors with practical instruments designed to take advantage of the attractive returns from low-volatility stocks. The ETFs differ somewhat in the specific strategies employed and in the benchmarks against which they should be measured. The SPDR Russell 1000 Low Volatility ETF (ticker LGLV) has been available only since early 2013. But the Power Shares S&P 500 Low Volatility ETF (ticker SPLV) and the iShares MSCI USA Minimum Volatility ETF (ticker USMV) have been available since 2011. None of the three ETFs have produced returns that have exceeded their capitalization-weighted benchmarks through the first quarter of 2014.

Momentum Strategies

The AQR Momentum Fund Class L ETF (ticker symbol AMOMX) has a longer history, having been available since 2009. Over its life through the first half of 2014, the ETF has failed to produce excess returns over either the Russell 1000 capitalization-weighted ETF or the Russell 1000 Growth ETF. While the time period for the low-beta and momentum ETFs is too short for definitive conclusions to be drawn, it is fair to say that thus far neither strategy has demonstrated superiority when the portfolios have been run with real money. Real money portfolios do not in general demonstrate the kind of effectiveness shown in academic simulations.

LOW-VOLATILITY (SPLV) AND MOMENTUM (AMOMX) VS. RUSSELL 1000 (IWB)

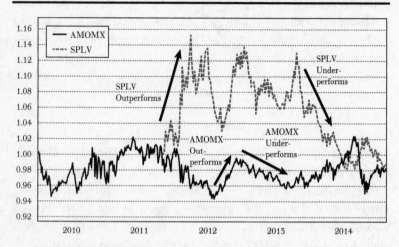

Low-Volatility Average Annual Return (since 05/05/2011): 14.59%
Russell 1000 Average Annual Return (since 05/05/2011): 15.29%

Momentum Average Annual Return (since 07/09/2009): 19.54%
Russell 1000 Average Annual Return (since 07/09/2009): 19.99%

The chart shows the return of the "smart beta" strategy divided by the return of the benchmark index. A number above (below) 1 indicates that the "smart beta" fund is outperforming (underperforming) the benchmark index.
Source: Morningstar.

IMPLICATIONS FOR INVESTORS

"Smart beta" strategies rely on a type of active management. They do not try to select individual stocks but rather tilt the portfolio toward various characteristics that have historically appeared to generate larger-than-market returns. In their favor, the "smart beta" portfolios provide these factor tilts at expense ratios that are lower than those charged by traditional active managers.

In general, the records of "smart beta" funds and ETFs have

been spotty. Many "smart beta" ETFs have failed to produce reliable excess returns, although a few have "beaten the market" over the lifetime of the funds. These funds are, however, less tax efficient than capitalization-weighted funds that do not require rebalancing.

To the extent that some "smart beta" strategies have generated greater-than-market returns, those excess returns should be interpreted as a reward for assuming extra risk. In departing from the market portfolio, investors are taking on a different set of risks. "Smart beta" portfolios do not represent a sophisticated better mousetrap for investors. Investors should be wary of getting caught in the riskier mousetrap themselves.

"Smart beta" portfolios have been the object of considerable marketing hype. They are a testament more to smart marketing than to smart investing. Whether "smart beta" strategies will perform well in the future depends crucially on the market valuations existing at the time the strategy is implemented. As noted above, "value" strategies performed extraordinarily well coming out of the Internet bubble when technology "growth" stocks were priced richly relative to most "value" stocks. Similarly, small stocks did particularly well when they were inexpensively priced relative to large caps. Investors should be aware that if "value" and "small size" become richly priced, as "smart beta" funds become increasingly popular, the results are likely to be disappointing. No strategy is likely to be effective irrespective of valuation relationships.

There is no reason to adjust the long-standing advice of the earlier editions of this book: The core of every portfolio should consist of low-cost, tax-efficient, broad-based index funds. If you do want to take a chance that some risk factor will generate excess returns in the future, you can do so most prudently if the core of your portfolio consists of capitalization-weighted broad-based index funds. And if you do wish to add an additional risk factor to your portfolio, such as some extra exposure to small-company stocks, you can do so most efficiently and effectively by purchasing a low-cost, capitalization-weighted fund that follows an index of small-cap stocks.

IMPLICATIONS FOR BELIEVERS IN
EFFICIENT MARKETS

From March 2008 through March 2009, the stock market declined by almost 50 percent. Did the stock market reflect all available information in March 2008, and could anyone reasonably argue that stocks were efficiently priced? For many observers, the collapse of 2008–09 and the subsequent world financial crisis sounded the death knell for the efficient-market hypothesis.

In 2009, George Soros wrote that "the Efficient Market Hypothesis has been truly discredited by the crash of 2008." The EMH was blamed as the villain in the financial crisis and was written off for dead by countless financial commentators. For example, the respected market strategist Jeremy Grantham opined that the EMH "is more or less directly responsible for the financial crisis." James Montier, global strategist at Société Générale, writing in the *Financial Times*, declared that the theory suggesting that markets are efficient was "utter garbage" and should be consigned to the dust bin.

Some supporters of "smart beta" portfolios believe that markets are inefficient and see their portfolio construction methods as a way of protecting investors from bubble-priced stocks. Moreover, they argue that smarter portfolios can be formed by a reliance on academic findings that there are many statistically significant predictable patterns in the stock market. We have seen, however, that these patterns are not dependable in every period, and that some of the patterns based on fundamental valuation measures of individual stocks may simply reflect a better proxy for measuring risk. In addition, many of these patterns could self-destruct in the future, as many of them have already done. Indeed, this is the logical reason why one should be cautious not to overemphasize these anomalies and predictable patterns or to put too much reliance on "smart beta" portfolios to enhance investment performance.

"Smart beta" portfolios will not protect you from market bubbles. I realize that some critics of the EMH and some managers of "smart beta" portfolios argue that the dot-com bubble was easy to identify as it was inflating. Robert Shiller published his book *Irrational Exuberance* in early 2000, just at the peak of the market. True, but the same models that identified a bubble in early 2000 also identified a vastly "overpriced" stock market in 1992, when low dividend yields and high price-earnings multiples suggested that long-run equity returns would be close to zero in the United States. In fact, from 1992 through 2013, annual stock-market returns were over 9 percent, approximately their historical average. In December of 1996, when the former Federal Reserve chairman Alan Greenspan gave his "Irrational Exuberance" speech, those same models predicted *negative* long-run equity returns. From the date of the chairman's speech through December 2013, the broad stock-market indexes returned about 7.5 percent per year, even after withstanding two sharp bear markets. It is only in retrospect that we know that it was during 1999 and early 2000 when stock prices were "too high." No one can help you time the market so that you avoid being invested when the market reaches a temporary top.

An exchange at an academic symposium between Robert Shiller, an economist who is sympathetic to the argument that stock prices are partially predictable and skeptical about market efficiency, and Richard Roll, an academic financial economist who was also a businessman managing billions of dollars of investment funds, is quite revealing. After Shiller stressed the importance of inefficiencies in the pricing of stocks, Roll responded as follows:

> I have personally tried to invest money, my client's money and my own, in every single anomaly and predictive device that academics have dreamed up. . . . I have attempted to exploit the so-called year-end anomalies and a whole variety of strategies supposedly documented by academic research. And I have yet to make a nickel on any of these supposed market inefficiencies. . . . [A] true market inefficiency ought to be an exploitable opportunity. If there's nothing investors can exploit in a systematic way, time in and time out, then it's very hard to say that information is not being properly incorporated into stock prices.

This lack of opportunities for extraordinary profits is often explained by a joke popular with professors of finance. A professor who espouses the EMH is walking along the street with a graduate student. The student spots a $100 bill lying on the ground and stoops to pick it up. "Don't bother to try to pick it up," says the professor. "If it was really a $100 bill, it wouldn't be there." Perhaps a better version of the story would be to remember that if any $100 bills are lying around, they will not be there for long.

As long as there are stock markets, mistakes will be made by the collective judgment of investors. And undoubtedly, some market participants are demonstrably less than rational. But even if price setting was always determined by rational profit-maximizing investors, prices can never be "correct." Suppose that stock prices are rationally determined as the discounted present value of all future cash flows. Future cash flows can only be estimated and are never known with certainty. There will always be errors in the forecasts of future sales and earnings. Moreover, equity risk premiums are unlikely to be stable over time. Prices are, therefore, likely to be "wrong" all the time. What the EMH implies is that we never can be sure whether they are too high or too low at any given time. Some portfolio managers may correctly determine when some prices are too high and others too low. But at other times such judgments will be in error. And, in any event, the profits that will be attributable to correct judgments will not represent unexploited extraordinary returns that were obviously apparent.

Pricing irregularities and predictable patterns in stock returns can appear over time and even persist for short periods. Andrew Lo* has argued that no engineer would ever devise a test to determine whether a particular motor was perfectly efficient. But engineers

---

*Lo has also argued that the existence of predictable stock-market patterns is not an all-or-nothing condition, but rather one that can vary over time, depending on the characteristics of existing limits to arbitrage, market imperfections, and psychological biases. These factors can give rise to periods when stock returns appear to be predictable and departures from the efficient market hypothesis (EMH) appear to exist.

would attempt to measure the efficiency of that engine relative to a frictionless ideal. Similarly, it is unrealistic to require our financial markets to be perfectly efficient in order to accept the basic tenets of the EMH. Indeed, as Sanford Grossman and Joseph Stiglitz have argued, the perfect efficiency of our financial markets is an unrealizable ideal. Those traders who ensure that information is quickly reflected in market prices must be able, at least, to cover their costs. But it is reasonable to ask whether our financial markets are relatively efficient, and I believe that the evidence is very powerful that our markets come very close to the EMH ideal. Information does get reflected rapidly in security prices. The EMH's basic underlying notion—that if there are obvious opportunities to earn excess risk-adjusted returns, people will flock to exploit them until they disappear—is as reasonable and commonsense as anything put forward by the EMH's critics. If any $100 bills are lying around, they will not be there for long.

CAPITALIZATION-WEIGHTED INDEXING REMAINS AT THE TOP OF THE CLASS

In conclusion, capitalization-weighted indexing is unlikely to be deposed as the overwhelming favorite in the battle for index supremacy. Even if markets were inefficient, departing from the weightings given by the market as a whole would have to be a zero-sum game. All the stocks in the market must be held by someone. If some investors hold portfolios that do better than the market, it must follow that some other investors hold portfolios that do worse. Because of their greater costs, however, active management or "smart" indexing must be a negative-sum game. On average, these higher-cost portfolios must underperform capitalization-weighted index funds that can be purchased at close to zero cost.

There is a remarkably large body of evidence suggesting that professional investment managers are not able to outperform index funds that simply buy and hold the broad stock-market portfolio. Two-thirds of professionally managed funds are regularly outperformed by a broad capitalization-weighted index fund with equivalent risk, and those that do appear to produce excess returns in one period are not likely to do so in the next. The record of professionals does not suggest that sufficient predictability exists in the stock market to produce exploitable arbitrage opportunities.

The core of every portfolio should consist of low-cost, tax-efficient, broad-based index funds. If you do want to take a chance that some risk factor will generate excess returns in the future, you can do so most prudently if the core of your portfolio consists of capitalization-weighted broad-based index funds.

Part Four

A PRACTICAL GUIDE
FOR RANDOM WALKERS
AND OTHER INVESTORS

12

A FITNESS MANUAL FOR RANDOM WALKERS AND OTHER INVESTORS

In investing money, the amount of interest you want should
depend on whether you want to eat well or sleep well.
—J. Kenfield Morley, *Some Things I Believe*

PART FOUR IS a how-to-do-it guide for your random walk
down Wall Street. In this chapter, I offer general investment advice that should be useful to all investors, even
if they don't believe that securities markets are highly efficient.
In chapter 13, I try to explain the recent fluctuations that have
occurred in stock and bond returns and to show how you might
estimate what the future holds. I also indicate how you can at least
roughly gauge the long-run returns you are likely to achieve from
different investment programs. In chapter 14, I present a life-cycle
investment guide indicating how the stage of your life plays an
important role in determining the mix of investments that is most
likely to enable you to meet your financial goals.

In the final chapter, I outline specific strategies for equity investors who believe at least partially in the efficient-market theory
or who are convinced that even if real expertise does exist, they
are unlikely to find it. But if you are sensible, you will take your
random walk only after you have made detailed and careful prepa-
rations. Even if stock prices move randomly, you shouldn't. Think
of the advice that follows as a set of warm-up exercises that will

enable you to make sensible financial decisions and increase your after-tax investment returns.

EXERCISE 1: GATHER THE NECESSARY SUPPLIES

A widely held belief is that the ticket to a comfortable retirement and a fat investment portfolio are instructions on what extraordinary individual stocks or mutual funds you should buy. Unfortunately, these tickets are not even worth the paper they are printed on. The harsh truth is that the most important driver in the growth of your assets is how much you save, and saving requires discipline. Without a regular savings program, it doesn't matter if you make 5 percent, 10 percent, or even 15 percent on your investment funds. The single most important thing you can do to achieve financial security is to begin a regular savings program and to start it as early as possible. The only reliable route to a comfortable retirement is to build up a nest egg slowly and steadily. Yet few people follow this basic rule, and the savings of the typical American family are woefully inadequate.

It is critically important to start saving now. Every year you put off investing makes your ultimate retirement goals more difficult to achieve. Trust in time rather than in timing. As a sign in the window of a bank put it, little by little you can safely stock up a strong reserve here, but not until you start.

The secret of getting rich slowly (but surely) is the miracle of compound interest. Albert Einstein described compound interest as the "greatest mathematical discovery of all time." It may sound complicated, but it simply involves earning a return not only on your original investment but also on the accumulated interest that you reinvest.

Jeremy Siegel, author of the excellent investing book *Stocks for the Long Run*, has calculated the returns from a variety of financial assets from 1800 to 2014. His work shows the incredible power of compounding. One dollar invested in stocks in 1802 would have grown to almost $18 million by the end of 2013. This amount far outdistanced the rate of inflation as measured by the consumer price index (CPI). The figure below also shows the much more modest returns that have been achieved by U.S. Treasury bills and gold.

TOTAL RETURN INDEXES

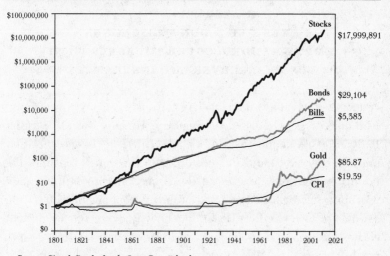

Source: Siegel, *Stocks for the Long Run*, 5th ed.

If you want a get-rich-quick investment strategy, this is not the book for you. I'll leave that for the snake oil salesmen. You can only get poor quickly. To get rich, you will have to do it slowly, and you have to start now.

What if you did not save when you were younger and find yourself in your fifties with no savings, no retirement plan, and burdensome credit card debt? It's going to be a lot harder to plan for a comfortable retirement. But it's never too late to make a plan. There is no other way to make up for lost time than to downsize your lifestyle and start a rigorous program of savings now. You may also have no other choice but to remain in the workforce and to push back retirement a few years. Fortunately, it is easier to play catch-up with tax-advantaged retirement plans that will be described below.

So put time on your side. Start saving early and save regularly.

Live modestly and don't touch the money that's been set aside. If you need further discipline, remember that the only thing worse than being dead is to outlive the money you have put aside for retirement. And if projections are to be believed, about one million of today's baby boomers will live to be at least one hundred.

EXERCISE 2: DON'T BE CAUGHT EMPTY-HANDED: COVER YOURSELF WITH CASH RESERVES AND INSURANCE

Remember Murphy's Law: What can go wrong will go wrong. And don't forget O'Toole's commentary: Murphy was an optimist. Bad things do happen to good people. Life is a risky proposition, and unexpected financial needs occur in everyone's lifetime. The boiler tends to blow up just at the time that your family incurs whopping medical expenses. A job layoff happens just after your son has totaled the family car. That's why every family needs a cash reserve as well as adequate insurance to cope with the catastrophes of life.

Cash Reserves

I know that many brokers will tell you not to miss investing opportunities by sitting on your cash. "Cash is trash" is the mantra of the brokerage community. But everyone needs to keep some reserves in safe and liquid investments to pay for an unexpected medical bill or to provide a cushion during a time of unemployment. Assuming that you are protected by medical and disability insurance at work, this reserve might be established to cover three months of living expenses. The cash reserve fund should be larger, the older you are, but could be smaller if you work in an in-demand profession and/or if you have large investable assets. Moreover, any large future expenditures (such as your daughter's college tuition bill) should be funded with short-term investments (such as a bank certificate of deposit) whose maturity matches the date on which the funds will be needed.

Insurance

Most people need insurance. Those with family obligations are downright negligent if they don't purchase insurance. We risk death every time we get into our automobile or cross a busy street. A hurricane or fire could destroy our home and possessions. People need to protect themselves against the unpredictable.

For individuals, home and auto insurance are a must. So is health and disability insurance. Life insurance to protect one's family from the death of the breadwinner(s) is also a necessity. You don't need life insurance if you are single with no dependents. But if you have a family with young children who count on your income, you do need life insurance and lots of it.

Two broad categories of life insurance products are available: high-premium policies that combine insurance with an investment account, and low-premium term insurance that provides death benefits only, with no buildup of cash value.

The high-premium policies do have some advantages and are often touted for their tax-saving benefits. Earnings on the part of the insurance premiums that go into the savings plan accumulate tax-free, and this can be advantageous for some individuals who have maxed out on their tax-deferred retirement savings plans. Moreover, individuals who will not save regularly may find that the periodic premium bills provide the discipline necessary for them to make sure that a certain amount will be available for their families if they die and that a cash value builds up on the investment part of the program. But policies of this kind provide the most advantages for the insurance agent who sells them and who collects high sales charges. Early premiums go mainly for sales commissions and other overhead rather than for buildup of cash value. Thus, not all your money goes to work. For most people, I therefore favor the do-it-yourself approach. Buy term insurance for protection and invest the difference yourself in a tax-deferred retirement plan. The recommendations that follow will provide an investment plan that is far superior to that available from "whole life" or "variable life" insurance policies.

My advice is to buy renewable term insurance; you can keep renewing your policy without the need for a physical examination. So-called decreasing term insurance, renewable for progressively lower amounts, should suit many families best, because as time passes (and the children and family resources grow), the need for protection usually diminishes. You should understand, however, that term-insurance premiums escalate sharply when you reach the age of sixty or seventy or higher. If you still need insurance at that point, you will find that term insurance has become prohibitively expensive. But the major risk at that point is not premature death; it is that you will live too long and outlive your assets. You can increase those assets more effectively by buying term insurance and investing the money you save yourself.

Shop around for the best deal. There is considerable variation in insurance company rates. Use quote services or the Internet to ensure that you are getting the best deal. For example, you can go to www.term4sale.com and see a number of alternative policies at varying prices. You do not need an insurance agent. Policies available from agents will be more expensive since they need to include extra premiums to pay the agent's sales commission. You can get a much better deal by doing it yourself.

Do not buy insurance from any company with an A.M. Best rating of less than A. A lower premium will not compensate you for taking any risk that your insurance company will get into financial difficulty and be unable to pay its claims. Don't bet your life on a poorly capitalized insurance carrier.

You can obtain A.M. Best's ratings of insurance companies by calling 908-439-2200. Insurance companies pay Best for the ratings. The A.M. Best Website is at http://www.ambest.com/. A somewhat more objective and critical rating is offered by Weiss Research, a consumer-supported company, which can be contacted at 800-291-8545. The Weiss website is at http://www.weissinc.com/.

Deferred Variable Annuities

I would avoid buying variable-annuity products, especially the high-cost products offered by insurance salespeople. A deferred variable annuity is essentially an investment product (typically a mutual fund) with an insurance feature. The insurance feature stipulates that if you die and the value of the investment fund has fallen below the amount you put in, the insurance company will pay back your full investment. These policies are very expensive because you typically pay high sales commissions and a premium for the insurance feature. Unless your mutual fund declines sharply with a fall in the stock market and you drop dead soon after purchasing a variable annuity, the value of this insurance is likely to be small. Remember the overarching rule for achieving financial security: keep it simple. Avoid any complex financial products as well as the hungry agents who try to sell them to you. The only reason you should even consider a variable annuity is if you are super wealthy and have maxed out on all the other tax-deferred savings alternatives. And even then you should purchase such an annuity directly from one of the low-cost providers such as the Vanguard Group.

EXERCISE 3: BE COMPETITIVE—LET THE YIELD ON YOUR CASH RESERVE KEEP PACE WITH INFLATION

As I've already pointed out, some ready assets are necessary for pending expenses, such as college tuition, possible emergencies, or even psychological support. Thus, you have a real dilemma. You know that if you keep your money in a savings bank and get, say, 2 percent interest in a year in which the inflation rate exceeds 2 percent, you will lose real purchasing power. In fact, the situation is even worse because the interest you get is subject to regular income taxes. Moreover, short-term interest rates were abnormally low during the mid-2010s. So what's a small saver to do? There are several short-term investments that are likely to help provide the best rate of return, although no very good alternatives existed at the end of 2014.

Money-Market Mutual Funds (Money Funds)

Money-market mutual funds often provide investors the best instrument for parking their cash reserves. They combine safety and the ability to write large checks against your fund balance, generally in amounts of at least $250. Interest earnings continue until the checks clear. Interest rates on these funds generally ranged from 1 to 5 percent during the first decade of the 2000s. In 2014, however, interest rates were very low and money-fund yields were near zero. Not all money-market funds are created equal; some have significantly higher expense ratios (the costs of running and managing the funds) than others. In general, lower expenses mean higher returns. A sample of relatively low-expense funds is presented in the Random Walker's Address Book and Reference Guide at the end of this book.

Bank Certificates of Deposit (CDs)

A reserve for any known future expenditure should be invested in a safe instrument whose maturity matches the date on which the funds will be needed. Suppose you have set aside money for junior's tuition bills that will need to be paid at the end of one, two, and three years. One appropriate investment plan in this case would be to buy three bank CDs with maturities of one, two, and three years. Bank CDs are even safer than money funds, typically offer higher yields, and are an excellent medium for investors who can tie up their liquid funds for at least six months.

Bank CDs do have some disadvantages. They are not easily converted into cash, and penalties are usually imposed for early withdrawal. Also, the yield on CDs is subject to state and local income taxes. Treasury bills (short-term U.S. government IOUs), which are discussed below, are exempt from state and local taxes.

Bank CD rates vary widely. Use the Internet to find the most attractive returns. Go to www.bankrate.com and search the site for the highest rates around the country. Deposits at all banks and credit unions listed at this site are insured by the Federal Deposit Insurance Corporation. Addresses and phone numbers are given for each listing, and you can call to confirm that the deposits are insured and learn what current rates of return are being offered.

Internet Banks

Investors can also take advantage of online financial institutions that reduce their expenses by having neither branches nor tellers and by conducting all their business electronically. Thanks to their low overhead, they can offer rates significantly above both typical savings accounts and money-market funds. And, unlike money-market funds, those Internet banks that are members of the Federal Deposit Insurance Corporation can guarantee the safety of your funds. To find an Internet bank, go to the Google search engine and type in "Internet bank." You will also see many of them popping up when you do a rate search on www.bankrate.com for the banks with the highest yields. The Internet banks generally post the highest CD rates available in the market.

Treasury Bills

Popularly known as T-bills, these are the safest financial instruments you can find and are widely treated as cash equivalents. Issued and guaranteed by the U.S. government, T-bills are auctioned with maturities of four weeks, three months, six months, or one year. They are sold at a minimum $1,000 face value and in $1,000 increments above that. T-bills offer an advantage over money-market funds and bank CDs in that their income is exempt from state and local taxes. In addition, T-bill yields are often higher than those of money-market funds. For information on purchasing T-bills directly, go to www.treasurydirect.gov.

Tax-Exempt Money-Market Funds

If you find yourself lucky enough to be in the highest federal tax bracket, you will find tax-exempt money-market funds to be the best vehicle for your reserve funds. These funds invest in a portfolio of short-term issues of state and local government entities and generate income that is exempt from both federal and state taxes if the fund confines its investments to securities issued by entities within the state. They also offer free checking for amounts of $250 or more. The yields on these funds are lower than those of the taxable funds. Nevertheless, individuals in the highest income tax brackets will find the earnings from these funds more attractive than the after-tax yields on regular money-market funds. Most of the mutual-fund complexes also offer selected state tax-exempt funds. If you live in a state with high state income taxes, these funds can be very attractive on an after-tax basis. You should call one of the mutual-fund companies listed in the Random Walker's Address Book to find out whether they have a money fund that invests only in the securities of the state in which you pay taxes.

EXERCISE 4: LEARN HOW TO
DODGE THE TAX COLLECTOR

One of the jokes making the rounds of the Internet goes as follows:

A couple, both age seventy-eight, went to a sex therapist's office. The doctor asked, "What can I do for you?" The man said, "Will you watch us have sexual intercourse?" The doctor looked puzzled, but agreed. When the couple finished, the doctor said, "There's nothing wrong with the way you have intercourse," and charged them $50. The couple asked for another appointment and returned once a week for several weeks. They would have intercourse, pay the doctor, then leave. Finally, the doctor asked, "Just exactly what are you trying to find out?" The old man said, "We're not trying to find out anything. She's married and we can't go to her house. I'm married and we can't go to my house. The Holiday Inn charges $93 and the Hilton Inn charges $108. We do it here for $50, and I get $43 back from Medicare."

By telling this story, I do not mean to suggest that you attempt to cheat the government. But I do mean to suggest that you take advantage of every opportunity to make your savings tax-deductible and to let your savings and investments grow tax-free. For most people, there is no reason to pay any taxes on the earnings from the investments that you make to provide for your retirement. Almost all investors, except those who are super wealthy to begin with, can build up a substantial net worth in ways that ensure that nothing will be siphoned off by Uncle Sam. This exercise shows how you can legally stiff the tax collector.

Individual Retirement Accounts

Let's start with the simplest form of retirement plan, a straight-forward Individual Retirement Account (IRA). In 2014, you could take $5,500 per year and invest it in some investment vehicle such as a mutual fund and, for people with moderate incomes, deduct the entire $5,500 from taxes. (Individuals who earn relatively high incomes cannot take an initial tax deduction, but they still get all the other tax advantages described below.) If you are in the 28 percent tax bracket, the contribution really costs you only $3,960 since the tax deduction saves you $1,540 in tax. You can think of it as having the government subsidize your savings account. Now suppose your investment earns 7 percent per year, and you continue to put $5,500 per year into the account for forty-five years. No taxes whatsoever are paid on the earnings from funds deposited in an IRA. The investor who saves through an IRA has a final value of more than $1.6 million, whereas the same contributions without the benefit of an IRA (where all the earnings are taxed at 28 percent each year) total just over $900,000. Even after paying taxes at 28 percent on what you withdraw from the IRA (and in retirement you might even be in a lower tax bracket), you end up with considerably more money. The chart below shows the dramatic advantage of investing through a tax-advantaged plan.

THE ADVANTAGE OF INVESTING THROUGH AN IRA
TAX-DEFERRED VS. TAXABLE INVESTING OF $5,500 A YEAR

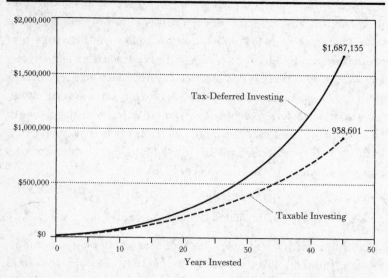

This chart compares the final values of two hypothetical accounts, one tax-deferred and one taxable. In both accounts, the investors contributed $5,500 annually for forty-five years and earned annual returns of 7 percent after expenses.

Source: Adapted from John J. Brennan, *Straight Talk on Investing*.

For those individuals who neglected to save early in life and must now play catch-up, the limits are even higher, as shown in the table below.

ANNUAL CONTRIBUTION LIMITS FOR IRAs

Tax Year	Under Age 50	Age 50 or Over
2015	$5,500	$6,500
Later	Indexed to Inflation	

Roth IRAs

Investors may also choose another form of individual retirement account called a Roth IRA. The traditional IRA offers "jam today" in the form of an immediate tax deduction (provided your income is low enough to make you eligible). Once in the account, the money and its earnings are taxed only when taken out at retirement. The Roth IRA offers "jam tomorrow"—you don't get an up-front tax deduction, but your withdrawals (including investment earnings) are completely tax-free. In addition, you can Roth and roll. You can roll your regular IRA into a Roth IRA if your income is below certain thresholds. You will need to pay tax on all the funds converted, but then neither future investment income nor withdrawals at retirement will be taxed. Moreover, there are no lifetime minimum distribution requirements for a Roth IRA, and contributions can continue to be made after age seventy and a half. Thus, significant amounts can be accumulated tax-free for the benefit of future generations.

The decision of which IRA is best for you and whether to convert can be a tough call. Fortunately, the financial services industry offers free software that lets you analyze whether or not conversion makes sense for you. Many mutual-fund companies and brokers have Roth analyzers that are reasonably easy to use. If you are close to retirement and your tax bracket is likely to be lower in retirement, you probably shouldn't convert, especially if conversion will push you into a higher bracket now. On the other hand, if you are far from retirement and are in a lower tax bracket now, you are very likely to come out well ahead with a Roth IRA. If your income is too high to allow you to take a tax deduction on a regular IRA but low enough to qualify for a Roth, then there is no question that a Roth is right for you, since your contribution is made after tax in any event.

Pension Plans

A variety of pension plans are available from your employer. In addition, self-employed people can set up plans for themselves.

401(k) and 403(b) Pension Plans. Check whether your employer has a pension profit-sharing plan such as a 401(k), available from most corporate employers, or a 403(b), available from most educational institutions. These are perfect vehicles for saving and investing since the money gets taken out of your salary before you even see it. Moreover, many employers match some portion of the employee's contribution so that every dollar saved gets multiplied. As of 2014, up to $17,500 per year can be contributed to these plans, and the contributions do not count as taxable income. For people over fifty, some of whom may need to play catch-up, contribution limits for 2014 were $22,500 per year.

Self-Employed Plans. For self-employed people, Congress has created the SEP IRA. All self-employed individuals—from accountants to Avon ladies, barbers to real estate brokers, doctors to decorators—are permitted to establish such a plan, to which they can contribute as much as 25 percent of their income, up to $52,000 annually. If you moonlight from your regular job, you can establish a SEP IRA for the income you earn on the side. The money paid into a SEP IRA is deductible from taxable income, and the earnings are not taxed until they are withdrawn. The plan is self-directed, which means the choice of how to invest is up to you. Any of the mutual-fund companies that I list in the Random Walker's Address Book can do all the necessary paperwork for you.

Millions of taxpayers are currently missing out on what is one of the truly good deals around. My advice is to save as much as you can through these tax-sheltered means. Use up any other savings you may have for current living expenses, if you must, so you can contribute the maximum allowed.

Saving for College: As Easy as 529

"529" college savings accounts allow parents and grandparents to give gifts to children that can later be used for college education. Named after the provision of the tax code that sanctioned them, the gifts can be invested in stocks and bonds, and no federal taxes will be imposed on the investment earnings as long as the withdrawals are made for qualified higher education purposes. Moreover, as of 2014, the plans allow an individual donor to contribute as much as $70,000 to a 529 plan without gift taxes and without reducing estate tax credits. For couples, the amount doubles to $140,000. If you have kids or grandchildren who plan to go to college and you can afford to contribute to a 529 plan, the decision to establish such a plan is a no-brainer.

Are there pitfalls to avoid? You bet. Most salespeople pushing these plans receive hefty commissions that eat into investment returns. Be an educated consumer and contact a company such as Vanguard for a no-load, low-expense alternative. While it's always nice to stiff the tax man, some high-expense 529 plans could end up shortchanging you. Also note that 529 plans are sanctioned by individual states, and some states allow you to take a tax deduction on your state income tax return for at least part of your contribution. Thus, if you live in such a state, you will want to get a plan from that state. If your state does not allow a tax deduction, choose a plan from a low-expense state such as Utah. Moreover, if you don't use the proceeds of 529 plans for qualified education expenses (including midcareer retooling or postretirement education), withdrawals are not only subject to income tax but also carry a 10 percent penalty.

Keep in mind that colleges are likely to consider 529 assets in determining need-based financial aid. Thus, if parents believe they will be eligible for financial aid when their child goes to college, they could be better off keeping the assets in their own names or, better still, in the names of the child's grandparents. Of course, if you won't qualify for need-based aid in any case, by all means establish a low-expense 529.*

*Comprehensive information about 529 plans can be found at www .savingforcollege.com.

EXERCISE 5: MAKE SURE THE SHOE FITS: UNDERSTAND YOUR INVESTMENT OBJECTIVES

Determining clear goals is a part of the investment process that too many people skip, with disastrous results. You must decide at the outset what degree of risk you are willing to assume and what kinds of investments are most suitable to your tax bracket. The securities markets are like a large restaurant with a variety of menu choices suitable for different tastes and needs. Just as there is no one food that is best for everyone, so there is no one investment that is best for all investors.

We would all like to double our capital overnight, but how many of us can afford to see half our capital disintegrate just as quickly? J. P. Morgan once had a friend who was so worried about his stock holdings that he could not sleep at night. The friend asked, "What should I do about my stocks?" Morgan replied, "Sell down to the sleeping point." He wasn't kidding. Every investor must decide the trade-off he or she is willing to make between eating well and sleeping well. The decision is up to you. High investment rewards can be achieved only at the cost of substantial risk-taking. That has been one of the fundamental lessons of this book. So what's your sleeping point? Finding the answer to this question is one of the most important investment steps you must take.

To help raise your investment consciousness, I've prepared a sleeping scale on investment risk (see pages 308–9) and expected rate of return, as of the early part of the twenty-first century. At the stultifying end of the spectrum are a variety of short-term investments such as bank accounts and money-market funds. If this is your sleeping point, you'll be interested in the information on these kinds of investments in Exercise 3.

Treasury inflation-protection securities (TIPS) come next in the safety scale. These bonds promise a low guaranteed rate that is augmented each year by the rate of increase of the consumer price index. Because they are long-term bonds, they can fluctuate in price with changes in real interest rates (stated interest rates reduced by the rate of inflation). But if held to maturity, they are guaranteed to preserve real purchasing power. In Exercise 7, I'll discuss the advantages of having a small portion of your portfolio invested in these bonds.

Corporate bonds are somewhat riskier, and some dreams will start intruding into your sleep pattern if you choose this form of investment. Should you sell before then, your return will depend on the level of interest rates at the time of sale. If interest rates rise, your bonds will fall to a price that makes their yield competitive with new bonds offering a higher stated interest rate. Your capital loss could be enough to eat up a whole year's interest—or even more. On the other hand, if interest rates fall, the price of your bonds will rise. If you sell prior to maturity, your actual yearly return could vary considerably, and that is why bonds are riskier than short-term instruments, which carry almost no risk of principal fluctuation. Generally, the longer a bond's term to maturity, the greater the risk and the greater the resulting yield.* You will find some useful information on how to buy bonds in Exercise 7.

No one can say for sure what the returns on common stocks will be. But the stock market, as Oskar Morgenstern once observed, is like a gambling casino where the odds are rigged in favor of the players. Although stock prices do plummet, as they did so disastrously in the early 2000s and in 2007, the overall return during the entire twentieth century was about 9 percent per year, including both dividends and capital gains. At their prices in 2014, I believe that a portfolio of domestic common stocks will have a 6 to 7 percent return, reasonably close to the annual rates of return during the twentieth century but somewhat lower. Comparable

*This isn't always the case. During some periods, short-term securities actually yielded more than long-term bonds. The catch was that investors could not count on continually reinvesting their short-term funds at such high rates, and later short-term rates had declined sharply. Thus, investors can reasonably expect that continual investment in short-term securities will not produce as high a return as investment in long-term bonds. In other words, there is a reward for taking on the risk of owning long-term bonds even if short-term rates are temporarily above long-term rates.

THE SLEEPING SCALE OF MAJOR INVESTMENTS

Sleeping Point	Type of Asset	2014 Expected Rate of Return Before Income Taxes (%)	Length of Time Investment Must Be Held to Get Expected Rate of Return	Risk Level
Semicomatose state	Bank accounts	0–1	No specific investment period required. Many thrift institutions calculate interest from day of deposit to day of withdrawal.	No risk of losing what you put in. Deposits up to $100,000 guaranteed by an agency of the federal government. An almost sure loser with high inflation, however.
Sound night's sleep	Money-market funds	0–1½	No specific investment period required. Most funds provide check-writing privileges.	Very little risk because most funds are invested in government securities and bank certificates. Not usually guaranteed. Rates vary with expected inflation.
	Certificates of Deposit (CDs)	½–2	Money must be left on deposit for the entire period to take advantage of a higher rate.	Early withdrawals subject to penalty. Rates geared to expected inflation and will vary.
	Treasury inflation-protection securities (TIPS)	0–1 plus inflation	These are long-term securities maturing in five years or longer. Base rates vary with maturity.	Prices can vary if sold before maturity.
An occasional dream or two, some possibly unpleasant	High-quality corporate bonds (prime-quality public utilities)	3½–5	Investments must be held until maturity (5–30 years) to be assured of the stated rate. (The bonds also need to be protected against redemption.) The bonds may be sold at any time, but market prices vary with interest rates.	Very little risk if held to maturity. Moderate to substantial fluctuations can be expected in realized return if bonds are sold before maturity. Rate geared to expected long-run inflation rate. "Junk bonds" promise much higher returns but with much higher risk.

Some tossing and turning before you doze, and vivid dreams before awakening	Diversified portfolios of blue-chip U.S. or developed foreign country common stocks	6–7	No specific investment period required and stocks may be sold at any time. The average expected return assumes a fairly long investment period and can only be treated as a rough guide based on current conditions.	Moderate to substantial risk. In any one year, the actual return could in fact be negative. Diversified portfolios have at times lost 25% or more of their actual value. Contrary to some opinions, a good inflation hedge over the long run.
	Real estate	Similar to common stock	Same as for common stocks in general if purchase is made through REITs.	Same as above but REITs are good diversifiers and can be a good inflation hedge.
Nightmares not uncommon but, over the long run, well rested	Diversified portfolios of relatively risky stocks of smaller growth companies	7–7½	Same as above. The average expected return assumes a fairly long investment period and can only be treated as a rough guide based on current conditions.	Substantial risk. In any one year, the actual return could be negative. Diversified portfolios of very risky stocks have at times lost 50% or more of their value. Good inflation hedge.
Vivid dreams and occasional nightmares	Diversified portfolios of emerging-market stocks	8–9	Plan to hold for at least 10 years. Projected returns impossible to quantify precisely.	Fluctuations up or down of 50% to 75% in a single year are not uncommon.
Bouts of insomnia	Gold	Impossible to predict	High returns could be earned in any new speculative craze as long as there are greater fools to be found.	Substantial risk. Believed to be a hedge against doomsday and hyperinflation. Can play a useful role in balancing a diversified portfolio, however.

returns are likely from the major companies in developed foreign markets. The actual yearly return in the future can and probably will deviate substantially from this target—in down years you may lose as much as 25 percent or more. Can you stand the sleepless nights in the bad years?

How about dreams in full color with quadraphonic sound? You may want to choose a portfolio of somewhat riskier (more volatile) stocks, like those in aggressive smaller-company mutual funds. These are the stocks in younger companies in newer technologies, where the promise of greater growth exists. Such companies are likely to be more volatile, and these issues can easily lose half of their value in a bad market year. But your average future rate of return for the twenty-first century could be 7 to 7½ percent per year. Portfolios of smaller stocks have tended to outperform the market averages by small amounts. If you have no trouble sleeping during bear markets, and if you have the staying power to stick with your investments, an aggressive common-stock portfolio may be just right for you. Even greater returns, as well as greater market swings, are likely from portfolios of stocks from many emerging markets such as China, India, and Brazil that have tremendous growth potential in the twenty-first century.

Commercial real estate has been an unattainable investment for many individuals. Nevertheless, the returns from real estate have been quite generous, similar to those from common stocks. I'll argue in Exercise 6 that individuals who can afford to buy their own homes are well advised to do so. I'll also show that it is much easier today for individuals to invest in commercial real estate. I believe that real estate investment trusts (REITs) deserve a position in a well-diversified investment portfolio.

I realize that my table slights gold and omits art objects, venture capital, hedge funds, commodities, and other more exotic investment possibilities. Many of these have done very well and can serve a useful role in balancing a well-diversified portfolio of paper assets. Because of their substantial risk, and thus extreme volatility, it is impossible to predict their rates of return; Exercise 8 reviews them in greater detail.

In all likelihood, your sleeping point will be greatly influenced by the way a loss would affect your financial survival. That is why the typical "widow in ill health" is often viewed in investment texts as unable to take on much risk. The widow has neither the life expectancy nor the ability to earn, outside her portfolio, the income she would need to recoup losses. Any loss of capital and income will immediately affect her standard of living. At the other end of the spectrum is the "aggressive young businesswoman." She has both the life expectancy and the earning power to maintain her standard of living in the face of any financial loss. Your stage in the "life cycle" is so important that I have devoted a special chapter (chapter 14) to this determinant of how much risk is appropriate for you.

In addition, your psychological makeup will influence the degree of risk you should assume. One investment adviser suggests that you consider what kind of Monopoly player you once were (or still are). Were you a plunger? Did you construct hotels on Boardwalk and Park Place? True, the other players seldom landed on your property, but when they did, you could win the whole game in one fell swoop. Or did you prefer the steadier but moderate income from the orange monopoly of St. James Place, Tennessee Avenue, and New York Avenue? The answers to these questions may give you some insight into your psychological makeup with respect to investing. It is critical that you understand yourself. Perhaps the most important question to ask yourself is how you felt during a period of sharply declining stock markets. If you became physically ill and even sold out all your stocks rather than staying the course with a diversified investment program, then a heavy exposure to common stocks is not for you.

A second key step is to review how much of your investment return goes to Uncle Sam and how much current income you need. Check last year's income tax form (1040) and the taxable income you reported for the year. For those in a high marginal tax bracket (the rate paid on the last dollar of income), there is a substantial tax advantage from municipal (tax-exempt) bonds. If you are in a high tax bracket, with little need for current income, you will prefer bonds that are tax-exempt and stocks that have low dividend yields but promise long-term capital gains (on which taxes do not have to be paid until gains are realized—perhaps never, if the stocks are part of a bequest). On the other hand, if you are in a low tax bracket and need high current income, you should prefer taxable bonds and high-dividend-paying common stocks so that you don't have to incur the transactions charges involved in selling off shares periodically to meet income needs.

The two steps in this exercise—finding your risk level, and identifying your tax bracket and income needs—seem obvious. But it is incredible how many people go astray by mismatching the types of securities they buy with their risk tolerance and their income and tax needs. The confusion of priorities so often displayed by investors is not unlike that exhibited by a young woman whose saga was recently written up in a London newspaper:

RED FACES IN PARK

London, Oct. 30

Secret lovers were locked in a midnight embrace when it all happened.

Wedged into a tiny two-seater sports car, the near-naked man was suddenly immobilized by a slipped disc, according to a doctor writing in a medical journal here.

Trapped beneath him his desperate girlfriend tried to summon help by sounding the hooter button with her foot. A doctor, ambulance men, firemen and a group of interested passers-by quickly surrounded the couple's car in Regents Park.

Dr. Brian Richards of Kent said: "The lady found herself trapped beneath 200 pounds of a pain-racked, immobile man.

"To free the couple, firemen had to cut away the car frame," he added.

The distraught girl, helped out of the car and into a coat, sobbed: "How am I going to explain to my husband what has happened to his car?"

—Reuters

Investors are often torn by a similar confusion of priorities. You can't seek safety of principal and then take a plunge with investment into the riskiest of common stocks. You can't shelter your income from high marginal tax rates and then lock in returns of 6 percent from high-yield taxable corporate bonds, no matter how attractive these may be. Yet the annals of investment counselors are replete with stories of investors whose security holdings are inconsistent with their investment goals.

EXERCISE 6: BEGIN YOUR WALK AT YOUR OWN HOME—RENTING LEADS TO FLABBY INVESTMENT MUSCLES

Remember Scarlett O'Hara? She was broke at the end of the Civil War, but she still had her beloved plantation, Tara. A good house on good land keeps its value no matter what happens to money. As long as the world's population continues to grow, the demand for real estate will be among the most dependable inflation hedges available.

Although the calculation is tricky, it appears that the long-run returns on residential real estate have been quite generous. We did have a bubble in single-family home prices during 2007 and 2008. By the second decade of the 2000s, however, home prices have returned to "normal," so it is again safe to enter the market. But the real estate market is less efficient than the stock market. Hundreds of knowledgeable investors study the worth of every common stock. Only a handful of prospective buyers assess the worth of a particular real estate property. Hence, individual pieces of property are not always appropriately priced. Finally, real estate returns seem to be higher than stock returns during periods when inflation is accelerating, but do less well during periods of disinflation. In sum, real estate has proved to be a good investment providing generous returns and excellent inflation-hedging characteristics.

The natural real estate investment for most people is the single-family home or the condominium. You have to live somewhere, and buying has several tax advantages over renting. Because Congress wanted to encourage home ownership and the values associated with it, it gave the homeowner two important tax breaks: (1) Although rent is not deductible from income taxes, the two major expenses associated with home ownership—interest payments on your mortgage and property taxes—are deductible; (2) realized gains in the value of your house up to substantial amounts are tax-exempt. In addition, ownership of a house is a good way to force yourself to save, and a house provides enormous emotional satisfaction. My advice is: Own your own home if you can possibly afford it.

You may also wish to consider ownership of commercial real estate through the medium of real estate investment trusts (REITs, pronounced "reets"). Properties from apartment houses to office buildings and shopping malls have been packaged into REIT portfolios and managed by professional real estate operators. The REITs themselves are like any other common stock and are actively traded on the major stock exchanges. This has afforded an excellent opportunity for individuals to add commercial real estate to their investment portfolios.

If you want to move your portfolio toward terra firma, I strongly suggest you invest some of your assets in REITs. There are many reasons why they should play a role in your investment program. First, ownership of real estate has produced comparable rates of return to common stocks and good dividend yields. Equally important, real estate is an excellent vehicle to provide the benefits of diversification described in chapter 8. Real estate returns have often exhibited only a moderate correlation with other assets, thereby reducing the overall risk of an investment program. Moreover, real estate has been a dependable hedge against inflation.

Unfortunately, the job of sifting through the hundreds of outstanding REITs is a daunting one. Moreover, a single-equity REIT is unlikely to provide the necessary diversification across property types and regions. Individuals could stumble badly by purchasing the wrong REIT. Now, however, investors have a rapidly expanding group of real estate mutual funds that are more than willing to do the job for them. The funds cull through the available offerings and put together a diversified portfolio of REITs, ensuring that a wide variety of property types and regions are represented. Moreover, investors have the ability to liquidate their fund holdings whenever they wish. There are also low-expense REIT index funds (listed in the Address Book), and I believe these funds will continue to produce the best net returns for investors.

EXERCISE 7: HOW TO INVESTIGATE A PROMENADE THROUGH BOND COUNTRY

Let's face it, from World War II until the early 1980s, bonds were a lousy place to put your money. Inflation ate away at the real value of the bonds with a vengeance. For example, savers who bought U.S. savings bonds for $18.75 in the early 1970s and redeemed them five years later for $25 found, much to their dismay, that they had actually lost real purchasing power. The trouble was that, although the $18.75 invested in such a bond five years before might have filled one's gas tank twice, the $25 obtained at maturity did little more than fill it once. In fact, an investor's real return was negative, as inflation had eroded purchasing power faster than interest earnings were compounding. Small wonder that many investors view the bond as an unmentionable four-letter word.

Bonds were a poor investment until the early 1980s because the interest rates they carried did not offer adequate inflation protection. But bond prices adjusted to give investors excellent returns over the next thirty years. Moreover, bonds proved to be excellent diversifiers with low or negative correlation with common stocks from 1980 through 2014. In my view, there are four kinds of bond purchases that you may want especially to consider: (1) zero-coupon bonds (which allow you to lock in yields for a predetermined length of time); (2) no-load bond mutual funds (which permit you to buy shares in bond portfolios); (3) tax-exempt bonds and bond funds (for those who are fortunate enough to be in high tax brackets); and (4) U.S. Treasury inflation-protection securities (TIPS). But their attractiveness for investment varies considerably with market conditions. And with the very low interest rates of the mid-2010s, investors must approach the bond market with considerable caution.

Zero-Coupon Bonds Can Be Useful to Fund Future Liabilities

These securities are called zero coupons or simply zeros because owners receive no periodic interest payments, as they do in a regular interest-coupon-paying bond. Instead, these securities are purchased at discounts from their face value (for example, 75 cents on the dollar) and gradually rise to their face or par values over the years. If held to maturity, the holder is paid the full stated amount of the bond. These securities are available on maturities ranging from a few months to over twenty years. They are excellent vehicles for putting money aside for required expenditures on specific future dates.

The principal attraction of zeros is that the purchaser is faced with no reinvestment risk. A zero-coupon Treasury bond guarantees an investor that his or her funds will be continuously reinvested at the yield-to-maturity rate.

The main disadvantage of zeros is that the Internal Revenue Service requires that taxable investors declare annually as income a pro rata share of the dollar difference between the purchase price and the par value of the bond. This is not required, however, for investors who hold zeros in tax-deferred retirement plans.

Two warnings are in order. High-commission brokers will charge small investors fairly large commissions for the purchase of zero-coupon bonds in small denominations. In addition, you should know that redemption at face value is assured only if you hold the bonds to maturity. In the meantime, prices can be highly variable as interest rates change.

No-Load Bond Funds Can Be Appropriate Vehicles
for Individual Investors

Open-end bond (mutual) funds give some of the long-term advantages of the zeros but are much easier and less costly to buy or sell. Those that I have listed in the Address Book all invest in long-term securities. Although there is no guarantee that you can reinvest your interest at constant rates, these funds do offer long-run stability of income and are particularly suitable for investors who plan to live off their interest income.

Because bond markets tend to be at least as efficient as stock markets, I recommend low-expense bond index funds. Bond index funds, which just buy and hold a broad variety of bonds, generally outperform actively managed bond funds. In no event should you ever buy a load fund (a fund with a commission fee). There's no point in paying for something if you can get it free.

The Address Book lists several types of funds: those specializing in corporate bonds, those that buy a portfolio of GNMA mortgage-backed bonds, those investing in tax-exempt bonds (which I will discuss in the next section), as well as some riskier high-yield funds appropriate for investors willing to accept extra risk in return for higher expected returns.

Tax-Exempt Bonds Are Useful for High-Bracket Investors

If you are in a very high tax bracket, taxable money funds, zeros, and taxable bond funds may be suitable only within your retirement plan. Otherwise, you need the tax-exempt bonds issued by state and local governments and by various governmental authorities, such as port authorities or toll roads. The interest from these bonds doesn't count as taxable income on your federal tax form, and bonds from the state in which you live are typically exempt from any state income taxes.

During 2014, good-quality long-term corporate bonds were yielding about 4½ percent, and tax-exempt issues of comparable quality yielded 4 percent. Suppose your tax bracket (the rate at which your last dollar of income is taxed) is about 36 percent, including both federal and state taxes. The following table shows that the after-tax income is $115 higher on the tax-exempt security, which is clearly the better investment for a person in your tax bracket. Even if you are in a lower tax bracket, tax-exempts may still pay, depending on the exact yields available in the market when you make your purchase.

TAX-EXEMPT VS. TAXABLE BONDS ($10,000 FACE VALUE)

Type of Bond	Interest Paid	Applicable Taxes (36% Rate)	After-Tax Income
4% tax-exempt	$400	$0	$400
4½% taxable	450	162	285

If you buy bonds directly (rather than indirectly through mutual funds), I suggest that you buy new issues rather than already outstanding securities. New-issue yields are usually a bit sweeter than the yields of seasoned outstanding bonds, and you avoid paying transactions charges on new issues. I think you should keep your risk within reasonable bounds by sticking with issues rated at least A by Moody's and Standard & Poor's rating services. Also consider so-called AMT bonds. These bonds are subject to the alternative minimum (income) tax and, therefore, are not attractive to individuals who have sheltered a significant part of their income from tax. But if you are not subject to the alternative minimum tax, you can get some extra yield from holding AMT bonds.

There is one nasty "heads I win, tails you lose" feature of bonds. If interest rates go up, the price of your bonds will go down. But if interest rates go down, the issuer can often "call" the bonds away from you (repay the debt early) and then issue new bonds at lower rates. To protect yourself, make sure that your long-term bonds have a ten-year call-protection provision that prevents the issuer from refunding the bonds at lower rates.

For some good tax-exempt bond funds, consult the list in the Address Book. If you have substantial funds to invest in tax-exempts, however, I see little reason for you to make your tax-exempt purchases through a fund and pay the management fees involved. If you confine your purchases to high-quality bonds, including those guaranteed by bond insurance, there is little need for you to diversify, and you'll earn more interest. If you have just a few thousand dollars to invest, however, a fund will provide convenient liquidity and diversification. There are also funds that confine their purchases to the bonds of a single state so that you can avoid both state and federal income taxes. Closed-end tax-exempt bond funds will be described in chapter 15.

Hot TIPS: Inflation-Indexed Bonds

We know that unanticipated inflation is devastating to bond-holders. Inflation tends to increase interest rates, and as they go up, bond prices fall. And there's more bad news: Inflation also reduces the real value of a bond's interest and principal payments. Now a lead shield is available to investors in the form of Treasury inflation-protection securities (TIPS). These securities are immune to the erosion of inflation if held to maturity and guarantee investors that their portfolios will retain their purchasing power. Long-term TIPS paid a basic interest rate of about 1 percent in 2014. But in contrast to old-fashioned Treasuries, the interest payment is based on a principal amount that rises with the consumer price index (CPI). If the price level were to rise 3 percent next year, the $1,000 face value of the bond would increase to $1,030 and the semiannual interest payment would increase as well. When the TIPS mature, the investor gets a principal payment equal to the inflation-adjusted face value at that time. Thus, TIPS provide a guaranteed real rate of return and a repayment of principal in an amount that preserves its real purchasing power.

No other financial instrument available today offers investors as reliable an inflation hedge. TIPS also are great portfolio diversifiers. When inflation accelerates, TIPS will offer higher nominal returns, whereas stock and bond prices are likely to fall. Thus, TIPS have low correlations with other assets and are uniquely effective diversifiers. They provide an effective insurance policy for the white-knuckle crowd.

TIPS do have a nasty tax feature, however, that limits their usefulness. Taxes on TIPS returns are due on both the coupon payment and the increase in principal amount reflecting inflation. The problem is that the Treasury does not pay out the increase in principal until maturity. If inflation were high enough, the small coupon payments might be insufficient to pay the taxes and the imbalance would worsen at higher rates of inflation. Thus, TIPS are far from ideal for taxable investors and are best used only in tax-advantaged retirement plans. Moreover, the interest rates on TIPS during 2014 were considerably lower than their historical averages.

Should You Be a Bond-Market Junkie?

Is the bond market immune to the maxim that investment risk and reward are related? Not at all! During most periods, so-called junk bonds (lower credit quality, higher-yielding bonds) have given investors a net rate of return 2 percentage points higher than the rate that could be earned on "investment-grade" bonds with high-quality credit ratings. In 2014 investment-grade bonds yielded about 4½ percent, whereas "junk" bonds often yielded 5 to 6 percent. Thus, even if 1 percent of the lower-grade bonds defaulted on their interest and principal payments and produced a total loss, a diversified portfolio of low-quality bonds would still produce net returns comparable to those available from a high-quality bond portfolio. Many investment advisers have therefore recommended well-diversified portfolios of high-yield bonds as sensible investments.

There is, however, another school of thought that advises investors to "just say no" to junk bonds. Most junk bonds have been issued as a result of a massive wave of corporate mergers, acquisitions, and leveraged (mainly debt-financed) buyouts. The junk-bond naysayers point out that lower credit bonds are most likely to be serviced in full only during good times in the economy. But watch out if the economy falters.

So what's a thoughtful investor to do? The answer depends in part on how well you sleep at night when you assume substantial investment risk. High-yield or junk-bond portfolios are not for insomniacs. Even with diversification, there is substantial risk in these investments. Moreover, they are not for investors who depend solely on interest payments as their major source of income. And they are certainly not for any investors who do not adequately diversify their holdings. However, at least historically, the gross-yield premium from junk bonds has more than compensated for actual default experience.

Foreign Bonds

There are many foreign countries whose bond yields are higher than those in the United States. This is particularly true in some emerging markets. Conventional wisdom has usually recommended against bonds from emerging markets, citing their high risk and poor quality. But many emerging economies have lower debt-to-GDP ratios and better government fiscal balances than are found in the developed world. The emerging economies are also growing faster. Hence, a diversified portfolio of higher-yielding foreign bonds, including those from emerging markets, can be a useful part of a fixed-income portfolio in a period of very low interest rates.

EXERCISE 7A: USE BOND SUBSTITUTES FOR PART OF THE AGGREGATE BOND PORTFOLIO DURING ERAS OF FINANCIAL REPRESSION

Extremely low interest rates present a daunting challenge for bond investors. All the developed countries of the world are burdened with excessive amounts of debt. Like that of the United States, governments around the world are having an extraordinarily difficult time reining in entitlement programs in the face of aging populations.

The easier path for the U.S. and other governments is to keep interest rates artificially low as the real burden of the debt is reduced and the debt is restructured on the backs of the bondholders. We have seen this movie before. At the end of World War II, the United States deliberately kept interest rates at very low levels to help service the debt that had accumulated during the war. By doing so, the United States reduced its debt-to-GDP ratio from 122 percent in 1946 to 33 percent in 1980. But it was achieved at the expense of bondholders. This is what is meant by the term "financial repression."

One technique to deal with the problem is to use an equity dividend substitution strategy for some portion of what in normal times would have been a bond portfolio. Portfolios of relatively stable dividend growth stocks have yields much higher than the bonds of the same companies and allow the possibility of growth in the future. An example of the sort of company in such a portfolio is AT&T. AT&T's fifteen-year bonds yield about 4¼ percent, its common stock has a dividend yield of 5¼ percent, and the dividend has been growing over time. Retired people who live off dividends and interest will be better rewarded with AT&T stock than with its bonds. And portfolios of dividend growth stocks may be no more volatile than an equivalent portfolio of bonds of the same companies. In the specific recommendations that follow, I recommend such a partial substitution of stocks for bonds in that part of the portfolio designed for lower risk and more stability. During periods of financial repression the standard recommendations regarding bonds need to be fine-tuned.

EXERCISE 8: TIPTOE THROUGH THE FIELDS OF GOLD, COLLECTIBLES, AND OTHER INVESTMENTS

In previous editions of this book I took different positions on whether gold belongs in a well-diversified portfolio. At the start of the 1980s, as gold had risen in price past $800 an ounce, I took a quite negative view of gold. Twenty years later, at the start of the new millennium, with gold selling in the $200s, I became more positive. Today, with gold selling at about $1,300 an ounce, I find it hard to be enthusiastic. But there could be a modest role for gold in your portfolio. Returns from gold tend to be very little correlated with the returns from paper assets. Hence, even modest holdings (say, 5 percent of the portfolio) can help an investor reduce the variability of the total portfolio. And if inflation were to reemerge, gold would likely produce acceptable returns. Small gold holdings can easily be obtained now by purchasing shares in one of the mutual funds or ETFs concentrating on gold.

The volatile movements in gold prices remind me of the story of the Chinese merchant who made an excellent living trading in sardines. His business was so successful that he hired a bright young college graduate to assist him in his endeavors. One day, when the young man was entertaining his in-laws for dinner, he decided to bring home a couple of cans of sardines to have as an appetizer. On opening the first can, he found, to his great chagrin, that the can was filled with sand. He then opened the second can and found that it, too, was filled with sand. When he informed the Chinese merchant of his experience the next day, the wily trader simply smiled and said, "Oh, those cans are for trading, not for eating."

In a sense, this story is very similar to the situation that occurs in gold trading. Practically all gold trading is for the purpose of hoarding or speculating so that the bullion can be sold later at a higher price. Almost none of the gold is actually used. In this kind of market, no one can tell where prices will go. Prudence suggests—at best—a limited role for gold as a vehicle for obtaining broader diversification.

What about diamonds, which are often described as everybody's best friend? They pose enormous risks and disadvantages for individual investors. One must remember that buying diamonds involves large commission costs. It's also extraordinarily hard for an individual to judge quality, and I can assure you that the number of telephone calls you get from folks wishing to sell diamonds will greatly exceed the calls from those who want to buy them.

Another popular current strategy is investment in collectibles. Thousands of salesmen are touting everything from Renoir to rugs, Tiffany lamps to rare stamps, Art Deco to airsick bags. And eBay has made buying and selling collectibles much more efficient. I think there's nothing wrong in buying things you can love—and God knows people do have strange tastes—but my advice is to buy those things because you love them, not because you expect them to appreciate in value. Don't forget that fakes and forgeries are common. A portfolio of collectibles also often requires hefty insurance premiums and endless maintenance charges—so you are making payments instead of receiving dividends or interest. To earn money collecting, you need great originality and taste. In my view, most people who think they are collecting profit are really collecting trouble.

"I'm putting all my money into 'things.'"

Another popular instrument these days is the commodities futures contract. You can buy not only gold but also contracts for the delivery of a variety of commodities, from grains to metals as well as foreign exchange. It's a fast market where professionals can benefit greatly, but individuals who don't know what they are doing can easily get clobbered. My advice to the nonprofessional investor: Don't go against the grain.

I would also steer clear of hedge-fund and private-equity and venture-capital funds. These can be great moneymakers for the fund managers who pocket large management fees and 20 percent of the profits, but individual investors are unlikely to benefit. The average performance of these funds is deeply disappointing. True, the best funds have done quite well, but unless you are an institutional investor who has established a clearly preferential position, your chance of investing with the best is realistically zero. Ignore these exotics—they are not for you.

EXERCISE 9: REMEMBER THAT INVESTMENT COSTS ARE NOT RANDOM; SOME ARE LOWER THAN OTHERS

Many brokers today will execute your stock orders at substantial discounts off standard commission rates. The discount broker usually provides a plain-pipe-rack service. If you want your hand held, if you want general portfolio advice and investment suggestions, the discount broker may not be for you. If, however, you know exactly what you want to buy, the discount broker can get it for you at much lower commission rates than the standard full-service house, especially if you are willing to trade online. Trading stocks online is easy and cheap. But let me warn you, few investors who try to trade in and out of stocks each day make profits. Don't let low commission rates seduce you into becoming one of the legion of unsuccessful former day traders.

While we are on the subject of commission costs, you should be aware of a Wall Street innovation called the "wrap account." For a single fee, your broker obtains the services of a professional money manager, who then selects for you a portfolio of stocks, bonds, and perhaps real estate. Brokerage commissions and advisory fees are "wrapped" into the overall fee. The costs involved in wrap accounts are extremely high. Annual fees can be up to 3 percent per year, and there may be additional execution fees and fund expenses if the manager uses mutual funds or REITs. With those kinds of expenses, it will be virtually impossible for you to beat the market. My advice here is: Avoid taking the wrap.

Remember also that costs matter when buying mutual funds or ETFs. There is a strong tendency for those funds that charge the lowest fees to the investor to produce the best net returns. The fund industry is one where you actually get what you don't pay for. Of course, the quintessential low-cost funds are index funds, which tend to be very tax efficient as well.

There is much about investing you cannot control. You can't do anything about the ups and downs of the stock and bond markets. But you can control your investment costs. And you can organize your investments to minimize taxes. Controlling the things you can control should play a central role in developing a sensible investment strategy.

EXERCISE 10: AVOID SINKHOLES AND STUMBLING BLOCKS: DIVERSIFY YOUR INVESTMENT STEPS

In these warm-up exercises, we have discussed a number of investment instruments. The most important part of our walk down Wall Street will take us to the corner of Broad Street—to a consideration of sensible investment strategies with respect to common stocks. A guide to this part of our walk is contained in the final three chapters, because I believe common stocks should form the cornerstone of most portfolios. Nevertheless, in our final warm-up exercise, we recall the important lesson of modern portfolio theory—the advantages of diversification.

A biblical proverb states that "in the multitude of counselors there is safety." The same can be said of investments. Diversification reduces risk and makes it far more likely that you will achieve the kind of good average long-run return that meets your investment objective. Therefore, within each investment category you should hold a variety of individual issues, and although common stocks should be a major part of your portfolio, they should not be the sole investment instrument. Just remember the teary-eyed ex-Enron employees who held nothing but Enron stock in their retirement plans. When Enron went under, they lost not only their jobs but all their retirement savings as well. Whatever the investment objectives, the investor who is wise diversifies.

Recall also the sinkholes and stumbling blocks covered in the section of chapter 10 entitled "What Are the Lessons for Investors from Behavioral Finance?" We are all too often our own worst enemy when it comes to investing. An understanding of how vulnerable we are to our own psychology can help us avoid the common pitfalls that can make us stumble on our walk down Wall Street.

A FINAL CHECKUP

Now that you have completed your warm-up exercises, let's take a moment for a final checkup. The theories of valuation worked out by economists and the performance recorded by the professionals lead to a single conclusion: There is no sure and easy road to riches. High returns can be achieved only through higher risk-taking (and perhaps through acceptance of lesser degrees of liquidity).

The amount of risk you can tolerate is partly determined by your sleeping point. The next chapter discusses the risks and rewards of stock and bond investing and will help you determine the kinds of returns you should expect from different financial instruments. But the risk you can assume is also significantly influenced by your age and by the sources and dependability of your noninvestment income. Chapter 14—"A Life-Cycle Guide to

Investing"—will give you a clearer notion of how to decide what portion of your capital should be placed in common stocks, bonds, real estate, and short-term investments. The final chapter presents specific stock-market strategies that will enable amateur investors to achieve results as good as or better than those of the most sophisticated professionals.

13

HANDICAPPING THE FINANCIAL RACE: A PRIMER IN UNDERSTANDING AND PROJECTING RETURNS FROM STOCKS AND BONDS

> No man who is correctly informed as to
> the past will be disposed to take a morose or
> desponding view of the present.
> —Thomas B. Macaulay, *History of England*

THIS IS THE chapter where you learn how to become a financial bookie. Reading it will still leave you unable to predict the course of the market over the next month or the next year—no one can do that—but you will be able to better the odds of constructing a winning portfolio. Although the price levels of stocks and bonds, the two most important determinants of net worth, will undoubtedly fluctuate beyond your control, my general methodology will serve you well in realistically projecting long-run returns and adapting your investment program to your financial needs.

WHAT DETERMINES THE RETURNS FROM STOCKS AND BONDS?

Very long-run returns from common stocks are driven by two critical factors: the dividend yield at the time of purchase, and the future growth rate of earnings and dividends. In principle, for the buyer who holds his or her stocks forever, a share of common stock is worth the "present" or "discounted" value of its stream of future dividends. Recall that this "discounting" reflects the fact that a dollar received tomorrow is worth less than a dollar in hand today. A stock buyer purchases an ownership interest in a business and hopes to receive a growing stream of dividends. Even if a company pays very small dividends today and retains most (or even all) of its earnings to reinvest in the business, the investor implicitly assumes that such reinvestment will lead to a more rapidly growing stream of dividends in the future or alternatively to greater earnings that can be used by the company to buy back its stock.

The discounted value of this stream of dividends (or funds returned to shareholders through stock buybacks) can be shown to produce a very simple formula for the long-run total return for either an individual stock or the market as a whole:

Long-run equity return = Initial dividend yield + growth rate.

From 1926 until 2013, for example, common stocks provided an average annual rate of return of about 10 percent. The dividend yield for the market as a whole on January 1, 1926, was about 5 percent. The long-run rate of growth of earnings and dividends was also about 5 percent. Thus, adding the initial dividend yield to the growth rate gives a close approximation of the actual rate of return.

Over shorter periods, such as a year or even several years, a third factor is critical in determining returns. This factor is the change in valuation relationships—specifically, the change in the price-dividend or price-earnings multiple. (Increases or decreases in the price-dividend multiple tend to move in the same direction as the more popularly used price-earnings multiple.)

Price-dividend and price-earnings multiples vary widely from year to year. For example, in times of great optimism, such as early March 2000, stocks sold at price-earnings multiples well above 30. The price-dividend multiple was over 80. At times of great pessimism, such as 1982, stocks sold at only 8 times earnings and 17 times dividends. These multiples are also influenced by interest rates. When interest rates are low, stocks, which compete with bonds for an investor's savings, tend to sell at low dividend yields and high price-earnings multiples. When interest rates are high, stock yields rise to be more competitive and stocks tend to sell at low price-earnings multiples. Common-stock returns were well below average from 1968 to 1982, when returns were only about 5½ percent per year. Stocks sold at a dividend yield of 3 percent at the start of the period, and earnings and dividend growth was 6 percent per year, a bit above the long-run average. Had price-earnings multiples (and dividend yields) remained constant, stocks would have produced a 9 percent annual return, with the 6 percent dividend growth translated into 6 percent capital appreciation per year. But a large increase in dividend yields (a large fall in price-earnings multiples) reduced the average annual return by about 3½ percentage points per year.

A perfectly dreadful period for stock-market investors was the first decade of the 2000s. The Age of Millennium turned out to be the Age of Disenchantment. At the start of April 2000, at the height of the Internet bubble, the dividend yield for the S&P 500 had fallen to 1.2 percent. (Price-earnings multiples were above 30.) Dividend growth was actually very strong during the period, averaging 5.8 percent per year. Had there been no change in valuation relationships, stocks would have produced a rate of return of 7 percent (1.2 percent dividend yield plus 5.8 percent growth). But price-earnings multiples plummeted and dividend yields rose over the decade. The change in valuation relationships lopped 13½ percentage points from the return. Hence, stocks did not return 7 percent—they lost an average of 6½ percent per year, leading many analysts to refer to these years as "the lost decade."

Many analysts question whether dividends are as relevant now as they were in the past. They argue that firms increasingly prefer distributing their growing earnings to stockholders through stock repurchases rather than dividend increases. Two reasons are offered for such behavior—one serves shareholders and the other management. The shareholder benefit was created by tax laws. The tax rate on realized long-term capital gains has often been only a fraction of the maximum income tax rate on dividends. Firms that buy back stock tend to reduce the number of shares outstanding and therefore increase earnings per share and, thus, share prices. Hence, stock buybacks tend to create capital gains. Even when dividends and capital gains are taxed at the same rate, capital-gains taxes can be deferred until the stocks are sold, or even avoided completely if the shares are later bequeathed. Thus, managers acting in the interest of the shareholder will prefer to engage in buybacks rather than increasing dividends.

The flip side of stock repurchases is more self-serving. A significant part of management compensation is derived from stock options, which become valuable only if earnings and the price of the stock rise. Stock repurchases are an easy way to bring this about. Larger appreciation benefits the managers by enhancing the value of their stock options, whereas larger dividends go into the pockets of current shareholders. From the 1940s until the 1970s, earnings and dividends grew at about the same rate. During the last decades of the twentieth century, however, earnings grew faster than dividends. Over the very long run, earnings and dividends are likely to grow at roughly similar rates, and, for ease of reading, I have elected to do the analysis below in terms of earnings growth.

Long-run returns from bonds are easier to calculate than those from stocks. Over the long run, the yield that a bond investor receives is approximated by the yield to maturity of the bond at the time it is purchased. For a zero-coupon bond (a bond that makes no periodic interest payments, but simply returns a fixed amount at maturity), the yield at which it is purchased is precisely the yield that an investor will receive, assuming no default and assuming it is held to maturity. For a coupon-paying bond (a bond that does make periodic interest payments), there could be a slight variation in the yield that is earned over the term of the bond, depending on whether and at what interest rates the coupon interest is reinvested. Nevertheless, the initial yield on the bond provides a quite serviceable estimate of the yield that will be obtained by an investor who holds the bond until maturity.

Estimating bond returns becomes murky when bonds are not held until maturity. Changes in interest rates (bond yields) then become a major factor in determining the net return received over the period during which the bond is held. When interest rates rise, bond prices fall so as to make existing bonds competitive with those that are currently being issued at the higher interest rates. When rates fall, bond prices increase. The principle to keep in mind is that bond investors who don't hold to maturity will suffer to the extent that interest rates rise and gain to the extent that rates fall.

Inflation is the dark horse in any handicapping of financial returns. In the bond market, an increase in the inflation rate is unambiguously bad. To see this, suppose that there was no inflation and bonds sold on a 5 percent yield basis, providing investors with a real (that is, after inflation) return of 5 percent. Now assume that the inflation rate increases from zero to 5 percent per year. If investors still require a 5 percent real rate of return, then the bond interest rate must rise to 10 percent. Only then will investors receive an after-inflation return of 5 percent. But this will mean that bond prices fall, and those who previously purchased 5 percent long-term bonds will suffer a substantial capital loss. Except for the holder of the inflation-protected bonds recommended in chapter 12, inflation is the deadly enemy of the bond investor.

In principle, common stocks should be an inflation hedge, and stocks are not supposed to suffer with an increase in the inflation rate. In theory at least, if the inflation rate rises by 1 percentage point, all prices should rise by 1 percentage point, including the values of factories, equipment, and inventories. Consequently, the growth rate of earnings and dividends should rise with the rate of inflation. Thus, even though all required returns will rise with the rate of inflation, no change in dividend yields (or price-earnings ratios) will be required. This is so because expected growth rates should rise along with increases in the expected inflation rate. Whether this happens in practice we will examine below.

FOUR HISTORICAL ERAS OF FINANCIAL
MARKET RETURNS

Before we attempt to project future stock and bond returns, let's examine four periods of stock- and bond-market history and see whether we can make sense of how investors fared in terms of the determinants of returns discussed above. The four eras coincide with the four broad swings in stock-market returns from 1947 to 2009. The table below indicates the four eras and the average annual returns earned by stock and bond investors:

**AN ERA VIEW OF U.S. STOCK AND BOND RETURNS
(AVERAGE ANNUAL RETURNS)**

Asset Class	Era I Jan. 1947– Dec. 1968 The Age of Comfort	Era II Jan. 1969– Dec. 1981 The Age of Angst	Era III Jan. 1982– March 2000 The Age of Exuberance	Era IV April 2000– March 2009 The Age of Disenchantment
Common stocks (S&P 500)	14.0%	5.6%	18.3%	–6.5%
Bonds (high-quality, long-term corporates)	1.8%	3.8%	13.6%	6.4%
Average annual inflation rate	2.3%	7.8%	3.3%	2.4%

Era I, the Age of Comfort, as I call it, covers the years of growth after World War II. Stockholders made out extremely well after inflation, whereas the meager returns earned by bondholders were substantially below the average inflation rate. I call Era II the Age of Angst. Widespread rebellion by the millions of teenagers born during the baby boom, economic and political instability created by the Vietnam War, and various inflationary oil and food shocks combined to create an inhospitable climate for investors. No one was exempt; neither stocks nor bonds fared well. During our third era, the Age of Exuberance, the boomers matured, peace reigned, and a noninflationary prosperity set in. It was a golden age for stockholders and bondholders. Never before had they earned such generous returns. Era IV was the Age of Disenchantment, in which the great promise of the new millennium was not reflected in common-stock returns.

With these broad time periods set, let us now look at how the determinants of returns developed during those eras and look especially at what might have been responsible for changes in valuation relationships and in interest rates. Recall that stock returns are determined by (1) the initial dividend yield at which the stocks were purchased, (2) the growth rate of earnings, and (3) changes in valuation in terms of price-earnings (or price-dividend) ratios. And bond returns are determined by (1) the initial yield to maturity at which the bonds were purchased and (2) changes in interest rates (yields) and therefore in bond prices for bond investors who do not hold to maturity.

ERA I: THE AGE OF COMFORT

Consumers celebrated the end of World War II with a spending spree. They had gone without cars, refrigerators, and countless other goods during the war, and they forked over their liquid savings with abandon, creating a mini-boom with some inflation. It was hard, however, to forget the Great Depression of the 1930s. Economists (those dismal scientists) were worried as demand began to slacken and became convinced that a deep recession, or perhaps a depression, was just around the corner. President Harry Truman was responsible for a widely used definition of the difference between the two: "A recession is when you're out of work. A depression is when I'm out of work." Investors in the stock market noted the economists' gloom and were clearly worried. Dividend yields at the start of 1947 were unusually high at 5 percent, and P/E multiples, which hovered around 12, were well below their long-term average.

It turned out that the economy did not sink into the depression many had feared. Although there were periods of mild recession, the economy grew at a quite reasonable rate through the 1950s and

1960s. President Kennedy had proposed a large tax cut in the early 1960s, which was enacted in 1964, after his death. With the stimulus from the tax cut and the increase in government spending for the Vietnam War, the economy was robust, with high employment levels. Inflation was generally not a problem until the very end of the period. Investors became progressively more confident; by 1968, P/Es were above 18, and the yield on the S&P 500-Stock Index had fallen to 3 percent. This created truly comfortable conditions for common-stock investors: their initial dividends were high; both earnings and dividends grew at reasonably robust rates of 6½ to 7 percent; and valuations became richer, further augmenting capital gains. The following table shows the different components of the returns from stocks and bonds over the 1947–68 period.

THE DEVELOPMENT OF STOCK AND BOND RETURNS (JANUARY 1947–DECEMBER 1968)

Stocks	Initial dividend yield	5.0
	Growth in earnings	6.6
	Change in valuation (increase in P/E ratio)	2.4
	Average annual return	14.0
Bonds	Initial yield	2.7
	Effect of increase in interest rates	−0.9
	Average annual return	1.8

Unfortunately, bond investors did not fare nearly as well. For starters, initial bond yields were low in 1947. Thus, bond returns were destined to be low even for investors who held to maturity. During World War II, the United States pegged long-term government-bond interest rates at no more than 2½ percent. The policy was implemented to permit the government to finance the war cheaply with low-interest borrowing, and it continued after the war until 1951, when rates were allowed to rise moderately. Therefore, bond investors suffered a double whammy during the period. Not only were interest rates artificially low at the start of the period, but bondholders suffered capital losses when interest rates were allowed to rise. As a result, bondholders received nominal rates of return below 2 percent over the period and real returns (after inflation) that were negative.

ERA II: THE AGE OF ANGST

From the late 1960s through the early 1980s, accelerating inflation made an unexpected appearance and became the major influence on securities markets. In the mid-1960s, inflation was essentially unnoticeable—running at a rate of just over 1 percent. When our involvement in Vietnam increased in the late 1960s, however, we had classic, old-fashioned "demand-pull" inflation—too much money chasing too few goods—and the rate of inflation spurted forward to about 4 or 4½ percent.

Then the economy was beset by the oil and food shocks of 1973–74. It was a classic case of Murphy's Law at work—whatever could go wrong did. The Organization of Petroleum Exporting Countries (OPEC) contrived to produce an artificial shortage of oil, and Mother Nature produced a real shortage of foodstuffs through poor grain harvests in North America and disastrous ones in the Soviet Union and sub-Saharan Africa. When even the Peruvian anchovy crop mysteriously disappeared (anchovies are a major source of protein), it appears that O'Toole's commentary had come into play. (Remember, it was O'Toole who suggested that "Murphy was an optimist.") Again, the inflation rate rose to 6½ percent. Then, in 1978 and 1979, a combination of policy mistakes—leading to considerable excess demand in certain sectors—and another 125 percent increase in the price of oil kicked the inflation rate up again, taking with it wage costs. By the early 1980s, the inflation rate went above 10 percent and there was considerable fear that the economy was out of control.

Finally, the Federal Reserve, under the leadership of its chairman at the time, Paul Volcker, took decisive action. The Fed initiated an extremely tight monetary policy designed to rein in the economy and kill the inflationary virus. Inflation did begin to subside in time, but the economy almost died as well. We suffered the sharpest economic decline since the 1930s, and unemployment soared. By the end of 1981, the U.S. economy suffered not only from double-digit inflation but from double-digit unemployment as well.

The table below shows the fallout in financial markets from the inflation and instability in the economy. Although nominal returns for both stockholders and bondholders were meager, the real returns, after factoring out the 7.8 percent inflation rate, were actually negative. On the other hand, hard assets such as gold, collectibles, and real estate provided generous double-digit returns.

THE DEVELOPMENT OF STOCK AND BOND RETURNS
(JANUARY 1969–DECEMBER 1981)

Stocks	Initial dividend yield	3.1
	Growth in earnings	8.0
	Change in valuation (increase in P/E ratio)	−5.5
	Average annual return	5.6
Bonds	Initial yield	5.9
	Effect of increase in interest rates	−2.1
	Average annual return	3.8

Because the inflation was unanticipated and allowance for it was not incorporated into yields, investors in bonds suffered disastrous results. In 1968, for example, thirty-year, long-term bonds offered a yield to maturity of about 6 percent. This provided protection against the going inflation rate of about 3 percent and an anticipated after-inflation real rate of return of 3 percent. Unfortunately, the actual rate of inflation over the period 1969–81 was almost 8 percent, wiping out any positive real rate of return. That's the good news part of this dreary story. The bad news was that there were capital losses. Who wanted to buy a bond yielding 6 percent in the late 1970s, when the rate of inflation was in double digits? No one! If you had to sell your bonds, you sold at a loss so that the new buyer could get a yield consonant with the higher rate of inflation. Yields rose even further as the risk premium on bonds rose to take into account their increased volatility. To make matters worse, the tax system delivered the unkindest blow of all to bond investors. Even though bond investors often actually earned negative pre-tax rates of return, their bond coupons were taxed at regular income tax rates.

The failure of bonds to protect investors against an unanticipated inflationary episode is hardly surprising. The common-stock flop was something else. Because stocks represent claims on real assets that presumably rise in value with the price level, stock prices—according to this line of logic—should have risen also. It's like the story of the small boy on his first trip to an art museum. When told that a famous abstract painting was supposed to be a horse, the boy asked wisely, "Well, if it is supposed to be a horse, why isn't it a horse?" If common stocks were supposed to be an inflation hedge, then why weren't they?

Many different explanations involving faltering dividends and earnings growth have been offered that simply don't hold up under careful analysis. One common explanation was that inflation had caused corporate profits to shrink drastically, especially when reported figures were adjusted for inflation. Inflation was portrayed as a kind of financial neutron bomb, leaving the structure of corporate enterprise intact, but destroying the lifeblood of profits. Many saw the engine of capitalism as running out of control, so that a walk down Wall Street—random or otherwise—could prove extremely hazardous.

The facts are, however, that there was no evidence that profits had been "sliding down a pole greased by cruel and inexorable inflation," as some in the financial community believed in the early 1980s. As the preceding table shows, profit growth accelerated over the 1969–81 period and increased to an 8 percent rate, comfortably ahead of inflation. Even dividends held their own, rising at close to the same rate as inflation.

Movie buffs should recall the marvelous final scene from *Casablanca*. Humphrey Bogart stands over the body of a Luftwaffe major, a smoking gun in his hand. Claude Rains, a captain in the

French colonial police, turns his glance from Bogart to the smoking gun to the dead major and finally to his assistant, and says, "Major Strasser has been shot. Round up the usual suspects." We, too, have rounded up the usual suspects, but we have yet to focus on who shot the stock market.

The major reason for the poor equity returns during the 1970s was that investors' evaluations of dividends and earnings—the number of dollars they were willing to pay for a dollar of dividends and earnings—fell sharply. Stocks failed to provide investors with protection against inflation, not because earnings and dividends failed to grow with inflation, but rather because price-earnings multiples quite literally collapsed over the period.

The price-earnings multiple for the S&P Index was cut by almost two-thirds during the 1969–81 period. It was this decline in multiples that produced such poor returns for investors in the 1970s and that prevented stock prices from reflecting the real underlying progress most companies made in earnings and dividend growth. Some financial economists concluded that the market was simply irrational during the 1970s and early 1980s—that multiples had fallen too far.

It is, of course, quite possible that stock investors became irrationally pessimistic in the early 1980s, just as they were possibly irrationally optimistic in the mid-1960s. But although I do not believe the market is always perfectly rational, if forced to choose between the stock market and the economics profession, I'd put my money on the stock market every time. I suspect that stock investors weren't irrational when they caused a sharp drop in price-dividend and price-earnings multiples—they were just scared. In the mid-1960s, inflation was so modest as to be almost unnoticeable, and investors were convinced that economists had found the cure for serious recessions—even mild downturns could be "fine-tuned" away. No one would have imagined in the 1960s that the economy could experience either double-digit unemployment or double-digit inflation, let alone that both could appear simultaneously. Clearly, we learned that economic conditions were far less stable than had previously been imagined. Equity securities (dare I say equity insecurities) were, therefore, considered riskier and deserving of higher risk compensation.*

The market provides higher risk premiums through a drop in prices relative to earnings and dividends; this produces larger returns in the future consistent with the new, riskier environment. Paradoxically, however, the same adjustments that produced very poor returns in the late 1960s and throughout the 1970s created some very attractive price levels in the early 1980s, as I argued in earlier editions of this book. The experience makes clear, however, that if one wants to explain the generation of returns over a decade, a change in valuation relationships plays a critical role. The growth rate of earnings did compensate for inflation during 1969–81, but the drop in price-dividend and price-earnings multiples, which I believe reflected increased perceived risk, is what killed the stock market.

ERA III: THE AGE OF EXUBERANCE

Let us now turn to the third era—the golden age of financial asset returns, from 1982 through early 2000. At the start of the period, both bonds and stocks had fully adjusted—perhaps even overadjusted—to the changed economic environment. Stocks and bonds were priced not only to provide adequate protection against the likely rate of inflation but also to give unusually generous real rates of return.

Indeed, in late 1981, the bond market was in disgrace. The *Bawl Street Journal*, in its 1981 annual comedy issue, wrote, "A bond

---

*Economists often put the proposition in terms of the risk premium—that is, the extra return you can expect from an investment over and above the return from perfectly predictable short-term investments. According to this view, the risk premiums in the 1960s were very small, perhaps 1 or 2 percentage points. During the early 1980s, risk premiums demanded by investors to hold both stocks and bonds expanded to a range of probably 4 to 6 percentage points, as I shall show below.

is a fixed-rate instrument designed to fall in price." At the time, the yield on high-quality corporate bonds was around 13 percent. The underlying rate of inflation (as measured by the growth of unit labor costs) was then about 8 percent. Thus, corporate bonds provided a prospective real rate of return of about 5 percent, a rate unusually generous by past historical standards. (The long-term real rate of return on corporate bonds has been only 2 percent.) To be sure, bond prices had become volatile, and it was therefore reasonable to suppose that bonds ought to offer a somewhat larger risk premium than before. But panic-depressive institutional investors probably overdiscounted the risks of bond investments. Like generals fighting the last war, investors had been loath to touch bonds because experience over the past fifteen years had been so disastrous. Thus, the initial conditions were such that bond investors could expect very generous returns in the years ahead.

What about stocks? As I mentioned above, it is possible to calculate the anticipated long-run rate of return on stocks by adding the dividend yield of the stock averages to the anticipated growth of earnings per share. The calculations I performed in 1981 suggested a total expected rate of return from common stocks of more than 13 percent—a rate well above the core rate of inflation and very generous by historical standards.

Common stocks were also selling at unusually low multiples of cyclically depressed earnings, at below-average price-dividend multiples, and at prices that were only a fraction of the replacement value of the assets they represented. Small wonder that we saw so many corporate takeovers during the 1980s. Whenever assets can be bought in the stock market at less than the cost of acquiring them directly, there will be a tendency for firms to purchase the equities of other firms, as well as to buy back their own stocks. Thus, I argued that in the early 1980s we were presented with a market situation where paper assets had adjusted and perhaps overadjusted to inflation and the greater uncertainty associated with it. The following table shows how returns developed during the 1982–2000 period.

THE DEVELOPMENT OF STOCK AND BOND RETURNS
(JANUARY 1982-MARCH 2000)

Stocks	Initial dividend yield	5.8
	Growth in earnings	6.8
	Change in valuation (increase in P/E ratio)	5.7
	Average annual return	**18.3**
Bonds	Initial yield	13.0
	Effect of decrease in interest rates	0.6
	Average annual return	**13.6**

This was truly an age of investor exuberance, with both stocks and bonds producing unusually generous rates of return. Although the nominal growth in earnings and dividends was not any greater during this period than in the unsatisfactory period of the 1970s, two factors contributed to produce spectacular stock-market returns. First, initial dividend yields of nearly 6 percent were unusually generous. Second, market sentiment went from despair to euphoria. Price-earnings multiples in the market almost quadrupled, from 8 to 30, and dividend yields fell to just over 1 percent. It was the change in valuation that lifted stock returns from unusually good to absolutely extraordinary.

Similarly, the initial yield of 13 percent in the bond market guaranteed that long-term holders would achieve double-digit returns. As I have said, what yield long-term holders see is what they get. In addition, interest rates fell, augmenting the returns further. Moreover, because the inflation rate moderated to the 3 percent level, real returns (returns after inflation) were well above their long-term average. The 1982–early 2000 period offered a once-in-a-lifetime opportunity to be invested in financial assets. Meanwhile, hard assets such as gold and oil produced negative rates of return.

ERA IV: THE AGE OF DISENCHANTMENT

The Age of Exuberance was followed by one of the worst decades for the stock market ever recorded. The period was widely considered to be "the lost decade" or "the naughties." It was a decade most stock-market investors would prefer to forget. The Internet bubble was followed by a crushing bear market. Later in the decade another bubble and crash rocked world stock markets as tumbling real estate prices destroyed the value of the complex mortgage-backed securities that were dependent on rising home prices. Investors were again reminded that the world was a very risky place. Valuation relationships changed accordingly.

Price-earning ratios fell and dividend yields rose. The investor who diversified her portfolio with bonds was able to mitigate the suffering, however, as bonds produced positive returns over the decade. The following table shows how returns developed during the Age of Disenchantment.

THE DEVELOPMENT OF STOCK AND BOND RETURNS (APRIL 2000–MARCH 2009)

Stocks	Initial dividend yield	1.2
	Growth in earnings	5.8
	Change in valuation (increase in P/E ratio)	–13.5
	Average annual return	**–6.5**
Bonds	Initial yield	7.0
	Effect of increase in interest rates	–0.6
	Average annual return	**6.4**

THE MARKETS FROM 2009 THROUGH 2014

By the trough in the market in 2009, the P/E multiple for the S&P 500 had fallen to less than 15 times cyclically depressed earnings. The dividend yield had increased to almost 3 percent. These changes in valuation relationships created the conditions for positive stock-market returns over the next five years. As earnings grew at double-digit rates, prices rose even more, aided by falling dividend yields and rising P/E multiples. Bonds also did reasonably well. U.S. Treasury yields ranged between 3 and 4 percent in 2009. In mid-2014, the ten-year U.S. Treasury bond yielded about

2½ percent. Thus, bonds offered some capital appreciation as their yields fell.

HANDICAPPING FUTURE RETURNS

So what's ahead? How can you judge returns from financial assets for the years ahead? Although I remain convinced that no one can predict short-term movements in securities markets, I do believe that it is possible to estimate the likely range of long-run rates of return that investors can expect from financial assets. And it would be unrealistic to anticipate that the generous returns earned by stock market investors during the 2009–14 period can be expected during the years ahead.

What, then, are the reasonable long-run expectations for returns? The same methods that I used in the past can be used today. I will illustrate the long-run return projections as of late 2014. The reader can perform similar calculations by using data appropriate for the time the projection is made.

Looking first at the bond market, as of late 2014, we can get a very good idea of the returns that will be gained by long-term holders. Holders of good-quality corporate bonds will earn approximately 4½ percent if they hold the bonds to maturity. Holders of ten-year Treasury bonds until maturity will earn just over 2 percent. Assuming that the inflation rate does not exceed 2 percent per year, both government and corporate bonds will provide investors with a positive but quite meager rate of return. These yields, however, are considerably lower than they have been since the late 1960s. Moreover, if inflation accelerates and interest rates rise, bond prices will fall and bond returns will be even lower. It is hard to imagine that bond investors will be well served by the yields available in 2014.

What returns can we project for common stocks as of late 2014? We can make reasonable estimates of at least the first two determinants of equity returns. We know that the 2014 dividend yield for the S&P 500 Index was about 1.9 percent. Suppose that earnings can grow at about 5 percent over the long term, a rate consistent with historical rates during periods of restrained inflation and similar to estimates made by Wall Street securities firms in late 2014. Adding the initial yield and growth rate together, we get a projected total return for the S&P 500 of just under 7 percent per year—higher than bond yields but somewhat below the long-term average since 1926, which had been close to 10 percent.

Of course, the major determinants of stock returns over short periods of time will be changes in the ways equities are valued in the market, that is, changes in market price-earnings multiples. Investors should ask themselves whether the valuation levels in the market during late 2014 will in fact hold up. Price-earnings multiples in late 2014 were in the high teens, higher than their long-run historical average. And dividend yields at 1.9 percent were well below their 4½ percent historical average.

To be sure, interest rates and inflation were both relatively low during 2014. When interest rates (and inflation) are low, somewhat higher price-earnings multiples and lower dividend yields are justified. Still, we can't simply assume that rates will always be so low and that inflation will always be benign. The unexpected frequently happens.

There is one predictable pattern in the stock market that also augurs for at best modest stock-market returns over the longer term. Depending on the forecast horizon involved, as much as 40 percent of the variability of future market returns can be predicted on the basis of the initial P/E multiple of the market as a whole.

An interesting way of presenting the results is shown in the diagram on page 347. The diagram was produced by measuring the P/E of the broad U.S. stock market each quarter since 1926 and then calculating the market's subsequent ten-year total return through 2014. The observations were then divided into deciles depending upon the level of the initial P/E multiple. In general, the exhibit shows that investors have earned higher total rates of return from the stock market when the initial P/E of the market portfolio was relatively low, and relatively low future rates of return when stocks were purchased at high P/E multiples.

MEDIAN TEN-YEAR ANNUAL COMPOUND TOTAL RETURN FROM HISTORIC P/E DECILES
1926 TO DATE

Returns Subsequent Ten Years

16.4% 15.2% 14.3% 11.8% 11.1% 9.7% 9.5% 7.5% 7.0% 3.7%

1st 2nd 3rd 4th 5th 6th 7th 8th 9th 10th

Deciles

Stocks Cheap   Stocks Expensive

P/E Decile	P/E Range For Decile	
1	Below	10.6x
2	10.6x to	11.6x
3	11.6x to	13.3x
4	13.3x to	15.1x
5	15.x to	16.8x
6	16.8x to	18.2x
7	18.2x to	19.8x
8	19.8x to	21.6x
9	21.6x to	25.1x
10	25.1x and above	

Source: The Leuthold Group.

In measuring the P/E for the market, these calculations do not use actual earnings per share but rather cyclically adjusted earnings. Thus, the measured P/Es are often referred to as CAPEs—cyclically adjusted P/E multiples. The CAPEs are available on Robert Shiller's website, and the earnings are calculated as average earnings over the last ten years. (Similar calculations can be obtained by averaging the past five years of earnings.) The Shiller CAPE in 2014 averaged just over 25. CAPEs do a reasonably good job of forecasting returns a decade ahead and confirm the expectation presented here of modest single-digit returns over the years ahead. But if your investment period is for less than a decade, no one can predict the returns you will receive with any degree of accuracy.

As a random walker on Wall Street, I am skeptical that anyone can predict the course of short-term stock-price movements, and perhaps we are better off for it. I am reminded of one of my favorite episodes from the marvelous old radio serial *I Love a Mystery*. This mystery was about a greedy stock-market investor who wished that just once he would be allowed to see the paper, with its stock-price changes, twenty-four hours in advance. By some occult twist his

A PRACTICAL GUIDE FOR RANDOM WALKERS

wish was granted, and early in the evening he received the late edition of the next day's paper. He worked feverishly through the night planning early-morning purchases and late-afternoon sales that would guarantee him a killing in the market. Then, before his elation had diminished, he read through the remainder of the paper—and came upon his own obituary. His servant found him dead the next morning.

Because I, fortunately, do not have access to future newspapers, I cannot tell how stock and bond prices will behave in any particular period ahead. Nevertheless, I am convinced that the moderate long-run estimates of bond and stock returns presented here are the most reasonable ones that can be made for investment planning decades into the twenty-first century. The point is not to invest with a rearview mirror projecting double-digit returns from the past into the future. We are likely to be in a low-return environment for some time to come.

14

A LIFE-CYCLE GUIDE
TO INVESTING

*There are two times in a man's life when he should not
speculate: when he can't afford it, and when he can.*
—Mark Twain, *Following the Equator*

INVESTMENT STRATEGY NEEDS to be keyed to one's life cycle.
A thirty-four-year-old and a sixty-eight-year-old saving for
retirement should use different financial instruments to
accomplish their goals. The thirty-four-year-old—just beginning
to enter the peak years of salaried earnings—can use wages to cover
any losses from increased risk. The sixty-eight-year-old—likely
to depend on investment income to supplement or replace salary
income—cannot risk incurring losses. Even the same financial
instrument can mean different things to different people depending on their capacity for risk. Although the thirty-four-year-old
and the sixty-eight-year-old may both invest in a certificate of
deposit, the younger may do so because of an attitudinal aversion
to risk and the older because of a reduced capacity to accept risk.
In the first case, one has more choice in how much risk to assume;
in the second, one does not.

The most important investment decision you will probably ever
make concerns the balancing of asset categories (stocks, bonds, real
estate, money-market securities, and so on) at different stages of your
life. According to Roger Ibbotson, who has spent a lifetime measur-

ing returns from alternative portfolios, more than 90 percent of an investor's total return is determined by the asset categories that are selected and their overall proportional representation. Less than 10 percent of investment success is determined by the specific stocks or mutual funds that an individual chooses. In this chapter, I will show you that whatever your aversion to risk—whatever your position on the eat-well, sleep-well scale—your age, income from employment, and specific responsibilities in life go a long way toward helping you determine the mix of assets in your portfolio.

FIVE ASSET-ALLOCATION PRINCIPLES

Before we can determine a rational basis for making asset-allocation decisions, certain principles must be kept firmly in mind. We've covered some of them implicitly in earlier chapters, but treating them explicitly here should prove very helpful. The key principles are:

1. History shows that risk and return are related.

2. The risk of investing in common stocks and bonds depends on the length of time the investments are held. The longer an investor's holding period, the lower the likely variation in the asset's return.

3. Dollar-cost averaging can be a useful, though controversial, technique to reduce the risk of stock and bond investment.

4. Rebalancing can reduce risk and, in some circumstances, increase investment returns.

5. You must distinguish between your attitude toward and your capacity for risk. The risks you can afford to take depend on your total financial situation, including the types and sources of your income exclusive of investment income.

1. Risk and Reward Are Related

Although you may be tired of hearing that investment rewards can be increased only by the assumption of greater risk, no lesson is more important in investment management. This fundamental law of finance is supported by centuries of historical data. The table below, summarizing the Ibbotson data presented earlier, illustrates the point.

TOTAL ANNUAL RETURNS FOR BASIC ASSET CLASSES, 1926–2013

	Average Annual Return	Risk Index (Year-to-Year Volatility of Returns)
Small-company common stocks	12.3%	32.3%
Large-company common stocks	10.1	20.2
Long-term government bonds	6.0	8.4
U.S. Treasury bills	3.5	3.1

Source: Ibbotson Associates.

Common stocks have clearly provided very generous long-run rates of return. It has been estimated that if George Washington had put just one dollar aside from his first presidential salary and invested it in common stocks, his heirs would have been millionaires more than ten times over by 2014. Roger Ibbotson estimates that stocks have provided a compounded rate of return of more than 8 percent per year since 1790. (As the table above shows, returns have been even more generous since 1926, when common stocks of large companies earned about 10 percent.) But this return came only at substantial risk to investors. Total returns were negative in about three years out of ten. So as you reach for higher returns, never forget the saying "There ain't no such thing as a free lunch." Higher risk is the price one pays for more generous returns.

2. Your Actual Risk in Stock and Bond Investing
Depends on the Length of Time
You Hold Your Investment

Your "staying power," the length of time you hold on to your investment, plays a critical role in the actual risk you assume from any investment decision. Thus, your stage in the life cycle is a critical element in determining the allocation of your assets. Let's see why the length of your holding period is so important in determining your capacity for risk.

We saw in the preceding table that long-term government bonds have provided an average 6 percent annual rate of return over an eighty-three-year period. The risk index, however, showed that in any single year this rate could stray far from the yearly average. Indeed, in many individual years, it was actually negative. Early in the first decade of the 2000s, you could invest in a 5¼ percent, twenty-year U.S. Treasury bond, and if you held it for exactly twenty years you would earn exactly 5¼ percent. The rub is that if you found that you had to sell it a year later, your rate of return could be 20 percent, 0 percent, or even a substantial loss if interest rates rose sharply, with existing bond prices falling to adjust to the new higher interest rates. I think you can see why your age and the likelihood that you can stay with your investment program can determine the amount of risk involved in any specific investment program.

What about investing in common stocks? Could it be that the risk of investing in stocks also decreases with the length of time they are held? The answer is a qualified yes. A substantial amount (but not all) of the risk of common-stock investment can be eliminated by adopting a program of long-term ownership and sticking to it through thick and thin (the buy-and-hold strategy discussed in earlier chapters).

The figure on page 353 is worth a thousand words, so I can be brief in my explanation. Note that if you held a diversified stock portfolio (such as the Standard & Poor's 500-Stock Index) during the period from 1950 through 2013, you would have earned, on average, a quite generous return of about 10 percent. But the range of outcomes is certainly far too wide for an investor who has trouble sleeping at night. In one year, the rate of return from a typical stock portfolio was more than 52 percent, whereas in another year it was negative by 37 percent. Clearly, there is no dependability of earning an adequate rate of return in any single year. A one-year U.S. Treasury security or a one-year government-guaranteed certificate of deposit is the investment for those who need the money next year.

RANGE OF ANNUAL RETURN RATES ON COMMON STOCKS FOR VARIOUS TIME PERIODS, 1950–2013

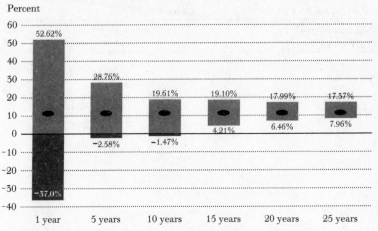

The ⬤ represents the average of the annual returns for various periods.

But note how the picture changes if you hold on to your common-stock investments for twenty-five years. Although there is some variability in the return achieved, depending on the exact twenty-five-year period in question, that variability is not large. On average, investments over all twenty-five-year periods covered by this figure have produced a rate of return of slightly more than 10 percent. This long-run expected rate of return was reduced by less than 3 percentage points if you happened to invest during the worst twenty-five-year period since 1950. It is this fundamental truth that makes a life-cycle view of investing so important. *The longer the time period over which you can hold on to your investments, the greater should be the share of common stocks in your portfolio.* In general, you are reasonably sure of earning the generous rates of return available from common stocks only if you can hold them for relatively long periods of time.*

Over investment periods of twenty or thirty years, stocks have generally been the clear winners, as is shown in the table below. These data further support the advice that younger people should have a larger proportion of their assets in stocks than older people.

PROBABILITY THAT STOCKS OUTPERFORM BONDS (PERCENTAGE OF PERIODS SINCE 1802 WHEN RETURNS OF STOCKS EXCEED THE RETURN FROM BONDS)

Investment Period	Percentage of periods when stocks have outperformed bonds
1 Year	60.2
2 Years	64.7
5 Years	69.5
10 Years	79.7
20 Years	91.3
30 Years	99.4

I do not mean to argue that stocks are not risky over long holding periods. Certainly the variability of the final value of your portfolio does increase the longer you hold your stocks. And we know that investors have experienced decades during which common stocks have produced near-zero overall returns. But for investors whose holding periods can be measured in twenty-five years or more, and especially those who reinvest their dividends and even add to their

*Technically, the finding that risk is reduced by longer holding periods depends on the reversion-to-the-mean phenomenon described in chapter 11. The interested reader is referred to Paul Samuelson's article "The Judgment of Economic Science on Rational Portfolio Management" in the *Journal of Portfolio Management* (Fall 1989).

holdings through dollar-cost averaging, common stocks are very likely to provide higher returns than are available from safe bonds and even safer government-guaranteed savings accounts.

Finally, perhaps the most important reason for investors to become more conservative with age is that they have fewer years of paid labor ahead of them. Thus, they cannot count on salary income to sustain them if the stock market has a period of negative returns. Reverses in the stock market could then directly affect an individual's standard of living, and the steadier—even if smaller—returns from bonds represent the more prudent investment stance. Hence, stocks should make up a smaller proportion of their assets.

3. Dollar-Cost Averaging Can Reduce the Risks of Investing in Stocks and Bonds

If, like most people, you will be building up your investment portfolio slowly over time with the accretion of yearly savings, you will be taking advantage of dollar-cost averaging. This technique is controversial, but it does help you avoid the risk of putting all your money in the stock or bond market at the wrong time.

Don't be alarmed by the fancy-sounding name. Dollar-cost averaging simply means investing the same fixed amount of money in, for example, the shares of some index mutual fund, at regular intervals—say, every month or quarter—over a long period of time. Periodic investments of equal dollar amounts in common stocks can reduce (but not avoid) the risks of equity investment by ensuring that the entire portfolio of stocks will not be purchased at temporarily inflated prices.

The table on page 356 assumes that $1,000 is invested each year. In scenario one, the market falls immediately after the investment program begins; then it rises sharply and finally falls again, ending, in year five, exactly where it began. In scenario two, the market rises continuously and ends up 40 percent higher. While exactly $5,000 is invested in both cases, the investor in the volatile market ends up with $6,048—a nice return of $1,048—even though the stock market ended exactly where it started. In the scenario where the market rose each year and ended up 40 percent from where it began, the investor's final stake is only $5,915.

DOLLAR-COST AVERAGING

	Volatile Flat Market			Rising Market		
Year	Amount Invested	Price of Index Fund	Number of Shares Purchased	Amount Invested	Price of Index Fund	Number of Shares Purchased
1	$1,000	$100	10	$1,000	$100	10
2	1,000	60	16.67	1,000	$110	9.09
3	1,000	60	16.67	1,000	$120	8.33
4	1,000	$140	7.14	1,000	$130	7.69
5	1,000	$100	10	1,000	$140	7.14
Amount invested	$5,000			$5,000		
Total shares purchased			60.48			42.25
Average cost of shares purchased	$82.67 ($5,000 ÷ 60.48)			$118.34 ($5,000 ÷ 42.25)		
Value at end	$6,048 (60.48 × $100)			$5,915 (42.25 × $140)		

Warren Buffett presents a lucid rationale for this investment principle. In one of his published essays he says:

A short quiz: If you plan to eat hamburgers throughout your life and are not a cattle producer, should you wish for higher or lower prices for beef? Likewise, if you are going to buy a car from time to time but are not an auto manufacturer, should you prefer higher or lower car prices? These questions, of course, answer themselves.

But now for the final exam: If you expect to be a net saver during the next five years, should you hope for a higher or lower stock market during that period? Many investors get this one wrong. Even though they are going to be net buyers of stocks for many years to come, they are elated when stock prices rise and depressed when they fall. In effect, they rejoice because prices have risen for the "hamburgers" they will soon be buying. This reaction makes no sense. Only those who will be sellers of equities in the near future should be happy at seeing stocks rise. Prospective purchasers should much prefer sinking prices.

Dollar-cost averaging is not a panacea that eliminates the risk of investing in common stocks. It will not save your 401(k) plan from a devastating fall in value during a year such as 2008, because no plan can protect you from a punishing bear market. And you must have both the cash and the confidence to continue making the periodic investments even when the sky is the darkest. No matter how scary the financial news, no matter how difficult it is to see any signs of optimism, you must not interrupt the automatic-pilot nature of the program. Because if you do, you will lose the benefit of buying at least some of your shares after a sharp market decline when they are for sale at low prices. Dollar-cost averaging will give you this bargain: Your average price per share will be lower than the average price at which you bought shares. Why? Because you'll buy more shares at low prices and fewer at high prices.

Some investment advisers are not fans of dollar-cost averaging, because the strategy is not optimal if the market does go straight up. (You would have been better off putting all $5,000 into the market at the beginning of the period.) But it does provide a reasonable insurance policy against poor future stock markets. And it does minimize the regret that inevitably follows if you were unlucky enough to have put all your money into the stock market during a peak period such as March of 2000 or October of 2007. To further illustrate the benefits of dollar-cost averaging, let's move from a hypothetical to a real example. The following table shows the results (ignoring taxes) of a $500 initial investment made on January 1, 1978, and thereafter $100 per month, in the shares of the Vanguard 500 Index mutual fund. Less than $44,000 was committed to the program. The final value was over $480,000.

ILLUSTRATION OF DOLLAR-COST AVERAGING WITH VANGUARD'S 500 INDEX FUND

Year Ended December 31	Total Cost of Cumulative Investments	Total Value of Shares Acquired
1978	$1,600	$1,669
1979	2,800	3,274
1980	4,000	5,755
1981	5,200	6,630
1982	6,400	9,487
1983	7,600	12,783
1984	8,800	14,864
1985	10,000	20,905
1986	11,200	25,935
1987	12,400	28,222
1988	13,600	34,080
1989	14,800	46,127
1990	16,000	45,804
1991	17,200	61,010
1992	18,400	66,818
1993	19,600	74,688
1994	20,800	76,780
1995	22,000	106,945
1996	23,200	132,769
1997	24,400	178,219
1998	25,600	230,621
1999	26,800	280,567
2000	28,000	256,274
2001	29,200	226,624
2002	30,400	177,505
2003	31,600	229,526
2004	32,800	255,481
2005	34,000	268,935
2006	35,200	312,320
2007	36,400	330,353
2008	37,600	208,942
2009	38,800	265,758
2010	40,000	306,758
2011	41,200	313,984
2012	42,400	364,935
2013	43,600	483,747

Of course, no one can be sure that the next forty-five years will provide the same returns as past periods. But the table does illustrate the tremendous potential gains possible from consistently following a dollar-cost averaging program. But remember, because there is a long-term uptrend in common-stock prices, this technique is not necessarily appropriate if you need to invest a lump sum such as a bequest.

If possible, keep a small reserve (in a money fund) to take advantage of market declines and buy a few extra shares if the market is down sharply. I'm not suggesting for a minute that you try to forecast the market. However, it's usually a good time to buy after the market has fallen out of bed. Just as hope and greed can sometimes feed on themselves to produce speculative bubbles, so do pessimism and despair react to produce market panics. The greatest market panics are just as unfounded as the most pathological speculative explosions. For the stock market as a whole (not for individual stocks), Newton's law has always worked in reverse: What goes down has come back up.

4. Rebalancing Can Reduce Investment Risk and Possibly Increase Returns

A very simple investment technique called rebalancing can reduce investment risk and, in some circumstances, even increase investment returns. The technique simply involves bringing the proportions of your assets devoted to different asset classes (e.g., stocks and bonds) back into the proportions suited to your age and your attitude toward and capacity for risk. Suppose you decided that your portfolio ought to consist of 60 percent stocks and 40 percent bonds and at the start of your investment program you divided your funds in those proportions between those two asset classes. But after one year you discovered that your stocks had risen sharply while the bonds had fallen in price, so the portfolio was now 70 percent stocks and 30 percent bonds. A 70–30 mix would then appear to be a riskier allocation than the one most suitable for your risk tolerance. The rebalancing technique calls for selling some stocks (or equity mutual funds) and buying bonds to bring the allocation back to 60–40.

The table below shows the results of a rebalancing strategy over the twenty years ending in December 2013. Every year (no more than once a year) the asset mix was brought back to the 60–40 initial allocation. Investments were made in low-cost index funds. The table shows that the volatility of the market value of the portfolio was markedly reduced by the rebalancing strategy. Moreover, rebalancing improved the average annual portfolio return. Without rebalancing, the portfolio returned 8.14 percent over the period. Rebalancing improved the annual rate of return to 8.41 percent with less volatility.

THE IMPORTANCE OF REBALANCING, JANUARY 1996–DECEMBER 2013
During This Period, an Annually Rebalanced Portfolio Provided Lower Volatility and Higher Return

	Average Annual Return	Risk* (Volatility)
60% Russell 3000/40% Barclays Aggregate Bond: Annually Rebalanced†	8.41	11.55
60% Russell 3000/40% Barclays Aggregate Bond: Never Rebalanced†	8.14	13.26

*Standard deviation of return.

†Stocks represented by a Russell 3000 Total Stock Market Fund. Bonds represented by a Barclays Aggregate Total Bond Market Fund. (Taxes not considered.)

What kind of alchemy permitted the investor who followed a rebalancing strategy at the end of each year to increase her rate of return? Think back to what was happening to the stock market over this period. By late 1999, the stock market had experienced an unprecedented bubble and equity values soared. The investor who rebalanced had no idea that the top of the market was near, but she did see that the equity portion of the portfolio had soared far above her 60 percent target. Thus, she sold enough equities (and bought enough bonds) to restore the original mix. Then, in late 2002, at just about the bottom of the bear market for stocks (and after a strong positive market for bonds), she found that the equity share was well below 60 percent and the bond share was well above 40 percent, and she rebalanced into stocks. Again, at the end of 2008, when stocks had plummeted and bonds had risen, she sold bonds and bought stocks. We all wish that we had a little genie who could reliably tell us to "buy low and sell high." Systematic rebalancing is the closest analogue we have.

5. Distinguishing between Your Attitude toward and Your Capacity for Risk

As I mentioned at the beginning of this chapter, the kinds of investments that are appropriate for you depend significantly on your noninvestment sources of income. Your earning ability outside your investments, and thus your capacity for risk, is usually related to your age. Three illustrations will help you understand this concept.

Mildred G. is a recently widowed sixty-four-year-old. She has been forced to give up her job as a registered nurse because of increasingly severe arthritis. Her modest house in Homewood, Illinois, is still mortgaged. Although the mortgage was taken out at a relatively low rate, it involves substantial monthly payments. Apart from monthly Social Security checks, all Mildred has to live on are the earnings on a $250,000 insurance policy of which she is the beneficiary and a $50,000 portfolio of small-growth stocks accumulated by her late husband.

It is clear that Mildred's capacity to bear risk is severely constrained by her financial situation. She has neither the life expectancy nor the physical ability to earn income outside her portfolio. Moreover, she has substantial fixed expenditures on her mortgage. She would have no ability to recoup a loss on her portfolio. She needs a portfolio of safe investments that can generate substantial income. Bonds and high-dividend-paying stocks, as from an index fund of real estate investment trusts, are the kinds of investments that are suitable. Risky (often non-dividend-paying) stocks of small-growth companies—no matter how attractive their prices may be—do not belong in Mildred's portfolio.

Tiffany B. is an ambitious, single twenty-six-year-old who recently completed an MBA at Stanford's Graduate School of Business and has entered a training program at the Bank of America. She just inherited a $50,000 legacy from her grandmother's estate. Her goal is to build a sizable portfolio that in later years could finance the purchase of a home and be available as a retirement nest egg.

For Tiffany, one can safely recommend an aggressive portfolio. She has both the life expectancy and the earning power to maintain her standard of living in the face of any financial loss. Although her personality will determine the precise amount of risk exposure she is willing to undertake, it is clear that Tiffany's portfolio belongs toward the far end of the risk-reward spectrum. Mildred's portfolio of small-growth stocks would be far more appropriate for Tiffany than for a sixty-four-year-old widow who is unable to work.

In the ninth edition of this book, I presented the case of Carl P., a forty-three-year-old foreman at a General Motors production plant in Pontiac, Michigan, who made over $70,000 per year. His wife, Joan, had a $12,500 annual income from selling Avon products. The Ps had four children, ages six to fifteen. Carl and Joan wanted all the children to attend college. They realized that private colleges were probably beyond their means but hoped that an education within the excellent Michigan state university system would be feasible. Fortunately, Carl had been saving regularly through the GM payroll savings plan but had chosen the option of purchasing GM stock under the plan. He had accumulated GM stock worth $219,000. He had no other assets but did have substantial equity in a modest house with only a small mortgage remaining to be paid off.

I suggested that Carl and Joan had a highly problematic portfolio. Both their income and their investments were tied up in GM. A negative development that caused a sharp loss in GM's common stock could ruin both the value of the portfolio and Carl's livelihood. Indeed, the story ended badly. General Motors declared bankruptcy in 2009. Carl lost his job as well as his investment portfolio. And this is not an isolated example. Remember the sad lesson learned by many Enron employees who lost not only their jobs but all their savings in Enron stock when the company went under. Never take on the same risks in your portfolio that attach to your major source of income.

THREE GUIDELINES TO TAILORING A LIFE-CYCLE INVESTMENT PLAN

Now that I have set the stage, the next sections present a life-cycle guide to investing. We will look here at some general rules that will be serviceable for most individuals at different stages of their lives. In the next section I summarize them in an investment guide. Of course, no guide will fit every individual case. Any game plan will require some alteration to fit individual circumstances. This section reviews three broad guidelines that will help you tailor an investment plan to your particular circumstances.

1. Specific Needs Require Dedicated Specific Assets

Always keep in mind: A specific need must be funded with specific assets dedicated to that need. Consider a young couple in their twenties attempting to build a retirement nest egg. The advice in the life-cycle investment guide that follows is certainly appropriate to meet those long-term objectives. But suppose that the couple expects to need a $30,000 down payment to purchase a house next year. That $30,000 to meet a specific need should be invested in a safe security, maturing when the money is required, such as a one-year certificate of deposit (CD). Similarly, if college tuitions will be needed in three, four, five, and six years, funds might be invested in zero-coupon securities of the appropriate maturity or in different CDs.

2. Recognize Your Tolerance for Risk

By far the biggest individual adjustment to the general guidelines suggested concerns your own attitude toward risk. It is for this reason that successful financial planning is more of an art than a science. General guidelines can be extremely helpful in determining what proportion of a person's funds should be deployed among different asset categories. But the key to whether any recommended asset allocation works for you is whether you are able to sleep at night. Risk tolerance is an essential aspect of any financial plan, and only you can evaluate your attitude toward risk. You can take some comfort in the fact that the risk involved in investing in common stocks and long-term bonds is reduced the longer the time period over which you accumulate and hold your investments. But you must have the temperament to accept considerable short-term fluctuations in your portfolio's value. How did you feel when the market fell by almost 50 percent in 2008? If you panicked and became physically ill because a large proportion of your assets was invested in common stocks, then clearly you should pare down the stock portion of your portfolio. Thus, subjective considerations also play a major role in the asset allocations you can accept, and you may legitimately stray from those recommended here depending on your aversion to risk.

3. Persistent Saving in Regular Amounts, No Matter How Small, Pays Off

One final preliminary before presenting the asset-allocation guide. What do you do if right now you have no assets to allocate? So many people of limited means believe that it is impossible to build up a sizable nest egg. Accumulating meaningful amounts of retirement savings often seems out of reach. Don't despair. The fact is that a program of regular saving each week—persistently followed, as through a payroll savings or 401(k) retirement plan— can in time produce substantial sums of money. Can you afford to put aside $23 per week? Or $11.50 per week? If you can, the possibility of eventually accumulating a large retirement fund is easily attainable if you have many working years ahead of you.

The table below shows the results from a regular savings program of $100 per month. An interest rate of 7 percent is assumed as an investment rate. The last column of the table shows the total values that will be accumulated over various time periods.* It is clear that regular savings of even moderate amounts make the attainment of meaningful sums of money entirely possible, even for those who start off with no nest egg at all. If you can put a few thousand dollars into the savings fund to begin with, the final sum will be increased significantly.

HOW RETIREMENT FUNDS CAN BUILD:
WHAT HAPPENS TO AN INVESTMENT OF $100 A MONTH,
EARNING A 7 PERCENT RETURN COMPOUNDED MONTHLY

Year	Cumulative Investment	Annual Income	Cumulative Income	Total Value
1	$1,200	$46	$46	$1,246
2	2,400	137	183	2,583
3	3,600	233	416	4,016
4	4,800	337	753	5,553
5	6,000	448	1,201	7,201
10	12,000	1,136	5,409	17,409
20	24,000	3,495	28,397	52,397
30	36,000	8,235	86,709	122,709

If you are able to save only $50 per month—only about $11.50 per week—cut the numbers in the table in half; if you can save $200 per month, double them. Pick no-load mutual funds to accumulate your nest egg because direct investments of small sums of money can be prohibitively expensive. Also, mutual funds permit automatic reinvestment of interest, or dividends and capital gains, as is assumed in the table. Finally, make sure you check whether

*I assume that the savings can be made in an IRA or other tax-favored savings vehicle, so income taxes on interest earnings are ignored.

your employer has a matched-savings plan. Obviously, if by saving through a company-sponsored retirement plan you are able to match your savings with company contributions and gain tax deductions as well, your nest egg will grow that much faster.

THE LIFE-CYCLE INVESTMENT GUIDE

The charts on pages 368–69 present a summary of the life-cycle investment guide. In the Talmud, Rabbi Isaac said that one should always divide one's wealth into three parts: a third in land, a third in merchandise (business), and a third ready at hand (in liquid form). Such an asset allocation is hardly unreasonable, but we can improve on this ancient advice because we have more refined instruments and a greater appreciation of the considerations that make different asset allocations appropriate for different people. The general ideas behind the recommendations have been spelled out in detail above. For those in their twenties, a very aggressive investment portfolio is recommended. At this age, there is lots of time to ride out the peaks and valleys of investment cycles, and you have a lifetime of earnings from employment ahead of you. The portfolio is not only heavy in common stocks but also contains a substantial proportion of international stocks, including the higher-risk emerging markets. As mentioned in chapter 8, one important advantage of international diversification is risk reduction. Plus, international diversification enables an investor to gain exposure to other growth areas in the world even as world markets become more closely correlated.

As investors age, they should start cutting back on riskier investments and start increasing the proportion of the portfolio committed to bonds and bond substitutes such as dividend growth stocks. The allocation is also increased to REITs that pay generous dividends. By the age of fifty-five, investors should start thinking about the transition to retirement and moving the portfolio toward income production. The proportion of bonds and bond substitutes increases, and the stock portfolio becomes more conservative and income-producing and less growth-oriented. In retirement, a portfolio heavily weighted in a variety of bonds and bond substitutes is recommended. A general rule of thumb used to be that the proportion of bonds in one's portfolio should equal one's age. Nevertheless, even in one's late sixties, I suggest that 40 percent of the portfolio be committed to ordinary common stocks and 15 percent to real estate equities (REITs) to give some income growth to cope with inflation. Indeed, since life expectancies have increased significantly since I first presented these asset allocations during the 1980s, I have increased the proportion of equities accordingly.

For most people, I recommend starting with a broad-based, Total Stock Market index fund rather than individual stocks for portfolio formation. I do so for two reasons. First, most people do not have sufficient capital to buy properly diversified portfolios themselves. Second, I recognize that most young people will not have substantial assets and will be accumulating portfolios by monthly investments. This makes mutual funds almost a necessity. As your assets grow, a U.S. stock-market fund should be augmented with a total international stock (index) fund that includes stocks from fast-growing emerging markets. You don't have to use the index funds I suggest, but do make sure that any mutual funds you buy are truly "no-load" and low cost. You will also see that I have included real estate explicitly in my recommendations. I said earlier that everyone should attempt to own his or her own home. I believe that everyone should have substantial real estate holdings, and some part of one's equity holdings should be in real estate investment trust (REIT) index mutual funds described in chapter 12. With respect to your bond holdings, the guide recommends taxable bonds. If, however, you are in the highest tax bracket and live in a high-tax state such as New York and your bonds are held outside of your retirement plan, I recommend that you use tax-exempt money funds and bond funds tailored to your state so that they are exempt from both federal and state taxes.

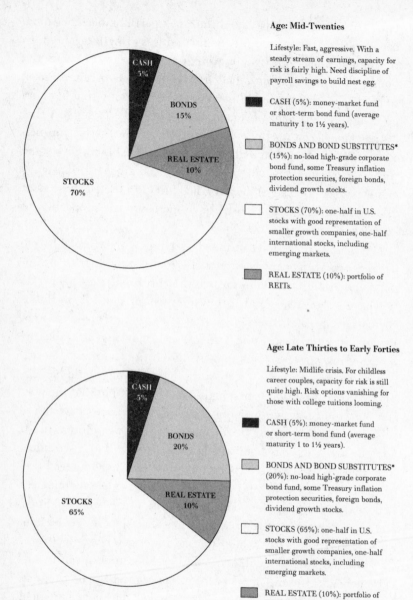

Age: Mid-Twenties

Lifestyle: Fast, aggressive. With a steady stream of earnings, capacity for risk is fairly high. Need discipline of payroll savings to build nest egg.

CASH (5%): money-market fund or short-term bond fund (average maturity 1 to 1½ years).

BONDS AND BOND SUBSTITUTES* (15%): no-load high-grade corporate bond fund, some Treasury inflation protection securities, foreign bonds, dividend growth stocks.

STOCKS (70%): one-half in U.S. stocks with good representation of smaller growth companies, one-half international stocks, including emerging markets.

REAL ESTATE (10%): portfolio of REITs.

CASH
5%

BONDS
15%

REAL ESTATE
10%

STOCKS
70%

Age: Late Thirties to Early Forties

Lifestyle: Midlife crisis. For childless career couples, capacity for risk is still quite high. Risk options vanishing for those with college tuitions looming.

CASH (5%): money-market fund or short-term bond fund (average maturity 1 to 1½ years).

BONDS AND BOND SUBSTITUTES* (20%): no-load high-grade corporate bond fund, some Treasury inflation protection securities, foreign bonds, dividend growth stocks.

STOCKS (65%): one-half in U.S. stocks with good representation of smaller growth companies, one-half international stocks, including emerging markets.

REAL ESTATE (10%): portfolio of REITs.

CASH
5%

BONDS
20%

REAL ESTATE
10%

STOCKS
65%

*BOND AND BOND SUBSTITUTES: If bonds are held outside of tax-favored retirement plans, tax-exempt bonds should be used.

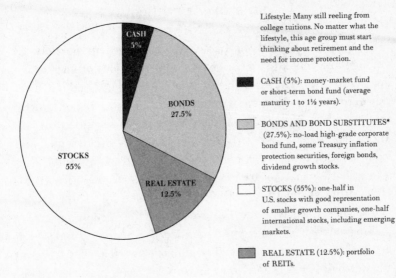

Age: Mid-Fifties

Lifestyle: Many still reeling from college tuitions. No matter what the lifestyle, this age group must start thinking about retirement and the need for income protection.

CASH (5%): money-market fund or short-term bond fund (average maturity 1 to 1½ years).

BONDS AND BOND SUBSTITUTES* (27.5%): no-load high-grade corporate bond fund, some Treasury inflation protection securities, foreign bonds, dividend growth stocks.

STOCKS (55%): one-half in U.S. stocks with good representation of smaller growth companies, one-half international stocks, including emerging markets.

REAL ESTATE (12.5%): portfolio of REITs.

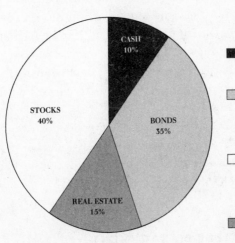

Age: Late Sixties and Beyond

Lifestyle: Enjoying leisure activities but also guarding against major health costs. Little or no capacity for risk.

CASH (10%): money-market fund or short-term bond fund (average maturity 1 to 1½ years).

BONDS AND BOND SUBSTITUTES* (35%): no-load high-grade corporate bond fund, some Treasury inflation protection securities, foreign bonds, dividend growth stocks.

STOCKS (40%): one-half in U.S. stocks with good representation of smaller growth companies; one-half international stocks, including emerging markets.

REAL ESTATE (15%): portfolio of REITs.

*BONDS AND BOND SUBSTITUTES: If bonds are held outside of tax-favored retirement plans tax-exempt bonds should be used.

LIFE-CYCLE FUNDS

Do you want to avoid the hassle of adjusting your portfolio as you age and rebalancing yearly as the proportions of your assets devoted to different asset classes vary with the ups and downs of the market? A new type of product has been developed during the 2000s just for those investors who want to set up a program and then forget about it. It is called the "life-cycle fund," and it automatically does the rebalancing and moves to a safer asset allocation as you age. Life-cycle funds are extremely useful for IRAs, 401(k)s, and other retirement plans.

You pick the particular life-cycle fund that is appropriate by picking a date when you expect to retire. For example, suppose you are forty years old in 2015, and you plan to retire at age seventy. You should then buy a life-cycle fund with a "target maturity 2045." Subsequent contributions can be directed to the same fund. The fund will be rebalanced annually, and the equity mix will become more conservative over time. The major mutual-fund complexes such as Vanguard, Fidelity, American Century, and T. Rowe Price all offer life-cycle funds. Details of the different maturities and the asset allocations offered may be found at the various company websites. When bond yields are extremely low, I tend to favor the life-cycle funds that are more aggressive—i.e., that start off with a larger allocation to equities. For those looking for the easiest way to manage their retirement monies, the automatic pilot aspect of life-cycle funds is a user-friendly feature. But before you sign up, check the fee schedule. Low fees mean more money in your pocket to enjoy a more comfortable retirement.

INVESTMENT MANAGEMENT
ONCE YOU HAVE RETIRED

More than ten thousand baby boomers are reaching the age of sixty-five each day, a pattern that will continue until year 2030.

According to the U.S. Census Bureau, more than one million baby boomers will live beyond the age of one hundred. A typical sixty-five-year-old has an average life expectancy of about twenty years. And half of all retirees will live longer than their average life expectancy. Yet most boomers have not heeded the advice in this book and have failed to save adequately for retirement. We have been a nation of consumers rather than savers. Given the long-run state of the federal budget, we can't rely on the government to bail us out.

Inadequate Preparation for Retirement

According to a survey of consumer finances conducted by the Federal Reserve Board of Governors, the typical American family has little money in the bank and considerable credit card debt. Only half of all Americans have any kind of retirement account, and only 11 percent of Americans in the bottom wealth quartile have a savings/retirement plan. While older Americans (between the ages of fifty-five and sixty-four) have, on average, $308,000 in retirement savings, that amount would not be sufficient to replace more than 15 percent of their household income in retirement. It's not a pretty picture. For many Americans, the golden years are likely to be extremely grim. Boomers approaching retirement who wish to avoid a life of privation have only two realistic choices. They can begin saving in a serious way. Alternatively, they can beat the odds and die early. As Henny Youngman used to say, "I've got all the money I'll ever need if I die by four o'clock."

For readers who find themselves in the situation I have described, I have no easy answers. You have no alternative but to work during your retirement years and to control expenses and save as much as possible. But there is a bright side even for you. There are many part-time jobs that can be done from home thanks to the Internet. And there are psychological and health benefits to working in retirement. Those who do some work have a better feeling of self-worth and connectedness, and they are also healthier. Indeed, I would recommend that everyone should delay retirement as long as possible and put off taking Social Security until full retirement age so as to maximize annual benefits. Only for those in very poor health with a short life expectancy would I recommend starting to take benefits at the earliest age at which you can start to collect.

INVESTING A RETIREMENT NEST EGG

If you've been prescient enough to save for your retirement, what investment strategies will help ensure that your money lasts as long as you do? There are two basic alternatives. First, one can annuitize all or part of one's retirement nest egg. Second, the retiree can continue to hold his investment portfolio and set up a withdrawal rate that provides for a comfortable retirement while minimizing the risk of outliving the money. How should one decide between the two alternatives?

Annuities

Sturgeon's Law, coined by the science fiction writer Theodore Sturgeon, states, "95 per cent of everything you hear or read is crap." That is certainly true in the investment world, but I sincerely believe that what you read here falls into the category of the other 5 percent. With respect to the advice regarding annuities, I suspect that the percentage of misinformation is closer to 99 percent. Your friendly annuity salesman will tell you that annuities are the only reasonable solution to the retirement investment problem. But many financial advisers are likely to say, "Don't buy an annuity: You'll lose all your money." What's an investor to make of such diametrically opposite advice?

Let's first get straight what annuities are and describe their two basic types. An annuity is often called "long-life insurance." Annuities are contracts made with an insurance company where the investor pays a sum of money to guarantee a series of periodic payments that will last as long as the annuitant lives. For example, during mid-2014 a $1,000,000 premium for a fixed lifetime annuity would purchase an average annual income stream of about $68,000 for a sixty-five-year-old male. If a sixty-five-year-old couple retired and desired a joint and survivor option (that provided payments as long as either member of the couple was alive), the million dollars would provide fixed annual payments of about $59,000.

Of course, with any inflation, the purchasing power of those payments would tend to decrease over time. For that reason, many people prefer to purchase "variable annuities." Variable annuities provide the possibility of rising payments over time, depending upon the type of investment assets (typically mutual funds) chosen by the annuitants. If the annuitant chooses common stocks, the payments will rise over time if the stock market does well, but they will fall if the stock market falters. Annuities can also be purchased with a guaranteed payment period. A twenty-year guaranteed period means that even if you die immediately after purchasing the annuity, your heirs will receive twenty years of payments. Of course, the annuitant will pay for that guarantee by accepting a substantial reduction in the dollar amount of the annual payments. The reduction for a seventy-year-old male is likely to be over 20 percent. Thus, if you are really bothered by the possibility of dying early and leaving nothing behind, it's probably better to scale back the proportion of your retirement nest egg used for an annuity purchase.

Variable annuities provide one approach to addressing inflation risk. Another possibility is an annuity with an explicit inflation-adjustment factor. For example, the Vanguard Group offers an annuity with an explicit inflation (consumer price index) adjustment up to 10 percent per year. Such a guarantee will naturally lower the initial payment substantially. A sixty-five-year-old couple desiring a joint and survivor option would find that $1,000,000 would provide an initial annual payment of only about $42,000 per year.

Annuities have one substantial advantage over a strategy of investing your retirement nest egg yourself. The annuity guarantees that you will not outlive your money. If you are blessed with the good health to live well into your nineties, it is the insurance company that takes the risk that it has paid out to you far more than your original principal plus its investment earnings. Risk-averse investors should certainly consider putting some or even all of their accumulated savings into an annuity contract upon retirement.

What, then, are the disadvantages of annuities? There are four possible disadvantages. Annuitization is inconsistent with a bequest motive, it gives the annuitant an inflexible path of consumption, it can involve high transactions costs, and it can be tax inefficient.

1. Desire to Leave a Bequest. Suppose a retiree has saved a substantial nest egg and can live comfortably off the dividends and interest from the investments. While an even larger amount of yearly income could be provided by annuitization, there would be no money left over for bequests when the annuitant dies. Many individuals have a strong desire to be able to leave some funds for children, relatives, or eleemosynary institutions. Full annuitization is inconsistent with such bequest motives.

2. Flexibility of Consumption. Suppose a couple retires in good health at age sixty-five and purchases an annuity that pays a fixed sum each year as long as either partner is alive. Such a "joint life" annuity is a common way for couples to structure their retirement. But right after signing the contract with the insurance company, both husband and wife learn that they have incurable diseases that are highly likely to reduce the period each will survive to a precious few years. The couple might reasonably want to take the around-the-world trip they had always dreamed of. Annuitization gives them no flexibility to alter their path of consumption if circumstances change.

3. Annuities Can Be Costly. Many annuities, especially those sold by insurance agents, can be very costly. The purchaser pays not only the fees and expenses of the insurance company but also a sales commission for the selling agent. Some annuities can thus be very poor investments.

4. Annuities Can Be Tax Inefficient. While there are some advantages to fixed annuities relative to bonds in terms of tax deferral, variable annuities turn preferentially taxed capital gains into ordinary income subject to higher tax rates. Also, partial annuitization of retirement account assets does not offset the required minimum distributions (RMDs) you must take. If you annuitize 50 percent of your IRA, you still have to take RMDs on the other half. This is no problem if you are spending at least that total amount, but tax inefficient if you are not.

So what should smart investors do? Here are my rules: At least partial annuitization usually does make sense. It is the only no-risk way of ensuring that you will not outlive your income. Reputable companies, such as Vanguard, offer annuities with low costs and no sales commissions. In order to make sensible decisions on annuities, you should do some comparison shopping on the Internet at http://www.valic.com. You will find considerable variation in rates from different providers.

THE DO-IT-YOURSELF METHOD

Many retirees will prefer to keep control of at least a portion of the assets they have saved for a retirement nest egg. Let's suppose the assets are invested in accordance with the bottom pie chart shown on page 369, that is, a bit more than half in equities and the rest in income-producing investments. Now that you are ready to crack open the nest egg for living expenses in retirement, how much can you spend if you want to be sure that your money will last as long as you do? I suggested in previous editions that you use "the 4 percent solution."*

---

*In the ninth edition of this book, I recommended a 4½ percent rule because bond yields were considerably higher than they were in 2014. Indeed, with interest rates as low as they are, a 3½ percent rule would give retirees even more assurance that they would not outlive their money.

Under the "4 percent solution," you should spend no more than 4 percent of the total value of your nest egg annually. At that rate the odds are good that you will not run out of money even if you live to a hundred. It is highly likely, too, that you will also be able to leave your heirs with a sum of money that has the same purchasing power as the total of your retirement nest egg. Under the 4 percent rule, you would need $450,000 of savings to produce an income in retirement of $1,500 per month or $18,000 per year.

Why only 4 percent? It is highly likely that a diversified portfolio of stocks and bonds will return more than 4 percent in the years ahead. But there are two reasons to limit the take-out rate. First, you need to allow your monthly payments to grow over time at the rate of inflation. Second, you need to ensure that you could ride out several years of the inevitable bear markets that the stock market can suffer during certain periods.

Let's see first where the 4 percent figure comes from. We suggested on page 346 that stocks might be expected to produce a long-run rate of return of about 7 percent per annum. A diversified bond portfolio including bond substitutes is likely to produce something like a 4 percent return. Hence we can project that a balanced portfolio of half stocks and half bonds should produce approximately a 5½ percent return per year. Now suppose that over the long pull the inflation rate is 1½ percent. That means that the corpus of the investment fund will have to rise by 1½ percent a year to preserve its purchasing power. Thus, in a typical year the investor will spend 4 percent of the fund, and the nest egg will grow by 1½ percent. Spending in the following year can also grow by 1½ percent so that the retiree will still be able to buy the same market basket of goods. By spending less than the total return from the portfolio, the retiree can preserve the purchasing power of both the investment fund and its annual income. The general rule is: First estimate the return of the investment fund, and then deduct the inflation rate to determine the sustainable level of spending. If inflation is likely to be 2 percent per year, then a 3½ percent spending rate would be more appropriate.

There is a second reason to set the spending rate below the

estimated rate of return for the whole fund. Actual returns from stocks and bonds vary considerably from year to year. Stock returns may average 7 percent, but in some years the return will be higher, whereas in other years it might be negative. Suppose you retired at age sixty-five and then encountered a bear market as severe as the one in 2008 and 2009, when stocks declined by about 50 percent. Had you withdrawn 7 percent annually, your savings could have been exhausted in less than ten years. But had you withdrawn only 3½ or 4 percent, you would be unlikely to run out of money even if you lived to a hundred. A conservative spending rate maximizes your chances of never running out of money. So if you are not retired, think hard about stashing away as much as you can so that later you can live comfortably even with a conservative withdrawal rate.

Three footnotes need to be added to our retirement rules. First, in order to smooth out your withdrawals over time, don't just spend 3½ or 4 percent of whatever value your investment fund achieves at the start of each year. Since markets fluctuate, your spending will be far too uneven and undependable from year to year. My advice is to start out spending 3½ or 4 percent of your retirement fund and then let the amount you take out grow by 1½ or 2 percent per year. This will smooth out the amount of income you will have in retirement.

Second, you will find that the interest income from your bonds and the dividends from your stocks are very likely to be less than the 3½ or 4 percent you wish to take out of your fund. So you will have to decide which of your assets to tap first. You should sell from the portion of your portfolio that has become overweighted relative to your target asset mix. Suppose that the stock market has rallied so sharply that an initial 50-50 portfolio has become lopsided with 60 percent stocks and 40 percent bonds. While you may be delighted that the stocks have done well, you should be concerned that the portfolio has become riskier. Take whatever extra moneys you need out of the stock portion of the portfolio, adjusting your asset allocation and producing needed income at the same time. Even if you don't need to tap the portfolio for spending income, I would recommend rebalancing your portfolio annually so as to keep the risk level of the portfolio consistent with your tolerance for risk.

Third, develop a strategy of tapping assets so as to defer paying income taxes as long as possible. When you start taking federally mandated required minimum distributions from IRAs and 401(k)s, you will need to use these before tapping other accounts. In taxable accounts, you are already paying income taxes on the dividends, interest, and realized capital gains that your investments produce. Thus, you certainly should spend these moneys next (or even first if you have not yet reached the age of seventy and a half when withdrawals are required). Next, spend additional tax-deferred assets. If your bequests are likely to be to your heirs, spend Roth IRA assets last. There is no required withdrawal for these accounts, and you can pass the assets to your heirs tax-free.

No one can guarantee that the rules I have suggested will keep you from outliving your money. And depending on your health and other income and assets, you may well want to alter my rules in one direction or another. If you find yourself at age eighty, withdrawing 4 percent each year and with a growing portfolio, either you have profound faith that medical science has finally discovered the Fountain of Youth, or you should consider loosening the purse strings.

15

THREE GIANT STEPS DOWN WALL STREET

Annual income twenty pounds,
annual expenditure nineteen six, result happiness.
Annual income twenty pounds, annual
expenditure twenty pounds ought and six, result misery.
—Charles Dickens, *David Copperfield*

THIS CHAPTER OFFERS rules for buying stocks and specific recommendations for the instruments you can use to follow the asset-allocation guidelines presented in chapter 14. By now you have made sensible decisions on taxes, housing, insurance, and getting the most out of your cash reserves. You have reviewed your objectives, your stage in the life cycle, and your attitude toward risk, and you have decided how much of your assets to put into the stock market. Now it is time for a quick prayer at Trinity Church and then some bold steps forward, taking great care to avoid the graveyard on either side. My rules can help you avoid costly mistakes and unnecessary sales charges, as well as increase your yield a mite without undue risk. I can't offer anything spectacular, but I do know that often a 1 or 2 percent increase in the yield on your assets can mean the difference between misery and happiness.

How do you go about buying stocks? Basically, there are three ways. I call them the No-Brainer Step, the Do-It-Yourself Step, and the Substitute-Player Step.

In the first case, you simply buy shares in various broad-based index funds or indexed ETFs designed to track the different classes of stocks that make up your portfolio. This method also has the virtue of being absolutely simple. Even if you have trouble chewing gum while walking randomly, you can master it. The market, in effect, pulls you along with it. For most investors, especially those who prefer an easy, lower-risk solution to investing, I recommend bowing to the wisdom of the market and using domestic and international index funds for the entire investment portfolio. For all investors, however, I recommend that the core of the investment portfolio—especially the retirement portion—be invested in index funds or ETFs.

Under the second system, you jog down Wall Street, picking your own stocks and perhaps overweighting certain industries or countries. This involves work, but also possibly a lot of fun. I don't recommend this approach for most investors. Nevertheless, if this is how you prefer to invest, I've provided a series of rules to help tilt the odds of success a bit more in your favor.

Third, you can sit on a curb and choose a professional investment manager to do the walking down Wall Street for you. The only way investors of modest means can accomplish this is to purchase managed mutual funds. I don't prefer actively managed funds, but later in the chapter I will at least present some suggestions that may help you choose the better ones if you insist on this option.

Earlier editions of my book described a strategy I called the Malkiel Step: buying closed-end investment company shares at a discount from the value of the shares held by the fund. When the first edition of this book was published, discounts on U.S. stocks were as high as 40 percent. Discounts are far smaller now, as these funds are more efficiently priced. But attractive discounts can arise, especially on international funds and municipal bond funds, and savvy investors can sometimes take advantage. The Malkiel Step is described later in this chapter.

THE NO-BRAINER STEP:
INVESTING IN INDEX FUNDS

The Standard & Poor's 500-Stock Index, a composite that represents about three-quarters of the value of all U.S.-traded common stocks, beats most of the experts over the long pull. Buying a portfolio of all companies in this index would be an easy way to own stocks. I argued back in 1973 (in the first edition of this book) that the means to adopt this approach was sorely needed for the small investor:

> What we need is a no-load, minimum-management-fee mutual fund that simply buys the hundreds of stocks making up the broad stock-market averages and does no trading from security to security in an attempt to catch the winners. Whenever below-average performance on the part of any mutual fund is noticed, fund spokesmen are quick to point out, "You can't buy the averages." It's time the public could.

Shortly after my book was published, the "index fund" idea caught on. One of the great virtues of capitalism is that when there is a need for a product, someone usually finds the will to produce it. In 1976, a mutual fund was created that allowed the public to get into the act as well. The Vanguard 500 Index Trust purchased the 500 stocks of the S&P 500 in the same proportions as their weight in the index. Each investor shared proportionately in the dividends and in the capital gains and losses of the fund's portfolio. Today, S&P 500 index funds are available from several mutual-fund complexes with expense ratios of about ⅟₂₀ of 1 percent of assets, far less than the expenses incurred by most actively managed mutual funds or bank trust departments. You can now buy the market conveniently and inexpensively. You can also buy exchange-traded S&P 500 index funds offered by State Street Global Advisors, BlackRock, and Vanguard.

The logic behind this strategy is the logic of the efficient-market hypothesis. But even if markets were not efficient, indexing would still be a very useful investment strategy. Since all the stocks in the market must be owned by someone, it follows that all the investors in the market will earn, on average, the market return. The index fund achieves the market return with minimal expenses. The average actively managed fund incurs an expense ratio of about 1 percent per year. Thus, the average actively managed fund must underperform the market as a whole by the amount of the expenses that are deducted from the gross return achieved. This would be true even if the market were not efficient.

The above-average long-run performance of the S&P 500 compared with that of mutual funds and major institutional investors has been confirmed by numerous studies described in previous chapters of this book. Yes, there are exceptions. But you can count on the fingers of your hands the number of mutual funds that have beaten index funds by any significant margin.

The Index-Fund Solution: A Summary

Let's now summarize the advantages of using index funds as your primary investment vehicle. Index funds have regularly produced rates of return exceeding those of active managers. There are two fundamental reasons for this excess performance: management fees and trading costs. Public index funds and exchange-traded funds are run at fees of ⅟₂₀ of 1 percent or even less. Actively managed public mutual funds charge annual management expenses that average 1 percentage point per year. Moreover, index funds trade only when necessary, whereas active funds typically have a turnover rate close to 100 percent. Using very modest estimates of trading costs, such turnover is undoubtedly an additional drag on performance. Even if stock markets were less than perfectly efficient, active management as a whole could not achieve gross returns exceeding the market. Therefore active managers must, on average, underperform the indexes by the amount of these expense and transactions costs disadvantages. Unfortunately, active managers as a group cannot be like the radio personality Garrison Keillor's fictional hometown of Lake Wobegon, where "all the children are above average."

Index funds are also tax-friendly. Index funds allow investors to defer the realization of capital gains or avoid them completely if the shares are later bequeathed. To the extent that the long-run uptrend in stock prices continues, switching from security to security involves realizing capital gains that are subject to tax.

Taxes are a crucially important financial consideration because the earlier realization of capital gains will substantially reduce net returns. Index funds do not trade from security to security and, thus, tend to avoid capital gains taxes.

Index funds are also relatively predictable. When you buy an actively managed fund, you can never be sure how it will do relative to its peers. When you buy an index fund, you can be reasonably certain that it will track its index and that it is likely to beat the average manager handily. Moreover, the index fund is always fully invested. You should not believe the active manager who claims that her fund will move into cash at the correct times. We have seen that market timing does not work. Finally, index funds are easier to evaluate. There are now over 5,000 stock mutual funds out there, and there is no reliable way to predict which ones are likely to outperform in the future. With index funds, you know exactly what you are getting, and the investment process is made incredibly simple.

"Leaping tall buildings in a single bound is nice, but can you outperform the S&P 500 Index?"

© 2002 by Thomas Cheney: Reprinted with permission.

Despite all the evidence to the contrary, suppose an investor still believed that superior investment management really does exist. Two issues remain: First, it is clear that such skill is very rare; and second, there appears to be no effective way to find such skill before it has been demonstrated. As I indicated in chapter 7, the best-performing funds in one period of time are not the best performers in the next period. The top performers of the 1990s had dreadful returns in the first decade of the 2000s. Paul Samuelson summed up the difficulty in the following parable. Suppose it was demonstrated that one out of twenty alcoholics could learn to become a moderate social drinker. The experienced clinician would answer, "Even if true, act as if it were false, for you will never identify that one in twenty, and in the attempt five in twenty will be ruined." Samuelson concluded that investors should forsake the search for such tiny needles in huge haystacks.

Stock trading among institutional investors is like an isometric exercise: lots of energy is expended, but between one investment manager and another it all balances out, and the trading costs the managers incur detract from performance. Like greyhounds at the dog track, professional money managers seem destined to lose their race with the mechanical rabbit. Small wonder that many institutional investors, including Intel, Exxon, Ford, American Telephone and Telegraph, Harvard University, the College Retirement Equity Fund, and the New York State Teachers Association, have put substantial portions of their assets into index funds. By 2014, about one-third of investment funds were "indexed."

How about you? When you buy an index fund, you give up the chance of boasting at the golf club about the fantastic gains you've made by picking stock-market winners. Broad diversification rules out extraordinary losses relative to the whole market. It also, by definition, rules out extraordinary gains. Thus, many Wall Street critics refer to index-fund investing as "guaranteed mediocrity." But experience shows conclusively that index-fund buyers are likely to obtain results exceeding those of the typical fund manager, whose large advisory fees and substantial portfolio turnover tend to reduce investment yields. Many people will find the guarantee of playing the stock-market game at par every round a very attractive one. Of course, this strategy does not rule out risk: If the market goes down, your portfolio is guaranteed to follow suit.

The index method of investment has other attractions for the small investor. It enables you to obtain very broad diversification with only a small investment. It also allows you to reduce brokerage charges. The index fund, by pooling the moneys of many investors, trades in larger blocks and pays minimal fees on its transactions. The index fund does all the work of collecting the dividends from all of the stocks it owns and sending you each quarter one check for all of your earnings (earnings that, incidentally, can be reinvested in the fund if you desire). In short, the index fund is a sensible, serviceable method for obtaining the market's rate of return with absolutely no effort and minimal expense.

A Broader Definition of Indexing

The indexing strategy is one that I have recommended since the first edition in 1973—even before index funds existed. It was clearly an idea whose time had come. By far the most popular index used is the Standard & Poor's 500-Stock Index, an index that well represents the major corporations in the U.S. market. But now, although I still recommend indexing, or so-called passive investing, there are valid criticisms of too narrow a definition of indexing. Many people incorrectly equate indexing with a strategy of simply buying the S&P 500 Index. That is no longer the only game in town. The S&P 500 omits the thousands of small companies that are among the most dynamic in the economy. Thus, I believe that if an investor is to buy only one U.S. index fund, the best general U.S. index to emulate is one of the broader indexes such as the Russell 3000, the Wilshire 5000 Total Market Index, the CRSP Index, or the MSCI U.S. Broad Market Index—not the S&P 500.

Eighty years of market history confirm that, in the aggregate, smaller stocks have tended to outperform larger ones. For example, from 1926 to 2014 a portfolio of smaller stocks produced a rate of return of about 12 percent annually, whereas the returns from larger stocks (such as those in the S&P 500) were about 10 percent. Although the smaller stocks were riskier than the major blue chips, the point is that a well-diversified portfolio of small companies is likely to produce enhanced returns. For this reason, I favor investing in an index that contains a much broader representation of U.S. companies, including large numbers of the small dynamic companies that are likely to be in early stages of their growth cycles.

Recall that the S&P 500 represents 75 to 80 percent of the market value of all outstanding U.S. common stocks. Literally thousands of companies represent the remaining 20 to 25 percent of the total U.S. market value. These are in many cases the emerging growth companies that offer higher investment rewards (as well as higher risks). The Wilshire 5000 Index contains all publicly traded U.S. common stocks. The Russell 3000 and MSCI Index contain all but the smallest (and much less liquid) stocks in the market. A number of mutual funds are now based on these broader indexes. Such index funds usually go by the name Total Stock Market Portfolio. Although past performance can never assure future results, the evidence clearly indicates that Total Stock Market index funds have provided higher returns than the average equity mutual-fund manager.

Moreover, unlike charity, indexing need not begin (and end) at home. As I argued in chapter 8, investors can reduce risk by diversifying internationally, by including asset classes such as real estate in the portfolio, and by placing some portion of their portfolio in bonds and bondlike securities, including Treasury inflation-protection securities. This is the basic lesson of modern portfolio theory. Thus, investors should not buy a U.S. stock-market index fund and hold no other securities. But this is not an argument against indexing because index funds currently exist that mimic the performance of various international indexes such as the Morgan Stanley Capital International (MSCI) index of European, Australasian, and Far Eastern (EAFE) securities, and the MSCI emerging-markets index. In addition, there are index funds holding real estate investment trusts (REITs). Finally, Total Bond Market index funds are available that track the Barclays Aggregate Bond Market Index. Moreover, all these index funds have also tended to outperform actively managed funds investing in similar securities.

One of the biggest mistakes that investors make is to fail to obtain sufficient international diversification. The United States represents only about one-third of the world economy. To be sure, a U.S. Total Stock Market fund does provide some global diversification because many of the multinational U.S. companies such as General Electric and Coca-Cola do a great deal of their business abroad. But the emerging markets of the world (such as China, India, and Brazil) have been growing much faster than the developed economies. China, for example, is still considered an emerging market. But it is now the second-largest economy in the world and is expected by the International Monetary Fund to continue to be the fastest-growing large economy in the world and to surpass the United States in size during the second decade of the twenty-first century. Hence, in the recommendations that follow, you will note that I suggest that a substantial part of every portfolio be invested in emerging markets.

Emerging markets are likely to sustain high growth rates well into the twenty-first century. Emerging markets tend to have younger populations than the developed world. Economies with younger populations tend to grow faster. Moreover, at the end of 2014, they had more attractive valuations than those in the United States. We have pointed out that cyclically adjusted P/E ratios (CAPEs) tend to have predictable power in forecasting longer-run equity returns in developed markets. The table below shows that the same relationship holds in emerging markets. Emerging market CAPEs were below 15 in late 2014. Future long-run returns have tended to be generous when stocks could be bought at those valuations.

CAPES AND FUTURE RETURNS IN EMERGING MARKETS (2005–2014)

CAPE	Future 5-Year Annual Equity Return
10–15	13%
15–20	11%
20–25	7%
25–30	1%
30–40	−3%

A PRACTICAL GUIDE FOR RANDOM WALKERS

Indexing also is an extremely effective strategy in emerging markets. The chart below indicates that the overwhelming majority of actively managed emerging-market equity funds are outperformed by the MSCI emerging-markets index. Even though emerging markets are not likely to be as efficient as developed markets, they are costly to access and to trade. Expense ratios of active funds are far higher than is the case in developed markets. Moreover, liquidity is lower and trading costs are higher in emerging markets. Therefore, after all expenses are accounted for, indexing turns out to be an excellent investment strategy.

EMERGING MARKET EQUITY FUNDS VERSUS MSCI EMERGING MARKET INDEX

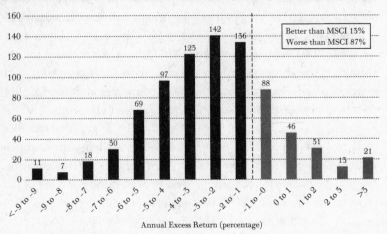

Annual Excess Return (percentage)

Ten years ended December 31, 2013 (net for fees, including survivorship bias).
Source: Morningstar.

A Specific Index-Fund Portfolio

The table on page 389 presents specific index-fund selections that investors can use to build their portfolios. The table shows the recommended percentages for those in their mid-fifties—the group I call the "aging boomers." Those who are not in their mid-fifties can use exactly the same selections and simply change the weights to those appropriate for their specific age group. Remember also that you may want to alter the percentages somewhat depending on your personal capacity for and attitude toward risk. Those willing to accept somewhat more risk in the hope of greater reward could increase the proportion of equities. Those who need a steady income for living expenses could increase their holdings of real estate equities and dividend growth stocks, because they provide somewhat larger current income.

A SPECIFIC INDEX-FUND PORTFOLIO FOR AGING BABY BOOMERS

Cash (5%)*

      Fidelity Money Market Fund (FXLXX)
      or Vanguard Prime Money Market Fund (VMMXX)

Bonds and Bond Substitutes (27½%)†

7½% U.S. Vanguard IntermediateTerm Bond (VICSX)
      or iShares Corporate Bond ETF (LQD)

7½% Vanguard Emerging Market Government Bond Fund (VGAVX)

12½% Wisdom Tree Dividend Growth Fund (DGRW)
      or Vanguard Dividend Growth Fund (VDIGX)†

Real Estate Equities (12½%)

      Vanguard REIT Index Fund (VGSIX)
      or Fidelity Spartan REIT Index Fund (FRXIX)

Stocks (55%)

27% U.S. Stocks
      Schwab Total Stock Market Index Fund (SWTSX)
      or Vanguard Total Stock Market Index Fund (VTSMX)

14% Developed International Markets
      Schwab International Index Fund (SWISX)
      or Vanguard International Index Fund (VTMGX)

14% Emerging International Markets
      Vanguard Emerging Markets Index Fund (VEIEX)
      or Fidelity Spartan Emerging Markets Index Fund (FFMAX)

---

*A short-term bond fund may be substituted for one of the money-market funds listed.

†Although it doesn't fit under the rubric of an index-fund portfolio, investors might consider putting part of the U.S. bond portfolio in Treasury inflation-protection securities. The dividend growth and corporate bond funds are also an exception since they are not standard index funds.

Remember also that I am assuming here that you hold most, if not all, of your securities in tax-advantaged retirement plans. Certainly all bonds should be held in such accounts. If bonds are held outside of retirement accounts, you may well prefer tax-exempt bonds rather than the taxable securities. Moreover, if your common stocks will be held in taxable accounts, you might consider tax-managed index funds. Finally, note that I have given you a choice of index funds from different mutual-fund complexes. Because of my long association with the Vanguard Group, I wanted also to suggest a number of non-Vanguard funds. All the funds listed have moderate expense ratios and are no-load. More information on these funds, including telephone numbers and websites, can be found in the Random Walker's Address Book, which follows this chapter. ETFs may be used in lieu of mutual funds.

ETFs and Taxes

One of the advantages, noted above, of passive portfolio management (that is, simply buying and holding an index fund) is that such a strategy minimizes transactions costs as well as taxes. Taxes are a crucially important financial consideration, as two Stanford University economists, Joel Dickson and John Shoven, have shown. Utilizing a sample of sixty-two mutual funds with long-term records, they found that, pre-tax, $1 invested in 1962 would have grown to $21.89 in 1992. After paying taxes on income dividends and capital gains distributions, however, that same $1 invested in mutual funds by a high-income investor would have grown to only $9.87.

To a considerable extent, index mutual funds help solve the tax problem. Because they do not trade from security to security, they tend to avoid capital gains taxes. Nevertheless, even index funds do realize some capital gains that are taxable to the holders. These gains generally arise involuntarily, either because of a buyout of one of the companies in the index, or because sales are forced on the mutual fund. The latter occurs when mutual-fund shareholders decide on balance to redeem their shares and the fund must sell securities to raise cash. Thus, even regular index funds are not a perfect solution for the problem of minimizing tax liabilities.

Exchange-traded index funds (ETFs) such as "spiders" (an S&P 500 Fund) and "vipers" (a Total Stock Market fund) can be more tax-efficient than regular index funds because they are able to make "in-kind" redemptions. In-kind redemptions proceed by delivering low-cost shares against redemption requests. This is not a taxable transaction for the fund, so there is no realization of gain that must be distributed to the fund's other shareholders. Moreover, the redeeming ETF shareholder pays taxes based on his or her original cost of the shares—not the fund's basis in the basket of stocks that is delivered. ETFs also happen to have rock-bottom expenses, sometimes even lower than those of equivalent mutual funds. A wide variety of ETFs are available not only for U.S. stocks but for international ones as well. ETFs are an excellent vehicle for the investment of lump sums that are to be allocated to index funds.

ETFs require the payment of transactions costs, however, including brokerage fees* and bid-asked spreads. No-load index mutual funds will better serve investors who will be accumulating index shares over time in small amounts. I suggest that you avoid the temptation to buy or sell ETFs at any hour of the day and to buy such funds on margin. I agree with John Bogle, founder of the Vanguard Group, who says, "Investors cut their own throats when they trade ETFs." If you are so tempted, follow the practice of Little Miss Muffet and run far away from the spiders and their siblings.

In the table on page 392, I list the ETFs that can be used to build your portfolio. Note that for investors who want to make their stock buying as easy as possible, there are Total World Index funds and ETFs that provide total international diversification with one-stop shopping.

---

* Some discount brokers offer commission-free trading of ETFs.

EXCHANGE TRADED FUNDS (ETFS)

	Ticker	Expense Ratio
Total U.S. Stock Market		
Vanguard Total Stock Market	VTI	0.05%
iShares Russell 3000	IWV	0.20%
Developed Markets (EAFE)		
Vanguard Europe Pacific	VEA	0.09%
iShares MSCI EAFE	EFA	0.35%
Emerging Markets		
Vanguard Emerging Markets	VWO	0.15%
iShares MSCI Emerging Markets	EEM	0.67%
Total World Ex-U.S.		
Vanguard FTSE All World (EX U.S.)	VEU	0.15%
SPDR MSCI ACWI (EX U.S.)	CWI	0.34%
Total World Including U.S.		
Vanguard Total World	VT	0.18%
iShares MSCI ACWI	ACWI	0.34%
Bond Market U.S.*		
Vanguard Intermediate-Term Corporate Bond	VCIT	0.12%
iShares Investment Grade Corporate Bond	LQD	0.15%

*Taxable investors should consider the closed-end municipal bond funds listed on page 405.

If you want an easy, time-tested method to achieve superior investment results, you can stop reading here. The indexed mutual funds or ETFs that I have listed will provide broad diversification, tax efficiency, and low expenses. Even if you want to buy individual stocks, do what institutional investors are increasingly doing: Index the core of your portfolio along the lines suggested and then take active bets with extra funds. With a strong core of index funds, you can take these bets with much less risk than if the whole portfolio were actively managed. And even if you make some errors, they won't prove fatal.

THE DO-IT-YOURSELF STEP:
POTENTIALLY USEFUL STOCK-PICKING RULES

Indexing is the strategy I recommend most highly for individuals and institutions. I do recognize, however, that indexing the entire portfolio may be considered by many to be a very dull strategy. Those with speculative temperaments will undoubtedly prefer using their own steps (and wits) to pick winners, at least for some portion of their investment funds. For those who insist on playing the game themselves, the Do-It-Yourself Step may be appealing.

Having been smitten with the gambling urge since childhood, I can well understand why many investors have a compulsion to try to pick the big winners on their own and a total lack of interest in a system that promises results merely equivalent to those in the market as a whole. The problem is that it takes a lot of work to do it yourself, and consistent winners are very rare. For those who regard investing as play, however, this section demonstrates how a sensible strategy might produce substantial rewards and, at the very least, minimize the risks in playing the stock-picking game.

Before putting my strategy to work, however, you need to know the sources of investment information. Most information sources can be obtained at public libraries. You should be an avid reader of the financial pages of daily newspapers, particularly the *New York Times* and the *Wall Street Journal*. Weeklies such as *Barron's* should be on your "must-read" list as well. Business magazines such as *Bloomberg Businessweek*, *Fortune*, and *Forbes* are also valuable for gaining exposure to investment ideas. The major investment advisory services are good, too. You should, for example, try to have access to Standard & Poor's *Outlook* and the Value Line *Investment Survey*. The first is a weekly publication that contains recommendations of stocks to buy; the second presents historical records, current reviews, and risk (beta) ratings of all the major securities. Finally, a wealth of information, including security analysts' recommendations, is available on the Internet.

In the first edition of *A Random Walk Down Wall Street*, over forty years ago, I proposed four rules for successful stock selection. I find them just as serviceable today. In abridged form, the rules, some of which have been mentioned in earlier chapters, are as follows:

Rule 1: Confine stock purchases to companies that appear able to sustain above-average earnings growth for at least five years. Difficult as the job may be, picking stocks whose earnings grow is the name of the game. Consistent growth not only increases the earnings and dividends of the company but may also increase the multiple that the market is willing to pay for those earnings. Thus, the purchaser of a stock whose earnings begin to grow rapidly has a potential double benefit—both the earnings and the multiple may increase.

Rule 2: Never pay more for a stock than can reasonably be justified by a firm foundation of value. Although I am convinced that you can never judge the exact intrinsic value of a stock, I do feel that you can roughly gauge when a stock seems to be reasonably priced. The market price-earnings multiple is a good place to start: Buy stocks selling at multiples in line with, or not very much above, this ratio. Look for growth situations that the market has not already recognized by bidding the stock's multiple to a large premium. If the growth actually takes place, you will often get a double bonus—both the earnings and the price-earnings multiple can rise. Beware of stocks with very high multiples and many years of growth already discounted in their prices. If earnings decline rather than grow, you can get double trouble—the multiple will drop along with the earnings. Following this rule would have avoided the heavy losses suffered by investors in the premier high-tech growth stocks that sold at astronomical price-earnings multiples in early 2000.

Note that, although similar, this is not simply another endorsement of the "buy low P/E stocks" strategy. Under my rule it is perfectly all right to buy a stock with a P/E multiple slightly above the market average—as long as the company's growth prospects are substantially above average. You might call this an adjusted low P/E strategy. Some people call this a GARP (Growth At A

Reasonable Price) strategy. Buy stocks whose P/Es are low relative to their growth prospects. If you can be even reasonably accurate in picking companies that do indeed enjoy above-average growth, you will be rewarded with above-average returns.

Rule 3: It helps to buy stocks with the kinds of stories of anticipated growth on which investors can build castles in the air. I stressed in chapter 2 the importance of psychological elements in stock-price determination. Individual and institutional investors are not computers that calculate warranted price-earnings multiples and then print out buy and sell decisions. They are emotional human beings—driven by greed, gambling instinct, hope, and fear in their stock-market decisions. This is why successful investing demands both intellectual and psychological acuteness. Of course, the market is not totally subjective either; if a positive growth rate appears to be established, the stock is almost certain to develop some type of following. But stocks are like people—some have more attractive personalities than others, and the improvement in a stock's multiple may be smaller if its story never catches on. The key to success is being where other investors will be, several months before they get there. So ask yourself whether the story about your stock is one that is likely to catch the fancy of the crowd. Can the story generate contagious dreams? Is it a story on which investors can build castles in the air—but castles in the air that really rest on a firm foundation?

Rule 4: Trade as little as possible. I agree with the Wall Street maxim "Ride the winners and sell the losers," but not because I believe in technical analysis. Frequent switching accomplishes nothing but subsidizing your broker and increasing your tax burden when you do realize gains. I do not say, "Never sell a stock on which you have a gain." The circumstances that led you to buy the stock may change, and, especially when it gets to be tulip time in the market, many of your successful growth stocks may become overweighted in your portfolio, as they did during the Internet bubble of 1999–2000. But it is very difficult to recognize the proper time to sell, and heavy tax costs may be involved. My own philosophy leads me to minimize trading as much as possible. I am merciless with the losers, however. With few exceptions, I sell before the end of each calendar year any stocks on which I have a loss. The reason for this timing is that losses are deductible (up to certain amounts) for tax purposes, or can offset gains you may already have taken. Thus, taking losses can lower your tax bill. I might hold a losing position if the growth I expect begins to materialize and I am convinced that my stock will eventually work out. But I do not recommend too much patience in losing situations, especially when prompt action can produce immediate tax benefits.

The efficient-market theory warns that following even sensible rules such as these is unlikely to lead to superior performance. Nonprofessional investors labor under many handicaps. Earnings reports cannot always be trusted. And once a story is out in the regular press, it's likely that the market has already taken account of the information. Picking individual stocks is like breeding thoroughbred porcupines. You study and study and make up your mind, and then proceed very carefully. In the final analysis, much as I hope that investors have achieved successful records following my good advice, I am well aware that the winners in the stock-picking game may have benefited mainly from Lady Luck.

For all its hazards, picking individual stocks is a fascinating game. My rules do, I believe, tilt the odds in your favor while protecting you from the excessive risk involved in high-multiple stocks. But if you choose this course, remember that a large number of other investors—including the pros—are trying to play the same game. And the odds of anyone's consistently beating the market are pretty slim. Nevertheless, for many of us, trying to outguess the market is a game that is much too much fun to give up. Even if you were convinced you would not do any better than average, I'm sure that most of you with speculative temperaments would still want to keep on playing the game of selecting individual stocks with at least some portion of the money you invest. My rules permit you to do so in a way that significantly limits your exposure to risk.

If you do want to pick stocks yourself, I strongly suggest a mixed strategy: Index the core of your portfolio, and try the stock-picking game for the money you can afford to put at somewhat greater risk. If the main part of your retirement funds is broadly indexed and your stocks are diversified with bonds and real estate, you can safely take a flyer on some individual stocks, knowing that your basic nest egg is reasonably secure.

Even if you use index funds for all your investments, you might choose to alter the weights of various portfolio components in an attempt to enhance returns. One adjustment that I make in my own indexed portfolio is to overweight China relative to its weight in the world index benchmark. I do so because I believe that China gets too low a weight relative to its economic importance. Certain peculiarities about China's stock markets lead to China's being underweighted both in emerging-markets index funds and in total world indexes.

Most indexes are "float" weighted. If some of a company's shares do not trade freely, they are not counted in the company's weight in the index. Float weighting means that China gets underweighted for two reasons. First, none of the shares traded in the local Chinese stock markets in Shanghai and Shenzhen get counted, because these shares have been available only to Chinese citizens (with minor exceptions). Only the freely tradable shares of Chinese companies listed in Hong Kong or New York are counted in the index. A second reason China gets underweighted is that the Chinese government owns a huge portion of the shares of many companies, and those shares are not counted in the float. As a result, China gets only about 2 percent of the weight in the world indexes, whereas, adjusted for purchasing-power parity, China's GDP is about 13 percent of the world's GDP and is growing rapidly.

Hence, I believe that investors need to put more China into their portfolios than is available in general world or emerging-market index funds. I am, however, true to my indexing beliefs and think the best way to do it is to buy a broad-based index fund of Chinese companies. Three of them that trade on the New York Stock Exchange are YAO (an index fund representing all Chinese companies available to international investors), HAO (a small-capitalization index fund that contains more entrepreneurial companies and ones with less government ownership), and TAO (a Chinese real estate fund).

THE SUBSTITUTE-PLAYER STEP: HIRING A PROFESSIONAL WALL STREET WALKER

There's an easier way to gamble in your investment walk: Instead of trying to pick the individual winners (stocks), pick the best coaches (investment managers). These "coaches" come in the form of active mutual-fund managers, and there are thousands of them for you to pick from.

In previous editions of this book, I provided the names of several investment managers who had enjoyed long-term records of successful portfolio management as well as brief biographies explaining their investment styles. These managers were among the very few who had shown an ability to beat the market over long periods of time. I have abandoned that practice in the current edition for two reasons.

First, with the exception of Warren Buffett, those managers have now retired from active portfolio management, and Buffett himself was well above retirement age in 2014. Second, I have become increasingly convinced that the past records of mutual-fund managers are essentially worthless in predicting future success. The few examples of consistently superior performance occur no more frequently than can be expected by chance.

Assuming that you prefer to invest in an actively managed equity mutual fund, is it really possible to select a fund that will be a top performer? One plausible method, favored by many financial planners and editors, is to choose funds with the best recent performance records. The financial pages of newspapers and magazines are filled with fund advertisements claiming that a particular fund is number one in performance. There are at least two problems with this approach. First, many fund advertisements are quite misleading. The number one ranking is typically for a self-selected specific time period and compared with a particular (usually small) group of common-stock funds. For example, one fund advertised itself as: "Now Ranked #1 for Performance. The Fund That's Performed Through Booms, Busts and 11 Presidential Elections." It is implied that this fund was a top performer over a period of forty-four years. The truth of the matter, revealed in a small footnote referenced by the asterisk, was that the fund was number one only during one specific three-month period and only compared with a specific category of funds with asset values between $250 million and $500 million.

The more important reason to be skeptical of past performance records is that, as I have mentioned earlier, there is no consistent long-run relationship between performance in one period and investment results in the next. I have studied the persistence of mutual-fund performance over more than forty years and conclude that it is simply impossible for investors to guarantee themselves above-average returns by purchasing those funds with the best recent records. Although there have been a few examples (such as Buffett's Berkshire Hathaway) of fairly consistent long-run superb performance, the general result is that there is no dependable long-term persistence. You can't assure yourself of superior performance by buying mutual funds that may have beaten the market in some past period. Once again, the past does not predict the future.

I have tested a strategy whereby at the start of each year investors would rank all general equity funds on the basis of the funds' records over the past twelve months. In alternative strategies, I have assumed that the investor buys the top ten funds, the top twenty funds, and so on. There is no way to beat the market consistently by purchasing the mutual funds that have performed best in the past.

I also tested a strategy of purchasing the "best" funds as ranked by the leading financial magazines. The clear implication of these tests in the laboratory of fund performance, as well as the academic work reported in Part Two of this book, is that you cannot depend on an excellent record continuing persistently in the future. Indeed, it's often the case that the hot performers of one period are the dogs of the next.

THE MORNINGSTAR MUTUAL-FUND
INFORMATION SERVICE

If recent performance is not a reliable indicator in choosing a mutual fund, what is? I have often said that the two best things that have happened to the mutual-fund industry are the arrival of Jack Bogle, who started the low-cost, consumer-friendly Vanguard Group of mutual funds during the mid-1970s, and Don Phillips, who in the early 1990s initiated the extremely useful Morningstar Service, which publishes information on mutual funds.

Basically, Morningstar is one of the most comprehensive sources of mutual-fund information an investor can find. For each mutual fund, it publishes a report crammed full of relevant data. Its reports show past returns, risk ratings, portfolio composition, and the fund's investment style (for example, the fund invests in established large companies or smaller growth companies; favors "value" stocks with low P/E ratios; buys foreign or domestic stocks or both; and so on). The reports indicate whether the fund has any sales charges (load fees) and show the annual expense ratios for the fund and the percentage of the fund's asset value represented by unrealized appreciation. If you buy actively managed funds you should look for no-load, low-turnover, low-expense funds with little unrealized appreciation to minimize future tax liability. For bond funds, Morningstar gives data on returns, effective maturity, quality of bonds held, and information on loads and expenses.

The Morningstar Service also uses a five-star rating system. It rates past performance, taking into account broad-market returns and the costs and risks associated with getting those returns. The top funds are given five stars—two more than Michelin assigns to the top restaurants in the world. The stars are useful in categorizing past performance. Unlike the Michelin stars, which virtually guarantee the diner a meal of the designated quality, however, the Morningstar ratings do not guarantee an investor continued superior performance. In the past, five-star funds have not done better than three-star or even one-star funds. The wise investor will look beyond the stars in making appropriate investment decisions.

Is there any way to select an actively managed fund that is likely to be an above-average performer? I have undertaken many studies of mutual-fund returns over the years in an attempt to explain why some funds perform better than others. As indicated earlier, past performance is not helpful in predicting future returns. The two variables that do the best job in predicting future performance are expense ratios and turnover. High expenses and high turnover depress returns—especially after-tax returns if the funds are held in taxable accounts. The best-performing actively managed funds have moderate expense ratios and low turnover. The lower the expenses charged by the purveyor of the investment service, the more there will be for the investor. As Jack Bogle, the founder of the Vanguard Group, puts it, in the mutual fund business, "you get what you don't pay for." I suggest that investors never buy actively managed funds with expense ratios above 50 basis points (½ of 1 percent) and with turnover of more than 50 percent. Expense ratios and turnover statistics are available on the funds' websites and from investment sources such as Morningstar.

THE MALKIEL STEP

As readers of previous editions know, I like to buy shares in a special type of investment fund called a closed-end fund (officially, a closed-end investment company) when they are available at attractive discounts. Closed-end funds differ from open-end mutual funds (the kind discussed in the preceding section) in that they neither issue nor redeem shares after the initial offering. To buy or sell shares, you have to go to a broker.

The price of the shares depends on what other investors are willing to pay for them; however, unlike shares in open-end funds or in ETFs, this price is not necessarily related to net asset value. Thus, a closed-end fund can sell at a premium above or at a discount from its net asset value. During much of the 1970s and at the start of the 1980s, these funds were selling at substantial discounts from their net asset value. Closed-end funds hire professional managers, and their expenses are no higher than those of ordinary mutual funds. So for those who believe in professional investment management, here was a way to buy it at a discount, and I told my readers so.

The beauty of buying these highly discounted closed-end funds was that, even if the discounts remained at high levels, investors would still reap extraordinary rewards from their purchase. If you could buy shares at a 25 percent discount, you would have $4 of asset value on which dividends could be earned for every $3 you invested. So even if the funds just equaled the market return, as believers in the random walk would expect, you would beat the averages.

It was like having a $100 savings account paying 5 percent interest. You deposit $100 and earn $5 interest each year. Only this savings account could be bought at a 25 percent discount—in other words, for $75. You still got $5 interest (5 percent of $100), but because you paid only $75 for the account, your rate of return was 6.67 percent (5 ÷ 75). Note that this increase in yield was in no way predicated on the discount narrowing. Even if you got only $75 back when you cashed in, you would still have received a big bonus in extra returns while holding the account. The discount on closed-end funds provided a similar bonus. You got your share of dividends from $1 worth of assets, even though you paid only 75 cents.

The strategy worked even better than expected. Discounts have narrowed significantly on U.S. closed-end funds. Although the publicity given closed-end funds in my books may have helped to close the discounts, I think the fundamental reason for the narrowing is that our capital markets are reasonably efficient. The market may misvalue assets from time to time, creating temporary inefficiencies. But if there is truly some area of pricing inefficiency that can be discovered by the market and dependably exploited, then value-seeking investors will take advantage of these opportunities and thereby eliminate them. Pricing irregularities may well exist and even persist for periods of time, but the financial laws of gravity will eventually take hold and true value will out.

With their discounts for the most part dried up at the time this edition goes to press, most domestic U.S. closed-end funds are no longer an especially attractive investment opportunity.* But discounts exist for some international funds, funds investing in emerging markets, and funds investing in municipal bonds. Diversified portfolios of emerging-market closed-end funds selling at discounts are a viable—and probably a preferable—alternative to an emerging-market index fund. When discounts of 10 percent or more exist, it is time to open your wallet to closed-end funds. The table on page 404 lists a few closed-end emerging-market funds with their discounts as of mid-2014. Check the discounts when you are ready to invest to determine whether they are greater than 10 percent. Discounts do vary from week to week.

---

*Indeed, when you buy a new closed-end fund at par value plus about 5 percent for underwriting commissions, not only do you get hit with the equivalent of a large loading fee but you also run the risk that the fund will sell at a discount at some time in the future. Never buy a closed-end fund at its initial offering price. It will almost invariably turn out to be a bad deal. It may be worth checking, however, to see whether discounts widen in the future during unsettled market conditions.

SELECTED EMERGING-MARKET CLOSED-END FUNDS SELLING AT DISCOUNTS FROM ASSET VALUES (JUNE 2014)

Fund Name (Ticker Symbol)	Net Asset Value (NAV)	Price	Discount	Description
Templeton Dragon (TDF)	$27.51	$24.41	–11.5%	Hong Kong, China, Taiwan
Morgan Stanley Asia Pacific (APF)	$17.82	$15.94	–10.5%	Asian markets
Aberdeen Latin America Equity Fund (LAQ)	$32.89	$29.54	–11.2%	All Latin American emerging markets
Korea Fund (KF)	$46.70	$41.84	–10.4%	Korean securities
Aberdeen Greater China Fund (GCH)	$11.30	$9.97	–11.8%	Equity securities of Greater China companies
Aberdeen Singapore Fund (SGF)	$14.69	$13.00	–11.5%	Singapore securities (at least 65%) and Pacific Basin countries
Morgan Stanley Emerging Market (MSF)	$17.12	$15.42	–9.9%	All emerging markets
Taiwan (TWN)	$20.94	$19.17	–8.5%	Taiwanese securities

There are also closed-end funds that hold tax-exempt municipal bonds. These funds have tended to sell at discounts at times when investors have been concerned about the creditworthiness of municipal securities. Worries about the indebtedness of Puerto Rico and the Detroit bankruptcy led to lower prices and higher yields for all state and local government securities. Those concerns also led to lower prices and bigger discounts for closed-end municipal bond funds. In 2014, many of these funds sold at discounts of 10 percent or more, and they provided investors with yields between 6 and 7 percent. The yield on regular long-term municipal bond funds was between 3½ and 4 percent in 2014.

The closed-end funds enhance their yields by using moderate leverage. They borrow moneys at very low short-term interest rates to buy higher-yielding long-term bonds. This increases their yields above those of mutual bond funds that do not use leverage. This is not a free lunch. Leverage increases the potential volatility and thus the riskiness of the closed-end funds.

SELECTED CLOSED-END MUNICIPAL BOND FUNDS SELLING AT DISCOUNTS FROM NET ASSET VALUES (JUNE 2014)

Fund Name (Ticker Symbol)	Net Asset Value (NAV)	Price	Discount	Description
BlackRock Municipal Income Investment (BBF)	$15.12	$13.77	−8.9%	National
Invesco Municipal Trust (VKQ)	$13.77	$12.43	−9.7%	National
Nuveen Quality Municipal Fund (NQI)	$14.66	$13.11	−10.6%	National
BlackRock CA Municipal (BFZ)	$15.92	$15.02	−5.7%	California
Nuveen NJ Municipal (NQJ)	$15.34	$13.60	−11.3%	New Jersey
Nuveen NY Dividend Advantage (NAN)	$15.20	$13.67	−10.1%	New York
Eaton Vance Municipal (MAB)	$14.90	$13.61	−8.7%	Massachusetts
BlackRock PA Municipal Yield (MPA)	$15.83	$14.24	−10.0%	Pennsylvania

A PARADOX

Although some emerging-market closed-end funds appeared attractive during 2014, domestic funds holding U.S. equities were no longer selling at the bargain-basement levels that existed in earlier periods. This illustrates an important paradox about investment advice, as well as the maxim that true values do eventually prevail in the market. There is a fundamental paradox about the usefulness of investment advice concerning specific securities. If the advice reaches enough people and they act on it, knowledge of the advice destroys its usefulness. If everyone knows about a "good buy" and everyone rushes in to buy, the price of the "good buy" will rise until it is no longer a good buy.

This is the main logical pillar on which the efficient-market theory rests. If the spread of news is unimpeded, prices will react quickly so that they reflect all that is known. This led me to predict in the 1981 edition that favorable discounts would not always be available. I wrote, "I would be very surprised to see the early-1980s levels of discounts perpetuate themselves indefinitely." For the same reason, I am skeptical that any simple popular investment techniques will be persistently successful.

I have recounted the story of the finance professor and his students who spotted a $100 bill lying on the street. "If it was really a $100 bill," the professor reasoned out loud, "someone would have already picked it up." Fortunately, the students were skeptical, not only of Wall Street professionals but also of learned professors, and so they picked up the money.

Clearly, there is considerable logic to the finance professor's position. In markets where intelligent people are searching for value, it is unlikely that people will perpetually leave $100 bills around ready for the taking. But history tells us that unexploited opportunities do exist from time to time, as do periods of speculative excess pricing. We know of Dutchmen paying astronomical prices for tulip bulbs, of Englishmen splurging on the most improbable bubbles, and of modern institutional fund managers who convinced themselves that some Internet stocks were so unlike any other that any price was reasonable. And when investors were overcome with pessimism, real fundamental investment opportunities such as closed-end funds were passed by. Yet eventually, excessive valuations were corrected and investors did snatch up the bargain closed-end funds. Perhaps the finance professor's advice should have been, "You had better pick up that $100 bill quickly because if it's really there, someone else will surely take it." It is in this sense that I consider myself a random walker. I am convinced that true value will out, but from time to time it doesn't surprise me that anomalies do exist. There may be some $100 bills around at times, and I'll certainly interrupt my random walk to stoop and pick them up.

INVESTMENT ADVISERS

If you follow the recommendations in this book carefully, you really don't need an investment adviser. Unless you have a variety of tax complications or legal issues, you should be able to accomplish the diversification required and do the rebalancing yourself. You might even find that it is fun to be able to take complete charge of your investment program.

The problem with investment advisers is that they tend to be quite expensive and are often conflicted. Many investment advisers will charge you 1 percent per year or more to manage your investment affairs. Brokers will frequently charge even more, costing you 2 or 3 percent per year in fees. As I suspect we are likely to live in a single-digit investment environment for some time, such high fees will do great harm to your net investment returns.

Many investment advisers are also often conflicted. Some will put you into certain funds that give extra kickbacks to the advisers. In other words, the advisers are actually paid to distribute the funds to you. Such funds may not be in your interest (indeed they tend to carry very high expense ratios). If you feel you must get an investment adviser, make sure that adviser is a "fee only" adviser. These advisers do not get paid for distributing investment products and thus are more likely to make decisions that are completely in your interest rather than in their interest.

If you feel that selecting a properly diversified set of investment products and rebalancing them over time as I have suggested on these pages is too much work, there is a low-cost alternative. I warn you at the outset that the service I am suggesting is one where I am the chief investment officer, and I therefore want to make my own conflict of interest crystal clear. The firm is called Wealthfront. It is the largest and fastest-growing automated investment service. Everything is done online. Wealthfront features a selection of broadly diversified exchange-traded index funds selected to be extremely low cost. The overall investment fee is only ¼ of 1 percent per year, and all brokerage fees are included. Wealthfront automatically rebalances the portfolio and even offers a tax loss harvesting program. If one of the ETFs in the diversified set of investments in your portfolio has declined, Wealthfront will sell it at a loss and replace it with a similar, but not identical, investment vehicle. Thus, rather than costing you a potentially significant tax bill at the end of the year (as many actively managed funds do), Wealthfront actually can provide you with some capital losses that can be used to offset capital gains or capital gain distributions and up to a limited amount can be deducted from your tax bill. Wealthfront can be contacted at www.wealthfront.com for more details.

SOME LAST REFLECTIONS ON OUR WALK

We are now at the end of our walk. Let's look back for a moment and see where we have been. It is clear that the ability to beat the averages consistently is extremely rare. Neither fundamental analysis of a stock's firm foundation of value nor technical analysis of the market's propensity for building castles in the air can produce reliably superior results. Even the pros must hide their heads in shame when they compare their results with those obtained by the dartboard method of picking stocks.

Sensible investment policies for individuals must then be developed in two steps. First, it is crucially important to understand the risk-return trade-offs that are available and to tailor your choice of securities to your temperament and requirements. Part Four provided a careful guide for this part of the walk, including a number of warm-up exercises concerning everything from tax planning to the management of reserve funds and a life-cycle guide to portfolio allocations. This chapter has covered the major part of our walk down Wall Street—three important steps for buying common stocks. I began by suggesting sensible strategies that are consistent with the existence of reasonably efficient markets. The indexing strategy is the one I recommend most highly. At least the core of every investment portfolio ought to be indexed. I recognized, however, that telling most investors that there is no hope of beating the averages is like telling a six-year-old that there is no Santa Claus. It takes the zing out of life.

For those of you incurably smitten with the speculative bug, who insist on picking individual stocks in an attempt to beat the market, I offered four rules. The odds are really stacked against you, but you may just get lucky and win big. I also am very skeptical that you can find investment managers who have some talent for finding those rare $100 bills lying around in the marketplace. Never forget that past records are far from reliable guides to future performance.

Investing is a bit like lovemaking. Ultimately, it is really an art requiring a certain talent and the presence of a mysterious force called luck. Indeed, luck may be 99 percent responsible for the success of the very few people who have beaten the averages. "Although men flatter themselves with their great actions," La Rochefoucauld wrote, "they are not so often the result of great design as of chance."

The game of investing is like lovemaking in another important respect, too. It's much too much fun to give up. If you have the talent to recognize stocks that have good value, and the art to recognize a story that will catch the fancy of others, it's a great feeling to see the market vindicate you. Even if you are not so lucky, my rules will help you limit your risks and avoid much of the pain that is sometimes involved in the playing. If you know you will either win or at least not lose too much, and if you index at least the core of your portfolio, you will be able to play the game with more satisfaction. At the very least, I hope this book makes the game all the more enjoyable.

A FINAL WORD

One of the most rewarding features for me in writing eleven editions of this book has been the many letters I have received from grateful investors. They tell me how much they have benefited from following the simple advice that has remained the same for over forty years. Those timeless lessons involve broad diversification, annual rebalancing, using index funds, and staying the course.

**BROADLY DIVERSIFIED PORTFOLIO OF MUTUAL FUNDS
(WITH ANNUAL REBALANCING) PRODUCED ACCEPTABLE RETURNS
EVEN DURING THE FIRST DECADE OF THE 2000s**

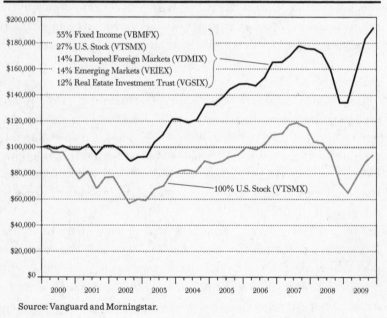

33% Fixed Income (VBMFX)
27% U.S. Stock (VTSMX)
14% Developed Foreign Markets (VDMIX)
14% Emerging Markets (VEIEX)
12% Real Estate Investment Trust (VGSIX)

100% U.S. Stock (VTSMX)

Source: Vanguard and Morningstar.

The first decade of the new millennium was one of the most challenging times for investors. Even a broadly diversified Total Stock Market fund devoted solely to U.S. stocks lost money. But even in this horrible decade, following the timeless lessons I have espoused would have produced satisfactory results. The chart above shows that an investment in the VTSMX (the Vanguard Total Stock Market Fund) did not produce positive returns in the "lost" decade of the "naughties." But suppose an investor diversified her portfolio with the approximate conservative percentages I suggested on page 369 for the "aging baby boomers." The diversified portfolio (annually rebalanced) produced a quite satisfactory return even during one of the worst decades investors have ever experienced. And if the investor also used dollar-cost averaging to add small amounts to the portfolio consistently over time, the results were even better. If you will follow the simple rules and timeless lessons espoused in this book, you are likely to do just fine, even during the toughest of times.

Supplement

HOW PORK BELLIES ACQUIRED AN IVY LEAGUE SUIT: A PRIMER ON DERIVATIVES

> The gambling known as business looks with austere disfavor
> upon the business known as gambling.
> —Ambrose Bierce, *The Devil's Dictionary*

ONCE UPON A time, long, long, long ago—at least 150 years—American farmers and other commodity producers worked out a market system to provide some financial sanity in their lives. In essence, it was a kind of insurance, and, like all insurance, it involved paying a relatively small price as a guarantee against future loss. The system, explained more fully below, became known as the futures market and was centered in Chicago. Because of that city's historical association with the processing and sale of sides of beef and pork, the catchy commodity component "pork belly" was used as a bellwether for all commodity futures trading. If the price of pork bellies went up, traders on LaSalle Street smiled; if it sank, they grimaced.

All that emotion—and the brokerage commissions that went with it—attracted the interest of those whose sole role in life was to buy and sell financial instruments. Why not, they successfully reasoned, create a system similar to commodity futures but restricted to stocks and other financial instruments? The result was an activity that became known as stock options and financial futures trading (also more fully explained below). Though options trading has been practiced in one form or another for centuries, it was considered such a minute, specialized aspect of investing that I devoted little attention to it in the first edition of this book in 1973.

How times do change! Those fat little pork bellies and those arcane options and financial futures now make up a multitrillion-dollar financial scramble. And they've also acquired a new name. After all, what self-respecting MBA—a person who sacrificed any personal life to work at least twelve hours every day—would publicly admit that all such effort was on behalf of pork bellies? Nary a one! This was big-time, sophisticated activity, and it deserved a big-time, sophisticated name: derivatives.

Dealing in derivatives was the most dynamic and rapidly growing part of the securities business during the first decade of the 2000s. It was the sure way to impress even the marginally financially literate at cocktail parties. Despite the complicated-sounding name, the term "derivative" is really self-explanatory. Derivatives are simply financial instruments whose value is determined by (or "derived" from) the price of some underlying asset, such as stocks, bonds, currencies, or commodities. As we shall see below, what they do is permit the transfer of risks and broaden the investment and hedging opportunities available to individuals and institutions. They also provide the means to undertake highly leveraged speculative positions.

This chapter seeks to present a proper perspective on derivatives by (1) explaining their function and history, (2) giving examples not only of how they work but also of how they can cause both tremendous gains and tremendous losses, and (3) presenting guidelines for their use.

THE BASIC TYPES OF DERIVATIVES

The two most popular forms of financial derivative securities are futures and options contracts. They are derivatives because they take their value from their connected underlying securities. While we will concentrate on simple options and futures, it should be noted that many other derivative-type instruments build upon these two basic forms. These complex derivatives have fancy and often forbidding names, such as swaps, inverse floaters, leaps, lookbacks, swaptions, quantos, rainbows, floors, caps, and collars. Then there are instruments that look as though they belong on an eye chart, such as REMICS, M-CATS, and TIGRS.

"I could be wrong, but you look like a man trapped in low-yielding financial instruments."

A futures, or forward, contract involves the obligation to purchase (or deliver) a specified commodity (or financial instrument) at a specified price at some specific future period. For example, suppose it is now June, and I want to get a delivery of 42,000 gallons of heating oil (the typical contract size) in December. I might buy a December heating oil future at a price of $2.50. This commits me to take delivery of 42,000 gallons of heating oil in mid-December at a price of $2.50 per gallon. The seller of the futures contract commits to make delivery of the oil at that time.*

---

*Futures contracts have standardized terms and are traded on organized futures exchanges. Forward contracts are individualized arrangements between two parties. Buyers (and sellers) of futures and forward contracts often close out their obligations by selling (or buying back) their contracts prior to the expiration date.

Futures are traded on single commodities such as gasoline, wheat, sugar, coffee, orange juice, corn, soybeans, and cattle. In addition, active markets exist in precious metals, such as gold, silver, and platinum. A burgeoning market exists in financial futures, where one can buy for future delivery a variety of bonds, currencies, and stock-market indexes such as the S&P 500. These financial futures are typically settled in cash on the basis of the difference between the initial contract price and the final cash market price of the financial instrument. No physical delivery is made. Not to be outdone in innovation on new contract designs and specifications, the options markets have developed options on futures contracts. If we can create derivatives, it is only natural to trade derivatives on derivatives.

A stock option, just as the name implies, gives the buyer the right (but not the obligation) to buy or sell a common stock (or group of stocks) at a specific price on or before a set date. For example, a call option on IBM might cost the buyer $15 a share (the option premium) expiring the third Friday in July (the expiration date) with an exercise price of $150 a share (the striking price). Thus, for a premium of $15, the buyer of this call option has the right to purchase a share of IBM at $150 at any time up through the third Friday in July. The seller (or writer) of the option receives the premium and takes on the corresponding potential obligation to sell the share at the contract price. A put option reverses the situation. A put on IBM gives the holder the right to sell IBM shares at a specific price. The seller of the put (called the writer) takes on the potential obligation to buy the shares.

Options exist on the major traded individual stocks as well as on a variety of stock indexes, bonds, and foreign currencies. Options on the S&P 500 Index, the NASDAQ 100, and the Dow Jones Industrial Average are traded in Chicago. In addition, options are traded on a variety of smaller capitalization indexes as well as on specific industry indexes. The volume of trading in basic options and futures has actually exceeded the volume of trading in the underlying assets. What makes the market important, however, is not simply its size but also the significant role it plays in providing new tools to manage risk.

THE FUTURES MARKETS: FUNCTIONS AND HISTORY

Despite their association in the financial press with speculation and gambling, futures markets have a valuable economic role. They permit both producers and consumers to transfer risks in such a way that all market participants can be better off. Contracts in the wheat futures markets, for example, typically stipulate the purchase and sale of specific quantities of wheat at fixed prices on a designated future date. At planting time, Farmer Jones might enter into a contract to sell his output of wheat at the end of the growing season at a fixed price. Knowing what he will receive for his wheat, Jones can then budget the purchase of supplies, such as fertilizer and irrigation equipment, offer labor contracts to his workers, and guarantee himself a profit—no matter what happens to the price of wheat over the season. Farmer Jones sleeps well at night with a wheat futures contract.

Baker Smith has a different problem. She has agreed to sell her output of bread to several elegant restaurants at a fixed price. Smith, knowing the revenues she will get for her bread, can guarantee herself a profit by entering into a futures contract to buy wheat at a fixed price. So both Smith and Jones are made better off by transacting in the futures market.

The concept of a futures market seems to have had its roots in the Book of Genesis. The Egyptian pharaoh had summoned Joseph to interpret a dream in which seven fat cows and seven plump ears of corn were succeeded by seven gaunt cows and seven thin, blighted ears of corn. Joseph said the dream meant that seven years of famine would follow seven years of great plenty. He also proposed a solution: Essentially, Egypt should initiate futures contracts to buy food products during the seven-year period of oversupply to avoid famine during the period of undersupply that would follow. Although the Egyptians did not open the first Nile Board of Trade, clearly the idea of futures contracting was born.

The origins of actual markets in futures are somewhat obscure, but it appears that such contracts have had a very long history. Some authors have suggested that futures trading began in India as early as 2000 BC. Others have traced the origins of the practice to Roman and even to classical Greek times. Strong evidence suggests that Roman emperors entered into futures contracts to assure their subjects an adequate supply of Egyptian grain. Whatever the actual origin, it seems clear that the immediate predecessor to modern futures trading was the "to arrive" contract used in Europe during the eighteenth century. These were contracts for the purchase of goods when they would be available in the future—for example, when a ship's cargo would arrive in port. Such contracts played an important role in the development of the United States' grain trade.

During the early stages of the development of American agriculture, grain prices were subject to seemingly perpetual cycles of boom and bust, as prices fell when farmers flooded the market with grain at harvest time and then rose later as shortages developed. Buyers and sellers began to contract for future delivery of specific quantities of grain at agreed-upon prices and delivery dates. These "to arrive," or forward, contracts were themselves bought and sold in anticipation of changes in market prices and became the basis for the standardized futures contracts traded on the Chicago Board of Trade, the first organized commodities futures market in the United States.

The Chicago Board of Trade was founded in 1848. It initially served as the exchange for all types of commodities trading, including grain, beef, and pork bellies. A rival exchange, the Chicago Mercantile Exchange, was established in 1874 as a successor organization to an organization trading butter and eggs. While several other futures exchanges have been formed in the United States, the two Chicago exchanges remain the major loci of trading.

Though they serve a beneficial economic function, futures exchanges have always looked somewhat like gambling casinos, and some of the traders have tried to manipulate the market. Perhaps the boldest futures manipulation of the twentieth century was Bunker and Herbert Hunt's attempt to corner the silver market. Together with their co-conspirators, the brothers at one time controlled over $17 billion worth of silver, in the process engineering a price rise from about $6 an ounce at the start of 1979 to a high of over $50 an ounce on one trading day in January 1980.

What the Hunts did was quite simple—and quite daring. They cornered the silver market by accumulating gigantic positions in the futures market to buy silver and then demanding delivery when the contracts came due. Simultaneously, they accumulated enormous stocks of silver in the spot market (the market in which physical quantities of the metal were bought for immediate delivery) and held this silver off the market, making it difficult for those who had sold silver futures to fulfill their obligations. Thus, they increased demand in the futures market while restricting supply in the spot market. The price of silver skyrocketed.

One amusing story reported by the author Stephen Fay recounts an incident about the Hunts' activities in hoarding and storing silver abroad that involved flying six million ounces of silver bullion across the Atlantic. The silver was carefully arranged around the hold of the aircraft to balance its weight. The large gap in the middle was filled by an enormous cage containing a circus elephant. Over the middle of the ocean, the plane began to yaw uncontrollably. One of the Hunts and a brother-in-law rushed back to discover that the elephant had pushed his trunk through the side of the cage and was playing with the wires controlling the aircraft's wing flaps. As Stephen Fay tells the tale, "Acting with the inspiration that is prompted only by impending death, our heroes opened the cage and threw a rubber tire at the elephant—which transferred its attention to its new toy—and thus saved their own lives and the family silver."

Corners have been a fact of life in the commodities markets since their inception, and so has the attempt at regulation. In the United States, the Commodity Futures Trading Commission (CFTC) attempts to avoid corners by ensuring that there are limits on the amount of futures contracts any individual or group can hold. The Hunts were able to avoid these constraints for a while. They did so by arguing that the two brothers were operating independently, so that any constraints were interpreted as applying to their individual rather than to their joint holdings. They also pointed out that they owned a significant interest in a silver mine, which was considered a member of the commercial silver market—not a speculator. And they denied categorically that their ownership of significant quantities of silver through various corporate entities, trusts, and partnerships (including one with a wealthy group of Saudi Arabians) was part of a global coalition engaged in a blatant attempt to corner the market.

The regulators and the courts finally saw it differently. Early in 1980, the CFTC ruled that no new purchases of silver contracts could be made in the futures markets. At the same time, the Chicago Board of Trade raised margin requirements on silver and lowered the amount of silver futures contracts any single speculator could hold. Traders were given until mid-February 1980 to liquidate their extra holdings. This prospective increase in supply came at the same time that high prices were bringing silver out of the woodwork as people began melting everything from coins to the family tea set to cash in. There was a dramatic loss of luster in the silver market, and prices plunged.

By early March 1980, the price of silver had declined to about $20 an ounce. Of course, as the price sank, those who had long positions in silver futures contracts (those who had bought silver for future delivery) suffered a financial loss and had to find additional cash to maintain their margin positions. Otherwise, they would have to sell some of their positions. The Hunts desperately struggled to come up with the required margin—even mortgaging hundreds of their prized racehorses. But as the price of silver continued to plummet, their efforts failed. On March 19, the Hunts defaulted on their margin obligation. Their brokers, Bache and Merrill Lynch, began selling off the collateral behind the loans, but this collateral was, of course, silver. In one final ploy to prop up the market, the Hunts announced a plan on March 26 to issue bonds backed by their holdings of silver. The market correctly interpreted this announcement as a desperation move. On March 27, a day that came to be known as Silver Thursday, silver opened at about $16 an ounce and plunged to about $10 by the end of the day. Rumors circulated that Bache and other Hunt creditors would fail.

Later a jury found that the Hunts had indeed manipulated the silver market. Monetary judgments and punitive damages were imposed against the Hunts, their co-conspirators, and their brokers. However, the full settlement was never collected against the Hunts. The two brothers—the world's richest men at the outset of the 1980s—sought protection in bankruptcy in 1990. So ended one of history's greatest corners of a commodities market. But the meltdown continued, and by the early 1990s silver was selling at $4 an ounce.

Though the shine was off silver, a new category of futures was making a sterling debut. A bevy of new products, called financial futures, propelled a spectacular growth of futures trading over the 1980s and 1990s. These came into being as a result of the increased price variability of many financial assets. And they were polished by the innovativeness and entrepreneurial abilities of the futures markets in designing products to cope with this variability.

The demise of the Bretton Woods system of fixed international exchange rates and the switch to a floating or flexible exchange rate regime dramatically increased the variability in foreign currency values. Leo Melamed, of the Chicago Mercantile Exchange, recognized that this new system, where markets rather than governments determined the prices of currencies, created the opportunity for the inception of futures trading. He introduced highly successful currency futures contracts in a variety of foreign currencies. At the same time, it became apparent that the forces of inflation would greatly increase the price volatility of fixed-income securities. Thus, in 1975 the Chicago Board of Trade initiated trading in bonds issued by the Government National Mortgage Association (GNMAs). This was the beginning of futures trading on a variety of fixed-income instruments. In January 1976, futures on ninety-day Treasury bills began trading, and in August of 1977 the first U.S. Treasury bond contract was introduced.

The next major landmark for financial futures occurred in the spring of 1982, when the Kansas City Board of Trade introduced a stock index futures contract based on the price of the Value Line Stock Index. Exchanges now trade contracts on the Standard &

Poor's 500-Stock Index, the NASDAQ 100 Index, and the Dow Jones Industrial Average. More recently, trading has commenced on a variety of foreign-stock indexes. These newer contracts also incorporated the feature of cash settlement. Thus, if one bought a futures contract on the S&P 500-Stock Index at a price of $2,000, the seller would not deliver a package of the 500 stocks on the expiration date. Rather, the contract would be settled in cash on the basis of the difference between $2,000 and the value of the index on the settlement date. Today, trading in financial futures represents well over half of the total futures trading. Most industry observers expect the continued growth of the futures market to center on such financial instruments, including futures on individual stocks.

THE OPTIONS MARKETS: FUNCTIONS AND HISTORY

Most people know of options as a device for speculating on an expected rise, or fall, in the price of a stock while putting up little money. For example, suppose IBM was selling at $150 a share, and you thought it would rise to $200 a share within a short period of time. If you purchased 100 shares of IBM, it would cost you $15,000 (plus commissions), and, if your forecast of the price increase was correct, you would be able to sell the shares later for $20,000 (less commissions). Your profit would be $5,000, or 33.33 percent of your initial investment, ignoring brokerage commissions. Suppose now, instead, you bought a call option on 100 shares of IBM at $150 per share at a premium of $15 per share. You would put up only $1,500 (plus commissions). If the price of IBM did rise to $200, you could simultaneously exercise your option, buying the 100 shares for $15,000 and selling them in the market for $20,000. Your profit, again ignoring brokerage commissions, would be $5,000 minus the $1,500 you paid for the option, or $3,500. Note that in percentage terms, however, your return would be 233.33 percent ($3,500 profit for a $1,500 investment) rather than the 33.33 percent return that you would have earned from an outright purchase. Thus, options allow an investor who makes correct forecasts about stock-price movements to increase substantially her percentage return. We shall see below, however, that options and futures can also play an extremely important role as a tool for risk reduction as well as risk enhancement.

Stock options can be used both to transfer risks and to broaden the investment opportunities available to individuals and institutions. Let us illustrate this by looking at the case of Widower White and Gambler Green. Widower White cannot afford to suffer a large drop in the value of his stock. He no longer works and depends on his investments as his major source of support. Gambler Green thinks White is a Nervous Nelson and is willing to bet money that she is right. White reduces some of his risk by selling a call option to Green. By purchasing the call, Green receives the right to buy White's shares at an agreed-upon price up to a fixed date. For this privilege, Green pays White a sum of money called the option premium.

By selling the call, White has transferred to Green the opportunity to profit if, by a specific time, the price of his stock has risen above the contract price, called the striking price. In turn, he has received an option premium that gives him some revenue and partially protects him if the stock declines in value. Thus, the option redistributes both some risk and all potential profit to Green. And Green may actually be a shrewd, rather than reckless, gambler because the call option can be used as a substitute for buying the stock outright and, therefore, as an efficient diversification strategy.

Options have a long and checkered history. Once again the Bible (Genesis 29) contains the earliest reference to a business option. The incident occurred when Jacob wished to marry Rachel, younger daughter of Laban. Laban agreed, provided that Jacob first pay him with seven years of labor. After that period, Jacob would have an option on Rachel's hand. One can see that options were already off to a bad start because Laban reneged on the contract and delivered to Jacob his elder daughter, Leah, instead.

Options are prominently mentioned in book 1 of Aristotle's *Politics*. Aristotle told the story of the philosopher Thales, who had been ridiculed by the populace for his poverty, which they took as proof that philosophy was of no practical use. But Thales, who possessed exceptional skill in reading the stars, had the last laugh. One winter, Thales foresaw that the next autumn's olive harvest would be a bumper crop, far above normal. He took the little money he had and quietly visited all the owners of olive presses in the area, placing small deposits with each for an option on the use of their presses at normal rents when fall arrived. Aristotle concludes the story as follows: "When the harvest-time came, and many [presses] were wanted all at once and of a sudden, he let them out at any rate he pleased, and made a quantity of money. Thus he showed the world that philosophers can easily be rich if they like."

Options made their first major mark on financial history during the tulip-bulb craze in seventeenth-century Holland, chronicled in chapter 2. Options were initially used in that time for hedging. By purchasing a call option on tulip bulbs, a dealer who was committed to a sales contract could be assured of obtaining a fixed number of bulbs for a set price. Similarly, tulip-bulb growers could assure themselves of selling their bulbs at a set price by purchasing put options. Later, however, options were increasingly used by speculators who found that call options were an effective vehicle for obtaining maximum possible gains per guilder of investment. As long as tulip prices continued to skyrocket, call buyers would realize returns far in excess of those they could obtain by purchasing tulip bulbs themselves. The writers (that is, sellers) of put options also prospered as bulb prices spiraled since writers were able to keep the premiums and the options were never exercised. Of course, when the tulip-bulb market collapsed in 1636, speculators lost everything. Hardest hit were the put writers who were unable to meet their commitments to purchase bulbs. As a result of the involvement of put and call options in this classic speculative mania, options acquired a bad name, which they have retained, more or less, to the present time.

Because of their association with excessive speculation, options were declared illegal in England by Barnard's Act of 1733 and continued to be illegal at various times until 1860. Opposition to options was particularly strong among members of the Labour Party, who regarded their use as prima facie evidence that the stock exchange was merely a den of gamblers. But Barnard's Act was even less effective than alcohol prohibition in the United States. Trading in options flourished on the London Stock Exchange despite their illegality, and London became the most important options market in the world.

As was the case in Britain, options have had a controversial history in the United States. The first mention of options in America dates back to 1790. By the time of the Civil War, options and futures trading flourished. As the progressive movement swept the country, however, all kinds of speculative activity fell into disfavor; at the beginning of the twentieth century, options on commodities came to be regarded as gambling contracts and, hence, illegal and unenforceable. Still, stock options were never banned, despite several attempts to abolish them as part of a general program to restrain speculation.

Interest in options increased dramatically in the United States during the bull market of the 1920s. The most flagrant abuses of these instruments also occurred during this period. As was described in chapter 3, options played an important role in several pools designed to manipulate stock prices. Trading in this period was largely in two- and three-day call options. There was even a one-day call option known as a "seven-cigar call," because it sold for one day's worth of stogies. In 1932 and 1933, a congressional investigation found that many of the financial abuses of the 1920s were related to the use of options. In 1934, a bill called for an outright ban on stock options, but the Securities Act of 1934 stopped short of forbidding options trading and only empowered the SEC to regulate it. In fact, the industry itself developed a highly organized, self-policing organization so that direct government regulation was averted.

Stock options began to be traded on organized options exchanges in 1973, following the formation of the Chicago Board Options Exchange (CBOE). In 1975, the American Stock Exchange initiated options trading, and later many of the regional exchanges followed suit. With the advent of exchange-traded options, many of the risks that formerly existed in options trading were eliminated. A centralized clearing entity, the Options Clearing Corporation (OCC), was organized as the issuer and guarantor of each option traded on a U.S. exchange. This essentially eliminated the credit risk that existed when traders had to rely on the counterparties to the transaction to live up to their obligations. In addition, the exchanges significantly reduced the transactions costs of dealing in options, and the existence of continuous options markets allowed investors both to initiate and to offset options transactions at competitively determined prices. These developments paved the way for a rapid expansion of the market that has continued to the present day.

THE EXCITING DANGERS OF DERIVATIVES

Probably the most important factor to keep in mind about derivatives is that their use can often entail considerable risk. If anyone tries to sell you a derivative strategy that involves a sure profit and no risk, watch out. He's selling snake oil. If something sounds too good to be true, it undoubtedly is too good to be true.

From one standpoint, buying a $500 call option on a specific stock involves limited risk because all you can lose is $500. Looked at another way, however, the strategy is extremely risky since that $500 can be 100 percent of your capital. A futures transaction can be even more disastrous. When you buy a $100,000 position in Treasury bonds for future delivery, you may have to put up an initial margin of as little as $1,000. But if the Treasury securities suddenly drop in price by just 2 percent, a movement that could happen in a single day, you will be liable for a loss of $2,000, double the amount of your initial capital. This explains how some traders can suffer extraordinary losses even if they put up relatively small amounts of money.

Even the pros can get badly burned. During the mid-1990s,

Procter and Gamble entered into a customized derivative transaction it thought would achieve its borrowing objectives. It turned out that the company lost over $100 million when German and U.S. interest rates both rose sharply. The company official responsible for the trade was placed on "special assignment," and P&G sued Banker's Trust (which it didn't trust anymore) for recommending the transaction. Not even staid public finance officials were immune from taking fliers in the derivatives market. Orange County, California, announced that its Christmas greeting in 1994 was to file for bankruptcy protection after taking a $2 billion loss in risky investments. While derivatives played only a part in the Orange County debacle, they came in for the most criticism in the media. At the end of February 1995, one of Britain's most venerable banks, Barings PLC—the oldest investment firm in the U.K.—collapsed after suffering more than a $1 billion loss from trading Japanese stock-index futures contracts.

The possibility that an ordinary investor can take a sum as small as $1,000 and, by shrewd trading, turn it into $100,000 in a few months is about as likely as going to Las Vegas, putting a dollar in a slot machine, winning the $50 million grand prize, and then walking away, never to enter a casino again.

The risk involved can be enormous even if the market participant is hedged, as some fund managers learned during the late 1990s. In a hedge fund, the manager, such as Long Term Capital Management, might sell short a derivative instrument on one stock or bond index and buy another instrument. Suppose, for example, you believed that the prices of stocks of smaller companies would rise relative to stocks of larger companies. You might buy a three-month future on the Russell 2000 index (an index of smaller firms) and sell an equivalent futures contract on the S&P 500 (an index of the biggest companies). Note that you would be hedged in the sense that if all stocks went down, you would lose on your Russell 2000 contract but gain on the S&P contract. As long as small stocks did better than large stocks on a relative basis, you could gain whatever the direction of the general market. However, if the relative performance figures went the other way—that is, big-company stocks did better than small-company stocks—you could lose substantial sums of money. This is so because futures markets allow you to control billions of dollars worth of securities while putting up a security deposit of only millions. Derivatives truly provide investors with staggering amounts of leverage.

George Soros, a famous hedge-fund manager, supposedly endowed with a "Midas touch," made hundreds of millions when he correctly "bet" that some currencies would be stronger than others and translated his bet into hedged-futures contracts. The Midas touch turned to a minus touch, however, when he lost more than half a billion dollars during 1994 on a single currency deal. Leverage is a double-edged sword.

Warren Buffett, arguably the world's greatest investor over a forty-year period well into the 2000s, has called derivatives "weapons of mass destruction." There can be little doubt of the correctness of that statement when one examines the 2007–08 period, when derivatives threatened to bring down the entire financial system. As was described in chapter 4, the enormous leverage associated with derivative contracts on mortgage-backed securities led to a near collapse of the banking system that was averted only by a government bailout of leading financial firms such as Citigroup, Bank of America, and Goldman Sachs. Another factor to keep in mind is that derivative transactions can entail substantial trading costs. If an option is quoted as 5 bid–5¼ asked, it means you buy the option at 5¼, whereas if you sell it, you get only 5. That ¼ point spread is a 5 percent transactions charge on the purchase or sale of that particular instrument (a so-called round-trip transaction) and does not include brokerage commissions. The experiences of the Princeton Students Investment Club in the early 1990s illustrate the potential pitfalls in dealing in derivatives. Four Princeton students, interested in learning about stock markets firsthand, put up $500 each and formed an investment club. Since it would be impossible to purchase a portfolio of individual stocks with only $2,000, they decided to pursue an options-buying strategy. At any one time, they would buy four or five call options on individual stocks they thought attractive and occasionally one or more put options on stocks considered overpriced and due for a fall. The students made some excellent choices during the club's two years of operation.

During a period when high-technology stocks were hot, they made lots of money in call options on Intel and Micron Technology. Similarly, they timed their put option purchases well, making a good profit betting that Snapple Beverages would retreat after a speculative frenzy drove its price to unsustainable levels. When Boston Chicken laid an egg and became Boston Turkey for a time, the club also benefited handsomely.

Of course, not all of their trades proved to be profitable. The club bought options on Paramount Communications and Grumman Aircraft, mistakenly predicting that a bidding war would erupt after initial tender offers were made for Paramount and Grumman shares. In both cases, their call options expired worthless. After two years of operation, the participants in the club graduated and divided their spoils. The final accounting showed that the original $2,000 had grown to $2,125 for an annual rate of return of approximately 3 percent. This was far below the 10 percent rate of return for the stock market as a whole over the same period. How could such brilliant pickers underperform the market? The answer: transaction costs, pure and simple. These totaled $980, almost 50 percent of their original stake. The budding entrepreneurs had done more to fatten the coffers of the financial community than to contribute toward their tuition bills.

SOME ILLUSTRATIONS OF THE POTENTIAL PROFITS AND PITFALLS FROM OPTIONS AND FUTURES

It is much easier to understand the potential profits and losses from derivative transactions with some simple numerical examples and charts. In this section, we will illustrate some basic strategies, using the Halliburton Company, an oil service company associated with the Gulf of Mexico oil spill of 2010.

Bullish on Halliburton Stock—Alternative Profit and Risk Positions

Suppose you believed that Halliburton would advance after the bad publicity following the oil spill and you wished to analyze the pros and cons of taking a position by buying the stock directly or by purchasing a three-month call "at-the-money" for $4 per share. (In the appendix to this supplement, I explain what determines the size of the option premium for different contracts.) "At-the-money" means that if the stock is currently selling at $40, the contract, or striking price, is also $40, right at the current market price. In options terminology, if the investor bought an option with a striking price of $45, that option would be "out-of-the-money" since the contract price was higher than the current market price. Alternatively, a call option with a $35 striking price and a market price of the stock at $40 would be $5 "in-the-money." For our purposes, and to keep the examples simple, all charts illustrate "at-the-money" calls.

Buying the stock outright results in gains or losses exactly equivalent to Halliburton stock's price movements. If Halliburton increases by 50 percent to 60, a 100-share investment—initially worth $4,000—will increase to $6,000, a 50 percent gain. (In this and future illustrations, we will also ignore brokerage costs to keep the numbers simple.) On the other hand, a 100-share investment in three-month options at $4 per share with a striking price of $40 increases in value by 400 percent, or $1,600. You can exercise your option at $40 and simultaneously sell the shares on the open market at $60. Your profit is the $2,000 of appreciation on the underlying stock minus the $400 you paid for the option. It is clear that if you are correct in your stock picks, the percentage gains are eye-catching, and you're even protected on the downside. If Halliburton declines, you let your option expire and the most you can lose is the $400 you spent to buy the contract.

The scenario is even more dramatic if you put all your money into options. Had you invested the whole $4,000 into Halliburton call options, profits from a 50 percent stock increase would be $16,000 ($1,600 times 10), as opposed to a $2,000 profit from direct ownership. As shown in chart 1, the leverage of options in enhanc-

Chart 1
The Allure of Fattening Your Purse with Call Options
Rather than Stocks

Haliburton–Current Price $40
Call option $4.00 Per Share: Striking Price $40

In percentage terms, the
call-option buyer can make
or lose considerably more
on an initial investment
than the stock buyer.

—— Buy Stock
..... Buy Call

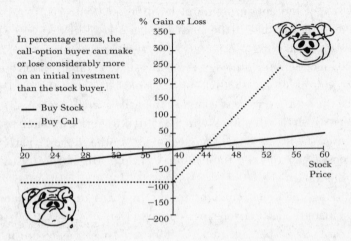

In dollar terms, however, the call-option
buyer has much less to lose if the price falls.

—— Buy Stock
..... Buy Call

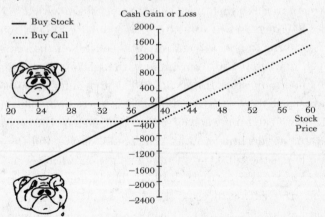

ing profits is beautiful to behold when everything goes well.

Leverage, as we all know, works two ways. Let's continue the example where the investor puts all $4,000 into call options, and let's suppose that Halliburton doesn't move within the three-month option period. The stock buyer still has his original stake intact and has lost nothing. Indeed, he has collected any dividends paid out during the three-month period. The option buyer, however, receives no dividends and has lost $4,000, 100 percent of his investment. Thus, anyone who tells you that buying options isn't risky is not telling the truth. Option buyers have to be right not only on the direction of the movement in the stock but also on the exact timing of when the move will take place. If Halliburton makes its move in four months, an option buyer can still lose everything, whereas the stock buyer would be fully rewarded. Before you engage in an options-buying strategy, consider how difficult it is not only to pick the right stock but also to time its upward move perfectly.

Bearish on Halliburton Stock—Alternative Profit and Risk Positions

Suppose you believe that Halliburton is now poised to decline. You can profit from this by buying a put option. A put gives you the right to sell the stock at a guaranteed price. If the price declines to $30, you can exercise your option to sell the stock at $40. How can you sell the stock if you don't own it? Simple. You buy it in the open market for $30 and sell it to the put writer for $10 more.* Thus, a put-option buyer profits only if the stock declines—and declines by more than the option premium. For example, if the put option costs $4 per share, the put option buyer will not make any money until the price of Halliburton stock falls below $36 a share. If the stock declines sharply, however, the put buyer can reap exciting gains. If the stock price stays even or advances, the put buyer will lose her entire stake.

---

* In practice, you would simply sell the put option rather than exercising it. The put would have risen in price to reflect the greater worth of an instrument that allows you to sell the stock at $10 more than its market value.

Put buying can also be combined with stock ownership. Suppose you own Halliburton but are having trouble sleeping at night because you are worried the price could decline sharply. In this case, you might buy a put option on Halliburton at $40. This is called a protective put. If the stock goes down, you exercise your option to sell the shares at $40. If the stock goes up, you allow the option to expire unexercised and profit from any rise in the price of the stock. Foolproof? Not quite. The put costs $4 per share. If the stock goes down, you would have been $4 per share better off to have sold in the first place. If the stock goes up, your profits are reduced by the $4 per share put premium. Think of the $4 as a three-month insurance premium. You pay for the peace of mind that comes from knowing you need not worry about losing money in the future from holding Halliburton. Like auto insurance, however, the protection is not cheap. Chart 2 shows the results for a put buyer who owns the underlying stock as well as for the purchaser of a put option who has no ownership position.

There is another way to gain some protection against a fall in the price of Halliburton. The owner of the stock can sell (write) a call against his position. This is called "covered" call writing and is explained in chart 3.

Compared with buying a put for protection, selling a call has both advantages and disadvantages, as can be seen from the visual summary shown in the bottom of the chart. If the price of Halliburton stock stays within 20 percent of the starting price within the three-month period, you are much better off selling a call option on the stock and collecting the premium as opposed to paying for a put. Indeed, even if the price of Halliburton declines to $32, a 20 percent decline, you are in exactly the same position using either strategy. Thus, as long as you think Halliburton will sell within a range of plus or minus 20 percent within a three-month period, writing covered calls offers some protection and is never a poorer strategy. Only if Halliburton stock rises or falls more than 20 percent would put buying be better. The put-buying strategy produces more protection against very severe price declines and allows the investor to profit more in the event of a very large price increase.

Chart 2

How to Put Your Best Foot Forward

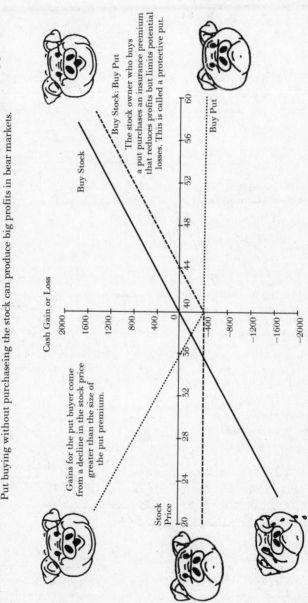

Halliburton—Current Price $40
Put Option $4.00 Per Share: Striking Price $40

An illustration of how buying a put while holding a stock protects against losses while not completely denying profits. Put buying without purchaseing the stock can produce big profits in bear markets.

Buy Stock

Buy Stock: Buy Put

The stock owner who buys a put purchases an insurance premium that reduces profits but limits potential losses. This is called a protective put.

Buy Put

Cash Gain or Loss

Gains for the put buyer come from a decline in the stock price greater than the size of the put premium.

Stock Price

Chart 3
How to Keep Your Shirt—and Only Your Shirt—in a Rising Market While Muting Agonized Squeals in a Plunging One

Haliburton–Current Price $40
Put option $4.00 Per Share: Striking Price $40

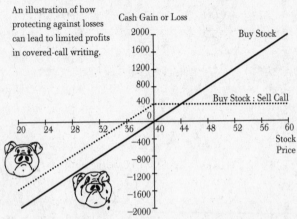

An illustration of how protecting against losses can lead to limited profits in covered-call writing.

This shows what happens when an individual who buys (or already owns) 100 shares of Halliburton at $40 per share writes (sells) a call option at $4 per share. This is called "covered" call writing. If the stock stays at $40 at the end of three months, the option will expire unexercised. The investor will own 100 shares worth $4,000 while keeping the $400 option premium in cash: a 10 percent return over a three-month period. Not bad for a stock that has gone nowhere. Now suppose the stock price goes up to $60. The covered writer does not benefit from the rise, because the option buyer will call the stock away at $40, the strike price. The writer ends up with $4,000 from the sale of the stock plus the $400 option premium—a 10 percent return. Should Halliburton fall in price, the owner of the stock would lose, but that loss would be reduced by the $400 premium on the option, which would expire unexercised.

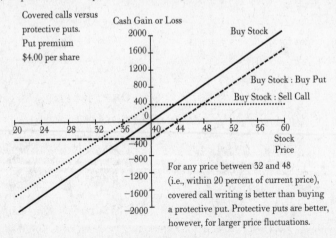

Covered calls versus protective puts. Put premium $4.00 per share

For any price between 32 and 48 (i.e., within 20 percent of current price), covered call writing is better than buying a protective put. Protective puts are better, however, for larger price fluctuations.

Of course, for every buyer of a call or put, there is a corresponding seller. And just as many option buyers do not own the stock in question, so there are sellers who write call and put options without ever owning a single share of stock. Selling a call option without owning the stock is called naked call writing. Remember that the call writer receives a lump sum for taking on the potential obligation to deliver 100 shares of stock to the option buyer at a set striking price (in all our examples, $40). Thus, if the stock price goes to $60, $1,600 goes out the window for the writer of a 100-share contract. The naked call writer must spend $6,000 to obtain 100 shares of Halliburton, which then must be turned over to the option buyer at the guaranteed price of $4,000. That $2,000 difference, minus the $400 option premium, makes up the $1,600 loss. Naked-call writers freeze when stocks go up. On the other hand, if Halliburton declines to $36 per share, the buyer would not want to pay $4,000 for a stock valued at $3,600 and thus does not exercise the option—permitting the seller of the naked call to pocket a $400 profit. Obviously, the risk associated with such profit is enormous.

The situation is similar for put writers. Put writers pocket the premium when stocks go up and lose heavily when stocks go down. It is actually difficult to figure out the percentage gains and losses from naked-option writing, because brokers will demand that the writer put up sufficient margin to give the broker comfort that the writer will be able to fulfill his contract obligation. It is clear, however, that naked writing is a very risky strategy. If the options remain unexercised, the gains to the writer are extremely large. But the potential losses can be staggering. Writers of naked puts were the ones who lost everything during the crash of 1987 and the sharp decline during 2008, while writers of naked calls lost heavily during the late 1990s when stock prices were soaring.

STRATEGIES INVOLVING FINANCIAL FUTURES

If you want a really flashily attired portfolio, dress it up in financial futures. The most popular of these instruments are futures on the Standard & Poor's 500-Stock Index and on long-term Treasury bonds. Recall that a futures contract represents an obligation to deliver or receive a commodity (in this case an underlying bond or basket of stocks) at a specified price at a designated future date. The price to be paid is the price at which the original contract is bought or sold in the open market. Unlike actual commodity transactions, financial futures transactions involve no physical delivery of goods. The settlement takes place by the payment of the cash difference between the price at which the contract was purchased and the value of the underlying asset on the final trading day. For example, suppose you purchase three-month futures contracts on the S&P Stock Index at $1,300 per contract and on settlement day the index stands at $1,280. You would be obligated to pay the seller of the contracts the $20 per contract that was lost on the transaction.

Both purchasers and sellers of futures contracts are subject to margin requirements, which determine both the initial deposit and the maintenance level. Not only that, financial futures have a special pay-as-you-lose system. At the end of each trading day, the value of a futures contract is determined and the party suffering the loss pays that loss to the gainer. (This is called marking to market.) Thus, whether a buyer or a seller of a financial futures contract, you must pay all losses as they accrue. Unless a trader closes out his futures position, he would be required, in the event of an uninterrupted market slide, to continue to pay unrealized losses as they occurred.

Obviously, as shown in chart 4, the ability to call turns in the stock market correctly can yield extraordinarily large profits. Economists disbelieve, and you should too, that such ability really exists. The results of managers seeking solely to profit from such transactions are as random as any other walk down Wall Street. It must be emphasized, however, that not all futures traders are speculators. S&P futures are widely used by index mutual funds as a method of investing a temporary influx of funds; in this way, the fund is always fully invested and can closely track the index. S&P futures are also widely used for hedging purposes. An investor who was very confident about the prospects for her stock holdings, but

Chart 4
How to Look into the Future and Wind Up a Sartorial Genius or an Out-of-Pocket Bum
Three-Month Future Bought $1,200; 2 Percent Margin Required

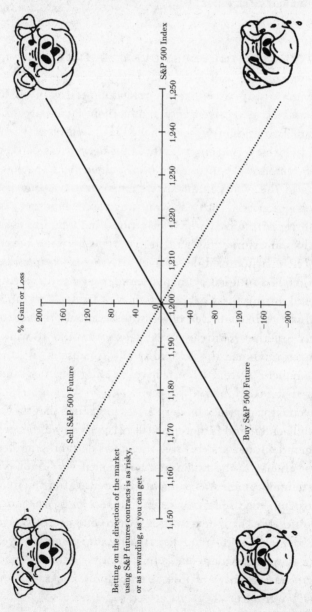

Betting on the direction of the market using S&P futures contracts is as risky, or as rewarding, as you can get.

In this example, an investor with $2,000 would control a $100,000 position in the S&P index. The percentage gains or losses are figured on the basis of the original investment. The buyer of an S&P future profits dollar for dollar from any rise in the price of the index while sustaining an equivalent loss in the future market price of the index declines below the price at which her contract was originally executed. Just the opposite is true for the futures seller.

very nervous about the overall level of stock prices, might sell S&P futures in the hope that even if the stock market declined sharply, the profit from the sale of the futures would exceed the losses from any individual stock holdings.

THE CONTROVERSY OVER DERIVATIVES

Controversy always accompanies great financial gains or losses. Derivatives have received more than their fair share of such attention. Two lines of criticism have been prominent. First, the squealing by players losing heavily in the derivatives markets led some regulators and politicians to worry aloud about the potential fragility of the whole financial system. While trading in standardized options and futures is centrally cleared and guaranteed by well-capitalized clearing corporations, individually designed derivatives are simply bilateral transactions between buyer and seller. These customized derivatives are the ones responsible for the large losses suffered by many market participants during the 1990s and during the financial crisis of 2007–08. And since the counterparties to some derivative transactions were institutions in many different countries, some people who like to wallow in doom even imagined the possibility of a collapse of the international financial system if derivatives trading was not somehow regulated and contained.

A second line of attack on derivatives proclaims that they make stock and bond markets more volatile. Critics viewed the leverage available to options and futures traders as destabilizing because large positions can be taken and abandoned very quickly. The search to find villains was particularly intense after the financial crisis of 2007–08. Today's wicked financial pigs are said to be the proliferation of index futures (where one can buy or sell a basket of stocks), high-frequency trading, and computer program trading strategies (where one automatically enters orders for the simultaneous purchase or sale of a group of stocks, such as the S&P 500). I disagree.

Options and futures have flourished as an inexpensive mechanism for tracking and adjusting positions in underlying securities. Institutions wishing to change a portfolio's equity mix or hedge against market declines can do so more quickly and at lower transactions costs in the futures market than in the underlying securities markets. This is why futures markets often react to new information first and give the impression that they cause price movements in the stock market.

I am particularly sorry to see the slop thrown at program trading. The technique follows the precept—advocated in every edition of this book—of using "passive portfolio management." Profits are eaten away by commissions and taxes when investors switch from security to security to catch good buying and selling opportunities. Indeed, two-thirds of active portfolio managers have consistently been outperformed by the unmanaged Standard & Poor's 500-Stock Index—a percentage that amply demonstrates the wisdom of simply buying and holding the index (as is done by many "index funds"). Program trading is the technique whereby index funds can add or subtract from their investment portfolios. It is a healthy development that has improved the effectiveness of portfolio management.

"Index arbitrage" is another form of program trading. The goal is to create a perfectly hedged position and an abnormally large return by combining a portfolio of stocks with an index futures contract. Arbitrage opportunities arise whenever the value of an index future (or an indexed exchange-traded fund) and the value of the underlying securities diverge. For example, suppose the value of the 500 stocks in the S&P index is $2,000 while the value of the S&P 500 future is $2,050. An index arbitrageur simultaneously sells the index at $2,050 and buys the underlying stocks through a program trade at $2,000 guaranteeing her a $50 profit, less commissions and carrying costs. The benefits of index arbitrage are twofold. First, by increasing trading, liquidity in the securities, futures, and ETF markets is enhanced. Second, arbitrage trades link markets together and ensure that both the underlying securities and the futures and ETFs are appropriately priced. When new information arises about the stock market, the futures market is the natural entry point for this information because of the low cost of futures trading. And such news (or change in sentiment) may well be carried into the stock market through computer-driven index arbitrage. But arbitrage is merely the medium—not the message. Technology does not move markets, people do.

As I indicated earlier, I think that much of the furor over the evils of "flash trading" (often called "high-frequency trading") is misguided. Flash trading involves the placement of high-speed computers as close as possible to the trading markets to allow trades to be executed within milliseconds. Although high-frequency trading can be used in an abrasive way (as when inside information about a large order comes to the attention of the flash trader, who then "front runs" this legitimate order by trading first), it can also serve a socially useful purpose. For example, suppose an ETF holding the S&P 500 portfolio sells at a small premium over the value of the underlying 500 stocks. The flash trader simultaneously sells the ETF short and makes a program trade to buy all 500 S&P stocks. He then exchanges the stock for a new ETF, which is used to cover his short position. By being able to complete the transaction in milliseconds, he can be assured of using arbitrage profits from the temporary price discrepancy. For the buyer of the ETF, the existence of flash trading ensures that the ETF will be appropriately priced at net asset value. These flash traders also bring liquidity into the market, and their activities have tended to reduce the spread between bid prices and actual ones substantially.

Futures markets arose to cope with underlying volatility. Blaming futures and related program trading for the volatility in the stock market is as illogical as blaming the thermometer for measuring uncomfortable temperatures. By making the market more quickly responsive to changes in underlying conditions or the sentiment of large institutions, rapid trading increases the efficiency of the stock market. To eliminate new instruments and techniques would be to make our markets less efficient. And because of the increasing integration of world financial markets, traders abroad would be sure to utilize any opportunities we discard.

After the 1929 crash, legislation was introduced to prohibit the use of telephones to transmit margin orders. Now derivatives and computer trading are often the target. But technology does not move markets; it merely facilitates the flow of orders. Program trading is not the mindless computer-driven technique that keeps the market from reflecting fundamental values. It reflects human decisions about the value of stocks, made easier to execute because of computers. If institutions decide to sell, they will do so whether by computers, telephones, or even hand signals from open windows to brokers outside, as was the case in earlier times.

Yes, sudden large movements in stock prices are upsetting to individual investors who feel at the mercy of large institutional traders. But to paraphrase a common expression, "If you can keep your head when those around you are losing theirs, you do understand the problem." The long-term investor can and should ignore short-term market volatility and not leave the stock market. The losers from volatility will be institutions that trade frequently in a futile attempt to time the market, not the steady investor who buys and holds for the long term.

SOME RULES FOR INDIVIDUAL INVESTORS

How can you as an individual investor take advantage of derivatives? It is not easy, because the risks are large and the transactions-cost savings available to institutions are usually unavailable for smaller players. Not surprisingly, many investment counselors suggest that individuals "just say no" to the futures market and "not exercise their options." I believe, however, that the following three situations provide acceptable opportunities for an individual's use of derivatives.

1. Options Buying as an Adjunct to Investing in Index Mutual Funds (or Exchange-Traded Funds)

As I have mentioned repeatedly, most investors would be far better off owning low-cost index mutual funds or ETFs (diversified to include bonds, smaller companies, and international stocks as well as the major U.S. stocks included in broad-based indexes). I recognize, however, that many investors, particularly those with a gambling temperament, will not be satisfied unless they do some picking of individual stocks. If you are one of these people, you might want to commit 95 percent of your funds to index mutual funds and ETFs and speculate with the remaining 5 percent. The options market allows you to buy a few positions for a moderate amount of money and the odds there are certainly better than at either the race track or your state lottery. Be prepared to lose your entire 5 percent stake because that is a real possibility, and take to heart the lessons of the Princeton Students Investment Club. You may well enrich only your broker by undertaking an option-buying strategy. Moreover, your gains, if any, will be taxed at ordinary income tax rates. And never forget, you are gambling and not investing.

2. Option Writing as an Adjunct to Portfolio Management

A strategy that is more likely to be profitable and may even save on taxes is an option-writing strategy undertaken in connection with the management of a diversified stock portfolio. As someone who believes largely in the efficient-market theory, I advocate a buy-and-hold strategy. Doing very little trading minimizes both transactions charges and taxes. The only time it makes sense to sell a stock is when it no longer fulfills your investment needs and it has declined in price. Selling a stock that has gone down will usually reduce your taxes.

Consider, however, the situation facing Dr. Brown. Dr. Brown was proud of her portfolio, which included a substantial number of pharmaceutical stocks that she knew from her work. Merck & Co., Inc. was her most successful holding at the start of 1999. It was trading at about $70 per share, while her cost was below $5 per share. Though proud of her overall portfolio, Dr. Brown became worried about Merck because appreciation in the stock had made it very much overweighted in her holdings. She also felt that a combination of competitive market pressures and governmental jawboning would restrain future increases in drug prices. Finally, she felt that Merck's vaunted research department had produced a less than blockbuster product pipeline of future drugs, and many of Merck's best drugs were soon to have their patents expire. This suggested a slowing of future earnings growth. Dr. Brown preferred not to have almost half of her portfolio in just one stock.

The dilemma facing Dr. Brown seemed insoluble. She was overinvested in a stock that she confidently believed would have a far less rosy future than its past. Moreover, industry changes and political pressures could make Merck's stock vulnerable to a substantial price decline. But selling all or part of her shares would generate a large capital gains liability. Figuring both the federal and the state capital gains tax, she would lose more than 25 percent of her investment to taxes.

Option writing gave Dr. Brown a way out of her dilemma. She began a program of writing call options of approximately three months in length "at-the-money," that is, with a striking price at or about the then current market price of $70. For this, she received an option premium of about $6 per share, or about 8½ percent of the market price. Because Merck is a relatively stable stock, its option premiums tend to be a smaller percentage of the price of the stock than options on a volatile stock such as Halliburton. The main determinants of option premiums "at-the-money" are (1) the stock's characteristic volatility and (2) the length of time the option runs. The appendix to this supplement presents a fuller discussion of what determines futures prices and option premiums.

At the end of the three-month period, the price of Merck stock remained at about $70. The option expired unexercised, and Dr. Brown then wrote (sold) another three-month call option for $600. At the end of the next period, her fears began to be realized. The price of Merck fell to $60, and again the option remained unexercised. Dr. Brown in effect lost $10 per share in the market value of the stock but pocketed the $600 option premium as well as the generous quarterly dividend paid by Merck. Hence, she largely avoided the loss she would have suffered if she had taken no offsetting action in the options market.

Dr. Brown continued to write call options on Merck stock every three months. At times the price of Merck actually rose during these periods. She had to cover her call (buy it back in the open market). She would lose money on the option transaction only if Merck rose by more than the amount of the option premium. And, of course, since she still owned the stock, any losses would be offset by her gain on the shares.

One year passed, and Dr. Brown then calculated the results from her strategy. It turned out she was correct in her worries about Merck's prospects during this period. Merck's stock declined from $70 to $63 a share, a $700 loss for each 100 shares she owned. Had Dr. Brown taken no action, she would have seen the value of her portfolio investment in Merck shrink by 10 percent. By continuously writing options, however, she actually came out ahead:

Value of premiums collected	$24.00
(4 call options written—average price	
$6.00/share net of transactions costs)	
Less cost to buy back options which did not expire	(–$4.00)
Dividends	<u>$1.16</u>
Total gain per share	$21.16

She collected $21.16 per share from the holding and option-writing strategy, which, even after she paid income taxes on the value of the expired option premiums, more than offset the capital loss from the shares.

3. The Use of Index Options and Futures as Hedging Instruments

Marcus Pincus, Esq., was named executor of a multimillion-dollar estate, invested in a diversified portfolio of stocks—

including the stocks of a number of very small companies. His assignment was a profitable but messy one. There were many beneficiaries, some who wanted to receive pro rata share in the stock, others who wished to receive cash. Moreover, a number of complicated legal challenges that had to be dealt with made it prudent to make no changes in the estate's assets. The problem was that Pincus was quite nervous about the high level of stock prices that prevailed in early 2007. He worried that since it would be a long time before the estate was settled, he would be criticized if stock prices declined sharply. He needed a hedge that would protect the corpus of the estate if the market took a nosedive.

Derivatives markets provided just such a hedge. Some alternatives were ruled out immediately. For example, it was not possible to sell call options against the entire portfolio, since many of the smaller stocks did not have active options markets. Pincus could have sold futures contracts against the portfolio, but he knew that would be likely to eliminate any chance for big gains if the market rose. While the portfolio might increase in value, losses would be suffered on the futures contracts. What Pincus wanted was simply an insurance policy that would insulate the portfolio from catastrophic losses during the time period that the estate was being settled. The vehicle that enabled Pincus to accomplish his objective was a deep "out-of-the-money" put option.

At the time of his decision, the S&P stock index was selling near the $1,200 level. Pincus could have bought three-month S&P puts with a striking price of $1,200 (at or slightly in-the-money), but they would have been very expensive. With each put option costing about 10 percent, a year's worth of protection for the entire portfolio would have cost about 40 percent of its total value. Pincus, however, wanted protection only against a major drop in the market. He found that deep out-of-the-money puts (puts with a striking price of $1,020, 15 percent below current market levels) could be bought for a cost of about ¾ of 1 percent, or for about 3 percent per year. Pincus knew that this bought him protection only from a disaster, that is, a 15 percent drop in the market. But the cost was low. And even if he never exercised the options prior to the settlement of the estate, he would be very happy for the protection. Just as he was happy to continue to pay premiums on his homeowners insurance policy, even though his house never burned down, so he was delighted to have been able to use the options market to buy catastrophe insurance for the estate. And since Pincus used such a strategy during 2007 and 2008, when the market did decline by more than 15 percent, he limited the losses suffered by the estate.

APPENDIX TO SUPPLEMENT:
WHAT DETERMINES PRICES
IN THE FUTURES AND
OPTIONS MARKETS?

ONE PROBABLY DOES need to be a rocket scientist to figure out the latest wrinkles in the pricing formulas used by professionals to determine the appropriate price to pay for any specific futures or options contract. It is possible, however, for any individual to understand the basic determinants of these prices and, therefore, to have at least a general idea why some options may sell at 15 percent and others at only 5 percent of the market value of the underlying stock.

Let's deal with the futures market first and see what is involved in the pricing of a silver future. Let's suppose that the spot price of silver for immediate delivery is $30.00 an ounce. Suppose further that the price of a silver future for delivery in three months' time is $30.35. Is the futures market some kind of con game in which buyers are, in effect, cheated out of an extra 35 cents? Not at all. Consider the situation faced by an individual who needs a certain quantity of silver in three months' time. He could buy the silver now at $30.00 per ounce and hold on to it until it was needed. This would involve two kinds of costs, however. First, he would have to store the silver for ninety days, and that would involve storage costs of perhaps $0.05 per ounce. Second, buying silver in the spot market would entail an immediate payment of the $30.00 price and, thus, what economists call an opportunity cost. By paying for the silver now, one forgoes the opportunity to invest the money for ninety days in a perfectly safe investment such as a Treasury bill. If Treasury bill yields were 4 percent per year (or 1 percent per quarter), the spot buyer would have forgone the opportunity to earn

$0.30 (the $30.00 times 1 percent). Hence, the buyer in need of silver would see no difference between buying silver in the spot market at $30.00 and buying it in the futures market at $30.35. Similarly, the seller would be equally happy to receive $30.00 now, which would enable her to save on storage costs and earn interest on the receipts, or to receive $30.35 at the end of the quarter.

From this simple illustration, the basic determinants of the spread between spot and futures prices can be made clear. Futures prices depend on the interest rate and storage costs. One additional factor is likely to enter the equation—the so-called "convenience yield" of having the inventory directly on hand. In general, the futures price will be above the spot price because of the interest and storage factors, but it could in some circumstances be lower when the convenience yield is very high, as might happen if the commodity was in very short supply.

Similarly, we can list the factors determining option prices. The factors have to do with the characteristics of the options contract and those of the underlying stock and the market. Five factors are important:

1. The Exercise Price

Suppose Halliburton is selling at $40 per share. A call option exercisable at $40 is clearly more valuable than one exercisable at $50 per share, well "out-of-the-money." The higher the exercise price, the lower the value of the option. Of course, the value of the option can never go below zero. As long as there is some probability that the market price of the stock can exceed the exercise price in the future, the option will have some value.

2. The Stock Price

All other things being the same, the higher the stock price, the higher the price of the call option. Obviously, if a stock is selling at $1 per share, the option could not possibly be worth more than $1, since purchasing the stock directly would allow the investor to realize whatever appreciation develops, whereas the investor's risk would be limited to the purchase price. An option premium on such a stock might run 5 or 10 cents per share. On the other hand, the value of an at-the-money call on a $100 stock could be $5 or $10 per share.

3. Expiration Date

The longer the option has to run, the greater its value. Consider two options on Halliburton with an exercise price of $40 per share. Obviously, a six-month option is worth more than a three-month option, since it has an additional three months within which the call on the stock can be exercised. Thus, if something good happens to the company, the buyer of the longer option will have a longer period over which she can take advantage of any favorable outcome.

4. The Volatility of the Stock

This is the key factor determining the value of a stock option. The greater the volatility of the underlying stock in question, the higher the cost of a call option. An at-the-money call on Halliburton, an extremely volatile stock, is likely to sell for very much more than an at-the-money call of similar length on a more stable stock such as AT&T. It is unlikely that the call buyer will make a killing with the stable stock, since it characteristically doesn't fluctuate much. Similarly, on the down side, buying the stock directly does not involve great risk. On the other hand, buying Halliburton, which is volatile, does involve considerable risk, which is limited when the investor buys the call option. At the same time, very favorable outcomes could lead to a big rise in Halliburton stock, making the potential worth of the option far greater than in the AT&T case.

5. Interest Rates

Call prices are also a function of the level of interest rates. The buyer of a call option does not pay the exercise price until and unless he exercises the option. The ability to delay payment is more valuable when interest rates are high and, therefore, earnings opportunities on cash are very attractive.

A model has been developed by Fischer Black, Myron Scholes, and Robert Merton to make quantitative estimates of options values on the basis of the factors just outlined. Merton and Scholes were awarded a Nobel Prize for the discovery. (Black would certainly have shared in the award, had it not been for his untimely death.) While the mathematics of these formulas are quite forbidding, they are easily programmed on a personal computer and are used extensively by option buyers and traders to determine the appropriate value of option premiums. It turns out that option premiums fluctuate reasonably closely around the values suggested by the Black-Scholes model.

BINOMIAL OPEN PRICING

Although the mathematics behind the Black-Scholes model will be inaccessible for most readers, a related model—the binomial model—can be easily understood by anyone familiar with high school algebra. Moreover, the general insights that inform Black-Scholes can all be found in the binomial model. Indeed, a multiperiod binomial model produces results equivalent to those of Black-Scholes. In describing the binomial model, we assume that only two future equally likely outcomes are possible. The stock in question can either go up or go down. A very volatile stock would go up or down a great deal. A more stable stock would have a narrower range of potential outcomes. We'll illustrate the binomial model with a volatile stock initially selling at $100 a share. We assume that at the end of a year the stock could either go up to $150 or fall to $75. We show how to price a one-year call option. The one-year riskless interest rate (on Treasury bills) is taken to be 10 percent. We diagram the present and future prices of the stock and the call option below.

ILLUSTRATION OF POSSIBLE FUTURE
STOCK AND CALL OPTION VALUES

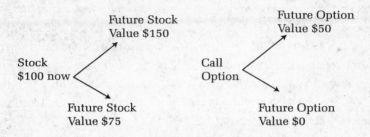

Note that if the stock rises to $150 at the end of one year, the call option will be worth $50, its intrinsic value. If the stock declines, however, the option will expire worthless. Obviously, an option to buy something at $100 when it can be purchased on the market at $75 is not worth anything. Now suppose an investor forms a perfectly hedged portfolio that has exactly the same terminal value whether the market rises or falls. Such a portfolio can be formed if the investor buys ⅔ of a share of stock and sells (writes) one call option with a striking price of $100, the initial stock price. Two-thirds is called the hedge ratio, and we will see in a moment how to find the correct ratio. Let's first confirm that the investor is perfectly hedged.

The illustration below shows that the investor who buys ⅔ of a share of stock and sells one call is indeed perfectly hedged. He obtains a payoff after one year of $50 whether the stock goes up or down.

ILLUSTRATION OF INVESTOR PAYOFFS

Stock rises to $150

	Payoff
Option exercised, investor receives	$100
Investor purchases ⅓ share	−50
Net Payoff	$ 50

Stock falls to $75

	Payoff
Option not exercised	
Investor owns ⅔ share	$ 50

If the stock rises, the call buyer exercises her option and presents $100 to buy a share of stock. The writer is obligated to deliver a share, but he owns only ⅔ of a share. Hence the writer must purchase ⅓ share at the then current price of $150. This costs him $50, for a net payoff of $50. If the stock falls to $75, the call is not exercised and the investor is left holding ⅔ of a share of a $75 stock, which is also worth $50. Thus, the investor has a final payoff of $50, irrespective of whether the stock rises or falls, and is thus perfectly hedged.

How does one determine the hedge ratio? Easy. The hedge ratio is simply the ratio shown in the illustration below.

DETERMINATION OF HEDGE RATIO

$$\frac{\textit{Value of Call if Stock Up} - \textit{Value of Call if Stock Down}}{\textit{Value of Stock if Up} - \textit{Value of Stock if Down}}$$

$$\frac{\text{Call (Up)} - \text{Call (Down)}}{\text{Stock (Up)} - \text{Stock (Down)}} = \frac{50 - 0}{150 - 75} = \frac{50}{75} = \frac{2}{3}$$

If the stock goes up, the call has an intrinsic value of $50. The right to buy a share of stock selling at $150 for only $100 is worth $50. If the stock goes down, the call is worthless. (The right to buy a share of stock for $100 while it is selling in the market at only $75 is worthless.)

Just one more insight is needed to determine the value of the call option. This insight lies behind the Black-Scholes as well as the binomial model. If an investor makes a riskless investment (that is, one that is perfectly hedged and has the same payoff whether the market goes up or down), that investment should earn the riskless rate of interest. The riskless interest rate is taken to be the rate of interest on perfectly safe Treasury bills. With this insight, we can easily determine the selling price of a call option, which we will designate as C.

We saw that the investor is perfectly hedged if he buys ⅔ of a share of stock and writes one call option. Such a purchase will cost

$66.67 (the cost of ⅔ share of a $100 stock) minus C, the value of the call option. (Remember, the buyer of the call pays the writer the option premium.) Such an investment, since it is perfectly hedged, should earn the one-year rate of interest, which we assumed was 10 percent. Hence, we can determine the price of the call option by solving the equation shown in the illustration below.

ILLUSTRATION OF THE DETERMINATION OF THE VALUE OF A CALL OPTION

Amount Invested (1+ Risk-Free Interest Rate) = Certain Payoff

[Hedge Ratio (Initial Stock Price) − C](1+ Interest Rate) = Certain Payoff

$$[⅔(100) − C](1+.10) = 50$$
$$(66.67 − C)(1.1) = 50$$
$$C = 21.22$$

The call option will be priced at $21.22.

The Black-Scholes option-pricing model uses precisely the same insight we just used in the binomial illustration above. Black-Scholes can be considered a multistage binomial model. We assumed that only two outcomes were possible after one year. But suppose we consider a two-stage (six-month) binomial model. After the first six months, the stock can go up or down. After the second six months, again two outcomes are possible. This leads to three possible outcomes at the end of one year. The stock can go up in both periods or down in both. Alternatively the stock could rise (fall) in the first period and fall (rise) in the second. Thus, three outcomes are possible. We could also do a four-stage binomial model where each quarter the stock price could rise or fall and several different outcomes would be possible. Or we could do a daily binomial or even an hourly or minute-by-minute model. As we break the binomial model into finer and finer subperiods, the binomial model and the Black-Scholes model converge. The basic insights remain the same. We form perfectly hedged portfolios of holding stock and writing call options. Such riskless portfolios should earn only the risk-free interest rate in an efficiently functioning market. It turns out that actual option premiums fluctuate reasonably closely around the values suggested by the Black-Scholes model. The model is also used extensively to determine the appropriate accounting charge against earnings from the granting of executive stock options.

A RANDOM WALKER'S
ADDRESS BOOK AND
REFERENCE GUIDE TO
MUTUAL FUNDS AND ETFs

DATA ON SELECTED TAXABLE MONEY-MARKET FUNDS (JULY 2014)

	Ticker	Year Organized	Net Assets ($ billion) 2014	Average Maturity in Days	Recent Expense Ratio (%)*
Fidelity Money Market Fund www.fidelity.com 800-544-8888	FSLXX	1985	$4.4	46	0.26
Schwab Value Advantage Money Market Fund www.schwab.com 800-435-4000	SWRXX	1994	$1.0	53	0.61
TIAA-CREF Money Market Fund www.tiaa-cref.com 800-927-3059	TIRXX	2006	$0.9	46	0.50
Vanguard Prime Money Market Fund www.vanguard.com 877-622-7447	VMMXX	1976	$129.2	58	0.17

DATA ON SELECTED NATIONAL TAX-EXEMPT MONEY-MARKET FUNDS (JULY 2014)†

	Ticker	Year Organized	Net Assets ($ billion) 2014	Average Maturity in Days	Recent Expense Ratio (%)*
Fidelity Municipal Money Market Fund www.fidelity.com 800-544-8888	FTEXX	1980	$28.5	31	0.41
T. Rowe Price Tax-Exempt Money Market Fund www.troweprice.com 800-225-5132	PTEXX	1981	$1.0	56	0.52
Vanguard Tax-Exempt Money Market Fund www.vanguard.com 877-622-7447	VMSXX	1980	$17.7	39	0.16

*Expense ratios have been inapplicable during periods of extremely low interest rates. Investment advisers have voluntarily waived expenses in excess of the contractual expense limitation to maintain positive net yields for the funds.

† State tax-exempt funds are available from the same fund sponsors.

DATA ON SELECTED GENERAL EQUITY INDEX FUNDS AND ETFs (JULY 2014)

Funds	Ticker	Index	Year Organized	Recent Expense Ratio (%)	Net Assets ($billion) 2014
Fidelity Spartan Total Index www.fidelity.com 800-544-8888	FSTMX	Dow Jones U.S. Total Stock Market	1997	0.10	$25.5
Schwab Total Stock Market Index www.schwab.com 800-435-4000	SWRXX	Dow Jones U.S. Total Stock Market	1999	0.09	$3.8
Vanguard 500 Index Admiral www.vanguard.com 877-622-7447	VFIAX	S&P 500	2000	0.05	$179.7
Vanguard Total Stock Market Index Admiral www.vanguard.com 877-622-7447	VTSAX	CRSP U.S. Total Market	2000	0.05	$347.4
Vanguard Small Cap Index Admiral www.vanguard.com 877-622-7447	VSMAX	CRSP U.S. Total Market	2000	0.09	$49.2
ETFs					
S&P 500 ETF www.vanguard.com 877-622-7447	VOO	S&P 500	2010	0.05	$179.7
Vanguard Total Stock Market Index ETF www.vanguard.com 877-622-7447	VTI	CRSP U.S. Total Market	2001	0.05	$347.4
iShares Russell 1000 ETF www.ishares.com 415-670-2000	IWB	Russell 1000	2000	0.15	$9.5
Schwab U.S. Large-Cap ETF www.schwab.com 800-435-4000	SCHX	Dow Jones U.S. Large-Cap Total Stock Market	2009	0.04	$2.9
SPDR Russell 2000 www.spdrs.com 866-787-2257	TWOK	Russell 2000	2013	0.12	$0.1

DATA ON SELECTED REAL ESTATE MUTUAL FUNDS AND ETFs (JULY 2014)

Funds	Ticker	Year Organized	Recent Expense Ratio (%)	Net Assets ($billion) 2014
Cohen & Steers Realty Shares Fund www.cohenandsteers.com 800-437-9912	CSRSX	1991	0.97	$5.9
Fidelity Real Estate Investment Portfolio www.fidelity.com 800-544-8888	FRESX	1986	0.81	$4.0
Vanguard REIT Index Fund Admiral www.vanguard.com 877-622-7447	VGSLX	2001	0.10	$44.1
Fidelity Spartan Real Estate Index Fund www.fidelity.com 800-343-3548	FRXIX	2011	0.23	$0.3
ETFs				
iShares Cohen & Steers REIT ETF www.ishares.com 415-670-2000	ICP	2001	0.35	$3.0
Vanguard REIT Index ETF www.vanguard.com 877-622-7447	VNQ	2004	0.10	$44.1
SPDR DJ Wilshire REIT ETF www.spdrs.com 866-787-2257	RWR	2001	0.25	$2.6
Schwab US REIT ETF www.schwab.com 800-435-4000	SCHH	2011	0.07	$1.0

DATA ON SELECTED INTERNATIONAL INDEX FUNDS AND ETFs (JULY 2014)

Funds	Ticker	Index	Year Organized	Recent Expense Ratio (%)	Net Assets ($billion) 2014
Fidelity Spartan International Index Fund www.fidelity.com 800-544-8888	FSHX	MSCI EAFE	1997	0.20	$14.3
Vanguard Developed Markets Index www.vanguard.com 877-622-7447	VTMGX	FTSE Developed ex North America	1999	0.09	$45.6
Vanguard Total International Stock Index Admiral www.vanguard.com 877-622-7447	VTIAX	FTSE Global All-Cap ex U.S.	2010	0.14	$130.0
Schwab International Index www.schwab.com 800-435-4000	SWISX	MSCI EAFE	1997	0.19	$2.6
Vanguard Emerging Markets Stock Index Admiral www.vanguard.com 877-622-7447	VEMAX	FTSE Emerging Markets	2006	0.15	$64.0
Vanguard Total World Stock Index www.vanguard.com 877-622-7447	VTWSX	FTSE Global All-Cap	2008	0.30	$5.5
ETFs					
Vanguard Total International Stock ETF www.vanguard.com 877-622-7447	VXUS	FTSE Global All-Cap ex U.S.	2011	0.14	$3.0
Vanguard FTSE All-World ex US Index Fund www.vanguard.com 877-622-7447	VEU	FTSE All-World ex U.S.	2007	0.15	$12.9

DATA ON SELECTED INTERNATIONAL INDEX FUNDS AND ETFs (JULY 2014) (continued)

ETFs	Ticker	Index	Year Organized	Recent Expense Ratio (%)	Net Assets ($billion) 2014
Vanguard Total World Stock Index www.vanguard.com 877-622-7447	VT	FTSE Global All-Cap	2008	0.18	$5.5
iShares Core MSCI EAFE www.ishares.com 415-670-2000	IEFA	MSCI EAFE	2012	0.14	$2.4
SPDR MSCI ACWI ex US www.spdrs.com 866-787-2257	CWI	MSCI ACWI ex US	2012	0.14	$2.4
Vanguard Emerging Markets www.vanguard.com 877-622-7447	VWO	FTSE Emerging	2005	0.15	$64.0

DATA ON ALTERNATIVE INCOME-PRODUCING FUNDS AND ETFs: CORPORATE AND FOREIGN BOND FUNDS AND ETFS (JULY 2014)

Funds	Ticker	Recent Expense Ratio (%)	Net Assets ($billion) 2014
Vanguard Emerging Markets Government Bond Index Fund Admiral www.vanguard.com 877-622-7447	VGAVX	0.34	$0.3
Vanguard Intermediate Term Corporate Bond Index Fund www.vanguard.com 877-622-7447	VICSX	0.12	$4.2
Vanguard High-Yield Corporate Fund Admiral www.vanguard.com 877-622-7447	VWEAX	0.13	$17.5
BlackRock Allocation Target Shares Series C www.blackrock.com 800-441-7762	BRACX	0.01	$0.3
Fidelity Corporate Bond Fund www.fidelity.com 800-343-3548	FCBFX	0.45	$0.8
ETFs			
iShares Emerging Markets Corporate Bond ETF www.ishares.com 415-670-2000	CEMB	0.60	$0.02
iShares JPMorgan USD Emerging Markets Bond ETF www.ishares.com 415-670-2000	EMB	0.60	$5.2
iShares iBoxx $ Investment Grade Corporate Bond ETF www.ishares.com 415-670-2000	LQD	0.15	$17.3
Vanguard Intermediate-Term Corporate Bond ETF www.vanguard.com 877-622-7447	VCIT	0.12	$4.2
Vanguard Emerging Markets Government Bond www.vanguard.com 877-622-7447	VWOB	0.35	$0.3

STOCK FUNDS AND ETFs WITH GROWING DIVIDENDS (JULY 2014)

Funds	Ticker	Recent Expense Ratio (%)	Net Assets ($billion) 2014
WisdomTree US Dividend Growth Fund www.wisdomtree.com 866-909-9473	DGRW	0.28	$0.1
Vanguard Dividend Appreciation Index Fund www.vanguard.com 877-622-7447	VDAIX	0.20	$24.5
Vanguard Dividend Growth Fund www.vanguard.com 877-622-7447	VDIGX	0.31	$21.3
Vanguard Equity Income Fund Admiral www.vanguard.com 877-622-7447	VEIRX	0.21	$17.7
ETFs			
Vanguard Dividend Appreciation ETF www.vanguard.com 877-622-7447	VIG	0.10	$24.5
iShares Core High Dividend ETF www.ishares.com 415-670-2000	HDV	0.12	$4.1
Schwab US Dividend Equity ETF www.schwabetfs.com 800-435-4000	SCHD	0.07	$2.0
Vanguard High Dividend Yield Index ETF www.vanguard.com 877-622-7447	VYM	0.10	$12.2
WisdomTree Large-Cap Dividend Fund www.wisdomtree.com 866-909-9473	DLN	0.28	$1.9
WisdomTree Total Dividend Fund www.wisdomtree.com 866-909-9473	DTD	0.28	$0.5

DATA ON SELECTED "SMART BETA" MUTUAL FUNDS AND ETFs

Funds	Ticker	Year Organized	Recent Expense Ratio (%)	Net Assets ($billion) 2014
AQR Momentum Fund	AMOMX	2009	0.49	$1.0
DFA US Large Cap Value Portfolio	DFLVX	1993	0.27	$14.6
DFA US Small Cap Value Portfolio	DFSVX	1993	0.52	$11.6
PowerShares FTSE RAFI US 1000 Portfolio	FRXIX	2011	0.23	$0.3
PowerShares S&P 500 Low Volatility Portfolio	SPLV	2011	0.25	$4.0
Vanguard Growth Index Fund	VIGAX	2000	0.09	$25.2
Vanguard Value Index Fund	VVIAX	2000	0.09	$17.4
Vanguard Small-Cap Value Index Fund	VBR	2004	0.09	$4.4
ETFs				
Guggenheim Russell 1000 Equal Weight ETF	EWRI	2010	0.40	$0.1
iShares Russell 1000 ETF	IWB	2000	0.15	$9.5
iShares Russell 2000 ETF	IWM	2000	0.20	$25.6
SPDR Russell 1000 Low Volatility ETF	LGLV	2013	0.20	$0.01
iShares MSCI USA Minimum Volatility ETF	USMV	2011	0.15	$2.7
iShares MSCI USA Momentum Factor ETF	MTUM	2013	0.15	$0.3
SPDR S&P 1500 Momentum Tilt ETF	MMTM	2012	0.35	$0.01
iShares Core US Value ETF	IUSV	2000	0.09	$0.6
Schwab US Small-Cap ETF	SCHA	2009	0.08	$2.1
iShares MSCI USA Minimum Volatility ETF	USMV	2011	0.15	$2.7
iShares S&P Small-Cap 600 Value	IJS	2000	0.30	$3.0
WisdomTree Earnings 500 ETF	EPS	2007	0.28	$0.1

INDEX